REVOLUTIONARY
WOMEN

REVOLUTIONARY WOMEN

Gender and the Socialist Revolutionary Role

Marie Marmo Mullaney

PRAEGER

PRAEGER SPECIAL STUDIES • PRAEGER SCIENTIFIC

Library of Congress Cataloging in Publication Data

Mullaney, Marie Marmo.
    Revolutionary women.

    Bibliography: p.
    Includes index.
    1. Women and socialism.   2. Women revolutionists—
Biography.   3. Communists—Biography.   I. Title.
HX546.M83   1983   335′.0088042   82-22437
ISBN 0-03-061927-0
ISBN 0-03-061928-9 (pbk.)

Photographs of
  Eleanor Marx (p. 14) courtesy of
  The Bettmann Archive
  Alexandra Kollontai (p. 54) courtesy of
  BBC Hulton Picture Library
  Rosa Luxemburg (p. 98) courtesy of
  BBC Hulton Picture Library
  Angelica Balabanoff (p. 148) courtesy of
  Wide World Photos

Published in 1983 by Praeger Publishers
CBS Educational and Professional Publishing,
a Division of CBS Inc.
521 Fifth Avenue, New York, NY 10175, U.S.A.

© by Praeger Publishers

3456789   052   987654321

Printed in the United States of America on acid-free paper.

To the Memory
of
My Grandmother

Preface and
Acknowledgments

My interest in revolutionary women was first aroused during a course entitled "Introductory History Workshop" given at Seton Hall University a decade ago. At that time I was rather startled by the instructor's suggestion that the subject of women in revolutionary movements might be a fruitful one for the class to pursue. Skeptical and unconvinced, I, along with the others, voted the suggestion down. Several years later, when as a graduate student in women's history I was feverishly involved in the doctoral research that became this book, I recalled that incident with a mixture of amusement and gratitude. Annoyed at myself that I hadn't recognized the significance of the topic as an undergraduate who prided herself on her properly raised consciousness, I resolved to one day inform Professor Phyllis Stock that I had finally come to appreciate the merits of her ill-fated proposal. This book stands as a fulfillment of that resolution.

I am deeply grateful to many others, especially Mary S. Hartman of Rutgers University, who chaired the dissertation committee under whose guidance the original draft of this manuscript was written. The other members of that committee, Seymour Becker and Lora D. Garrison, were also particularly helpful and supportive in offering their insights and advice and in encouraging me to revise the dissertation for publication. Mary Boutilier of Seton Hall University deserves special acknowledgment for she also served on that committee and her work on the socialization of political women has greatly influenced my own. Special thanks also to John Osborne of Rutgers, who read the manuscript; to librarians Hedy Seitz and Wanda Gawienowski of Rutgers, who helped me gather materials from all over the country; to E. E. Larson of the Library of Congress and Professors Francisco Pena of Caldwell College and Temma Kaplan of UCLA, who assisted with sources; and to Edith Wynner, consultant to the Schwimmer-Lloyd collection of the New York Public Library Archives, who granted permission to use that collection in my research. Generous fellowships awarded by the Danforth Foundation and the Graduate School of Rutgers University made this work possible.

Finally, I owe my greatest debt to Lynda Sharp of Praeger for her faith in this project; to my parents, for their constant love and support; and to my husband Ken for his patient willingness to share his life with the women of this study for the past four years.

Table of Contents

BIBLIOGRAPHY

Introduction:
The Study of
Revolutionary Women

The central characters of this study are all women, all socialists, and all revolutionaries, bold and impassioned crusaders who were bent on making the world anew in the movements they joined over the course of the last century. As revolutionary socialists, they shared an ideology and a political commitment with male comrades. As women, however, they struggled alone, breaking from familial and social expectations of proper feminine behavior, suffering intense personal conflicts and personal tragedies, enduring the sneers of the "bourgeois" world and the condescending snickers of patronizing political contemporaries. Nonetheless, all persevered, dedicating their lives to a cause and an ideal in which they yearned to find a place.

Interest in women revolutionaries has recently become quite popular. The proliferation of studies examining the role played by women in an assortment of revolutionary movements has served, first of all, a revisionist function.[1] By rescuing and resurrecting forgotten women from the dustbin of history, and by emphasizing the contributions many did make to political and revolutionary struggles, historians of women have "desexed," so to speak, events and causes that have traditionally been regarded as all-male affairs. In the process they have also answered the flippant, if genuine, query of the nonbeliever: "How many female revolutionaries have there been, anyway?"

This, however, is not such a study. Its intent is neither to prove that vast numbers of women were active in socialist revolutionary movements in modern Europe nor to search out their names. Placing revolutionary women back into history must begin to assume more than a simply compensatory dimension. Although numerous studies have demonstrated that women could be found in the revolutionary movements of the past, no study has ever described the how and why of their participation, the pain, disillusionment, frustration, tragedy, and at times even blatant prejudice that revolutionary women confronted. No study, before this one, has ever examined the key question of how gender itself affected women's revolutionary participation.

This study hopes to move beyond the realm of compensatory history into the area of comparative, critical, and analytical biography, to identify and define certain commonalities of the female revolutionary experience. Dealing with five prominent women, it illustrates the kinds of roles that women have played within Marxist socialism, the first political movement to admit women to its leadership councils. It looks at their revolutionary careers in a new way, putting their lives into a context, drawing and isolating connections, similarities, and resemblances among them. Most importantly, it focuses on these revolutionary women as women, not simply as revolutionaries. It aims to develop some substantial theoretical conclusions about the female revolutionary experience, and to distinguish that experience from the better-known male variant.

One of the most important results of the growing interest in women's history is the opportunity it has afforded historians to rethink and reassess many of the discipline's standard theories, conceptions, and generalizations. The study of individual female revolutionaries is important because the uniqueness—or, more precisely, even the *question* of the uniqueness—of the female revolutionary experience has never been raised in the standard literature on individual revolutionary behavior. Through the study of prominent revolutionaries, social scientists and historians have produced a model of the so-called revolutionary personality, a general composite portrait of the distinctive psychological, emotional, and behavioral characteristics of revolutionary figures across time and space.[2] Considered as a whole, these studies have produced a basic model of revolutionary behavior, a model that includes some significant hypotheses about the socialization of revolutionaries, their motivations in entering political activity, and certain recognizable features of their behavior once they have entered a revolutionary role.

Admittedly, the model has had its share of detractors. What makes this literature so intriguing is also what makes it most controversial. Opponents of psychohistory have attacked its methodology, while others have condemned its highly speculative and intuitive nature. The model, they say, is a generalized and schematized one that sacrifices the particular for the sake of the universal. It provides us with questions but not proof. Above all, it wrongly focuses on the agent of revolutionary change rather than on the backdrop against which the revolutionary activity occurred.[3]

The recent wave of interest in revolutionary women, however, makes it apparent that the biggest problem with the available literature on revolutionary behavior is neither its unscientific quality nor its reductionist nature, but rather its unstated assumptions regarding the gender of revolutionary participants. Although the factor of sexist bias has never yet been targeted by the model's critics, this, indeed, is its most glaring flaw.

The established model has never been identified as a male model as such. Both by their silence on the question of gender and by the fact that individual revolutionaries studied in the course of constructing the model have all been men, existing studies either ignore the historical existence of women revolutionaries entirely, or implicitly assume that the woman revolutionary would simply have acted like her male counterpart. The studies become even more problematic when applied to women because of their use of a Freudian psychoanalytic base. All have highlighted the importance of childhood experiences to future personality development, and all center on the Oedipal relation with the father as being the critical determining factor in the decision to embark on a revolutionary role. Certainly their conclusions become highly speculative if one abandons the traditional Freudian underpinning, a psychology that, it is now commonly recognized, is loaded with biases and prejudices in its assessment of what constitutes "normal" female behavior.[4]

There are even larger problems with the established model of the revolutionary as a type. Defined in male terms and rooted in Freudian psychology, it does not touch on any of the wider questions of female revolutionary involvement. Throughout history the adoption of revolutionary behavior by women has never been a simple, one-step process as it may have been for men, a process psychologically triggered by a conflict with authority or an authority figure. Critical personal choices have been involved for those women who decided to adopt public roles. Since the average woman must have first challenged a traditional sex role ideology before she chose to adopt a revolutionary ideology, the more important question to be raised about the socialization of female revolutionaries is how these women came first to adopt an activist sex role ideology,[5] a code of behavior atypical for their sex, and certainly a nontraditional one in terms of their culture and historical milieu.

Entrance into revolutionary behavior by women has involved at least a two-tiered process: an initial decision to embark on a public, activist role, thus breaking from traditional social and familial expectations of proper behavior for women; and a second decision, in the adoption of that public role, to embark on revolutionary as opposed to reformist political behavior. Because self-conscious political activity has not been the common historical experience of women, additional factors—such as the historical period in which the woman acted and the revolutionary ideology she embraced—must be examined and identified when studying the careers of those women who did become politically involved. In certain historical periods the adoption of revolutionary behavior by a woman would have been the only kind of public political activity that her culture and society would have made available to her. On the other hand, if various opportunities for public behavior were available to a woman during the period in which she lived, she would have been more inclined to adopt a particular revolutionary ideology if, from the start, that ideology itself appeared to offer her a ready place.

By the late nineteenth century, both of these components—a growing popular acceptance of public behavior by women, and the rising power and prominence of a revolutionary ideology, Marxist socialism, that specifically attempted to attract women to its ranks—were present in the European world, making this an especially fruitful period for a general study of women revolutionaries. Women's emergence as a self-conscious force in cultural, political, and economic life dates from these years,[6] as industrialization gradually transformed traditional family life for women of all classes. Mass migration to urban centers was accompanied by the large-scale employment of wives and daughters, not only in factories but also in any number of new careers—as nurses, retail clerks, secretaries, stenographers, and schoolteachers—then opening up. Women's heightened visibility in public life also stemmed from the efforts of leisured middle class housewives to correct the abuses that massive industrialization had made inevitable. Acting from altruistic and reformist motivations, they banded together to achieve "moral betterment," and to work in philanthropic and activist causes: temperance, social purity, prison reform, and charitable and missionary organizations. Liberal feminism—specifically, the suffrage movement—was itself born from this milieu, for with their new self-assertiveness women came to demand civil, political, and legal rights, equal opportunities in education, business and professional careers, and political life. Virtually all the major and most of the minor countries of Europe saw the birth of a variety of feminist organizations during this period,[7] and the woman question became a recognized topic for debate and argument. Thus, women intent on entering a public role in these years had a variety of options from which to choose, one of which was becoming a revolutionary.

The rise and spread of Marxist socialism constituted a second significant development of the waning decades of the nineteenth century. The Paris Commune of 1871 marked the birth of the modern socialist era and ushered in a half century that saw European socialism grow ideologically and mature politically, a period that culminated in the Russian Bolshevik Revolution of 1917 and an abortive communist revolution in Germany two years later. In between, revolutionary socialism rose and fell in Italy, and England and Spain witnessed the birth of militant labor movements impregnated with Marxist principles.

From the first, women supporters were specifically welcomed by the new ideology. European socialism, from its earliest theoretical beginnings in the nineteenth century, showed itself to be particularly sympathetic to the question of women's emancipation.[8] A standard tenet of the developing creed was that the radical restructuring of society along socialist lines would bring with it full personal, political, social, economic, and legal equality for women. The French utopians, Owenites, and Saint-Simonians all welcomed the participation of women in their movements, addressing propaganda to them, and dealing with the question of women's role in the future societies they hoped to create. Along with other early socialists like Flora Tristan and Etienne Cabet, they demanded changes in social organizations and institutions that would allow women to become the full and equal partners of men in the new socialist world. Charles Fourier was especially sensitive to the needs and oppression of women, and he forged a powerful ideological alliance between socialism and feminism. With his bold decree that the stage of development of any society could be gauged by the position of its women, he gave the new movement a dictum that came to be adopted almost verbatim by Marx himself.[9]

Marx followed in the spirit of the utopians without, however, troubling himself with any of the niceties of practical detail. Connecting women's emancipation with socialist revolution alone, he took female oppression to be a manifestation of the evils of capitalist society in general. Capitalism wrecked traditional family life, drove women and children into the atrocious atmosphere of the factory, and caused both men and women to sell their souls for the tenuous security of a starvation wage. Female prostitution became for Marx the most glaring of all symbols of the "cash nexus" that bound human beings to each other in the capitalist world. Although Marx dealt with women's problems only tangentially, he enunciated what was to become the socialist movement's standard position on the woman question. Since class alliances would always separate women from each other, "bourgeois feminist" movements, with their demands for the vote, equal pay for equal work, and civil and legal rights, were meaningless without wider societal restructuring. True salvation for working women lay in fighting alongside the men of their class for the achievement of socialism.[10]

Frederick Engels echoed Marx's moral outrage at the factory employment of women and children, providing in *The Condition of the Working Class in England* a poignant and powerful description of the disintegration of family life among the poor. Even more importantly, in *The Origin of the Family, Private Property, and the State*, he gave Marxist thought on the woman question a theoretical and quasi-historical underpinning. "The first class opposition that appeared in history," he wrote, "was the antagonism between man and woman in monogamous marriage." Rooting the causes of women's oppression in a marriage system developed to enshrine and protect private property, he tied female emancipation to the destruction of all societies based on the private ownership of the means of production.[11]

As Marxism matured into an organized political movement, the German leader August Bebel completed socialism's commitment to the woman question with a final bold attempt to draw women to the cause. His monumental work, *Woman Under Socialism*, was destined to become the classic statement on this issue. Beginning his book with a historical survey of the position of women, Bebel connected sexual oppression with the rise of capitalism itself, and explained that the subjection of women would always remain symptomatic of the pervasive oppression of class society. Attributing female subordination to the evils of wage slavery, private property, and the marriage market, Bebel insisted that only the future socialist society could guarantee women's full equality, and grant them all political, social, and economic rights. With this persuasive assurance, *Woman Under Socialism* was a sensational success. Reprinted in several million copies and translated into more than a dozen languages, it was a powerful motivating factor in attracting women to the socialist cause.[12]

Drawing sustenance from this inspirational ideological heritage, many women came to revolutionary socialism in this period, women whose task it became to interpret the theoretical language of the socialist tradition and translate it into practical terms. The socialist women chosen for this study were five of the most famous. While the selection was admittedly arbitrary and makes no claim to being based on a scientifically representative sample, certain important considerations dictated the choices made. Women selected were those who had left written records of their revolutionary involvement, and who were recognized by their contemporaries as having taken leading roles. These women were among the leading socialist personalities of Europe in their day, and no study of female revolutionaries of the period could justifiably leave them out. Each of their careers represents and illustrates a different facet of the female revolutionary experience. Although they acted within five different national contexts, they were all heirs to a common Marxist tradition, and despite national differences, similar themes emerge in the study of their lives. All joined socialist parties that had to deal with the real, rather than the rhetorical, equality of women. The problems and prejudices that each of them confronted expose the often glaring discrepancy between socialist theory and socialist reality.

This study begins, appropriately enough, with Karl Marx's daughter Eleanor, the only one of his three daughters to become an important political personality in her own right. Active in the British labor movement in the years when it was first emerging into institutional maturity, she brought the banner of revolution to Marx's adopted homeland, the nation where he expected the revolutionary movement first to triumph. Seeking to carry on after her famous father, Eleanor remains critically important to a study of female politicization, radicalization, and organizational acceptance. The intense personal conflicts she suffered illuminate the kinds of problems that have been faced by women in their attempts to embark on a public role. Surely political advantages, but also disadvantages, came from being the daughter of Karl Marx.

Because Marx's revolution triumphed first, of all places, in Russia, a study of the Bolshevik Revolution provides a wealth of possibilities for examining how revolutionary socialism actually began to carry out its promises to women. One woman, Alexandra Kollontai, was most vocal of all in her demands that the victorious Bolsheviks begin to deliver the long-heralded millennium for women. Kollontai's contributions to the Bolshevik cause illustrate her special concerns as a female revolutionary. Even more importantly, however, they highlight the difference between her priorities, as a woman, and those of Lenin, long identified as the perfect example of the "classical revolutionary." The far-reaching and nontraditional nature of Kollontai's proposals conflicted with those of the revolutionary hierarchy, and the indignities she suffered for her beliefs, dreams, and personal lifestyle all exposed the pretensions of this revolution's real commitment to women.

In the wake of the Bolshevik example, socialist revolutions were also attempted in Germany and Italy. Both failed. Yet both were important because of the presence in their ranks of two women, Rosa Luxemburg and Angelica Balabanoff, who each exemplified opposite poles of the female revolutionary experience. Of all the women selected for this study—indeed, of all women revolutionaries in history—Rosa Luxemburg is probably the best known, for in her theoretical accomplishments and political successes, she comes closest to fitting the mold of rigorous "political" behavior as typically defined. What is not so well known, however, is how much and how deeply Rosa Luxemburg, as a woman, suffered both for her political beliefs and for her attempts to serve a movement that was blatantly reluctant to take its advice from women. In her suffering, Luxemburg shared much with Balabanoff, even though the latter's theoretical understanding and practical contributions were of a markedly different caliber. Both women were foreigners who came to serve socialist movements in adopted countries. Why one was accepted and the other was not had as much to do with the kinds of tasks each was willing to shoulder as with the needs and state of development of the movement she sought to join.

Nowhere is this better seen than in the career of Dolores Ibarruri, the famed Pasionaria of the Spanish Civil War. By the opening decades of the twentieth century, women's usefulness to the socialist cause had become readily apparent, and Ibarruri stood out from all the rest in her fervor, loyalty, and unflinching acceptance of the demands made upon her. Saluted by revolutionary comrades and feared by opponents, she came to embody better than anyone else the spirit of the left's crusade against fascism, and became in the process a powerful rallying symbol for a nascent Spanish communist movement sorely in need of one. In her vaunted symbolic role, she exemplified the dilemma revolutionary women have faced not only in Spain but in European socialist and communist movements as a whole.

While any attempt to generalize from such a small, admittedly arbitrary sample has obvious risks, it also has certain clear and undeniable advantages. The question of how socialism—or any ideology, for that matter—dealt with and regarded its most important women leaders can best be answered in this fashion. Only sharply defined personal profiles can show how revolutionary activity satisfied or failed to satisfy each individual woman's needs, what desperations drove her to reject traditional female roles, and what expectations caused her to seek personal emancipation within the revolutionary movement. What did their adopted ideology promise women? What did the movement mean to them, and they to it? What motivations propelled them, what social and psychological problems helped or hindered them along the way, and what kinds of personal traumas and conflicts did they suffer in the process? Was there a dichotomy between the kinds of roles they sought to fill in the revolutionary movement, and those they were given—willingly, or begrudgingly—by male comrades? Most importantly, did the revolutionary movement give them more personal latitude, respect, and freedom as women than the societies they chose to break away from?

In joining revolutionary movements, the goals of revolutionary women have been totally different from those of revolutionary men. Although in the final analysis, revolutions are all about the seizure and consolidation of political power, these women were seeking power of a totally different sort: the chance to exercise power not over others but finally over themselves. In certain historical periods it was only within radical movements that women could prove their usefulness to society and hope to be treated as the equals of men. By choosing to revolt against the authority structure of her society, a woman may implicitly have felt that she was working toward a newer world where the opportunities available to her as a woman would be quite different. When studying the motivations of revolutionary women—as distinct from revolutionary men—historians cannot ignore this psychological dimension. They must repeatedly remind themselves that the role options historically available to men and women have not been the same.

In seeking to place revolutionary women back into history, historians must develop new concepts and new questions that touch more intimately and directly the real core of women's lives. The established model of the revolutionary as a type, precisely because it is male, has not explored any of the larger issues of female revolutionary involvement—issues like socialization experiences, personal needs, psychological conflicts, family and social pressures, revolutionary expectations, and relationships with male political contemporaries. This study hopes to demonstrate not only that revolutionary women have acted differently from revolutionary men but, more importantly, that different criteria must be used to look at them. Although limiting this study to only five women may raise questions about the validity of the generalizations posed, it is hoped that the hypotheses made here will guide research into the lives of various revolutionary women, women inspired by differing ideologies and active in different periods.

Heightened research into the lives of revolutionary women may inspire others to rethink the standard model of the revolutionary personality, rooted as it is in Freudian psychology and based on male examples. Perhaps the established model may actually be inapplicable to most men, founded as it is on revolutionaries recognized as having been outstanding political successes—Trotsky, Lenin, and Mao among them. What about men—and women—who have not fit this mold, the second and third stringers in the revolutionary hierarchy, so to speak, or the less than familiar names? The world does not need another biography of Lenin. History would be better served if future researchers devoted their efforts to resurrecting the "maverick men"[13] and fallen visionaries of the past, those individuals whose artistic or aesthetic sensibilities placed them outside the inherently practical and hard-nosed political mainstream as typically defined.

Finally and most importantly, an examination of the roles played by these revolutionary women may give historians an opportunity to rethink the meaning of the word "revolution" itself. Recently, sociologists, biologists, psychologists, anthropologists, and theologians have begun to study the basic and innate differences that do exist between the two sexes, asking in what ways these differences do contribute to the divergences between the masculine and feminine character and orientation.[14] Although a controversial philosophical question with a long history is involved here, research of various kinds has suggested that women could be a humanizing element in political life if given the chance. Yet, because of their continued absence, politics has traditionally overvalued dominant male traits like competitiveness and aggressiveness, and concurrently denigrated feminine ones like kindness, gentleness, and compassion, and society itself has been the loser.[15] The women of this study did seek to impart a humanizing element first to their movements and then to their world. When celebrating their contributions, we must also lament their failures. We can only ponder what the greater entrance of women into socialist life, and the socialist movement's more open and sincere embrace of their involvement, might have meant for the softening and civilizing of human life in general, for the creation of a *novus ordo saeculorum* for men and women both.

Two important tasks remain for historians. Not only do they need to examine the lives of those pioneering men and women whose revolutionary contributions have so far been either ignored or minimized, but they must also take the first halting steps toward introducing the female revolutionary, as a type, to the theoretical literature of social science. It is hoped that this study will begin to pave the way.

Chapter • One

Eleanor Marx

The Female Revolutionary
as Tragic Heroine

I

The coming to revolutionary consciousness of some women is rather easy to explain. Eleanor Marx, the most talented and politically minded child of Karl Marx, inherited the mantle of revolutionary socialism from her famous father. Schooled in political consciousness from girlhood and sharing his sympathy and love for the working class, she was active in the English socialist movement in the years when it was first emerging. Her life in the service of her father's cause was marked by dedication, devotion, and self-sacrificing zeal, and she was generally considered to be one of the most famous women in the socialist movement of her day.

Eleanor Marx's career as a socialist personality is highly instructive for many reasons. Most importantly, it demonstrates the kinds of doubts, insecurities, and problems women have had to overcome in seeking to enter socialist movements as the equals of men. Although she was welcomed and accepted as the daughter of her famous father, even Eleanor Marx had to grapple with feelings of self-doubt and inadequacy, finding it virtually impossible to transcend both cultural expectations of her role as a woman and the widely held opinion, even in the allegedly enlightened socialist movement, that leadership and theorizing roles should belong rightfully to men rather than to women. Paradoxically, she never achieved the status, renown, influence, or power to which her role as Marx's daughter should have entitled her.

Her heritage was a hindrance as much as a help. It was not the quality of her life as such but the terms of both her birth and death that made her a heroine in the socialist revolutionary drama. In life she was accepted as the daughter of her famous father; in death she was remembered more for the gruesome details of her personal life than for her assorted political activities. A romantic legacy haunts her and many other women revolutionaries. While the circumstances of her glorious birth and tragic death have guaranteed her fame, those same circumstances also served to minimize her real political contributions in the socialist world of late-nineteenth-century England.

Although Marx's entry into revolutionary socialist circles was naturally eased by the lucky accident of her birth, the English revolutionary tradition, socialist and otherwise, promised a place to all women ready and willing to join in the struggle. The roots of female revolutionary activity within the English tradition can be traced to the revolution and civil war of the seventeenth century. While women's activity in the actual course of the revolution was minimal and peripheral, small groups of women did attempt to bring direct pressure upon Parliament by public agitation, and by demanding their right to free public expression by drafting and presenting petitions.[1]

Even more important than these political demands were claims for women's spiritual equality put forth by the civil war sects. From the very beginning, the separatists placed great emphasis on the spiritual equality of the two sexes, explaining that the soul was "sexless" and presenting a new view of marriage as a spiritual union between equals.[2] While such arguments were admittedly very far from being bold feminist calls for political, legal, and social change, they proved in the long run to be central to the birth of feminism in the English context. Insofar as the civil war period marked the ascendancy of a political theory that took the individual as its primary unit of analysis, the groundwork for modern feminism was laid here. Mary Wollstonecraft's monumental treatise on women's rights grew from such roots, a direct response to male philosophers who somehow did not see that the concept of individual human importance could also be applied to women.[3]

British socialism's treatment of the woman question also built on this heritage. Socialist theorists addressed themselves to women and promised them a place in the revolution to come. In any account of the native development of British socialism, a special place must be reserved for Robert Owen, the self-made cotton manufacturer whose scheme for a programmed socialist community was unveiled at New Lanark in Scotland in 1821. A concern for female emancipation was central to Owen's plan for social restructuring.[4] Individual family life, he felt, victimized woman, and made her a household drudge, the property of her husband, and a child-bearing machine. All Owenite schemes included plans for communal kitchens and dining rooms, to free women from the "tyranny" of housework, and schools for infant children, to release them from the burden of child care. Owen went even further, however. He attacked loveless marriages and advocated both easy divorce and birth control as remedies—radical views that made him a convenient target for conservatives eager to shackle all socialists with charges of immorality.[5]

Early British socialism showed itself to be particularly sympathetic to the woman question because of the import of advanced feminist ideas from France. Both Saint-Simonian and Fourierist "missionaries" were active in England in the early decades of the nineteenth century, and both of these socialist sects addressed themselves to female emancipation from the outset.[6] Saint-Simonian propaganda, some of it geared to female audiences, circulated widely, and frequently appeared in Owenite periodicals.

All three utopian socialist groups, Owenites, Fourierists, and Saint-Simonians, addressed themselves to woman's position as a producer within the isolated household and demanded marriage and divorce reform as a necessary first step on the road to change. Yet, because they all centered their attack on the destructive nature of capitalist society in general, their real commitment to women's emancipation always remained a secondary one. Committed to the emancipation of "every human being," they consistently linked women's emancipation to larger social and political events. Female emancipation was not to be sought as an end in itself, but would come as a concomitant result of the birth of a new social order.

This problem of establishing revolutionary priorities can be clearly seen in an examination of what the most latently revolutionary movement of mid-nineteenth century England promised its female supporters. "Peaceably if we may, forcibly if we must," was the bold motto of Chartism, a predominantly working class movement with a detailed six-point program for political and social reform. Women's sections were established in most of the main centers of Chartist activity, and certain pieces of Chartist propaganda were written specifically for them.[7] However, as in the case of utopian socialism, women were promised only a share in the better world that the men of their class were making. Exclusively feminist problems were never emphasized. Although many Chartist leaders believed in the vote for women, and although women's suffrage had been included in the original demands upon which the People's Charter was based, it never became part of the movement's program. Again it was a question of priorities. Demanding the vote for women, many Chartists feared, might retard working men's chances of gaining the franchise.[8] Despite such vacillation on feminist issues, however, there is no record of antimale agitation among the female Chartists. Chartist women did not see themselves as any more oppressed than the men of their class, but were content to fight together with them, combatting the twin issues of hunger and economic oppression.[9] Neglecting women's special needs, the Chartists developed no outstanding female leaders.[10] This fact is significant, for the legacy of women's supportive role in the primarily class struggle was to color the developing British labor movement from then on.

The workers became quiescent after the failure of Chartism, and organized revolutionary ferment would not crystallize again until the 1880s. Then a variety of causes were responsible: the Irish national question, the influx of political refugees from the repressive empires of Europe, economic depression, the stimulus of upheavals in France, the decline of agriculture, and a general disillusionment with the electoral reforms of the last decades.[11]

By that time Marx was dead, but his daughter Eleanor—the only one of his children to be born, to work, and to die in England—inherited his legacy. No female revolutionary of the period had a clearer claim to acceptance and authority in the socialist world. None had such a clear-cut mandate to work out the kinks in socialism's treatment of the woman question. Yet Eleanor Marx's role as a revolutionary was limited by the traditions of her society, and no woman epitomized the traditional English heritage of the revolutionary helpmate better than she. What became of the mantle bequeathed to her is alarmingly significant in any attempt to explain why women have failed to attain positions of real leadership in modern revolutionary movements.

II

Eleanor Marx's attraction to revolutionary socialism cannot be totally explained by the simple fact that she was the daughter of Karl Marx. Marx had three daughters who lived to adulthood, yet she was the only one who chose to devote herself wholeheartedly to the movement that had been her father's creation. Her sisters Laura and Jenny, through their heritage, their personal correspondence, and their marriages to French socialists, kept in touch with political events of the period, but neither attained the prominence and public acclaim that Eleanor did. Contemporaries noted that her political involvement was always in sharp contrast to theirs. Although Engels often tried to press them into action, they were blissfully content to play the role of housewives and mothers in France.[12] While the circumstances of Eleanor's birth, then, certainly predisposed her to revolutionary involvement, her acceptance of that legacy was neither inevitable nor automatic.

Eleanor was born in London on January 16, 1855, the sixth child of Karl Marx and Jenny von Westphalen. A son and a daughter had died previously, and Eleanor's birth was followed closely by the death of another son, Edgar. Marx was severely affected by the loss of his son and deeply troubled by the recognition that he would probably never have a male heir.[13] He came to be consoled, however, by the fact that his infant daughter seemed to be so much like him. "Tussy is me," he proudly proclaimed, often joking with his wife that the girl's female gender must have been an accident.[14] Identifying Eleanor with his dead son, Marx treated her as the little boy he never had. Through his lavish care, concern, and attention, he consciously and deliberately heightened Eleanor's sense of self-importance.

Poor health in early childhood also added to the fawning adulation that the young girl received. Since the grinding poverty of the Marx family in these years was held to have been responsible for Edgar's death,[15] a determined effort was made to keep Eleanor alive. So weak and sickly was she at birth that she was fed on nothing but milk to age five, and mainly on milk to age ten.[16] Such excessive attention must have ingrained a sense of specialness in Eleanor from early childhood. This sense of specialness, coupled with the unconscious identification with her dead brother, and the conscious recognition that she was so much like Marx himself, were all important factors in her political socialization and in her subsequent decision to embark on a political life.

Her sisters were ten and eleven years, respectively, older than she was, and Eleanor, by common admission, became the darling of the household. All contemporary accounts admit she was spoiled. Her mother called her the "idol of the whole house," "Marx's pet," and freely admitted that the family's love and grief for Edgar were lavishly showered on his little sister.[17]

As critical factors in her political socialization, this inordinate sense of specialness must be added to the tremendous political education that the child received from the simple fact of being brought up in the household of Karl Marx.[18] Eleanor and *Capital*, it has been said, grew up together.[19] Although her scholastic attainments were poor, the value of having Karl Marx as an informal tutor was immense. As Eleanor's sisters approached adolescence, their concerns drifted to other areas, and Marx was free to lavish his tremendous tutorial powers on his youngest daughter.[20] She, for her part, showed an exceptional willingness to imbibe this political education.

In later life Eleanor fondly recalled how Marx had always made time for her, and never complained of her interruptions. She "was never allowed to think she was in the way,"[21] never taught to believe that politics should not be her concern. Some of her childhood letters are startling, both for their political awareness and for their bold tone. At age eight she wrote to an uncle—interestingly enough, whom she had never met:

> I hear from papa that you are a great politician, so we are sure to agree. How do you think Poland is getting on? I always hold up a finger for the Poles those brave little fellows. Do you like A. B.? [Auguste Blanqui] He is a great friend of mine. . . . I dare say you will hear from me again.[22]

True to her word, she wrote again, six months later.

> What do you think of affairs in America? I think the Federals are safe. . . . Were you not delighted about the Alabama? Of course you know all about it; at all events a Politician like you ought to. As for poor Poland, I am afraid there is no help for it.[23]

Convinced that Abraham Lincoln "badly needed" her advice on the Civil War, she wrote long letters to the American president, which her father dutifully "agreed" to mail.[24] Many of Marx's political friends and acquaintances were so amused by the little girl's bold ventures that they made special note, in their letters, to give her their regards.[25] She frequently accompanied her father on both pleasure trips and political jaunts, and met many of the biggest leaders of international socialism while she was still a child.[26] Although for a time she maintained a fleeting correspondence with the daughter of German socialist leader Wilhelm Liebknecht, it was Liebknecht himself who became her life-long friend.[27]

Frederick Engels was another of Eleanor's personal political tutors. He remained her political mentor and confidant all his life, becoming, in the years after Marx's death, like a second father to her. Here again, in her love and friendship for Engels, Eleanor showed herself to be markedly different from her two older sisters. She was the only one of the three who ever spent time with Engels on extended vacations in Manchester. Although the invitation was also extended to the others, there is no evidence that either ever responded.[28] Eleanor was with Engels in Manchester on that fateful day when he permanently ended his association with his father's textile firm. Witnessing the sense of triumph and celebration with which he ended his "forced labor,"[29] Eleanor was schooled in the evils of capitalism from an early age—a schooling that was intensely intimate, personal, and emotional.

Along with a deliberately fostered feeling of importance and the tremendous value of her personal political education, a third factor is significant in any attempt to assess the quality of Eleanor's political socialization: the character and kind of female role models presented to her in childhood and adolescence. Her early political interest might have proven to be nothing more than a natural and childlike response to the pervasive political atmosphere of her surroundings, nipped in the bud by the time she reached young womanhood, had it not been for three strong female figures who presented her with at least ambivalent notions of what a woman's "proper" role in life should be.

When Wilhelm Liebknecht was to write his reminiscences of Marx, Eleanor begged him not to forget her mother in his account, so aware was she of the decisive part that Jenny had played in Marx's success.[30] Eleanor's assessment of her mother's contributions extended well beyond Jenny's role as dutiful and efficient household manager. Not only did Eleanor emphasize the companionate nature of her parents' marriage, and their tremendous love and utter devotion to one another, but she also called attention to the respect that Marx accorded his wife's political opinions.[31]

Although Jenny Marx was greatly concerned with raising her daughters in respectable Victorian fashion,[32] she was never quite so imbued with a traditional sex role ideology to accept the view that politics was a male domain alone. She copied Marx's manuscripts before they were sent to the printer, and, in her memoirs, referred with an obviously clear understanding to many of her husband's writings.[33] In her own correspondence she made frequent reference to political events,[34] and even on her deathbed remained vitally interested in the socialists' fate in the recent German elections.[35] Engels and others praised her "penetrating intellect," "political tact," and "clear and brilliant mind."[36]

Yet, a tension existed within Jenny Marx, a struggle between her roles as private woman and political wife. Never known to have taken an independent political stance, she insisted that her one published piece, a literary and not a political work, be published anonymously.[37] First and foremost, she always remained Marx's wife, "his life-long helpmate in the truest and fullest sense of the word."[38] It was this aspect of her mother's life that Eleanor considered most important. After her parents' deaths, Eleanor poignantly recalled the beautiful complementary nature of their lives together,[39] and she took these idyllic memories as the model for her own. Shared devotion to a cause in such a companionate marriage, and not an independent political existence of her own, became her ideal.

The second important female role model in Eleanor's youth was another strong, politically conscious woman, but one whose life also revolved around self-sacrifice and devotion to others. She was Helene "Lenchen" Demuth, the Bavarian peasant woman who spent her lifetime as a maid-of-all-work in the service of the Marx family. Lenchen loved the family blindly. She became the "bosom friend" of Jenny Marx and a second mother to the girls. Marx respected her "innate" sense of political judgment and often asked her advice on "difficult and complicated" party matters.[40] So highly was she regarded as an integral and respected member of the household that she was even buried in the Marx family plot. Engels paid her the supreme compliment at her funeral: "For my part, I owe all the work I have been able to do since Marx's death largely to the sunshine and help that her presence brought to my house, where she did me the honour of coming to live after Marx's death."[41]

Both Jenny Marx and Lenchen Demuth had a lasting effect on Eleanor Marx. When called upon to write a tribute to Engels upon his seventieth birthday, Eleanor included tributes to them as well, so strongly did she feel that neither Marx nor Engels could have succeeded without the help of both of these strong, devoted, self-sacrificing women.[42] The helpmate mold obviously appealed to her.

The third important female influence on Eleanor Marx also evidenced these same qualities of limited political consciousness and self-sacrificing devotion, but to these she added the element of an unconventional but nonetheless attractive sexuality. She was Lizzie Burns, the Irish-born factory girl who became Engels' common-law wife. Not only did Lizzie acquaint Eleanor with the free and easy unrespectability of a nontraditional sexual liaison, but she also introduced her to what was to become the first of many burning political issues in her life: the Irish national question. Although Marx and Engels were both intensely interested in the revolutionary potential of Irish nationalism,[43] it was from Lizzie that Eleanor acquired a personal and emotional attachment to the movement. Lizzie was an ardent patriot, and many "Sinn Feiners" found refuge and hospitality in her house.[44] Her enthusiasm and patriotism were infectious, and the adolescent Eleanor took to wearing only green, buying copies of *The Irishman*, the organ of the Irish nationalists, and signing her letters "Eleanor, F. S. (Fenian Sister)."[45]

In Eleanor's early political education the Irish question was soon superseded by another much more monumental event. In 1871 revolutionary convulsions rocked the city of Paris. The decaying empire of Louis Napoleon had revealed its helplessness in the Franco-Prussian War, but when the Germans sought to impose a humiliating *Diktat*, the French took to fighting among themselves. Starved and frozen by the Germans, revolutionary Parisians refused to accept the new republican government that, in their opinion, had surrendered French honor, was dominated by a predominantly monarchist assembly, and had too quickly and unfeelingly cancelled many wartime emergency relief measures. A fierce civil war erupted between the national government and the city of Paris, which proclaimed its autonomy and proceeded to organize itself as a self-governing municipal council or "commune."[46]

The Paris Commune affected the entire Marx family intimately. Famous for its protosocialist legislation and revolutionary fervor, it was hailed as a possible precursor of the long-awaited dictatorship of the proletariat. Because of its proletarian character, conservative circles were quick to accuse the "diabolical" Marx of directing the whole affair from the London headquarters of the International,[47] the workers' association he had established to popularize his doctrines of proletarian solidarity and working class revolution the world over. With the brutal repression of the Commune, streams of refugees invaded the family apartments, and Jenny Marx wrote poignant letters inquiring after the safety of friends and associates.[48] Eleanor's sister Laura had by that time married the Frenchman and Communard Paul Lafargue, and for her the fate of the Parisian revolution became a question of survival itself. Through such personal involvement, the Commune's influence on Eleanor Marx became long-lasting. All her life the fires of her revolutionary faith were stoked by the debt she felt was owed to the Commune's martyrs. In later years she became a regular speaker at the annual commemorative services held by London radical groups to honor the victims of the short-lived Parisian uprising.[49]

During the episode of the Commune, Eleanor received her first taste of what it meant to be the daughter of the infamous Dr. Marx. In May 1871, Eleanor, then 16, and her sister Jenny traveled to France to visit Laura, who had only recently given birth to her third child. Paul's involvement in the Commune made the Lafargues fear for their political safety, and after the victory of the government forces they crossed the border into Spain. When Jenny and Eleanor left to return to London, they were arrested at the border and accused of acting as "emissaries" of the International on the Spanish and French frontiers. Forced to submit to a lengthy interrogation, they spent the night in jail, and were able to return to London only after further difficulties with the Spanish authorities. Despite what Marx considered to be the "tragicomical" and "farcical" nature of the whole affair, the incident must be taken as a decisive one in arousing Eleanor's political consciousness.[50]

After her return from the Continent, Eleanor's interest in the Commune and its aftereffects mounted, due to the steady flow of Parisian refugees who made the pilgrimage to Marx's door. The plight of the Communards affected her deeply. "There are a great many members of the Commune here," she wrote to a friend, "and the poor refugees suffer frightfully—they have none of them any money, and you can't think how difficult it is for them to get work. I wish they'd taken some of the millions they're accused of having stolen."[51]

It was also during this period that Eleanor first attempted to link her personal devotion to a cause with her emotional desires as a young woman. Among the refugees who came to call on Marx were two French socialists and ex-Communards, Charles Longuet and Hippolyte-Prosper-Olivier Lissagaray. After Longuet had made his interest in Jenny apparent, Eleanor was quite jealous of their engagement and eager to follow suit.[52]

Despite the difference in their ages—Lissagaray, at 34, was almost twice Eleanor's age—she felt herself deeply attracted to him. Perhaps his career as a revolutionary journalist and member of the Commune National Guard excited her revolutionary sympathies, but more probably there was an element of adolescent rebellion in her prolonged infatuation. With one sister engaged and the other married, Eleanor was becoming disenchanted with her role as dutiful daughter, yearning for excitement and some sort of independent existence.

Marx was opposed to the relationship from the start.[53] Certainly his persistence in continually referring to Eleanor as "the child" revealed his attitude on the question of the age difference, but it also demonstrated a protective father's reluctance to hand over his favorite daughter to a political exile with no resources and apparently no future. Marx also opposed Lissagaray for political reasons, seeing the Frenchman's egoistic and individualistic approach to socialism as a direct challenge to his own philosophical authority.[54]

In spite of all objections, Eleanor defiantly entered into what she considered to be an "engagement" to Lissagaray. Those anxious to establish a conflict with the father as being the determining element in the making of the revolutionary, male or female, may perhaps hope to make more out of this affair than the facts warrant. But if Eleanor were indeed "rebelling" against Marx, her rebellion was certainly grounded in a very traditional area. History is full of father-daughter quarrels on this and similar questions, and the birth of revolutionary women by the thousands has not been the inevitable result. Neither did Eleanor ever consider committing the ultimate act of rebellion and running off with the Frenchman. Her acceptance of her father's authority was in fact so conventional that she even went so far as to beg Marx's permission to see Lissagaray, after he had ordered and enforced a long separation between them. The pleadings of such a respectful daughter can certainly not be used as evidence by those who might seek to attribute her later revolutionary activity to a rejection of her father as an authority figure. Marx's role in the positive political socialization of his daughter was much more important to her assuming a future revolutionary role than was any psychological or psychosexual conflict between them.

The pseudo-engagement, with all its allegedly rebellious character, eventually died quietly after nine long years. When the general amnesty for ex-Communards was proclaimed in 1880, Lissagaray returned to France and there was no mention of Eleanor's returning with him. Nonetheless, their relationship was important for several reasons. It marked the first time in Eleanor's life that she assumed the role of helpmate, dedicating herself, in a shared union with a lover, to a cause in which they both believed. The model of Jenny Marx as the devoted political wife continued to be inspirational. United to Lissagaray by the legacy of the Parisian insurrection, Eleanor spent years of her life preparing an English translation of his monumental *History of the Commune*.[55] Significantly, in this her first explicitly political labor, she was content to satisfy herself with the painstaking task of translator, a subsidiary, behind-the-scenes role to which she was to return again and again the rest of her life.

Second, the Lissagaray affair can be regarded as Eleanor's first bid for independence out from the shadow of her famous father. Although this need for independence troubled her until Marx's death in 1883, her quest always remained ill-defined. Beset by an urge to be and to do, she could never take the critical leap from ambition to accomplishment. Recurrent emotional and health problems were convenient excuses that prevented her from making a serious decision as to the course her life would take. Marx, in the fashion of the day, was inclined to label her "hysterical."[56]

Eleanor struggled to establish her independence in a variety of ways, but her dabbling activities were characterized by a lack of intensity and serious commitment. All her life she was plagued by the conflict between living as a private woman or assuming the political legacy to which her birthright entitled her. This conflict, manifested in a wavering dilettantism, served to dilute her political contributions. Although she retained her interest in politics during this period, it was a shared and divided one. She canvassed for radical candidates in school board elections,[57] wrote reviews on the Russian political situation,[58] and did piecework for her father in the

British Museum. As her mother's health failed, she came more and more to assume the role of hostess in the Marx household.

Yet, despite her frequently acute political observations,[59] Eleanor retained a fatal attraction for the nonpolitical life. Captivated by the literary and dramatic world of late Victorian society, she maintained a stubborn desire to be an actress.[60] If her nascent career had indeed shown signs of promise, she would have been more than content to abandon the political calling. "One of the sorest disappointments of her life was that she never became an actress," one of her friends recalled.[61] Thwarted in her theatrical ambitions, she became depressed, even suicidal,[62] but continued her literary dabblings in other areas. She joined a variety of literary societies, hosted drama club meetings, and did limited amounts of literary research and translating.[63]

Obviously, Eleanor's reluctance to accept the political legacy to which her role as Marx's daughter entitled her was not born of any Victorian sense of squeamishness as to the propriety of a woman's entering political life. She was not one to be troubled by such niceties. The Victorian actress was no "lady,"[64] yet Eleanor would gladly have accepted that career had she shown herself capable. Her turning from revolutionary socialism in these years may be explained by a variety of reasons. Elements of resentment against her father may have been a lingering legacy of the Lissagaray affair. "For long, miserable years there was a shadow between us . . . ," she admitted to a friend.[65] Perhaps conscious of her own political and theoretical inadequacy vis-à-vis Marx, she was anxious to establish her worth in her own area and on her own terms. As both her parents grew old and sick, she was expected to bear the burden of keeping the household together. Even Marx was aware of the strain that nursing duties were placing on her, confiding to Engels that he never wanted Eleanor to become a martyr, "sacrificed on the family altar."[66] Embittered by the demands that were made of her as the last unmarried daughter living at home, she may have identified her rejection of politics with her rejection of this dutiful daughter role.

After the death of both her parents, however, Eleanor was finally freed of any sense of sacrifice, duty, and resentment under which she may have labored. Yet at this time, rather than embark on an independent political or literary course of her own, she chose to substitute wifely responsibilities for filial ones. In the summer of 1884 she entered into a free union with the socialist and freethinker Dr.

Edward Aveling, in the hope, it appears, of following her parents' model of a marriage both companionate and political.

Edward Aveling was a well-known figure in London radical, literary, and scientific circles. Holding a doctorate in natural science from the University of London, he was a popular atheist lecturer, active in the secularist movement, one of the most important intellectual currents of late Victorian Britain. With its profession of atheism, attack on the power of the national church, emphasis on social welfare, and respect for freedom of thought, secularism was a formative influence on the development of British socialism,[67] and Aveling himself found that his secularist past provided him with an especially useful background for the socialism he also came to adopt.

At the time of Marx's death, Aveling was the editor of the secularist journal *Progress*, for which he asked Eleanor to write an obituary tribute.[68] This event is usually taken to mark the beginning of their relationship. The attraction was strong and immediate. "Our tastes were much the same," she explained. "He knew more than I about Darwin and evolution. . . . We agreed on socialism. We both loved the theatre. Neither of us cared for money. My father liked him. We could work together effectively."[69]

Surely Eleanor would have married Aveling had she been legally able, but since his first wife was unwilling to grant him a divorce, he was not in the position to marry Eleanor had he so desired. Thus, her decision to live openly with him without benefit of clergy should be taken as proof neither of her blazing radicalism or pioneering nonconformism. Although an attachment to the principle of "free love" was not the direct cause of their common-law union, Eleanor did come to believe that free love would and should be the standard form of human relationships in the future socialist world, where freedom in all aspects of life would be the rule. Her own lifestyle was to bear witness to the radical sexual ideology that she did eventually champion.[70]

Pathetically—and tragically—however, her life within this free union was more oppressed and submissive than it might have been in the worst of traditional marriages. Her liaison with Aveling was destined to be an ill-fated one, the source of the romantic legend that still surrounds her life. Contemporaries remained baffled at the attraction between the "dutiful and good" daughter of Karl Marx and that "disreputable dog" Aveling.[71] Although it was acknowledged that he would "go to the stake" for his political beliefs,[72] his personal reputation was dreadful. Page after page after page of memoirs by contemporaries recount his moral perversion, his financial extravagance and irresponsibility, his alcoholism, and his freewheeling sexual encounters.[73] Only his "mysterious force of seductive sexuality" could have drawn Eleanor to him.[74]

Yet it is not difficult to justify her attraction on rational grounds. The two shared interests in many areas, as Eleanor herself admitted. Aveling's literary and dramatic penchants paralleled her own, and even his somewhat tenuous claims to Irish ancestry may have appealed to her earlier Fenian leanings. Although his socialism was of relatively recent vintage, he was ready and eager to succumb to Marxian orthodoxy, proud and not in the least reluctant to present himself as the "son-in-law" of Karl Marx. He boasted of how Marx and even the young Eleanor had attended his university lectures years earlier, and of how he had basked in the great man's praise.[75] Marx was a great admirer of Darwin, on whose theories Aveling himself was quite an authority. His rightful role as a link between the two great minds, he asserted, was therefore quite obvious.[76] Despite such posturing, Engels and the Lafargues liked and accepted Aveling, and Engels even entrusted parts of the English translation of *Capital* to his hand.

At this period of her life, when Eleanor found herself alone and economically forced to pursue an independent career, it is easy to understand why this shared realm of interests attracted her to Aveling. Obviously, she did not feel confident enough in her own abilities to assume alone what should have been her rightful place in the international socialist movement. Regardless of her motivations, however, it was with Aveling that she embarked on her helpmate role as the bearer of revolutionary socialism to the nation that had been her father's adopted home, and upon whose industrial system all his theories about the coming crisis of capitalism were based.

III

Despite a promising revolutionary heritage, the presence of Marx and Engels, and the London base of the International, revolutionary socialism never came to England in one major upheaval. The story of the "revolution" in England—if, indeed, the story is even worthy of that name—was one of trial-and-error efforts to create a climate favorable to a revolutionary future. In a nation where the average worker appeared to have no taste for barricades and street fighting,[77] even the word "revolution" came to be redefined. The bringing of revolutionary socialist consciousness to England consisted of a series of attempts to educate and to organize, conducted in the hope of forging a sense of class among workers hitherto divided from each other. Although peppered with riotous strikes and bloody demonstrations, the struggle for a socialist transformation of society and a shift of power to the working class came to be an increasingly peaceful one, characterized by reformist political demands and by an ever-widening search for institutional maturity and international respectability. How could the female revolutionary—especially one whose name happened to be Marx—act in such a context?

The socialism that developed in England after 1880 remained conscious of its native roots and traditions, but also acknowledged the international character of the revolutionary movement. Old Chartists lingered in London radical clubs, but their numbers were swelled by French, German, and Russian refugees escaping from a hardening conservative backlash in their respective countries. These refugees brought not only numerical strength but also theoretical maturity to the young movement.[78]

British radicalism was also fed in its beginning stages by members of the intellectual middle class, that group whose development of essentially counterclass sympathies has historically provided impetus to all modern revolutionary movements. In England, disillusionment was bred in such circles by the recognition that unemployment was growing, agriculture was in crisis, industrialism was threatened, and Britain's economic and political supremacy could no longer be assured. It was one of these middle class intellectuals, a wealthy barrister, journalist, and politician named Henry Mayers Hyndman, who really must be credited with creating England's first socialist political organization.[79]

Hyndman had become acquainted with European Marxism through German socialists in London, and one of these, Karl Hirsch, introduced him to Marx.[80] In subsequent meetings, Hyndman tried to interest Marx in a plan to build a revolutionary organization through remnants of the old Chartists and the London radical clubs. Marx, finding Hyndman personally offensive, held aloof from the scheme.[81] Hyndman persisted in the plan, however. In June 1881 he formed the Democratic Federation, a self-proclaimed socialist group actually characterized by a wide diversity of political opinions.[82]

From the start, the major problem encountered by the Democratic Federation seemed to be Hyndman's tyrannical and dictatorial personality. The inspiration behind the organization, he believed, was his and his alone, and no one, not even Marx himself, should rob him of the limelight to which his accomplishment entitled him. His egotism was not only to prove fatal to the institutional success of British socialism, but also was to earn him the eternal enmity of both Marx and Engels. Marx's initial dislike for Hyndman increased after Hyndman published a socialist textbook entitled *England for All*. Although certain chapters of this work amounted to a virtual summary of Marx's *Capital*, Hyndman had merely acknowledged his debt to "a great thinker and original writer" whom he chose not to name.[83] Marx was outraged by such blatant "plagiarism," and the lasting significance of the affair was that he never gave his blessing to Hyndman's allegedly Marxist organization.

In spite of these shaky beginnings, the Democratic Federation—or the Social Democratic Federation (SDF), as it was later rechristened—was the "first modern socialist organization of national importance in Britain."[84] By January 1884 it had adopted a clearly socialist program, premised on both the class struggle and dreams of the social revolution.[85] In sharp contrast to the Fabian Society, which eschewed all notions of the class struggle in its hope for a peaceful and gradual evolution to socialism,[86] the SDF was a force with which any self-proclaimed revolutionary socialist would soon have to reckon.

Eleanor Marx, therefore, with her father dead, her dramatic hopes frustrated, and her "marriage" partner a willing believer, soon chose to throw in her lot with Hyndman's organization. The alliance was a stormy one, at best. Eleanor was well aware of Marx's distaste for Hyndman, and Hyndman was forever suspicious that the Avelings, backed by Engels, would challenge his claims to supremacy by establishing their own organization. His fears were well founded. The Avelings, along with William Morris, Belfort Bax, and others, did in fact secede from the SDF in December 1884, to form their own organization, the Socialist League. The overriding cause of the split, however, was not Engels' jealousy—as Hyndman liked to believe—but his own high-handedness and dictatorial pretensions.[87]

The creators of the Socialist League attacked the spirit of opportunism, reformism, and "electioneering" that they claimed had come to color the SDF. Its emphasis on parliamentary action, they felt, was premature and inappropriate. The working classes needed to be educated to their future role before they could even hope of seizing power by political means. From the start, the Socialist League characterized itself as a revolutionary body. Although not averse to political methods, it aimed at the "realization of complete revolutionary socialism."[88] Such an aim encompassed a determined commitment to internationalism, a goal that Eleanor believed had been decidedly lacking in the SDF. "We wish to make this a really international movement," she wrote to Wilhelm Liebknecht. "Mr. Hyndman, whenever he could do so with impunity, has endeavoured to set English workmen against 'foreigners.'"[89]

Eleanor's presence in the League brought it international renown, and on the Continent it was regarded as a genuine Marxist group.[90] Despite its early promise, however, the Socialist League never became a truly national organization. Its largest membership never amounted to more than a few hundred, and its official journal, *Commonweal*, never had a large circulation.[91] Engels, referring to both the SDF and the Socialist League, consistently warned his European colleagues not to be misled as to the real strength of the movement in England. "I am very glad," he wrote to Lafargue, "that what passes for socialism here is not advancing at all."[92]

From the start, the Socialist League was doomed by factional disputes, but its founders were reluctant to create a spurious unity through the imposition of centralized control. Repulsed by Hyndman's domineering, the creators of the League went full circle and never endowed any one of their members with administrative power or leadership authority. Eleanor Marx, revolted by Hyndman's tyrannical posturing, always refused to assume power for herself.

Her relationship to the socialist movement was not marked by a conscious and deliberate search for a political role, but was, on the contrary, consistently determined and shaped by the influence of certain men in her life. Although she was accepted as Marx's daughter, her heritage could serve to hurt her as well, for Hyndman's jealousy of both Marx and Engels also extended to her.[93] While Engels, for his part, always tried to protect Eleanor with the care and concern he felt he owed to the child of his dearest friend, his protection could be detrimental insofar as it deprived her of an identity of her own. Because Engels always chose to isolate himself from the organizational aspects of British socialism, he was never able to use his personality and prestige in a positive way, to help her find a niche in a viable political organization.

The problems that Eleanor encountered from being Marx's daughter and Engels' protégé were only magnified by her stubborn resolve to call herself "Mrs. Aveling." If the Marx-Engels liaison provided her with dubious advantages at best, the Aveling affair could, at worst, have written her out of the international socialist movement entirely.

Nowhere were the sorry results of her attachment to Aveling better seen than in the lingering scandal that came to be associated with what should rightfully have been considered one of her first political triumphs and independent political acts. In August 1886 the Avelings departed on a 15-week tour of the United States as guests of the Socialist Labor Party of North America (SLP). Their tour coincided with a critical period in the growth of the American labor movement.[94] In the spring immediately preceding their arrival, a mounting wave of strikes and agitation for an eight-hour day had peaked in the famous incident in Chicago's Haymarket Square, where an explosion of dubious origin served to shackle the incipient labor movement with charges of conspiracy, terrorism, and anarchism. The eight men arrested for the deed, commonly known as the "Chicago Anarchists," became the focus of an international crusade for clemency in which Eleanor Marx was herself active.[95]

Because the Haymarket incident created confusion between anarchism and socialism in the American mind, one of the major aims of the Avelings' lectures was to distinguish socialist demands from bomb-throwing and random violence. Eleanor led the attack against anarchism, calling it "dangerous and useless." She urged her listeners instead "to throw three bombs among the masses—agitation, education, and organization."[96]

Eleanor's role as Marx's daughter won her ready acceptance among the Americans. Even the nonsocialist press was infatuated with this nontraditional woman who was not only daring enough to preach in public, but bold enough to utter revolutionary proclamations in the process.[97] The trip in general was widely hailed as a success. The Avelings lectured in most of the industrial centers of the Northeast and Midwest,[98] met a wide variety of American labor leaders, contributed to working class papers, gathered enough material to write two books based on their experiences and observations,[99] and clarified, they felt, what should be the role of a united American proletariat in the international socialist movement. As they departed for England in December, it seemed that the trip had indeed gone a long way toward establishing their claims to leadership not only in international socialist circles but, more importantly, in British ones. Surely the trip would enhance the prestige of their Socialist League vis-à-vis Hyndman's SDF.[100]

They were to be sorely disappointed. No sooner had the Avelings departed for England than a scandal erupted in the pages of the New York *Herald*. The Executive Committee of the SLP charged that Aveling had "padded" his own expense account over the course of the tour so as, in effect, to cover the cost of his wife's accompanying him, even though her expenses were explicitly not part of the original bargain with the SLP. Aveling's bill for $1,300, although considered rather steep for one with proclaimed socialist sensibilities, was accepted, but the goodwill of the Executive Committee broke down when they were presented with a supplementary bill for $600 to cover an assortment of questionable expenses. These included $50 for cigars, $25 for corsages, $26 for stamps, $100 for theater tickets, and $42 for wine at a first-class Baltimore hotel.[101]

The whole affair eventually blew over when it was discovered that the SLP had reasons of its own for being disenchanted with the socialist visitors. Before their departure, the Avelings had called attention to and criticized the predominantly German nature of the movement in America, and they predicted that it would fail unless and until it broadened its scope to appeal both to native Americans and other immigrant workers. The few who were anxious to "boss the show" had to be made aware of "how essential it is that the movement be American as well as international."[102] Although their comments were not only well taken, but also in substantial agreement with earlier statements made by Engels,[103] the Avelings were not necessarily wise to be quite so blunt to the leaders of the very organization that had financed their extended stay. They should at least have waited until returning to England to launch their attack.

Nonetheless, the scandal served to put Aveling, and by implication Eleanor, in a very discreditable light. Aveling's extravagance in money matters was already well known, and despite his denials it was generally accepted that he could have been guilty of at least the kind of behavior that the charges specified. Eleanor's guilt in the matter was more difficult to assess. After all, the bill was thought to have been padded to cover her expenses, and certain of these, such as corsages and cigarettes, were items that were specifically designated as having been for her. Yet, even if the daughter of Karl Marx were innocent of any wrongdoing, the entire sorry episode stands as one more example of how her own reputation was adversely affected by the man with whom she had thrown in her lot.

Engels of course stood by both of them in the controversy, but his excessive protectiveness served to highlight the weakness of Eleanor's own political identity.[104] If only Aveling's reputation had been at stake, perhaps Engels would have chosen not to get involved, but the fact that the charges impugned her integrity made it imperative that he rush to her defense:

> Had he [Aveling] tried to swindle the party, how could he do that during all his tour without his wife being cognizant of it? And in that case the charge includes her too. And then it becomes utterly absurd, in my eyes at least. Her I have known from a child, and for the last 17 years she has been constantly about me. And more than that. I have inherited from Marx the obligation to stand by his children as he would have done himself, and to see, as far as lies in my power, that they are not wronged. And that I shall do, in spite of 50 Executives. The daughter of Marx swindling the working class—too rich indeed![105]

Duped by one man, and protected by another because of her role as child of a third, Eleanor Marx was consistently plagued by the problem of establishing her identity as an independent socialist personality in her own right. Her birthright may have won her ready acceptance in international socialist circles, but in Britain she was never able to find a satisfactory institutional base from which to operate. Moreover, in the wake of the American affair, the Socialist League proved to be an increasingly weak and ineffective vehicle by which to do so. Beset by leadership and ideological controversies, it came more and more to be dominated by an increasingly vocal anarchist section infatuated with random acts of crude and thoughtless violence.[106] Disgusted by the League's deterioration, and disenchanted most of all by the continuing bitter squabbles and power plays between self-proclaimed socialists, Eleanor withdrew entirely from League affairs and chose to devote herself to other pursuits.

Consciously deciding to separate herself from an institutional base, she embarked on those activities for which she is still best remembered: agitating and organizing among the British poor. For Eleanor, socialism always meant much more than theorizing or leading. A woman deeply troubled by the "factory hell" and by an "inhuman" industrial system that showed a "real contempt for the value of human life,"[107] she believed socialism to be a real means to deal with the inequality and misery she saw around her. Genuinely shocked and alarmed that in "quiet, respectable, happy England" millions of people were on the verge of starvation,[108] she sought to harness their despair by working for any and all practical reforms that might stand to improve their lot in life.

With this end in mind, Eleanor Marx became one of the leading figures in the New Unionism of the late 1880s, a wave of labor agitation considered to be new and novel because it was marked by a changed position on the revolutionary potential of the unskilled laborer.[109] While older craft unionists had always been suspicious of revolutionary socialist infiltration and elitist in their attitudes toward the common and untrained laborer, new unionists like Eleanor Marx came to be convinced that the unskilled needed broad-based unions with militant, class-conscious programs, organizations dedicated to winning political victories and social and industrial reforms. Although Eleanor Marx was repeatedly insistent that the workers must never lose sight of the larger struggle, she felt unions were critically important, both as vehicles to achieve vital reforms and as a means to organize the working classes for independent labor politics.[110] Her activities here were important for several reasons. They demonstrate her individualistic conception of socialism, her eagerness to obliterate poverty and despair in the concrete rather than in the abstract, and her faith in the spontaneity and revolutionary potential of the masses. Her work among the unionists both appealed to and satisfied her in a way that socialist politics never could, for it allowed her to make actual contact with the laboring masses to whose liberation she had chosen to dedicate her life.

The formation of the Gasworkers and General Labourers Union in March 1889 is the event generally taken to herald the advent of the New Unionism. It was organized by Will Thorne, an uneducated stoker, who had been introduced to socialism in the early days of the SDF.[111] Once organized, the union's mere threat to strike at a time of full employment and expansion in the gas industry had maximum impact, and the Gasworkers were immediately successful in winning their demand for an eight-hour day.[112]

Eleanor Marx was intimately involved in several aspects of the Gasworkers' struggle. Significantly, the support she had given in her own quiet, behind-the-scenes way was at least indirectly responsible for Throne's own success. She taught him to read and, more than anyone else, helped him to improve his very bad handwriting and broaden his general knowledge.[113] As his Gasworkers Union grew, he continued to rely on her to help him with the "morass of paperwork."[114] Marx and Thorne represented the new union at the Brussels Congress of the recently founded Second International in 1891. There she delivered an address on labor activities in Great Britain and Ireland, the first time that one of the main international reports was ever written and delivered by a woman.[115] Along with Aveling, she drafted the Gasworkers' General Statement of aims at their first annual convention, a document that highlighted the class nature of the workers' efforts.[116] She was so popular with the Gasworkers that many simply called her "our Mother."[117] Beloved by the members for her sensitive and emotional nature and deep concern for their needs and interests as individuals, "Sister Aveling" was elected to the union's Executive Committee, one of the few middle class socialists to be invited to join the leadership councils of a great union.[118]

The Gasworkers' success proved an inspiration to workers in other trades. Marx formed the union's first women's branch, the result of a strike of East End rubber workers that she led.[119] Very much in demand as an orator and organizer, she spoke daily, sometimes twice daily, using chairs and even tables as her platform, enthusiastically haranguing the strikers to keep the faith.[120] Organizing women workers was particularly important to her. When the revolution came, she believed, it would be made by workers without distinction of "sex, or trade, or country."[121] Although she was highly sensitive to the difficulties of organizing women who had little time or inclination for attending meetings or listening to speeches, she was insistent that women must, "above the rest, bestir themselves,"[122] and unite not only for increased wages at present but for the future battle when they would fight alongside the men of their class for the achievement of socialism. Besides the rubber workers, Marx also helped other groups of women to organize, among them typists and women employed in the tailoring trades.

She was also a prominent figure in two other activities of the late-nineteenth-century British labor movement: the formulation of plans for the first English celebration of May Day, and the initiation of organized agitation for the eight-hour day. Here she demonstrated her staunch fidelity to the international character of the labor movement, for these activities were directly sponsored by the Second Socialist International. In 1889 the Paris Congress of the International had called for one day of working class demonstration that would be celebrated worldwide and would press for a variety of necessary reforms. With Marx's help, the first British May Day was an "epoch-making success."[123] Some 250,000 workers participated in socialist celebrations in London alone.[124] Engels was so impressed by the "grandsons of the old Chartists" that he grew skeptically optimistic about the prospects of a mass English socialist movement.[125] "It was a great victory for us," he beamed, "specially for Tussy and Aveling who with the help of the Gasworkers . . . have done it all."[126] Under Eleanor's leadership, the May Day committee became the nucleus of a new organization, the Legal Eight Hours and International Labour League. Composed of socialists, radicals, and trade unionists, its express purpose was agitation and propaganda both to secure the legal enactment of the eight-hour day and to establish an independent labor party that could represent British socialism in the International.[127]

The vitality of the British socialist movement quickened in the 1890s, but that movement came more and more to be defined not as a revolutionary insurrection but as a labor movement. The English experience of socialism was markedly different from the continental one. In Europe, large socialist parties had created trade union consciousness, but in England it was trade union activity that laid the groundwork for working class political success.[128] The most important result of the New Unionism and related agitation was the creation of a political party, formed by and for trade unionists, to work independently for the political aims of the working class and elect workingmen to Parliament. Born in January 1893, the Independent Labour Party (ILP) adopted a socialist program based on collective ownership and control of the means of production, but it sought to achieve its goals not through violent revolution but through parliamentary action.[129] Although Marx was present at the founding congress of the ILP, she never played a vital part in its affairs,[130] content to continue in her loner role as a labor agitator and organizer. But the divisions among British socialists continued. Marxism in Britain lost its theoretical coherence and revolutionary connotation despite the best efforts of the daughter of Karl Marx.

IV

Besides her educational and organizational activities among the working classes, Eleanor Marx also contributed to the socialism of her day as an author, editor, and translator. Although she labored diligently in all these areas—certainly to an extent far greater than either of her sisters—the most politically active daughter of Karl Marx never took that bold leap to establish herself as an important theoretician, biographer, or historian in her own right. Her most important contributions to the field of socialist literature were editions and collections of certain of her father's unpublished pieces,[131] as well as translations of several works by other noted Marxists.[132] Yet, the translation of more monumental works eluded her. She was not called upon to assist in the English translation of Marx's *Capital*,[133] although she was entrusted with the hackwork of checking the accuracy of Marx's original English citations.[134] Even when Sam Moore, Engels' self-appointed translator, was in desperate need of assistance, Aveling, not Eleanor, was selected for the assignment. She herself suggested him for the role, and Engels, despite some lingering doubts, agreed.[135]

Although Eleanor did write for several socialist periodicals of the day, her contributions were mainly reviews or comments upon the works of others.[136] Her one fairly regular and most substantial contribution was a column entitled "Record of the International Popular Movement," which appeared for a time in a variety of journals, *To-Day* and *Commonweal* among them.[137] This regular feature was a collection of news items relating to socialist activities in America and on the Continent, mailed to Eleanor by socialist correspondents and friends. Here again she seemed to be exhibiting the role, to use Liebknecht's words, of "predestined mediatrix between the proletarians of different countries."[138] Although this column not only manifested but also contributed to her wide knowledge of international socialism, there was a tedious element of secretarial collection and cataloguing entailed in her labors. The column was popular and certainly important, but it did not require great theoretical insight to produce. When Eleanor ceased to contribute to *Commonweal*, her successor was no socialist heavyweight, but another woman, William Morris' daughter May[139]—an interesting comment upon the kind of work Eleanor, as a woman, either was called upon to do, or chose to do of her own volition.

Significantly, those of her writings that were original pieces, not editions or translations, were coauthored with Aveling.[140] Her one independent work, *The Working Class Movement in England*,[141] was a short historical summary only, lacking both analysis and scholarly rigor. Even though Engels had high hopes for her project, optimistically proclaiming that no one could expect to write a better history of British socialism than Eleanor,[142] the pamphlet revealed her curious reluctance to deal with questions vital to the current state of the English movement. She had made a few timid, halting forays into socialist theory—the introductory prefaces to her father's works and a short piece on surplus value written for *Progress*—that had clearly demonstrated her easy familiarity with Marxism's philosophical essentials.[143] Then why was she so stubbornly reticent to base a claim to socialist prominence on substantial theoretical contributions?

Here again, it seems that the Marxian legacy that she inherited was a mixed blessing. Living in the shadow of her famous father left her with feelings of painful inadequacy. Plagued by doubts and insecurities in many aspects of her life, she wrote poignantly to a friend that she had, unfortunately, "only inherited my father's nose . . . and not his genius."[144] Even Hyndman recognized that some obstacle blocked her from living up to the promise of her birthright, and in the end he also attributed it to this sense of inferiority vis-à-vis Marx.[145]

Although as a young woman Eleanor had expressed doubts as to the true extent of her intellectual abilities, she was confident enough to know that she wanted some career other than housewife and mother.[146] Thus her literary activities followed a middle course—translating the original works of others and the securities of joint authorship with Aveling. Obviously she felt that she could perform her most valuable services to socialism by adopting what was essentially a supportive role, the editing and translating of her father's more obscure manuscripts.

The supportive, subsidiary nature of her activities was a pattern she followed in other areas of her life. Although she was a noted delegate to a variety of international congresses, the main task she was repeatedly called upon to undertake was not one that required tremendous theoretical insight, administrative skill, oratorical power, or leadership capacity. Her main role at such congresses was as translator and interpreter, and it was for this service that she was most consistently recognized and praised.[147] Able to speak English,

French, and German equally well, she was called "unrivalled as a translator,"[148] and contemporaries emphasized her "able and untiring efforts in this field."[149] The greatest tribute to her linguistic skills was paid by German socialist Eduard Bernstein, who recalled her "superhuman" labors at the Paris Congress of 1889:

> She was constantly busy, from morning to night, usually working in three languages. She never took a break, nor missed a session. Despite the intense heat, she stayed the length of the congress, doing this thankless and grueling labor: the real "proletarian" of the congress in the truest sense.[150]

The "real proletarian" of these congresses, however, was also the daughter of Karl Marx, and somehow she seemed deserving of a better fate. Although contemporaries repeatedly emphasized her unselfish and tireless devotion to the cause and her cheerful willingness to take up, as Bernstein noted, the "thankless and grueling work," they never quite made clear why she was attracted to such tasks. Was it because of her own insecurity, and her lingering sense that she could never live up to her father's greatness, or was it because such supportive and plodding roles were perfunctorily assigned to her as a woman—even though her name happened to be Marx? Contemporaries admitted that although many socialists proudly boasted of their radical and progressive views, "few of them had any patience with such advanced women as Eleanor."[151] Antiwoman sentiment was rife among some segments of British socialism.[152]

There are also other explanations for Marx's cheerful willingness to shoulder the peripheral duties. Feelings of inadequacy, the model of her self-sacrificing mother, what her contemporaries called her "infinitely good nature,"[153] and the pattern of silent female self-sacrifice inherited from the ages all played a part in the modest and often tedious chores she chose to undertake, "the drudgery of clerical work," typing, translating, and literary hackwork among them.[154] She was the one who balanced the Socialist League's budget, bought window cleaner for the premises, and sold tickets for various socialist events[155]—duties more in keeping with traditional sex role stereotyping than with her illustrious heritage. Modest and self-effacing, she was willing and eager to shoulder whatever tasks she was called upon to do, if, by so doing, she thought she could help the movement. For Marx, socialism and service were synonymous. Her patient devotion, tireless energy, unceasing work for the cause, and admirable self-abnegation were in sharp contrast, contemporaries recognized, to the "struts" and "boasting" of many socialist men who had clearly lost sight of what socialism was all about.[156]

Willingly given ceremonial duties, Marx was frequently denied really meaningful ones. One of the saddest stories of her career was the way in which she was actually cheated out of one of her most rightful roles, the authorship of her father's biography.

In the wake of Karl Marx's death, the leaders of the German Socialist Party came to be selfishly preoccupied with what would become of his vast collection of unpublished papers, books, and letters. Although it was the legal property of Marx's daughters and their heirs, there was no question that during Engels' lifetime the job of sorting and making sense of these documents would fall to him. As Engels' own health waned, however, the Germans descended upon his London home like vultures in search of prey, in an attempt to influence him to will to them as much of the collection as was legally within his power to do.[157] Eleanor's estrangement from Engels in the last months of his life is one of the saddest parts of her tragic story,[158] the more tragic since it appears to have been deliberately planned by leading German socialists. Eleanor was not consulted by Engels in the final preparation of his will,[159] a document that certainly affected her since it dealt with the disposition of many of her father's literary remains.

Upon Engels' death, his collection of books, manuscripts, copyrights, and letters—including all those between Marx and himself—was willed to the German party. Eleanor inherited only those letters that did not fall into that category, and the least important of Marx's manuscripts, those still in his original hand. The upshot of the whole affair was that Marx's papers were hopelessly divided, and neither Eleanor nor the German party had enough material to publish an authoritative biography. She hoped for a time to be able to write one nonetheless—and issued an urgent plea to the holders of any of her father's letters—but, like the promise of her life in general, this project also fell by the wayside.

It would be wrong, however, to view the actions of the German party in this affair as having been simply villainous or manipulative. They feared that Eleanor's undivided inheritance of the collection would be tantamount to its inheritance by Aveling, and that they could never accept. His wasteful extravagance and greed might cause him to sell the collection haphazardly to the highest bidder. The whole episode merely illustrates again how Eleanor's tragic association with Aveling must certainly be regarded as one of the most important factors in her failure to emerge as one of the leading figures of international socialism.

Yet Eleanor was determined to find a place for herself in public life. As her commitment to socialism waxed and waned depending on the successes or failures of the moment, she returned to the literary world that had always been her second love, writing literary and dramatic reviews for London periodicals, translating plays and stories, or popularizing the views of a favorite playwright.[160] She never considered these endeavors to be a detraction or distraction from her socialist labors, however, for she deeply believed that drama, literature, and art could be powerful educational tools, that the rich panorama of human relationships, old and new, real and ideal, could be seen most clearly there. Because she never held a narrowly economic or political view of what socialism was all about, she felt that socialists had much to learn from the new literary currents of the 1880s and 1890s, where radical political, social, and cultural views were clearly fused.[161]

Eleanor was especially affected by the vogue of Ibsen in late-nineteenth-century radical circles, feeling compelled "to do something to make people understand our Ibsen a little more than they do."[162] The attraction was understandable. Ibsen's attacks on the smothering, destructive, and dishonest character of bourgeois morality and married life seemed to provide justification for her own non-traditional lifestyle. Eleanor produced the first English translation of several of Ibsen's works,[163] and collaborated in writing a satirical sequel to *A Doll's House* that could not "fail to satisfy the English sense of morality and decency."[164]

In her enthusiasm for Ibsen and other authors whose literary works reflected the revolt of women in late-nineteenth-century Europe, Eleanor came to realize more strongly than ever that for women, personal lifestyle becomes a political statement. Her own quest for personal and political emancipation seemed to parallel that of the literary heroines who so intrigued her, women like her who were assertive, determined, and willing to fight for their share of life's happiness and opportunities. One of her closest friends was Olive Schreiner, whose autobiographical *Story of an African Farm* took its place alongside *A Doll's House* as a classic illustration of the new woman of the period. The saga of an adolescent girl's passionate rejection of a traditional female role, the work created a sensation among women, enthusiastically hailed by Eleanor and many others.

Eleanor was also fascinated by Flaubert's *Emma Bovary* for similar reasons, and she produced the first English translation of this feminist masterpiece. Emma's search for personal fulfillment paralleled Eleanor's own, and she herself seemed to recognize the similarity between their lives. "This strong woman," she wrote in the preface to her translation, "feels there must be some place for her in the world: there must be something to do—and she dreams. . . ."[165]

Emma Bovary's disenchantment with her lot in life was a feeling that was coming to be shared by many women in the England of Marx's day. It was an alienation that Eleanor not only felt but also acted upon. She was vitally concerned with the woman question, and what was probably her most important theoretical work was written on this issue. "The Woman Question: From a Socialist Point of View" was coauthored by the Avelings to coincide with the appearance of an English translation of August Bebel's *Woman Under Socialism*.[166] Their essay was an important one, they believed, for it brought together the complementary viewpoints of a man and a woman working together on this problem.

Although the Avelings followed the orthodox socialist line on the oppression of women—claiming, in familiar fashion, that its source was predominantly economic—their grappling with the real issues involved was more forthright than that of any of the other theorists who had also dealt with the matter—Marx, Engels, and Bebel included. They discussed the question of sexual gratification and condemned the "unnatural chastity" that the late marriages of the bourgeoisie foisted on respectable women. The prevailing double standard, they wrote, gave young men the means to gratify their urges, but respectable women had no alternative before marriage but to suffer the unhealthfulness of prolonged virginity. The Avelings also attacked false modesty and the Victorian sense of propriety that made the discussion of all such topics taboo. Most importantly, they attacked the "nonhuman" separation of the sexes and bemoaned society's failure to utilize and celebrate the unique and complementary qualities of men and women both.

Although all socialists agreed that capitalist marriage was a "commercial transaction," and that only in the truly free socialist society would marriage be freed of its "cash nexus" and based on love alone, no theorist had actually dealt with the translation of this prediction into practical terms. In their essay, the Avelings had hinted that polygamous relationships might be possible in the socialist society, but not until their American tour were they asked to take a candid stand on the issue. Aveling grew angry and impatient when pressured, but Eleanor was courageous enough to admit that the free love that socialism implied might, unfortunately, lead to unpleasant results. She frankly acknowledged that, under socialism, there would be no obligation for a man and woman to stay together, and no force to bind them. Yes, "a man could at any time put away an old wife for a younger one, or a sickly wife for a healthy one."[167] Perhaps a dissatisfaction with her own personal life had led her to realize that the rote repetition of socialist panaceas did not hold the real answer to the woman question.

Nor, however, did she believe contemporary British feminists had the answer. In spite of her frank treatment of such issues, there are problems in affixing a "feminist" label on Eleanor Marx, because that word usually connotes a liberal brand of legal and political reformism from which she clearly separated herself.[168] All the ideas of "advanced" women, she believed, didn't touch the "bedrock" issue of economics. The vote was not enough to achieve women's emancipation in the fullest sense. Furthermore, she recognized that the demands of suffragists were elitist and selfishly class based. The early suffragists were pressing not for universal adult suffrage, but for the eradication of the sex barrier to the franchise—the property qualifications could stay. To the extent that Eleanor agreed with Engels that the English suffragists were mainly "interested in the capitalist exploitation of both sexes,"[169] her commitment to socialism always took precedence over her commitment to feminism. Both the oppressed classes—women and workers—would profit from the eventual victory of socialism and should be natural allies in the struggle toward that end.

Marx was especially anxious that other women join the socialist cause for she deeply believed that the movement would benefit from the profoundly human qualities that women would bring to it. Her own definition and vision of socialism was decidedly different not only from her father's but from that of most of the other male socialists of her day. Neither couched in cold political formulas nor preoccupied with the seizure and conquest of political power, it emphasized and called attention to socialism's ethical aspects and the cultivation of humane sensibilities in the men and women who both embraced it and benefited from it. Marx's socialism was profoundly moral in tone and stressed self-sacrifice and devotion to others. There was an almost religious essence to her view of human responsibility for one another: "Though each one must work out his own salvation, we can make the work perhaps a little less hard for those that shall come after...."[170] Although she had no children of her own, she was greatly concerned that the tenets of socialism reach and touch the younger generation. "We too want the 'little children to come unto us,'" she wrote when planning a Socialist League Christmas party in 1885. "We cannot too soon make children understand that socialism means happiness."[171] Anxious to reach future workers while they were still young, she also taught for a time at a socialist Sunday school in Battersea, where she explained socialist principles in the language of traditional Christian ethics.

As she became more and more disenchanted with the petty factionalism and theoretical squabbles of British socialism, she emphasized socialism's moral underside and the promise of hope that it held out to individual human beings. For her, socialism came to have a human face. Vitally affected by the misery, poverty, and suffering in London's East End, she made increasingly frequent trips to the area, not only to agitate and organize, but also to explore and investigate the conditions of the real human beings who lived and suffered there. Although she was very much aware that her own father had considered works of individual personal charity to be useless, she knew that he had never visited a slum house.[172] Because she had, she found it very difficult to maintain, for herself, his veneer of theoretical hardheartedness for the sake of the larger cause.

Eleanor's experiences in the East End not only caused her to rethink the proper Marxian attitude on the charity issue, but also to redefine her sense of pride in her own ancestry. One of the most conspicuous of suffering groups in the East End were Jewish immigrants from central and eastern Europe, whose exodus from tsarist persecutions had reached flood-tide proportions by the late nineteenth century.[173] Despite the poverty and economic oppression of these immigrants, English socialists as a group had neglected their revolutionary potential.[174] The Fabians had no significant opinion on the Jewish question, while the SDF under Hyndman was even accused of covert antisemitism. Marx's relationship to his own

Jewishness also remained problematic; his expressed views on the subject were ambivalent at best.[175]

Although Eleanor recognized that her father had taken no interest in Jewish affairs and had kept aloof from London Jewry, her own feelings on the matter were different. She came to manifest a fierce sense of pride in her own Jewishness. Her "happiest moments," she maintained, were spent among the Jewish workers of the East End,[176] and for a time she even toyed with the idea of learning Yiddish, so as to be more effective in her labors among them. Although she actually played only a small part in Anglo-Jewish socialism, the leaders of that movement—men like Aaron Rosebury, Abraham Cahan, and Morris Winchevsky—all recalled her fondly in their memoirs.[177]

The reasons for her reawakened sense of pride can only be guessed at. It certainly had its roots in her humanistic conception of socialism, and was inspired by the general sympathy that she felt for the poor of East London. Perhaps as she grew increasingly conscious of women's oppression, she became more acutely aware of the oppression that had been inflicted indiscriminately on other readily identifiable groups such as Jews. Finally, as her own personal life with Aveling deteriorated, she may have searched for solace in the family traditions of her past, finding it in that "intergenerational sense of connectedness" which has been identified as a special female property.[178]

It was this sense of connectedness with the movement her father had created—duty, loyalty, and family pride—that kept Eleanor going in the dark days of her relationship with Aveling. Her nature craved love, she had once confessed,[179] and as Aveling showed himself to be less and less willing to fulfill her needs, her devotion to the cause gave her life meaning and purpose. Certainly it would be incorrect to see her socialist activities as having been compensatory alone, or to attribute them to her loveless and childless state, for politics had been a fixture of her life since childhood. Yet she had always hoped to be able to combine her personal and political selves, to recreate in her adult life the warmth and intimacy of her childhood. Haunted by this ideal, she never stopped yearning for happiness and fulfillment, for loving companionship and a home of her own "ringing with a child's laugh."[180] Had she been more centrally and directly involved in the socialist world, perhaps she would have been able to rise above her sorrows and disappointments.[181] In the end, however, the movement alone was not enough to satisfy her. Longing for a child she was never to have, she wrote to a friend, "You have your boy—I have nothing; and I see nothing worth living for. . . ."[182]

V

Eleanor's relationship with Aveling undoubtedly served to retard the recognition of her real political achievements, stifle her revolutionary enthusiasm, and dampen her revolutionary ardor. One of the greatest tragedies of the liaison was that it separated her from her friends. She came to find doors "closed against her," said Eduard Bernstein, not because she lived in a free union, but because her chosen partner was Edward Aveling. "His reputation in the radical and democratic world of London was already very bad, and it grew worse year by year."[183] Because of Aveling's presence, several socialists boycotted the Sunday social and political gatherings at Engels' London home.[184] "When we run down Marxism," quipped Sidney Webb, "we mean Aveling."[185] His financial escapades in America had hurt Eleanor as well, and there was a certain element of ostracism involved in the Avelings' departure from the SDF and later from the Socialist League. Hyndman summed up the situation best when he remarked: "Eleanor Marx does good work. She would wear the mantle of her father among us if not for her . . . choice of the Irishman."[186]

The "horror" with which Aveling was regarded cannot be easily or neatly explained. Eduard Bernstein was himself so frustrated by his failure to ascertain its precise cause that he was often tempted, he later wrote, to be shockingly blunt: "What's the truth about them, really? Have they murdered their children, or what?"[187] Contemporaries accused Aveling of a multitude of sins.[188] Although he was, in Hyndman's words, "ugly and repulsive," women found him irresistibly attractive, and he was said to have "seduced every woman he met." A "supercilious dandy," Aveling fed his attraction for luxury in numerous ways. He was accused of embezzlement, and of pocketing funds earmarked for the defense of the Chicago Anarchists. His borrowing, even from the poorest workman, was legendary, and his debts were paid with bounced checks or not at all. Financially extravagant himself, he expected socialist comrades to foot his costly bills at the local pub. Small wonder, then, that his political career was checkered with a string of expulsions from political organizations on a variety of counts.

"Dreading" Aveling themselves, Eleanor's friends could not understand her continued devotion to a man whom a contemporary blatantly described as an "unmoral human animal."[189] For some reason, Eleanor clearly believed their relationship to be as indissoluble as any legal marriage, always maintaining that their free union was a "true and real one nonetheless."[190] While a friend attributed her fidelity to her "Jewish reverence for the sacred bond of wedded life,"[191] there may be other explanations. Her apparent eagerness to disbelieve the rumors about Aveling grew from her staunch recognition that all great men, her father among them, had been slurred by their enemies.[192] Her stubborn persistence in the liaison shows how closely she identified with her ever-supportive mother. Marital fidelity had not been one of Karl Marx's qualities, as Eleanor herself knew.[193] Referring to her relationship with Aveling, she once admitted that if she had sacrificed something, "it was no more than my mother had done."[194]

To Aveling's credit, it can be said that he did something very few others did—he treated Eleanor as herself, not as the daughter of Karl Marx. He never addressed her as "Tussy," the childhood nickname by which she continued to be known all her adult life.[195] "My father," Eleanor explained, "used to say that I was more like a boy than a girl. It was Edward who really brought out the feminine in me. I was irresistibly drawn to him."[196]

As Aveling's physical health worsened in the last years of their relationship, Eleanor's attachment and devotion grew. Her "maternal" nursing of him after a serious operation in February 1898 only increased her contemporaries' praise for her saintly goodness and heightened their disgust with the "downright scoundrel" who was the cause of her "martyrdom."[197] Understanding both his physical and moral disease, Eleanor didn't need to forgive him, she wrote, she could "only love."[198]

Yet Aveling did not recognize or appreciate her efforts. Vicious infidelity topped the list of sins of which he could be accused. Despite their 14-year common law union, it was not Eleanor whom Aveling chose to marry upon the death of his first wife, but a 22-year-old actress named Eva Frye. The secret marriage of "Alec Nelson," as Aveling called himself in dramatic circles, was kept from Eleanor, with whom Aveling continued to live. She heard of the event only months later, receiving news of it mysteriously in the mail on the morning of March 31, 1898.

Eleanor Marx committed suicide that same morning.[199] The immediate cause of her death—universally labelled a "tragedy"[200] — was prussic acid poisoning. She was 43 years old. Faced with the news, Aveling exhibited the same callousness towards Eleanor that he had shown her in life, caring, it was said, only "for her property and her money."[201] He did not claim her ashes and was rumored to have attended a cricket match the day before her funeral. Some of Eleanor's friends, recognizing his responsibility in the affair, sought to have him tried for murder, but the matter was dropped by the public prosecutor for lack of evidence.[202] A few months later, Aveling himself died, in disgrace, of kidney disease and complications from his February operation.

Though he performed valuable services for the developing British socialist movement,[203] Edward Aveling's victimization of Eleanor Marx has made him one of the supreme villains of international socialism, while she, in turn, has become perhaps its greatest tragic heroine. Her death had within it the seeds of melodrama and, as such, led to her deification not as a significantly important revolutionary figure but as a romantic, semilegendary character. The story of her life has been told more often in fictionalized accounts than in serious scholarly ones. As early as 1906, George Bernard Shaw drew upon her relationship with Aveling for his play *A Doctor's Dilemma*, the tale of a poor long-suffering wife devoted to her morbidly evil husband.[204] More recently, novelists have seized upon Marx's daughter as a fitting subject for titillating tales, centered not on her serious revolutionary contributions but on the prurient nature of her affair with Aveling.[205] The worst of these have portrayed the dutiful daughter of Karl Marx as a sex-starved wanton, seduced by Lissagaray, attracted to the sinful life of the theater, and plied with opium by the diabolical Aveling.[206]

Remembered as the daughter of one man, Eleanor Marx has been immortalized as the victim of another. After her death it was almost impossible to get an accurate contemporary assessment of her character and contributions, since all accounts centered on Aveling's demonic evil.[207] She, in contrast, was credited with an almost unbelievable array of saintly virtues. If she had only lived, her contemporaries mourned, she would have done great things.[208] Those she did accomplish were conveniently overshadowed by her tragic end.

Eleanor Marx was a dauntless and courageous woman, full of life and energy, a woman of "great charm, radiating intelligence, and loving kindness."[209] Had she been able to overcome both her own doubts and hesitations at assuming the rightful role to which her heritage entitled her, as well as the rigid sex role stereotyping of the era in which she lived, she might have been able to stamp the developing socialist movement with the sympathetic tenderness that was her special mark. But this was not to be the case. After her death, contemporaries chided her for her sensitivity and idealism, mocking the emphasis she had placed on love both in her own life and in the movement as a whole. Her life was a cruel disappointment, several noted, a "waste," its value to be measured only by its inspiration to others.[210]

In this way, Karl Marx's beloved daughter came to fill the role of bloodless symbol only. Eulogized as a martyr to the cause rather than a serious contributor, she failed to provide the Marxist movement with the lasting legacy of a strong female revolutionary, but socialism was the poorer for the loss of her spirit and example.

Chapter • Two

Alexandra Kollontai

The Female Revolutionary
as Visionary

I

> Love must not crush the woman's individuality, not bind her wings.
> If love begins to enslave her, she must make herself free, she must step
> over all love tragedies, and go her own way.[1]

With these words, Alexandra Kollontai, the "Red Rose of the
Russian Revolution," grasped the essence of the tragedy of Eleanor
Marx. As a revolutionary and theoretician, she felt her main task was
to teach women not to put "their hearts and souls into love for a
man, but into the essential thing, creative work"[2] —precisely that
conflict which had troubled Eleanor Marx all her life. Kollontai's
heightened awareness of the difficulties women face in combining
love, work, and politics stemmed from her own experiences and led
her to demand that socialists recognize and grapple with these
issues in their policies.

In her career as a Bolshevik agitator, propagandist, theoretician,
and commissar of social welfare in Lenin's first cabinet, Alexandra
Kollontai always remained extremely sensitive to women's problems
and needs, but she was inspired above all by an idealistic and radical

Portions of this chapter were first published in an article, "Alexandra
Kollontai and the Vision of a Socialist Feminist Utopia," *Alternative Futures:
The Journal of Utopian Studies* 4, no. 2/3 (1981): 73-84.

vision of a totally new society, where all human beings, men and women both, would be truly free. Going further than any previous socialist thinker, even Marx himself, she sought to give shape and substance to socialist dreams, definition and practical detail to what the communal nature of life under socialism would really mean. Even more importantly, with her speculations on social and sexual relations under communism, she tried to add a new dimension to Marxist theories on the woman question, theories that had become stale and somewhat mechanical by the opening years of the twentieth century. Although women had long been promised equality in the new society that would be the fruit of the socialist revolution, they had never been provided with a detailed or exact description of the forms that equality would take. Repeatedly, women had simply been told to join in the struggle for the liberation of the proletariat; the glorious day of their own liberation would shortly follow.

As the leading woman Bolshevik of her generation, Alexandra Kollontai saw and gloried in that day. After the victory of the Bolsheviks, she hoped to share in the creation and design of the new socialist society that would bring the long-promised millennium for women. Yet, with the consolidation of Lenin's revolution, her theorizing on the woman question was stillborn; her revolutionary contributions came to an abrupt halt. Disgraced, alone, and isolated from decision-making centers by the mid 1920s, she lost all chance of formulating a precise and far-reaching amplification of Marxist thought on the woman question. Insofar as Kollontai was unable to enact real and lasting changes in the new revolutionary world, her failures must be understood in the light of a preexisting Russian tradition of female revolutionary involvement, a tradition that had implicitly circumscribed the outer limits of acceptable revolutionary behavior by women.

Recognition of the woman question came early to Russia. Pre-Marxist socialists like Alexander Hertzen, in embracing the utopian socialism of Western Europe, had introduced Russia to Saint-Simonian thought on the equality of the sexes. Fourier had his Russian adherents as well: The Petrashevists of the 1840s echoed their "master's" cries for the liberation of women and attacked women's subordinate position in marriage and family. Another important factor in stimulating support for female emancipation among Russian socialists were the novels of George Sand, with their ethos of freedom in love, that virtually "flooded" Russia after 1836.[3]

Feminism as a movement, however, was not born until the decade following the Crimean War, a crucial period in modern Russian history. Russia's humiliating defeat in that war spawned a sincere and well-meaning crusade to isolate the reasons for the nation's weakness and backwardness. Censorship was lifted, serfdom was abolished, and the nation embarked on a short-lived period of intellectual revival and soul searching. Taking its place among the burning issues of the day was the woman question, born in these years for a variety of reasons.[4] Psychologically, the emancipation of some 50 to 60 million "souls" had left the nagging sensation of unredeemed oppression in the minds of many women. Russian feminism was also the product of practical economic concerns. The liberation of the serfs had dislocated the lifestyles of many gentry families, and, in many households, formerly dependent daughters now sought for ways to support themselves or supplement the family income. When they entered the economic marketplace, however, these women found the channels to economic, professional, and educational advancement closed to them because of their sex. As happened elsewhere in Europe, Russian feminists soon began to demand equal opportunities for women in all of these areas.

Another kind of women's movement was also born in Russia during this period. By the 1870s, certain radical women had come to oppose this limited, purely feminist vision. Despising narrow reformist questions, they chose to dedicate themselves to the larger challenges of the common cause, peasant problems, and the overthrow of the tsarist autocracy. Women's eagerness to join the revolutionary movement was encouraged by male radicals of the 1870s and 1880s, who anxiously recruited women into populist organizations and offered to treat them as equals in the preparation of an agrarian revolution that would bring about a redistribution of land to the peasants. Of all individuals arrested for political crimes between 1873 and 1879, 15 percent were women. When terrorism came to be accepted as a revolutionary strategy, women joined the ranks of the terrorists as well; 30 percent of the members of the People's Will, the most important terrorist group of the period, were women.[5]

The populist and terrorist women of the 1870s and 1880s left a rich legacy of female revolutionary involvement to their Bolshevik granddaughters. "We have begun a great thing," beamed Sophia Perovskaya, the leader of the successful plot to assassinate tsar Alexander II in 1881, and the first woman in Russian history ever to receive capital punishment for a political crime.[6] On the basis of that legacy, women were to continue to demand a role in the revolutionary transformation of Russian society. Yet the peculiar character of that heritage was to color women's acceptance—and rejection—by the Bolshevik hierarchy of the next generation.

From the first, feminism and female revolutionary involvement were separate and distinct components of the Russian tradition. Revolutionary women scorned "feminism," seeing it as the vapid preoccupation of those who had no conception of the overarching "human question." Most radical women considered female emancipation to be a personal, individual struggle only. Because they had managed to resolve that struggle for themselves, successfully overcoming their own insecurities and doubts to join predominantly male revolutionary organizations, they felt there was no need for a separate women's cause.[7] Believing others could easily follow in their paths, radical women remained silent on the large and important issue of how to bring revolutionary consciousness, self-confidence, and political awareness to those women who had not yet been able to make that "existential leap" for themselves.

Radical women, however, may actually have been deluding themselves as to the true extent of the equality and emancipation they had really received. While accepted as equals, women were welcomed into revolutionary movements for their possession of certain moral qualities highly valued by Russian radical men of the nineteenth century—qualities such as selflessness, devotion, and a willingness to sacrifice. These were qualities that, "let us admit it," wrote the populist Sergei Kravchinsky, "women possess in a much greater measure than men. That is why the Russian revolutionary movement owes its almost religious fire above all to them. . . . "[8] Female radicals wrote and spoke of each other in similar terms. The moral underside of the radical movement was the unique preserve of its female members, in whom, wrote Catherine Breshkovskaya, feelings such as "love, tenderness, grace, beauty, courage, and abnegation for the sake of large ideals" were "innate."[9] Such traits, she continued, were the exception rather than the rule among men. Thus, because of their perceived possession of such qualities, women were idealized as near-perfect revolutionaries in terrorist movements like the People's Will, which placed such a premium on self-abnegation, self-sacrifice, and willingness to die a martyr for the cause.

Vaunted as the equals if not superiors of their male comrades in bomb throwings and assassinations, populist and terrorist women were the decided underlings, however, in the theoretical backbone of the movement. Not one populist woman emerged as an important theoretician in her own right. Men dominated the movement's journalistic, theoretical, and decision-making sides.[10] Since Russian populism prided itself on activism, not theory, the deficiencies of women in this area did not impair their status or reputation. In a highly theory-conscious movement, however, the result would be different. Women's reticence in the theoretical realm remained an important characteristic of the female revolutionary tradition in Russia.

Finally, in the area of personal and sexual freedom, Russian radical women of the nineteenth century left an ambivalent legacy.[11] While the nihilists of the 1860s claimed to believe in "free love," their definition of that term stressed the freedom of women to choose their own marriage partners, not promiscuity or even boldness in sexual relations. Prominent radical women themselves were strict, if not ascetic, in their private lives. These were the women whom Kravchinsky praised as having learned to "transcend" the "petty right of free love."[12] Personal life and romance were luxuries that radical women did not allow themselves. "In accordance with the ideals of our epoch," wrote Vera Figner, Perovskaya "was a rigid ascetic."[13] The great cause of love for which Vera Zasulich longed was the revolution itself.[14] In her autobiography, Catherine Breshkovskaya wrote of a female colleague's indifference to men, and of her "love" for the movement alone.[15]

Alexandra Kollontai and the other Bolshevik women of her generation inherited a ready-made tradition of female revolutionary involvement. They shared a tradition that saw feminist separatism as a dangerous diversion from the cause, that stressed women's moral qualities in the service of the revolution, that allowed women few theoretical opportunities, and that looked askance at bold sexual experimentation. Insofar as Alexandra Kollontai overstepped the bounds of that tradition, she would have trouble winning real acceptance from the men of her own party. Indeed, her treatment at the hands of the victorious Bolsheviks exposed the shallowness of Marxist pretensions on the issue of women's equality. More importantly, her quarrels with Lenin, long identified as the classic example of the revolutionary personality, highlight her deviations, as a woman, from the standard—and male—models of revolutionary behavior.

II

Like other revolutionary women, Alexandra Kollontai attributed her later political involvement to a childhood sense of being "chosen," the feeling from her earliest years that she had a "mission" to fulfill in life.[16] As the "petted" daughter of a noble gentry family, Kollontai's missionary urges may be interpreted as typical *noblesse oblige* sentiments common to women of her class and station in life, but the particular circumstances of her birth and upbringing also contributed to fostering this sense of specialness and ordained purpose.

Her mother, Alexandra Masalina, had been married for ten years and was the mother of three children when she decided to divorce her husband and marry Mikhail Domontovich, a general in the tsarist army. Alexandra, born in St. Petersburg on March 19, 1872, was the first child of their rebellious union. Since all the other children born of this second marriage died in early infancy, she soon became the object of very special care and attention, "the living expression of the deep and lasting love" that held her parents together.[17] Fussed over for health reasons, Alexandra also enjoyed much of the status of an only child, since her mother's children from the previous marriage were considerably older than she. They themselves spoiled their half-sister and treated her almost like a "toy."[18]

The fawning adulation that Alexandra received not only strengthened her sense of specialness and mission, but also awakened the pangs of social conscience within her. Recognizing early on the contrast between her own privileged lifestyle and that of the servant children who became her playmates, she grew to resent the fact that her clothes and food were different from theirs. "Outraged" that her best friend, an assistant maid, was not allowed to sit down in her mother's presence, Alexandra assuaged her feelings of guilt and resentment by smuggling food from the kitchen to feed the neighborhood children who came to her door. Grieved at the inequality she saw around her, she "tormented" herself with wondering how the scheme of things could be so arranged so that "all could go well with everybody."[19]

While there certainly appears to be an element of romanticization in such nostalgic memoirs written in later life, Kollontai described a process that was common to gentry women of her generation. The implantation of a social conscience was an experience shared by leisured European women of the late nineteenth century, Alexandra's mother among them.[20] Thus, the perceived recognition of social injustice alone is not enough to explain Alexandra Kollontai's later revolutionary status, since her pangs of social conscience could have found an outlet in charitable or philanthropic endeavors. That Kollontai's memoirs also hint of a sense of rebellion at her privileged status, and of disgust with the smothering and oppressive overprotectiveness of her mother, may be more important in understanding her inclination to revolutionary activity.

Although she was to remember her childhood as a happy one, Kollontai lamented and resented her mother's constant supervision.[21] She had no freedom of maneuver, but was excessively sheltered and fussed over. Shielded from dangerous games and pastimes, she had few friends her own age and lived a lonely life in an adult world. She was not even allowed to attend school with other children, since her parents were afraid that their delicate child could not endure two hours away from home daily. Kollontai's feelings of resentment and inner frustration were common to nihilist and radical women of earlier generations, who, in embracing political activity, had also sought release from the traditionally oppressive and sheltered lifestyles of middle and upper class women.

For all her excessive protectiveness, however, Alexandra Masalina herself provided her daughter with an important model of nontraditional, active female behavior. Strong-willed and independent, she had shocked her parents and relatives by her divorce and remarriage. Not only had she flouted convention by her desire to marry for love alone, but she also enjoyed a measure of economic independence through her ownership of an estate in Finland. Alexandra Masalina proved to be a shrewd businesswoman. Having inherited heavy debts along with the property, she cleared them by successfully managing a dairy farm and selling the products in the Finnish capital—certainly unorthodox behavior for the wife of a tsarist officer.

The legacy of rebellion and independence that Alexandra Kollontai inherited from her mother came to be tinged with feelings of political consciousness drawn from the example of her father. "If ever a man had an influence on my mind and development," she later wrote, "it was my father."[22] As her conflicts with her mother increased, Alexandra drew closer to her father, a progressive and liberal thinker with strong commitments to English constitutionalism. Later in life he secretly financed his daughter's Marxist studies and helped her hide illegal pamphlets from the tsarist police.

Mikhail Domontovich was a member of the Russian staff stationed in Sofia, Bulgaria, after the Russo-Turkish War, and the family moved there for a year when Alexandra was five. Later she attributed her first antitsarist sentiments to this period. The memory of seeing a group of Bulgarian partisans arrested and shot on the tsar's orders never left her.[23] Her hatred of the tsar increased when her father was ordered to leave Sofia in disgrace after having advocated a liberal constitution for Bulgaria. As the tsarist autocracy continued to touch her personal life, Alexandra's sense of political awareness grew. After the assassination of Alexander II in 1881, her mother's first husband was arrested and convicted for complicity in the deed,* and the Domontoviches were snubbed by St. Petersburg society both for their connections with the accused and for their suspected liberal sentiments.

An important role in Kollontai's coming to political consciousness must also be assigned to her tutor and governess, Maria Ivanovna Strakhova, who provided the young girl with a strong model of female political activity. An outspoken advocate of female emancipation, Strakhova had connections with underground revolutionary circles, and under her influence Alexandra came to regard Sophia Perovskaya as her favorite romantic heroine. Alexandra was also much impressed that her father enjoyed discussing politics with Strakhova, and that he treated her as an equal.[24]

Yet, despite Kollontai's early exposure to the political life, her voracious appetite for reading, and her interest in learning, Alexandra Masalina was determined that her daughter's life follow the traditional pattern of a girl of her class—that she choose an appropriate marriage partner and settle down to a life of quiet domesticity. Alexandra rebelled at both suggestions. Vowing to continue her education, she enrolled at the famous Bestuzhev lectures in history and literature, which provided the equivalent of a university curriculum for young women then denied the benefits of higher education in Russia.[25] At the same time, she declared herself to be "revolted" at the prospects

---

*Aware of terrorist plots to plant dynamite under the streets of St. Petersburg, the police hired the engineer Mravinskii to inspect the plumbing and underground sewer systems of the city. When the assassination attempt was successful, he was convicted—with no evidence—of the charge of having deliberately misled police.

of a marriage for convenience as had been arranged for her oldest half-sister. Alexandra was determined to "marry only for love, out of a great passion."[26]

The chosen object of her affection came to be her impoverished second cousin, Vladimir Ludvigovich Kollontai, who had come to St. Petersburg to study engineering. Vladimir's romantic revolutionary heritage was a factor in attracting Alexandra to him. The knowledge that his father had been banished from Poland following an abortive rebellion against tsarist rule made her heart "swell with indignation and warm sympathy."[27] Despite such sentimental proclamations, however, her attachment to Kollontai was as much a protest against the wishes of her parents as it was an act of love.[28] Insistent that their daughter "make a good match," they were opposed to the relationship from the start, but their opposition only heightened Alexandra's resolve. She married Kollontai in 1893—in her mother's words, the "stupid" and "obstinate" folly of a stubborn girl.[29] Her rebellious behavior, however, revealed not her future revolutionary inclinations, but—as had been the case with Eleanor Marx—her need and longing for independence.

Alexandra soon discovered, however, that marriage was not to fulfill that need. Especially after the birth of her son Mikhail in 1894, she grew more and more to hate her "idiotic" and "meaningless" routine.[30] While she loved her son and husband, she could never hope to content herself with the "cage" of married life, nor could motherhood ever become the "kernel" of her existence. Tired of domestic concerns, she entered into a period of social activism, working with her former governess at a library and museum for factory workers. Since such cultural-educational societies often served as covers for illegal underground activity, especially the circulation of populist and Marxist tracts, Alexandra made her first acquaintance with radical politics during this time. She also came into contact with many political prisoners at the famed Schlusselberg Fortress, for whom her group provided educational exhibits and reading materials.

Kollontai was very specific about the event that "decided" her fate and marked her resolute entry into rigorous and determined revolutionary activity. In 1896 her husband was called upon to inspect the Kremholm textile plant at Narva, and Alexandra, who accompanied him, was provided with her first real glimpse of the "terribly enslaved" plight of the workers. The trip changed her whole life. Horrified by the sight of a dead child on the factory floor, she was convinced she could not go on living the life she had been leading "while other people live like animals." "I went away feeling that I could not live unless I did something to help change the condition of the Russian workers."[31]

Recognizing that her own political ideas were not especially clear or well developed, she began to study Marxist journals. These, she later wrote, "opened" her eyes. "The path for which I had been searching with particular insistence since Narva was found."[32] The famous strike of St. Petersburg textile workers in 1896, in which she participated by collecting funds and other aid for the strikers, also contributed to the clarification of her political views. This "visible sign" of the growing consciousness of the proletariat caused her to join the Marxists. Considering herself insufficiently prepared for future revolutionary activity, she made a bold decision soon after. Both committed to activism and longing for personal fulfillment, she chose to make an irrevocable break from her life as a married woman and mother. Placing herself squarely within the tradition of radical women who had been attending foreign universities for 30 years seeking personal and political emancipation,[33] Kollontai abandoned husband and child to study political economy at the University of Zurich.

At Zurich her revolutionary sentiments grew. Educating herself in Marxist theory, traveling across Europe, and meeting the leading socialists of the day, she discovered the great cause to which she had hoped to devote herself since girlhood. Silently she divorced her husband—although she retained his name the rest of her life—and resolved to raise her son alone.

Kollontai then proceeded to establish her credentials within the international socialist movement. Significantly, she had a theoretical bent from the outset. Her publication of *The Life of the Finnish Workers*, a massive study of the Finnish economy written from the orthodox Marxist perspective, and an article in Germany's *Die Neue Zeit* on the same theme served as her entry card into European Social Democracy.[34]

When she finally returned to Russia in 1903, Kollontai entered the ranks of a Marxist movement that had matured well beyond the transitional period of the 1890s.[35] The rapid growth of Social Democratic groups, the spread of capitalism, and the rising class consciousness of the proletariat as manifested through the great strike waves of the 1890s all served to establish Marxism as a clearly defined alternative to older revolutionary traditions based on the peasants. Russian Marxism had developed differently from that in the West. Charges of opportunism and electioneering were meaningless in Russia, where there was as yet no Parliament for Social Democrats to conquer. The intransigence of the tsarist autocracy made it inevitable that Marxism be nothing but revolutionary in Russia. Thus, the cleavages in Russian Social Democracy centered not on the quarrels between reformists and revolutionaries but on the question of how and by whom that inevitable revolution was to be made.

Kollontai was eager to avoid the political infighting between Bolsheviks and Mensheviks on these issues. Disdaining political labels, she was content to work independently, as a labor agitator and organizer, political speaker, teacher, and writer, moving in both camps. Nonetheless, her sympathies with the Mensheviks soon became apparent. Not only did she admire their leaders, but she was also emotionally more in line with their ideological position. From the start it was the millenarial side of the future revolution that attracted Kollontai. Her passionate faith in the revolutionary potential and intrinsic good of the masses separated her from the Bolsheviks, whose insistence on what she termed a "managed" revolution alienated and disgusted her.[36] By 1905—that eventful year when the Russian working classes first erupted into revolution—her dislike of the Bolshevik formula was clear. Lenin's group was skeptical and distrustful of the workers' spontaneous independence, adamant that unions and factory committees be subject to party directives, but Kollontai, along with the Mensheviks, welcomed any and all signs of self-conscious working class activity.

The events of 1905 marked a watershed both in Russian political history and in Kollontai's personal revolutionary development. Not only did the revolution cause her to clarify her own ideas and sympathies, but it also led directly to her assumption of that role for which she is best remembered: the active organization of women in support of the socialist movement.

Kollontai's attention to this issue grew slowly, the product both of her own experiences and convictions and of external political circumstances in Russia. The resulting thaw in the political climate after 1905 led to a rise in activity by middle class liberal feminist organizations. Fed by the general feeling that the tsar had ignored women in the promised reforms of his October Manifesto, the burgeoning Russian suffrage movement of this period took its place alongside those of England, the United States, and Western Europe.[37] While Russian feminists had been agitating and working since the 1860s in the fields of philanthropy, social welfare, and educational reform, it was not until after 1905 that a variety of feminist groups began to demand civil and political rights for women.

What upset Kollontai about this new surge of feminist energy was the women's resolve to shed the old genteel, philanthropic character of their cause, and their eagerness to win supporters from the peasantry and working classes. Not only did Kollontai identify this new supraclass appeal as alien to all Marxist principles—the lady and her maid, she cried, could be nothing but enemies—but she also recognized earlier than any other Russian Social Democrat of the period that feminist inroads among women of the working classes could seriously sap the strength of proletarian unity. Since Marxists had always insisted that the woman question was one not of gender but of economics, the women of the proletariat were urged to support their husbands in the larger fight. Women's goals were to be met and could only be met by joining hands with the men of their class.

Kollontai's unique contribution to Russian Social Democracy after 1905 was to recognize the flaws in this neat argument. If the standard Marxist line on the woman question persisted in characterizing any special attempt to organize working women as "separatist, deviationist, and dangerous" to the larger cause, then how were women workers to be brought to the cause to begin with? A question even more critical to the post-1905 Russian situation was this: What were Social Democrats to do in the face of increasingly aggressive attempts by feminists to recruit working women to their side? Kollontai's understanding of the problem was simple and straightforward: If women's concerns and needs were not adhered to, women would not join the class struggle.

Kollontai was highly sensitive to the special difficulties women faced if they tried to enter political life: hostility from husbands with traditional attitudes on woman's place; burdens of home and child care that left little time or inclination for political meetings; household budgets hard-pressed to provide for political tracts and club dues; and finally, the attitude among women themselves that politics was not for them.[38] Determined to correct that misconception, she worked tirelessly among factory women for the next two years, organizing lectures, discussion groups, and reading clubs. Her efforts were geared toward demonstrating the absurdity of an alliance between working women and "bourgeois feminists." The issue at base, she cried in a powerful metaphor, was one of a "crust of bread."[39] "Women's righters," with their "hypocritical" cries for equal educational and professional opportunities, were seeking only to attain parity with their bourgeois husbands and brothers. They were blind to questions of hunger and survival that were daily facts of life for working women. Kollontai's attacks on the charity women were scathing: "They cannot empty out the ocean of pain and misery created by the capitalist exploitation of hired labor with the teaspoon of charity."[40]

Despite the importance of her observations, however, in 1905-1906 Kollontai was a lone prophet of the need to organize working women. In later life she wrote bitterly of her years of fighting both Bolsheviks and Mensheviks on this issue.[41] Both sides greeted her ideas with skepticism and indifference, seeing in her proposals a "harmful deviation towards feminism." While the party did not explicitly forbid her activity, it gave her no help whatsoever. "The truth was that this question did not interest them."[42]

Attributing her lack of support to a basic male hostility to women even in her allegedly enlightened party, Kollontai herself became frustrated and disgusted with her work in this area. She was most disheartened by her failure to obtain help from other prominent Social Democratic women. Vera Zasulich, for example, the renowned former terrorist then affiliated with the Mensheviks, refused to assist Kollontai, calling her efforts a useless waste of time and a diversion of party strength.[43] Adding to Kollontai's dismay was her growing notoriety as a revolutionary. Wanted by police for a pamphlet she had written calling for revolution in Finland, she silently slipped into exile in 1908. She was to remain abroad for the next nine years, traveling across Western Europe, writing and agitating, not to return to Russia again until her homeland was afire with revolution.

Her own lingering sense of failure and frustration notwithstanding, Kollontai's efforts in these years were important. She had sown the seeds for future work among women, and others were soon to see the truth of her arguments. The growing number of strikes by women workers after 1910 caused the party to reassess its position on the issue of framing separate and special appeals to women. Although the Bolsheviks remained opposed to any separate organization by and for women workers, after 1913 their attitude on the publication of special literature geared to women softened.[44] While Lenin tried to ensure that work in this area would be directed by two women who could always be subject to his control—his wife Krupskaya and his devoted friend and alleged mistress Inessa Armand—it was Kollontai's book, *The Social Bases of the Woman Question*, published in 1909, that has remained to this day the major work on the subject by a Russian Marxist.[45]

The outbreak of war in Europe put an end to all discussion of the woman question. Kollontai was horrified by the war, calling it "an abomination, a madness, a crime."[46] What appalled her even more, however, was the total and utter collapse of a socialist movement that had pledged itself to the principle of international proletarian solidarity. Marxists had always believed that all workers were brothers, that French and German workers had more in common with each other than with capitalists who shared their language and cultural heritage. Yet the war proved the Marxists wrong, as socialists on both sides of the trenches queued up to support the "fatherland." For Kollontai this was a "calamity without parallel."[47] She recoiled at the spectacle of socialists supporting an imperialist war fanned and fomented by international finance capital. Revolted by "anything that smacked of super patriotism," she found herself alienated from her former Menshevik comrades, many of whom defended Russian involvement in the war as a do-or-die struggle against German aggression.

Kollontai's attitude on the war finally drove her into the Bolshevik camp. Lenin's views on the war were similar to hers, and the war was her most pressing concern. She did not become a Bolshevik by choice—she had not resolved her earlier doubts about Lenin's plans for a managed revolution and his distrust of mass spontaneity—but the war and the war alone decided the issue. Her fears and suspicions would one day return to haunt her.

Although Kollontai had met Lenin as early as 1905, they never corresponded or worked together until this period. He, for his part, was "delighted" that she had come around to the Bolshevik side, for he recognized that her talents could be useful to him and to his party.[48] Because of Kollontai's contacts and linguistic abilities, she became Lenin's agent in Scandinavia, following his detailed instructions, from 1914 to 1917, to transport people, literature, and letters through the "Northern Underground," the main route for lines of communication between Lenin in Switzerland and his supporters in Russia.[49]

While Lenin was anxious to make use of Kollontai's abilities and contacts among the Scandinavian socialists, he was not inclined to look kindly on her adoption of independent theoretical views. Horrified both by the carnage of war and by the disintegration of socialist solidarity, Kollontai at this time supported the efforts of the so-called "Zimmerwald movement," an *ad hoc* grouping of European socialists who were working feverishly to demand immediate peace and to restore the integrity of the old Second International, which had been torn asunder in the nationalistic rivalries unleashed by the capitalist war. Lenin, however, was critical both of Kollontai's antimilitarist stance and of the Zimmerwaldians under whose influence she had fallen. His letters to her from this period were replete with lengthy and detailed instructions, criticisms of her opinions, and corrections of her pamphlets and writings. Fearful that Zimmerwald's aims masked a dangerous inclination toward pacifism, he chastised Kollontai's failure to understand the usefulness of the war as such, that the imperialist war could and must be transformed into a civil war between proletarian and capitalist. He also opposed her utopian and emotion-laden calls for unity among socialists. The old International was dead, he proclaimed, and calls for "indiscriminate" unity could only damage his plans for a new Third International—an International that would be subject to his will and whim from the start.

Eager to quash Kollontai's theoretical pretensions, Lenin was quick to point out, however, those areas in which she could be most useful. Above all, he was anxious that she translate his pamphlets and various Bolshevik position papers into Swedish, Norwegian, and the other languages with which she was familiar[50] —supportive and subsidiary roles that would guarantee her allegiance to the proper Bolshevik line.

With such careful tutoring, Kollontai did eventually draw closer to Lenin's views on the correct juxtaposition between war and revolution. She became a prominent "Left Zimmerwaldian," a member of the radical faction within the socialist anti-war group who, directly inspired by Lenin, came to call not for immediate peace but for the transformation of the war into an international social revolution. It was as their representative that Kollontai was invited by the German Federation of the American Socialist Party to tour the United States in the fall of 1915, and to speak to German groups about the state of European socialism and the war. Lenin hoped that Kollontai's tour would arouse support for the Left Zimmerwald movement in the United States and raise money for his cause.

During her three-month tour, Kollontai traveled from coast to coast, speaking in four languages to audiences in major U.S. cities. The main theme of her speeches and articles was the bankruptcy of the Second International and the need of all socialists to form a new Third International dedicated to the principles of international proletarian solidarity and working class revolution. Besides denouncing the imperialist war, she also condemned the opportunism and cowardly stagnation infecting European socialist parties.[51] Although her fund-raising efforts were not successful, Kollontai's speeches and writings served to acquaint American socialists with the character and shape of the European movement. More importantly, her trip secured and established her reputation as an internationally renowned socialist personality.

In December 1916, representatives of the American party again urged Kollontai to begin another lecture tour. Fearing the revolution was too imminent, she refused. Kollontai was right. The outbreak of revolution in Russia ended her nine long years of exile. After the tsar's abdication, the new Provisional Government declared an amnesty for all political exiles, and on March 18, 1917, "one of the happiest hours" of her life,[52] Alexandra Kollontai returned to St. Petersburg.

III

Kollontai was to remember 1917 as the high point of her life, the period of her greatest achievements and highest degree of acceptance by the Bolshevik hierarchy.[53] Upon her return to Russia she threw herself into full-scale revolutionary activity, agitating among the troops and attacking the Provisional Government's decision to continue the war. Both Trotsky and Lenin highlighted her usefulness to the Bolshevik cause during this period. Trotsky praised her "brilliant" agitational efforts, while Lenin appreciated her unflinching support for his tactical revolutionary position.[54] Alone among Bolsheviks, she wholeheartedly supported the program outlined in his *April Theses*, which demanded the transfer of power to the soviets, immediate peace, and noncooperation with other political parties. Arrested after the abortive Bolshevik attempt at an uprising in July, Kollontai was freed in September and resumed her revolutionary efforts. Elected to the Central Committee of the party at the Sixth Party Congress, she attended the Central Committee meeting where the Bolshevik seizure of power was decided on. With tears in her eyes, she heard the All-Russian Congress of Soviets declare the new government, describing the meeting as "the greatest, most memorable hour of my life."[55]

With the seizure of power by the Bolsheviks, Kollontai was named Commissar of Social Welfare in Lenin's new government. Although the men of his party were eager to hail Kollontai's selection as proof of the new regime's commitment to women, perhaps her appointment was not really as groundbreaking as it first appeared. Not only had the Ministry of Social Welfare been headed by a woman, the Countess Sophie Panina, under the previous Kerensky government, but the department's concerns with orphans, invalids, the unemployed, needy, and homeless seemed to mark it out as a proper political extension of the traditional female sphere.

Nonetheless, Kollontai enthusiastically accepted the challenge of social welfare work, and what she did with the power and authority given her is significant. Both her administrative style and the kinds of jobs she chose to undertake serve as important keys to uncovering her own revolutionary priorities as a female close to the centers of power.

The ministry Kollontai was called upon to head was a melange of social welfare institutions inherited from the tsarist bureaucracy and the Provisional Government. Many employees were openly hostile to the new regime, but Kollontai, from the start, was inclined to use novel approaches to gain their loyalty. Inspired by a real faith in the revolutionary creativity and good sense of the masses, she drew all levels of the ministry into policy making, asking the opinions even of "janitors and messenger boys" on a wide range of issues. Meetings of the ministry were held frequently, and all employees were expected to be present. Everyone was to have an equal chance of promotion.[56] Although Lenin was angered by these actions, by what he took to be her vacillation and by her unwillingness to use "brutal measures," like arrest and imprisonment, to establish control over her employees,[57] Kollontai insisted on the real importance of her practices.[58] Humane administration was the first of her contributions to the new revolutionary society.

In her work at the ministry, Kollontai also attempted to implement a wide variety of social welfare reforms: the establishment of shelters for the crippled, handicapped, and war wounded; the creation of homes for orphans and others left homeless by the war; the reorganization of sanatoria; the institution of self-government in schools and old age homes; and the seizure of church buildings and their conversion into more socially useful institutions like hospitals and asylums.[59]

Such activities alone, however, were not enough to satisfy her. As a woman in a position of power, she felt that her greatest responsibility was to deal with the special problems and needs of women. Here she manifested a significant difference of opinion from Lenin. While he had always been determined to bring women into the service of the revolution, his interest in women's issues stemmed from his recognition that their support was vital to the revolution's survival.[60] According to Kollontai, however, women had already given that support and the time had come for the promised fruits of that revolution to begin affecting the lives of its female supporters. As she saw it, the long-delayed discussion of the woman question should properly end—the proverbial day after the revolution had arrived—and the task of that revolution should now be to consider the much-postponed problem of female emancipation.

On one level, the reforms in women's situation over the old regime were easy and clear to see. Women had been decreed equal in all civil, political, and legal rights. They had been given the vote, and the principle of equal pay for equal work had been established. Divorce laws had been eased, and the distinction between religious and civil marriage had been eradicated. Abortion had been legalized, and contraceptive information was to become available. All discrimination between legitimate and illegitimate children was to end.[61]

Although Lenin and the Bolsheviks were rightly proud of these accomplishments, seeing them as the first stage in the promised Marxist millennium for women, to Kollontai they were not enough, nor were they the essence of female emancipation as she defined it. She reprimanded the Bolsheviks for taking false pride in such purely legal decrees, for in reality their enactments had actually gone no further than those in most of the advanced "bourgeois" countries.[62] The revolution, Kollontai demanded, had to affect the lot of women in daily life, in daily social relations. Revolutionary changes in daily life were at the core of women's liberation as she saw it, and these were the kinds of changes that she was determined to bring about by her work in the commissariat.

While Lenin focused on the work women owed to a new communist society badly in need of their labor power,[63] Kollontai, on the other hand, emphasized what that new society owed to its female members. Women, she insisted, served a critical social function in all societies, not only in the area of production but more importantly in reproduction. Because motherhood, the provision of new workers for the republic, was a social service, the protection of motherhood and maternity should in return be established as a legitimate government priority.

Kollontai regarded her work in setting up a comprehensive system of prenatal care as her most momentous accomplishment.[64] In her plans and decrees at the commissariat, she had the opportunity to implement ideas she had formulated in the prerevolutionary period, especially in her book, *Society and Maternity*, published in 1916. Her ideas have a triple importance. Not only do they demonstrate her sensitivity, as a woman revolutionary, to basic human issues as well as women's special problems and needs, but they also mark her attempt to implement in a concrete way the new collectivist society that was to be at the very core of the Marxist revolution.

One of the more vague and troubling elements of Marxist theory was the idea that the family, like the state itself, would wither away in the new society. Although Marx had paid little attention to the real meaning of this neat phrase, Engels, in *The Condition of the Working Class in England*, had attempted to clarify its meaning. For the proletariat, he explained, the institution of the family, at least as understood by the middle and upper classes, was a myth. Any vestige of family life had been wrecked by child and female labor. Certainly childhood was not sacred for the poor, whose children worked in factories and were educated on the street. Insofar as the socialist revolution would abolish these problems, the family, in its bourgeois sense, would also be done away with.[65]

In her writings Kollontai echoed Engels, but she emphasized not so much the myth of childhood among the proletariat as the myth of maternity. While the bourgeoisie proudly chanted praises to the sanctity of maternity, such odes to motherhood were unknown to the women of the proletariat. For them pregnancy was not a period of anxious and pampered expectation but a "cross."[66] Driven by that "relentless taskmaster, need," pregnant working class wives slaved in factories until the last possible moment. Small wonder, then, that babies died "like flies" because of the harmful and unhealthy conditions to which their mothers had been exposed during pregnancy.

If the working mother were relieved of the physical burdens of caring for her child, however, then she too could share in the "joys" of motherhood. Inspired by this perception, Kollontai's vision of the family under the new society gave shape and form to the old Marxist slogans. She clearly identified Marx's call for the "withering away of the family" with the adoption of former familial functions by society itself: "Society, that big happy family, will look after everything."[67]

Kollontai was very specific as to how society was to take over those old family functions. Her plans called for a system of free maternity hospitals and state-guaranteed and -supported child care facilities. Paid maternity leave, both before and after delivery, would ensure the health of mother and child and provide sound and healthy workers for the workers' state. Since modern science, she wrote, had demonstrated the advantages of nursing one's own child, crèches should be set up in all factories, "so that each nursing mother could easily visit and feed her baby in breaks from work."[68]

Kollontai's analysis was strictly rooted in the standard Marxist theory on the woman question: the view that woman's subordinate status was at base the result of her economic dependency. State support for mother and child would allow women to combine motherhood and economically productive labor. The working mother, therefore, was serving herself at the same time that she was contributing to the economic needs of society. The mother who fulfilled her duties to the state was in turn rewarded by the state, which, by freeing motherhood of its economic anxieties, allowed the woman to share in its natural joys.

On a larger level, the social protection of maternity was the answer to the problem of the family in the new society. A collectivist ethos, not the private egotism of the nuclear family, was to be the hallmark of the new socialist world. By providing for all children, the social collective would make the individual family as a child-rearing institution obsolete. Children would be taught the virtues of comradely love and solidarity while their mothers would lose their smothering and overprotective possessiveness. The great slogan of Kollontai's ministry encouraged women to be "mothers not only to your own children but to all children of the workers and peasants."[69]

Kollontai's vision of the collective form of the new society extended beyond provisions for the protection of maternity. Her boldest reforms called for an end to the drudgery, waste, and inefficiency that she considered characteristic of individual family life. Economically productive labor, she realized, was not an automatic route to emancipation for women who had to shoulder the double burden of work in factory and home. While Lenin shared Kollontai's contempt for housework, calling it "barbarously unproductive . . . stultifying and crushing drudgery,"[70] it was Kollontai who gave the fullest expression to the picture of communal life under communism. Her plans called for public kitchens and dining rooms, collective apartments, children's colonies, central laundries and clothes-mending shops, all staffed by women who would be paid for their domestic labors. Not only would these workers become economically independent themselves, but they would also free other women from the "mindless and inefficient" repetition of these identical tasks in their individual homes, releasing them for productive labor and recreational and educational pursuits.[71] Kollontai envisioned not only a society that promised to touch intimately the lives of women, but a truly revolutionary new order in which comradeship, solidarity, and mutual devotion to the collective would become real ideals. In the new socialist world, individuals would be bound to one another not by ties of blood, but by "community of work, unity of interests, aspirations and problems." These would firmly unite all people and "train them to be true brothers in spirit."[72]

Despite such vision, Kollontai was greatly disillusioned by obstacles that blocked fulfillment of her bold plans. Economic problems and the dislocations of war, revolution, and civil war thwarted her repeatedly. Nor was she prepared for popular hostility to her formulas, fed by rumors that she envisioned the "nationalization" of women and the wrenching of infant children away from their mothers and families.[73] She eventually came to be demoralized by her own utopianism, by the "magnificent illusions" of those days.[74] The growing disparity between her revolutionary dreams and her practical successes soured Kollontai on the political life. She came to feel that it was "no fun to be people's Commissar . . . ," and longed for the time when she had been only "an ordinary party agitator traveling around the world and dreaming of revolution."[75]

Adding to Kollontai's difficulties during this period were growing personal problems, arising from that critical dilemma common to revolutionary women of combining love, work, and politics. In January 1918, Kollontai, then 45, married Pavel Efimovich Dybenko, the Commissar of the Navy, a man of peasant extraction 17 years her junior. The two had met in the spring of 1917, on one of her agitational tours among the sailors of Helsingfors, and by early November, according to Trotsky, party gossip had it that they were lovers.[76]

Kollontai's attempt to carve out a private life for herself was not looked upon kindly in revolutionary circles. Her liaison created sensational rumors, the most spectacular being a story that she and Dybenko had gone off together for a tryst in the Crimea in the midst of the November Revolution itself[77] —an act that, if true, would have exposed her less-than-total devotion to the revolutionary cause and compromised her reliability in the eyes of the party faithful. Much of the salacious interest in her affair centered on the obviously passionate and erotic side of her romance. There was much tittering about the 45-year-old aristocrat's attraction to the virile sailor who was also her social inferior. For all their vaunted revolutionary proclamations, Bolshevik men were a puritanical lot with staid, if not Victorian, attitudes on sexuality, female behavior, and married life. Lenin was especially harsh on those women who overstepped the bounds of "proper" respectability. In later years he was to be quite blunt about the true extent of his commitment to women's emancipation from the repressive mores of the past, announcing, in a direct reference to Kollontai, that he could not "vouch for the reliability or the endurance of those women whose love affair is intertwined with politics."[78]

Kollontai's association with Dybenko hurt her in other ways, for the scandal of the liaison itself was worsened by the stigma of her husband's arrest in March 1918. As Commissar of the Navy, he was initially held responsible for the defection of several ships of the Baltic fleet to the Germans at Narva.[79] Although he was subsequently acquitted of all charges of treason and complicity, the disgrace of the Dybenko affair, on both levels, marked the beginning of the "dark period" of Kollontai's life, the beginning of her fall from grace in party circles.[80] Or, more accurately perhaps, the ease with which she did fall proved that her acceptance by the Bolshevik hierarchy had always been a tenuously based one. Her isolation in this period was only worsened when she began to adopt an increasingly independent line of political thought. Just as the war had brought Kollontai into the ranks of the Bolsheviks, the war also marked the beginning of her separation from them.

Lenin's insistence on immediate peace with Germany infuriated Kollontai. Although she had been a staunch antimilitarist all her life, by 1917 she had come to hope that the war with Germany could be transformed into a great war against capitalism itself, an international revolution of workers and peasants of which the Bolshevik Revolution was only a part. In her genuine revolutionary zeal, Kollontai continued her allegiance to the program to which the party had been pledged throughout 1917, even though Lenin himself was willing to compromise with the concept of revolutionary war to save the revolution in Russia. According to Kollontai, however, the revolution in Russia was not worth saving if the price were compromise with all earlier principles.[81] She accused Lenin of opportunism, of betraying the proletariat of the world, and of compromising with imperialism.

Kollontai's opposition to the Treaty of Brest-Litovsk marked the beginning of an irrevocable split with Lenin. In the party's debates over ratification of the treaty, Lenin reprimanded Kollontai for her romantic vision, scolding her for her failure to recognize the need to temper her revolutionary ardor with considerations of practicality. The Germans were on the verge of taking Petrograd, and the Bolsheviks had no army with which to deal both with domestic enemies and foreign forces. Like a master to an apprentice, he ridiculed Kollontai's idealized concepts of revolution. It was not easy to be a revolutionary, he preached, as if to imply that her earlier efforts had been mere play-acting. "The path of revolution is not strewn with roses, with marches from victory to victory, with waving flags to the strains of 'Internationale!'"[82]

In protest against the Treaty of Brest-Litovsk, Kollontai resigned her post at the Ministry of Social Welfare. Lenin, in one respect, had been right: Kollontai's idealism would not allow her to adjust to the prosaic demands of political life. During the civil war she continued her revolutionary work, serving as an agitator and propagandist for the Bolshevik cause, but her talents, wrote Jacques Sadoul, a member of the French military mission to Russia, were "wasted" in such pursuits.[83]

Perhaps Kollontai's most bitter punishment came in the fall of 1919. In that year, after years of controversy on the issue, the party finally authorized the establishment of a special bureau to mobilize women in support of the government. The Section for Work Among Women, or Zhenotdel, was never viewed as a concession to separatist feminist sentiment, however, but was justified as a practical political expedient in the face of the civil war.[84] Despite her years of work in support of the cause of working women, Kollontai was not chosen to head Zhenotdel. The top leadership position was bestowed instead on Inessa Armand, whose most impressive political credentials included utter loyalty and obedience to Lenin, and whose reliability had never been tainted by oppositionist activity. As the reward for independence, Kollontai was given a relatively minor—some might say insulting—position organizing peasant women.

Kollontai finally did assume the top post at Zhenotdel after Armand's death in 1920. Although the bureau remained understaffed and underfinanced, and continued to be plagued by hostility from many men who resented special work among women, she retained a vigorous vision of what Zhenotdel should and must accomplish. Its task, she insisted, was not to bring women to the service of the state, but to represent and defend the interests of women and children before the state. While Armand had devoted her efforts during the Civil War to organizing wartime auxiliary work among women, re-cruiting them to care for wounded soldiers, to sew bandages, and to distribute food, Kollontai used her leadership position to challenge and to question the extent of the government's real commitment to women. She demanded that women achieve full and actual equality; that they sit on economic and political decision-making boards, and that they, as a group, achieve political power. Willing to undertake bold criticism of the party for not doing enough in these areas, Kollontai was courageous enough to call the bluff of Bolshevik leaders. Even a self-proclaimed "revolutionary" regime could be run too largely by men, she admitted to an American newspaper reporter. As long as their interests continued to be overlooked, women would simply have to "keep stirring up the government."[85]

Unfortunately, however, Kollontai's brief tenure as the head of Zhenotdel did not give her this opportunity. While she did have some spectacular successes—among them the theatrical unveiling and emancipation of groups of veiled Moslem women from the Russian provinces of Central Asia[86] —her leadership of the women's section hinged on her willingness to toe the party line. Her sudden dismissal from Zhenotdel in February 1922 was the direct result of her reentry into political opposition, and her opposition resulted from her grow-ing disgust with the direction the revolution was taking.

With the pressures of the civil war dying down and the virtual assurance of Bolshevik victory, discussions in party circles came to center on the consolidation of the Soviet regime, most especially in the area of economic development and productivity. While Lenin's use of the magic slogan "workers' control of industry" had played an important role in the Bolshevik rise to power,[87] the exact nature and meaning of that phrase remained to be defined. Where workers' control via factory committees had actually existed during the civil war period, it had proven to be a dismal failure.[88] The inadequate technical and administrative knowledge of these committees—coupled with inflation, the decay of machinery, shortages of materials, and the breakdown of the transport system—had had a devastating effect on production.

Despite the glaring failures of workers' control, the government's decision to return to one-man management and the use of "bourgeois specialists" in industry after the civil war erupted into a new controversy, centering on the party's reluctance to clarify the exact role of workers and trade unions in building the new Soviet state. Discontent came to be centered in a group known as the Workers Opposition, a trade union movement whose membership was drawn mostly from the metal-workers, a union known for revolutionary militancy. The extent of its real support among other workers was difficult to ascertain, and until 1921 it existed as a "somewhat colorless" oppositionist faction,[89] with no talented leaders or publicists until Kollontai joined its ranks in January of that year. Although party gossip attempted to impugn her motives for joining the opposition—Lenin, for one, attributed her involvement to an infatuation with Alexander Shlyapnikov, a metal worker, oppositionist, and old Bolshevik with whom she had lived and loved in Norway before the revolution—the ideas that formed the kernel of oppositionist thought had long been central to Kollontai's revolutionary thinking. In her hands the platform of the Workers Opposition came to have a potentially wider appeal, becoming the focus of all latent discontents within the party. With her passionate and eloquent oratorical style, she seemed the appropriate person to deliver the platform of the Workers Opposition before the upcoming Tenth Party Congress in March 1921, where a debate on the increasingly central trade union controversy had been scheduled.

The ideas Kollontai expressed in her speech before the Congress and in her pamphlet, *The Workers Opposition*, were imbued with the same intense faith in natural proletarian goodness that had long made her an advocate of revolutionary spontaneity. In identifying the proletariat with the unions and not the party, she revealed her continued commitment to the view that real political wisdom flowed from below and not from above. The Workers Opposition was "wonderful" precisely because it had no prominent leaders, but was the product of healthy grass roots sentiments arising from among the working classes.[90] Since the masses felt alienated from the leadership of the party, the party, she warned, would do well to listen to their criticisms.

The key question raised by the Workers Opposition, outlined Kollontai, was this: "Who shall develop the creative powers in the sphere of economic reconstruction—the trade unionists themselves, or petty bourgeois specialists and managers?"[91] Current problems within the party could be attributed to its reliance on bureaucracy, its lack of a democratic spirit, its distrust of workers' initiative, and its infusion with nonproletarian elements. Those who loved the party, as she did, could not close their eyes to the evils they saw within. They were not advocating a split, but sounding a clarion call for the return to true Marxist principles.

"The creation of communism belongs to the workers," Marx had written in the *Communist Manifesto.* By ending her oration with these words, Kollontai sought to justify her entry into opposition. Yet despite her claims to be following in the footsteps of Marx, prospects for the party's acceptance of her views were poor. Kollontai had failed to see that the party had become not only the manager of the revolution but the molder and creator of new Soviet life as well. While her observations on the ideological hardening of the arteries within the party were well taken, she was destined to be the victim of her own accuracy.

The Workers Opposition had selected a particularly inauspicious time to launch its attack. A recent sailors' revolt at Kronstadt, a major naval base on an island in the Finnish Gulf, 17 miles west of Petrograd, had made the party especially sensitive both to criticism and to threats of counterrevolution.[92] Although the Workers Opposition had played no role in the recent revolt, that revolt was a symptom of the kind of discontent of which the oppositionists spoke. While Lenin stopped short of accusing the Workers Opposition of having fomented the rebellion, he tried to discredit the group by linking its criticisms to other dangerous counterrevolutionary tendencies like anarchism and anarchosyndicalism. Arguing that groups like the Workers Opposition played into the hands of enemies of the state, Lenin chose not to deal with the charges of the oppositionists but simply to decree the danger of criticism itself.

Yet there were problems with the oppositionist position, problems that Lenin could and should have addressed. Although the oppositionists were united in their high ideals and in their disapproval of certain tendencies in the party, they possessed no realistic sense of the pressing economic problems Russia faced, and they posed no practical economic development program of their own. Had Lenin dealt directly with these problems, his attack would have seemed more reasoned and more rational. Instead, however, he decided to launch into a furious and vicious attack on Kollontai as the group's representative—a tactic that demonstrated the extent to which he felt threatened by her powerful and effective oratory.

Rather than choosing to engage Kollontai in a sound intellectual debate on the issues, Lenin sought to discredit her views by ridiculing her as a woman, and by drawing attention to her former relationship with Shlyapnikov. Casting aspersions at her sexual reputation, he deviously used her own words against her. In her speech, Kollontai had termed the Workers Opposition "class united and class conscious." To this, Lenin replied, "Well, thank God, so we know that Comrade Kollontai and Comrade Shlyapnikov are class united and class conscious."[93] There was much snickering in the audience from those delegates who knew the hidden meaning of Lenin's remarks.[94] Kollontai at this time was legally married to Dybenko, and although she worked closely with Shlyapnikov during this period, there is no evidence that they had resumed their earlier romantic involvement. Lenin's charges were not only in poor taste, therefore, but also untrue. More importantly, they reveal his real opinion of emancipated women—or, more accurately, of those daringly independent revolutionary women who remained beyond his control.

The attempt to disparage Kollontai's revolutionary credentials was continued by party leader Nikolai Bukharin, whose response to the actual charges raised by the oppositionists was even more irrelevant than that of Lenin. Bukharin's attack on Kollontai centered on an article she had published in January of that year, entitled "The Cross of Motherhood." The article dealt with the difficulties of being a mother, and in it Kollontai had made reference to a play she had once seen in Germany, "The Miracle," whose three main characters were a young nun, the Mother Superior of a convent, and the Virgin Mary. Bukharin's discussion of the article out of context made it and its author both seem ludicrous and foolish. "Obviously," he charged, anyone who wrote such "disgusting, sentimental Catholic banalities" about motherhood shouldn't be taken seriously. Perhaps Kollontai would argue that he couldn't understand the article since he was a man, but, Bukharin continued, even if he could be turned into a woman he would still think it ridiculous, just like the "clear class line" she claimed for the Workers Opposition.[95]

Kollontai's involvement with the Workers Opposition left her isolated and attacked within the party. While the masculinity of the other oppositionists had not been impugned, she had felt the sting of sarcasm and ridicule because of her sex. Lenin's response to her independence had been "implacable and unjust" anger and slander. Contemporaries reported that he could never hear her name again without flying into a rage.[96] Blinded by her sacred vision of the revolution, Kollontai failed to realize that organized oppositional activity within Soviet Russia had become impossible. Threatened with explusion from the party after her attempt to bring the platform of the Workers Opposition before the new Third International, she was rewarded with dismissal from her post at Zhenotdel. From then on, Alexandra Kollontai was never again in a position to influence the course of the revolution in Russia with her ideas or ideals.

IV

Kollontai's estrangement from Lenin and the Bolsheviks was the result of her fundamentally different view of the party and its role in the revolution. Her boundless faith and trust in the ability of the masses was matched in its exuberance only by Lenin's distrust of unchanneled mass activity. Although she had theoretical goals herself, she criticized Lenin for being "too theoretical,"[97] too far removed from the masses he was hoping to lead. In her own work at the Ministry of Social Welfare, she had always been determined not to let herself lose contact with the workers whom she considered to be the lifeblood of the revolution, giving, she always claimed, the same consideration to suggestions from scrubwomen as to those from her closest colleagues.[98]

While the war may have caused Kollontai to forget temporarily her differences with the Bolsheviks, her own view of the party itself had never changed. Her criticisms of the Russian party in 1921 were basically the same as those she had leveled against the German party during the war, when she charged the leaders of German socialism with having destroyed the creative revolutionary potential of the masses. German workers were silent and sheepish upon the outbreak of the war because they had been educated in the tradition of blind submission to their leaders, leaders who had preached caution, discipline, and routine, who had never developed or strengthened the revolutionary energy of the masses.[99]

The German Socialist Party, Kollontai explained, had lost its revolutionary spirit because its members had become infected with the vile disease of careerism. Fawning obedience and obsequiousness, not critical independence, had become the only way to get ahead in the party. Those "colorless toers-of-lines" who used the party as a springboard to personal power were rewarded with deputy's seats, while those who chose not to play the game—like Rosa Luxemburg, she noted—were kept at a distance.[100] Careerism, bureaucracy, and the seductive influence of power had wrecked the German party during the war, and in 1921 were on the verge of wrecking a Russian party where stifled criticism had become the price one paid for advancement.

Although she knew the consequences of oppositional activity, Kollontai chose to pursue it anyway, because, by her own admission, she had never been obsessed by the quest for power or political influence. She had entered revolutionary life to implement her vision of a new society, not to secure power or political positions for herself. In fact, in the aftermath of the October Revolution, she had even appeared to show some hostility to entering bureaucratic life. When asked about plans for her ministry, she seemed amused. "Heavens, I have no plans. If I became a minister, I would be just as stupid as all other ministers."[101] In an interesting generalization, Kollontai attributed women's failure to obtain positions of influence in Russia to their greater political integrity. Since women had "more conscience" than men, they had no desire to obtain positions "for which they were not fitted by previous training."[102]

Just as Kollontai did not gauge political success by the usual guidelines, that is, a string of political posts and appointments, her measure of the success of the revolution itself was not ends- or goal-oriented. Not for her was the "ends justifies the means" rationale of Lenin. His familiar metaphor—"You can't get an omelette without breaking eggs"—repulsed her. Success for Kollontai was in the attempt itself, in the formulation of the vision, in framing issues and raising questions, in keeping the faith. She was never willing to compromise her principles to "save" the revolution. "Even if we are conquered," she told American journalist Bessie Beatty, "we have done great things. We are breaking the way, abolishing old ideas. . . ."[103] By her own standards, then, Kollontai's life as a revolutionary was a success, even though the majority of her ideas were not implemented, and her vision of the new society was not in line with that of the party leadership.

All her life, Kollontai's socialist faith was marked by a sincere commitment to two ideals that communism was supposed to be all about—communalism and revolution, the creation of a truly new human society made up of people linked together by "innumerable psychological and emotional bonds," people inspired by "delicacy, sensitivity, and the desire to be useful to one another."[104] This was the essence of Kollontai's vision. By describing in detail what the new communist society could be like and should be like, she made a serious and pioneering attempt to add a new dimension to Marxist thought.

The most important element of the new society, according to Kollontai, would be the acceptance of the principle of collective responsibility by and for all its members. This principle had inspired her work at the commissariat, and it was again in pursuit of this ideal that she entered her last public debate in 1926, the party debate over the proposed new family code. The issues in question here gave Kollontai the opportunity to unite her two paramount interests— work for women and work for the collective.

The partial restoration of free market conditions under Lenin's New Economic Policy had led to the rapid growth of unemployment among women, because as the least skilled segment of the labor force, they were the initial victims of resulting job cutbacks. Problems of female unemployment, however, were magnified because many of these same women, in the heady days after the revolution, had neglected to register their marriages with the civil authorities. Deprived of legal status, they found themselves with neither means of support nor legal recourse if abandoned by their husbands. The new code was an attempt to protect this increasingly large number of "unprotected" women. By declaring previously unregistered marriages legal and binding, it increased the husband's obligations to pay alimony.

The proposed code offended Kollontai because it betrayed the time-honored socialist principle of collective responsibility. She accused party leaders of being too quick to abandon the vision of the new socialist family, and of being too eager to fall back on the old outworn solutions of the past. Horrified by the spectacle of wives being reduced to begging alimony in court from men who in most cases probably couldn't afford to pay, she attacked alimony as demeaning to women because it perpetuated their dependent status.

Kollontai's alternative to the proposed code was new and novel, in keeping with her deeply felt vision of communal life under communism. She called for the abolition of alimony entirely, and for the establishment of a General Insurance Fund to which the entire adult working population would contribute on a graduated scale. This fund would provide for the support of unemployed and deserted wives with young children, and create children's homes and crèches so that mothers could easily return to work if employment became available. Kollontai's plan, therefore, encompassed her two main aims—the principle of collective responsibility for members in need, and the creation of new independent women, freed from the debilitating support of men.[105]

The campaign was Kollontai's last struggle. Isolated by her earlier oppositionist activity, she now found herself out of touch not only with the government's economic priorities but also with popular opinion. Her plan, seen as a dangerous encouragement of promiscuity and a protection for male licentiousness, was rejected by all but a small group of her supporters.[106]

Kollontai's contribution to the marriage law debate is understandable only in the context of her larger quest—her search for new socialist family forms and for a new morality by which communist individuals would frame their lives. Sensitive to charges that her efforts in this area were "utopian, dreaming, or idealistic," she deliberately framed her discussion of the "new communist morality" against an orthodox Marxist backdrop. It was an "old truth," she wrote, that every new economic class develops its own ideology, of which the accepted code of sexual behavior was an important part.[107] The victorious proletariat, therefore, should develop a new code of sexual behavior appropriate to its needs.

By her attention to the moral and psychological changes that would occur under communism, Kollontai hoped to open up a neglected, but important, side of Marxist thought. She insisted that her work was necessary and worthwhile, vital, in fact, to the emancipation of women, because the sudden release from centuries of legal and economic oppression would have a radical effect on the female mind.[108]

Kollontai was the only Bolshevik of her generation who attempted to deal with these issues, and her analysis showed a much greater sophistication than that of any earlier socialist writer on the woman question—Marx, Engels, and Bebel included. Her treatment of the woman question went well beyond the rote and pat formulas, the calls for economic and legal equality, and the attacks on the "cash nexus" of prostitution. She had always insisted that a woman's perspective was necessary to deal adequately with women's issues, that only a woman could creatively complement masculine beliefs. Her writings demonstrate the validity of this view. She wrote about women's problems and needs as men never could, both because she was a woman herself, and because she had lived the problems she so sensitively discussed.

Over and above women's economic and legal oppression, Kollontai recognized that their problems stemmed in large part from their dependence on love, from their need and longing for love that kept them from productive and useful work—economic, political, revolutionary, or otherwise. Women depended upon love, she analyzed, because over the centuries little else of substance or importance had been left to them. Nonetheless, she respected the place of love in women's lives. Plagued by loneliness and repeated romantic disappointments herself (her marriage to Dybenko had also crumbled), she had often longed "to be enveloped by love, warmth and understanding."[109] Because both work and love were important, the answer to the female dilemma, she believed, was in the ability of women to combine love and work, and in the education of men so as to allow women to do this.

Kollontai chose to develop these themes not only in essays and articles but also in novels and short stories. While not averse to purely theoretical activity, she, unlike Lenin, put it in proper pertive. "One must write not only for oneself, but for others," she believed,[110] recognizing the special ability of fiction to appeal to the hearts and minds of those women she was most trying to touch.

Her novels and stories were simple tales of women struggling to combine political work with love for party comrades.[111] Although Kollontai's plots and characters were simple and one-sided, her depiction of women was especially interesting. Drawn from her own experiences, the "new woman" she presented was not only strong-willed, politically active, and economically independent, but also possessed of a fierce and pure revolutionary intensity, a purity of revolutionary vision not shared by her male characters.[112] In the end, the men of Kollontai's fiction misunderstood and disappointed their former lovers, lost sight of larger revolutionary ideals, and became corrupted by power and the pursuit of their own pleasure, but the women persevered.

The new woman of Kollontai's depiction was marked first and foremost by her desire for inner freedom, her demand for both economic and spiritual independence. While her ideal remained the "great love," that "complete wordless understanding existing between two human beings united in their mutual respect, harmony, and passion,"[113] she was not absorbed by that desire alone. Her motivation, rather, came from her work, her self-esteem, and her absorption in the collective. The loss or absence of love was much less disastrous than would be the loss of that most precious commodity, her personal identity. Love for the new woman, said Kollontai, far from being her whole existence, was only a step, the way to finding her true self.[114]

Precisely because the new woman's life was not exhausted in love, new criteria were necessary to evaluate and appraise her "moral personality."[115] For centuries, women's value had been judged by such standards as "moral purity" and virtuousness, but these precepts of the old morality should no longer apply in the new society, where women and men alike would be judged by their achievements and their contributions to the collective.

Kollontai began her call for a new morality with an attack on the double standard that allowed free sexual expression to men but denied it to women. One of the characteristic traits of the new woman, she wrote, was that she didn't deny her natural physical drives or hide behind a "mask of immaculateness."[116] While Kollontai recognized and admitted that the drive for sexual satisfaction was a natural human need common to both men and women, she condemned as "wingless Eros" all sexual relations based on physical desire alone, with "no inner moral obligations."[117] These, she insisted, were vulgar, crude, and worse than prostitution itself.

Far from preaching "free love" as an appropriate moral code for the new woman of the new society, Kollontai firmly separated herself from any ideological tradition that identified free love with female emancipation. Free love, she insisted, was not the answer to the woman question, but only a "bourgeois illusion." The "daring heroines of free love" failed to recognize that sexual emancipation meant nothing without larger social changes.[118] Kollontai advocated not free love, but a new society in which larger social and economic changes would ensure that all human beings would be free to love: freed from economic dependency in love; from economic concerns; and from worries about child support and child care. Women would no longer need love to establish their identity, nor would they need to fear that love itself would rob them of that identity.

Although Kollontai never recommended free love, neither marriage nor permanency in love was ever very important to her. Recognizing that complicated psychological changes take place in each individual in the course of a lifetime, she envisioned instead of one permanent union a series of monogamous relationships.[119] The establishment of the principle of collective responsibility for child care ensured that children of all such relationships would be well provided for.

Yet the one "great love," when it could be found, always remained Kollontai's ideal. She christened it "winged Eros," and characterized it as a great creative force, "woven of delicate strands of every kind of emotion."[120] Far from being all-demanding, all-possessing, or all-embracing, the great love was based on mutual respect and sympathy between the partners, a sensitivity and responsiveness to each other's needs, and a desire to help each other. Since these qualities enriched the collective, Kollontai felt, it would joyously welcome "all loving hearts" who, in loving each other, tightened the bonds of mutual respect, harmony, and devotion between the members of the collective itself. This process led to the formation of the final and highest form of human love, the "love collective."[121]

Kollontai's bold pronouncements were sensitive and far-reaching statements that went well beyond both standard Marxist formulas on the woman question and earlier sketchy descriptions of human relations under communism. Demonstrating her concerns as a woman, as a socialist, and as a revolutionary, her ideas touched the very core of the woman problem in all its complexity. Rooted in the purest socialist ideals, they were also truly revolutionary, advocating the abandonment of habits, customs, and beliefs that had imprisoned men and women for centuries, "We still live and think under the heavy hand of an unavoidable loneliness of the spirit,"[122] she wrote. Yet she was perplexed by the "unforgivable indifference" shown to that question, angered by the troubling refusal to grapple with some of the most essential problems of human life.

Kollontai's ideas were maligned, derided, and criticized. Her attempt to frame a new code of human relationships for the new revolutionary world was not seen as an important supplement to Marxist theory, but was grossly misunderstood, mocked, and ridiculed as an excessively bold and outrageous attempt to justify her own "unorthodox" sexual views. The Bolsheviks may have made a political revolution in Russia in 1917, but their attachment to traditional values and practices continued. The erroneous perception that Kollontai was obsessed with sex and free love alone was considered "disgusting" to party leaders. To them, her writings "reeked of pornography and the gutter."[123]

Although a careful reading of Kollontai's articles certainly makes it clear that she never advocated promiscuity, her earlier criticisms of the regime had done little to encourage a reasoned and careful appraisal of her ideas. She was also a vulnerable target. A courageous and emancipated woman in all respects, she had rejected a traditional female lifestyle years earlier when she decided to join the revolutionary cause. Yet, even within that cause, her own nontraditional lifestyle, the very real difficulty of combining her private and political selves, left her open to attack.

Above all, Kollontai's concern with sexual, moral, and psychological problems was widely regarded as frivolous and silly because such issues frankly wcrc not considered serious or worthy of discussion by party leaders. Lenin himself set the tone here. Both before and after the revolution he had feared and criticized the wasteful expenditure of energy. "Do not expend your forces on unimportant things," he admonished the party in 1907.[124] In 1921 his advice was the same: "The main thing is not to squander one's energy."[125] Lenin had always been contemptuous of those who chose to concentrate on "beautiful fairy tales," rather than concern themselves with the grim realities of everyday life.[126] When those fairy tales took a sexual direction, his scorn and contempt knew no bounds. In his famous 1920 interview with the German socialist Clara Zetkin, Lenin attacked those "who are always absorbed in sex problems, the way an Indian saint is absorbed in the contemplation of his navel." The revolution, he decreed, "called for concentration and rallying every nerve by the masses and by the individual. . . . There must be no dissipation of energy."[127] Clearly, the conflict between Lenin and

Kollontai centered on their very different perception of what was truly important, of what the human side of revolutionary creation was all about.

After the civil war the "revolutionary" Bolsheviks came to stress traditional morality more than ever before, as an attempt to introduce a stabilizing influence into Soviet life. In the early days of the revolution, irresponsible sexual behavior had created serious problems, when misconceptions about the freedom the revolution had brought wreaked havoc on personal and family relations.[128] Easier divorce laws led to the wholesale abandonment of wives and families. Sexual experimentation among youth with little or no knowledge of birth control produced thousands of unwanted children, and the larger cities came to be flooded with wandering hordes of homeless or abandoned orphans. Not only was the government concerned with the social and economic problem of caring for the deserted and homeless, but Lenin also feared that the disease of rampant promiscuity afflicting youth was diverting them from revolutionary fervor and industry.

Bukharin, Trotsky, and others held the "heresies" of Kollontai to be directly responsible for the sexual anarchy and degeneracy among the "decadent and semihooligan" groups of Russian youth.[129] Other vicious attacks on Kollontai followed. She was called an "un-Marxist petty-bourgeois philistine" whose obsession with love prevented her from focusing on more pressing problems and concerns. Although she had tried to "pass off" her ideas about marriage and love as the "last word in Marxism," she was really wasting her time, "shooting at sparrows with a cannon."[130] The cruellest of all remarks were those that used her sexual views to impugn the quality of her earlier revolutionary contributions. "The real question to be asked," one scathing attack concluded, "is how she could have been considered for so long to be one of the leaders not only of the Russian, but also of the international communist women's movement?"[131]

This slander campaign ensured that Kollontai would be prevented from having any influence on the future course of Russian developments. More tragic, however, was the role it played in wrecking her confidence in herself, in convincing her that the search to combine personal happiness with active political involvement, both for herself and for others, had been unimportant and unnecessary. "It was an expenditure of precious time and energy," she wrote in her autobiography, "fruitless, and, in the final analysis, utterly worthless."[132]

V

Despondent at the thought of remaining an impotent and disgraced oppositionist, in the summer of 1922 Kollontai wrote to Joseph Stalin, then secretary of the party, asking him to reassign her to some kind of party work. His response—that she await appointment to a diplomatic post abroad—was tantamount to a sentence of exile; separation from the field of the revolution was meant as punishment for her sins. Although Kollontai recognized this, she could no longer bear the stigma and frustration of continuing political isolation. Her willingness to enter diplomatic life was not the result of what she herself would have chosen to do, but was the product of her desire to be of service to her party and her country in whatever capacity she would be allowed.

Kollontai's career as a diplomat spanned 23 years and was characterized by a wide diversity in her fields of activity.[133] Her aristocratic upbringing, schooling in the social graces, and linguistic abilities all made her a promising candidate for diplomatic work. Entering diplomatic life as a member of the Soviet trade delegation to Norway, she also served for brief periods as official Soviet representative to Mexico and Norway, and was a member of the Soviet delegation to the League of Nations. Her last and most famous appointment came in 1930, when she became Soviet ambassador to Sweden, the first woman in modern history to hold such a position.

During her years as a diplomat, Kollontai negotiated commercial and trade treaties between the Soviet Union and the countries where she was accredited, fostered improved Soviet-Scandinavian relations, and played a major role in negotiating a settlement between Finland and the Soviet Union in the Winter War of 1941, and the Continuation War of 1943–1944. So highly were her peacemaking efforts regarded that she was nominated for a Nobel Peace Prize in 1946.[134]

Despite these accomplishments, however, any analysis of the life and work of Alexandra Kollontai must deal with the nagging, perplexing question of how this militant revolutionary, this prophetess of visionary idealism, could have made such an ostensible about-face and abandoned her earlier ideals to serve the Stalinist bureaucracy. Kollontai's entry into diplomatic service amazed and disgusted other European socialists opposed to developments in Russia. Many regretted that Kollontai was "lost to the revolution."[135] "Such a gifted person," lamented one, "and now she is to busy herself with buying herring."[136] "For some unaccountable reason," wrote another, "she accepted the dictatorship in Russia and remained in Stalin's good graces."[137]

Yet the reasons for Kollontai's acceptance of diplomatic life were not really so "unaccountable" as they might at first appear. In a curious way it was Kollontai's idealistic love of the revolution in Russia that prevented her from breaking all ties with her heritage. For 24 years she had had no personal life or work not somehow related to the service of the revolution, and her decision to remain in that service in whatever capacity was a measure of the extent to which she had fused her personal identity with the revolutionary cause. "The strongest of us are loathe to give up a long cherished dream," another similarly disillusioned socialist once wrote.[138] A life of obedience and suffering silence, Kollontai had painfully and tragically come to realize, was better than one of impotence and isolation.

Kollontai admitted that she no longer had the strength to remain in opposition; she had no means with which to continue the "hopeless struggle" against the "machine."[139] Certainly she was tremendously disillusioned by the growing trend toward dictatorship in Russia, but her recognition of the ills that plagued her country and her party also made her painfully aware of her own powerlessness. One so assured of the purity and righteousness of her high ideals could not take the intense vilification, slander, "insults and lies" that were the "murder weapons" that had been used against others who had dared to criticize the regime.[140] Her entry into diplomatic service was the result not of self-seeking accommodation to the new centers of power in the party but of her realization that the "romantic revolutionary epoch" in Russia was dead.[141] "I put my principles in a corner of my conscience," she told French communist Marcel Body, "and do what I am told as well as I can."[142]

Shattered by Stalin's methods of dealing with criticism in the party, Kollontai actually expected to be among the victims of the purges. Two days before leaving for a visit to Moscow in July 1937, she wrote a letter to an intimate friend, asking her to guard all her personal notes and papers "in case I become the victim of an accident."[143] Although Kollontai was under surveillance by Stalin—the memoirs of secret police agent Vladimir Petrov reveal how he was sent to join the staff of the Soviet Embassy in Stockholm to keep watch on Kollontai's loyalty[144] —she, along of course with Stalin himself, was the only member of the Central Committee of 1917 to survive the great purges of the 1930s. For whatever reason, Kollontai may have escaped arrest, but in the words of one dissident, she suffered enough—"pushed out of the leadership, terrorized . . . , deprived of any influence," and treated by Stalin with "undisguised contempt."[145]

In 1945 poor health forced Kollontai's retirement from diplomatic life, and she lived obscurely in a Moscow apartment until her death on March 9, 1952. Although she had been highly decorated for her diplomatic and wartime services, receiving the Red Banner of Labour, both first and second orders, *Pravda* announced neither her death nor her funeral.[146] No eulogy appeared in the party press for this woman who had once embodied the highest ideals of the revolution.

Despite her diplomatic achievements, after 1922 Kollontai always maintained a tenuous political existence in the Soviet Union. Contemporary opinion persisted in seeing her not as a high-minded idealist who had made sound and substantial contributions to the revolutionary cause, but as an ultraradical and militant prophetess of free love. Pitirim Sorokin, a one-time revolutionary later to become a prominent sociologist, remembered her as "the mistress of a dozen men," attributing her revolutionary enthusiasm not to reasoned political judgment, but to her sexual "satyriasis," that is, her abnormal, uncontrollable sexual desire.[147] Marguerite Harrison, a reporter for the Baltimore *Sun*, observed that Kollontai had "any number of husbands,"[148] while Walter Duranty, Moscow correspondent for the New York *Times*, emphasized that she had as much "experience" in sexual relations with men as the legendary Isadora Duncan. "Two past masters," he called them both, "in the art of life, love, and men."[149]

By all accounts, Alexandra Kollontai was a colorful and charming woman who cared about her appearance, a woman whose aristocratic background, natural elegance, cultivated refinement, and flair for clothes made her a "heartbreaker" in the eyes of many.[150] Obviously, the allegedly enlightened men of her party were unable to deal with a woman like her in their midst, or, even more importantly, to treat her as an equal. An erroneous and exaggerated picture of her private life fueled the myth that she was the "high priestess of rampant sexuality." Yet the tally sheet on this attractive and vivacious woman actually revealed not "numerous husbands," but two failed marriages—one with Kollontai, the other with Dybenko—and two disappointing love affairs—one with Shlyapnikov in Norway, and one with a prestigious Menshevik economist in her émigré days before the revolution.[151] If there were other romantic liaisons in her life, contemporary gossip never targeted or discussed the particulars.

All these depictions dimmed Kollontai's political importance and minimized her revolutionary contributions, serving, at the same time, to justify the party's not having taken seriously her ideas and ideals. The most sensational popularization of her views was one that portrayed Kollontai as the advocate of the "glass of water" theory on sexual relations, the flippant attitude that one makes love "just as you drink a glass of water, to relieve yourself."[152] This vulgar perversion of her real ideas has been even more damaging than attacks on her private affairs, since it is this aspect of Kollontai's revolutionary activity that historiographical opinion, until very recently, has chosen to emphasize.

Even the best scholarly accounts of modern Russian history can be criticized for their distorted and inaccurate portrayals of Kollontai. She has been introduced to readers as a "somewhat unstable figure," an "impulsive" "left-wing hothead" who "preached the uninhibited satisfaction of the sexual impulse."[153] Her difficulties with Lenin have been attributed not to their theoretical differences but to her "libertinism." Lenin, it has been said, found her "personally odious" because "she not only practiced but preached free love."[154] Not only have her theories been made to appear absurd and ridiculous, but her sincerity in adopting them has also been questioned. Attempts to explain her involvement in the Workers Opposition controversy by calling her the "mistress" or "paramour" of Shlyapnikov have been a serious distortion of history.[155]

In recent years Alexandra Kollontai has undergone a curious and troubling rehabilitation both in Soviet public opinion and in Western historiography. Two revitalized images have appeared, for two different reasons, yet neither image touches the essence of the work she attempted to do in the service of the revolution.

In the Soviet Union the resurgence of interest in Kollontai, the appearance of biographies, editions of her works, and even a film on her life, have all been geared toward establishing her as a highly touted symbol of female achievement and emancipation under communism.[156] She has been remembered for her diplomatic contributions and hailed as the first fully accredited woman ambassador of modern times. Diplomacy, however, was certainly far from being the most important of her political contributions. Her oppositional activity, criticisms of the regime, and calls for a new morality have remained downplayed and forgotten.

Alexandra Kollontai broke with the Russian revolutionary tradition of the devoted female comrade and wife. She was never content to sit on the sidelines like Lenin's wife Krupskaya, or the wives of the other commissars who busied themselves with nursing, educational, or secretarial pursuits. Reaching the highest levels of any woman involved in the Bolshevik Revolution, she was the best orator, strongest theorist, and most prolific writer. That she attained the zenith of her prestige at the time she most supported Lenin and the party line is a sad commentary, however, on the real extent of Bolshevik commitment to women and their emancipation.

In the West, Kollontai has been discovered by contemporary feminists who have sought to set her up as a brave precursor of their own calls for sexual liberation. One sign of her adoption by the women's movement was the appearance, in 1970, of German and English translations of her autobiography under the bold title, *The Autobiography of a Sexually Emancipated Communist Woman.* Kollontai, however, in writing the short piece in 1926, had christened it with a far less titillating rubric: "The Aims and Worth of My Life."[157]

Kollontai neither preached free love nor did she actually consider herself a "feminist" in the usual sense of the term. In fact, certain of her ideas—that women are intrinsically different from men; that motherhood is their unique social obligation; and that abortion on demand is a selfish evasion of responsibility and a deprivation to the collective—are decidedly alien to contemporary Western feminist thought.[158] Any attempt to make Kollontai too relevant by seeing her as the champion of modern ideologies serves only to cheapen the extent and the content of her real revolutionary involvement.

A revolutionary socialist with profoundly human hopes and convictions, Alexandra Kollontai was a woman who felt deeply about what she believed and worked untiringly and persistently for its achievement as long as she was able. Propelled by a flaming intensity, she was moved by a romantic vision of the revolution, a glowing idealism that was at once her weakness and her strength. While it may have blinded her to the practical economic and political side of revolutionary consolidation as Lenin understood it, it also served as a powerful inspirational force, causing her to make a strong and lasting impression on all who heard her speak. Typical was this comment by a young girl who attributed her own later work for the party to Kollontai's mesmerizing influence. Kollontai, she recalled, "pictured a future so beautiful as never before seen on earth."[159]

Chapter • Three

Rosa Luxemburg

The Female Revolutionary
as Martyr

I

In a world where the exploits of women have remained hidden from history, Rosa Luxemburg is an anomaly. Even among those generally unfamiliar with the history of European socialism, her name is well known. She has been hailed as the "only woman ever to achieve greatness in politics";[1] the "most remarkable woman the international socialist movement ever produced."[2] Active as an orator, agitator, journalist, and pamphleteer, she is most remembered for her starring role in the abortive German Communist Revolution of 1919. Above all else, however, it was her remarkable intellectual ability that clearly elevated her above her contemporaries, men and women both. Her theoretical works were like Marx at his best, political comrades acknowledged.[3] Undoubtedly, she was the "greatest genius among the scientific heirs of Marx and Engels."[4]

Because Rosa Luxemburg has been generally taken to be a highly touted female version of the successful male revolutionary, she has, unlike Eleanor Marx and Alexandra Kollontai, been the subject of a number of studies. These have analyzed her monumental theoretical accomplishments, focused on her quarrels with Lenin, and presented her, for the most part, as a consummate political actor in the proper male mold. Thus she has been portrayed as a typically ruthless politico "out to make a career for herself," motivated and inspired by "nicely calculated self-interest."[5] Historians and political scientists have pointed to Luxemburg's career as living proof that women can achieve greatness in politics if they so desire.

99

Because the historiographical treatment of Rosa Luxemburg has been so bloodless and one-dimensional, recent attempts to "humanize" "Red Rosa" have been gleefully received. The publication, in English, of her love letters to revolutionary socialist Leo Jogiches sensationally demonstrate that even the awesome Luxemburg had a female side, that she loved babies and flowers, clothes and furniture, and really yearned above all else for a home of her own.[6] The pendulum of Luxemburgist scholarship has indeed swung both ways.

None of these wide-ranging studies, however, has sensitively presented a clear and accurate picture of Luxemburg both as woman and as revolutionary. Despite her enormous political stature, Luxemburg shared much with other revolutionary women of her day, women who never came close to achieving the lasting fame and recognition she did. She also suffered because she was a woman, and the painful details of her suffering deserve to be told. Like Kollontai, her theoretical forays were resented by male contemporaries who vilified and mocked her "aggressive" and "quarrelsome" championing of her ideas. Scorned and hated in life by those who feared her revolutionary proclamations, in death she experienced that sentimental deification common to revolutionary women. Her fate was in many ways like that of Eleanor Marx, for the particular circumstances of her death elevated her to martyr status in the revolutionary socialist pantheon. The recent interest in her love affair with Leo Jogiches also stands ready to rival the Marx-Aveling liaison for the distinction of being considered the greatest human tragedy of European socialism.

Like other revolutionary women, Rosa Luxemburg was both shaped and confined by the tradition of female revolutionary involvement imposed by her culture. Yet, unlike the cases of Marx and Kollontai, to identify the cultural heritage within which Rosa Luxemburg operated is not an easy procedure. No single country can claim her. Born a Jew in Russian Poland,* and raised in a family that was

---

*Three territorial divisions of Poland by its more powerful neighbors—Russia, Prussia, and Austria—erased the ancient nation from the map by the end of the eighteenth century. Although Napoleon raised Polish hopes for a time with his creation of a purely Polish "Duchy of Warsaw," the failure of his war with Russia in 1812 meant that, by 1813, the Duchy of Warsaw came under Russian administration. The settlement made by the Congress of Vienna, 1814–1815, confirmed the territorial division of Poland until 1918. Rechristening the main

highly assimilated into the surrounding Russo-Polish community, Luxemburg chose Imperial Germany as her main field of political operation. While she remains most closely associated with the German socialist movement, the revolutionary traditions of all three countries—Poland, Russia, and Germany—colored and affected the opportunities and options open to her as a female revolutionary.

"Poland has never perished, as long as we're alive," sang the revolutionary faithful in this, the most popular Polish folksong of the partition period. Although she was later to denounce such sentimental patriotism, Luxemburg could never deny or minimize the role played by the rebellious tradition of undying Polish nationalism in the molding of her own revolutionary consciousness. Rosa Luxemburg literally breathed the air of rebellion in the Russified Poland where she grew up. A burning conception of political injustice and a seething sense of rebellion against century-old oppression were the legacy carried in the hearts of all Poles who vowed to avenge the rape and murder of their fatherland. This seemingly hereditary politicization was a powerful inspirational factor for Polish women as well as for Polish men.

Despite the "unspeakably pathetic, medieval, oriental, and atrocious" condition in which the ninteenth-century Polish peasant woman found herself,[7] Polish women of the educated middle and upper classes shared in the enlightened, cosmopolitan culture of Western Europe. Especially important to the growth of the female revolutionary heritage in Poland was Poland's traditional affection for France, the mother of revolutions, whose star-struck patriots of 1789, 1830, and 1848 had repeatedly promised to restore Poland to the map of Europe. Sharing in the French Enlightenment tradition, Poland was familiar with French revolutionary ideals like freedom of thought and conscience, individual rights, and human dignity.

---

part of the Duchy of Warsaw the "Kingdom of Poland," the Congress united this so-called Congress Kingdom of Poland with the Russian Empire. Rosa Luxemburg was born in Russian or Congress Poland. When she wrote or spoke of Poland, she meant Congress Poland. References later in this chapter to a united Poland refer to the unification of the Polish nucleus of the Congress Kingdom with formerly Polish areas under Austrian or Prussian (later German) administration. An independent Republic of Poland was recreated after World War I.

Also from France came the emancipatory ideas of George Sand, the mistress of Poland's celebrated Chopin, and the French inheritance was a powerful factor in the birth of the woman question in Poland. Educated Polish women shared the aspirations of their French counterparts, and several made substantial contributions to the political and feminist campaigns of the Paris Commune of 1871. The great Polish heroines of the Commune, Paule Minck and Lodoyska Kawecka, were both names with which the youthful Rosa Luxemburg was familiar.[8]

Equally important to the framing of the Polish female revolutionary heritage was the legacy that Russian radical women of the nineteenth century bestowed upon their sisters in Russian Poland. Both shared a hatred of tsarist oppression, a hatred that intensified in Poland as the web of tsarist repression tightened after the abortive Polish insurrection of 1863. In the period immediately following the insurrection, the Kingdom of Poland lost one-half of its male population, through death in battle, exile, or emigration.[9] Polish radicals, therefore, were quick to follow their Russian counterparts in recognizing that their struggle against the tsarist autocracy could not afford the luxury of discriminatory sex barriers. Due to the particular circumstances of her birth in Russian Poland, Rosa Luxemburg could claim the mantle not only of the Polish heroines of the Commune but also of the Russian nihilist and populist women of her generation. The image of the female rebel was a familiar facet of Luxemburg's childhood. She was seven years old when Vera Zasulich rose to prominence for her attempted assassination of St. Petersburg's General Trepov; ten, when the populist Sophia Perovskaya was executed. Rosa Luxemburg came out of the same revolutionary milieu as did Alexandra Kollontai, a tradition that welcomed and encouraged female revolutionary involvement.

Inspired by this legacy, Luxemburg entered the revolutionary socialist movement of her day with a self-assured and insistent demand that she be taken seriously. She chose, however, not to confine her revolutionary activity to the Russo-Polish heritage to which she had been born, but rose to international socialist prominence in the proverbial land of *küche, kirche, und kinder*, a nation where political intrusions by women, Poles, Jews, and foreigners were regarded with a jaundiced eye. Since her most outstanding successes and failures occurred in the socialist movement of Imperial Germany, those successes and failures must be understood in the context of the struggle between the heritage that inspired her and the tradition of that nation that became her main area of political activity, a nation where cultural distrust of the political female was combined with a tradition of female political and revolutionary activism that was ambivalent at best.

Certainly the German states, along with the rest of Europe, were affected by the gospel of equality that was the legacy of the French Revolution, democratic sentiments that grew and flowered during the wars of liberation against Napoleon.[10] Also from France came the social and political pronouncements of the Saint-Simonians, whose teachings exercised a considerable influence in Germany.[11] The Saint-Simonian demand for complete legal, political, and social equality for women was adopted by the Young German movement of the 1830s, whose followers urged women to emerge from their confining roles in the home and partake of the "higher things" in life.[12] As happened in Poland and Russia, the vogue of "George Sandism," with its critique of society and marriage, also contributed to the nascent German movement for female emancipation.

The real birth of German feminism, however, the first stirrings of organized German feminist activity, date from the upheavals of 1848.[13] Diaries and memoirs of women of the period reveal that they shared in the general revolutionary fervor of the day. History records German women fighting valiantly on the barricades and drawing praise from their contemporaries for their contributions.

Yet these feminist stirrings were decidedly narrow and limited ones. The rights of women were not specifically discussed in the national assembly that was elected that year to draft a constitution for the united German Empire. No great names emerged as symbols of women's revolutionary ardor. Compared to Russia, the German revolutionary heritage remained glaringly lacking in revolutionary heroines.

Most important to the stillborn character of the German feminist movement was the death of German democracy itself in 1848. The recognition that democratic men had fallen short of realizing their goals for a united and liberal Germany attracted pioneering women to the politics of the possible, and caused them to focus on such narrow concerns as education reform alone. Furthermore, the repressive mechanisms of the German states quickly moved to ensure that the civic equality of women would be slow in taking root. Inspired by the view that the politicization of women was somehow threatening and dangerous, the reactionary Prussian *Vereinsgesetz* of March 1850 prohibited women from belonging to organizations that police authorities defined as "political." Soon enacted by other states, such laws, until their repeal in 1908, were critical elements in the smothering of female political consciousness.

While the political woman was seen as an imported, somehow un-German creature, a powerful cult extolled the virtues of the model German woman, wife, and mother. The "true German woman" was an "emotional, subordinate, and motherly" character, a "naive, sweet, and simple" soul who served her intellectually superior husband and master with selfless and devoted abandon.[14] Feminism, especially of the socialist "free love" variety, was condemned and hated for the threat it was thought to pose to the patriarchal German home.

Yet even the German socialist movement, with its theoretical commitment to female emancipation, was not one that welcomed women with open arms. There was a serious discrepancy between the theoretical claims and practical activities of many German socialist men, who, according to one contemporary account, were "every bit as backward as any petty bourgeois philistine on the issue of women's equality."[15] These subtle attitudinal barriers, which would prevent women from ever achieving true equality in the party, existed among both leaders and rank and file. Even August Bebel, the highly acclaimed author of *Woman Under Socialism*, found it difficult to rise above the patriarchal, artisanate mentality into which he had been born. For all its pioneering dimensions, his book betrayed his deep-rooted sentiments and prejudices on the woman question. Bebel accepted and repeated the traditional clichés about women's stereotypical behavior. Women, he wrote, were more impulsive than men, and less able to get along well with each other. Their more passionate natures left them with less capacity for reflective thought. Since women's abilities were clearly different from men's, women should perform only those tasks best suited to their abilities,—and, Bebel was quick to note—the roles for which women were "naturally" suited were motherhood and the rearing of children.[16]

Bebel believed that with the coming of socialism, women would no longer have to ruin themselves "physically and morally" in factory labor that placed them "in competition" with men. They could then assume the position in which, "according to nature and the law," they belonged—"in the family in order to educate the children and run the household."[17] Convinced it was a woman's duty to society to bear children, he condemned abortion and the increasing use of contraceptives, and he held both responsible for the "calamitous" drop in the national birth rate.[18]

In his private life, Bebel subscribed to conventional German notions of the "cosiness" and "poetry" of middle class domesticity. His wife Julie was no model of blazing feminism or vigorous political involvement, but a "helpmate" who embodied the German ideal of the middle class woman anchored firmly in the home. In his autobiography, Bebel recalled Julie in touching terms, praising this traditional woman as one who had provided him with a happy haven and solace against the public world of political enemies.[19]

Other leaders of German socialism joined Bebel in idealizing the true German woman. Karl Kautsky eulogized Julie Bebel in similar terms. He praised the "strong support" she had given her husband, and the "intelligent, untiring dedication with which she kept the small daily worries away from him. . . . Her ambition was to rule over an area which was cut out for her. She was a . . . faithful and understanding housewife and mother."[20]

If the leaders of German socialism remained so enamored of traditional patriarchal ideals, the rank and file of the German Social Democratic Party (SPD) were even more strongly imbued with what has been termed "proletarian anti-feminism."[21] Sympathy for the patriarchal, preindustrial family was firmly rooted in the members of a German party that was long in overcoming the artisanate character of its early years.

The real founder of the German labor movement was not Karl Marx, but a lawyer named Ferdinand Lassalle, whose attempt to improve working class conditions through the action and support of existing governments drew the wrath of Marx. German socialism, in its formative years, was a movement not of consciously Marxist proletarians but of radical artisans with democratic aspirations, socialist ideals, and reactionary attitudes toward the position of women in economy and in society. The Lassalleans did not reject every type of female labor, only that which they considered to be outside the "female sphere." All occupations that endangered feminine "purity and chastity" were condemned as "morally objectionable." Hostile to the economic competition of women, they sought to exclude them from factory and workplace. The resulting drop in the number of wage earners, they argued, would guarantee higher wages for men.[22]

Even after 1875, the year in which Marxist socialism formally triumphed over this powerful challenger, the Lassallean heritage remained strong in Germany. The merger of the two wings of the German labor movement to form a united German Social Democratic Party did not automatically ensure that Lassallean ideas, especially among the rank and file, would quickly vanish. Although the SPD committed itself to a program of female emancipation, old attitudes died hard. While it recognized and accepted women's contributions to modern industry, the party clearly regarded women as second-class citizens within its own ranks.

Most SPD members accepted the need for strict sex role differentiation in their private lives. When women's issues were discussed at party meetings, they were approached with a "jovial, condescending, and lighthearted tone."[23] Few men brought their wives and daughters to political gatherings. Even the wives of party leaders, for the most part, held aloof from political concerns. German men, socialist or otherwise, simply felt that women didn't belong in political clubs. "Most men don't praise women because they go to a meeting or join a club," a working woman told a socialist organizer. "They're supposed to stay home and mend stockings."[24] According to one leading socialist feminist, the SPD's leader, Wilhelm Liebknecht, would have "preferred by far to have all the women thrown out of the party."[25]

Only if women agreed to assume auxiliary roles, such as mutual aid, secretarial, or organizational work, was the party anxious to accept their services.[26] Strongly committed in theory to the emancipation of women, the SPD hedged in practice, and this boded ill for the political aspirations of Rosa Luxemburg. Steeped in a more egalitarian revolutionary heritage, she had no intention of shouldering peripheral duties.

II

Rosa Luxemburg was born on March 5, 1871, in the small provincial town of Zamosc in Russian Poland, a town with one of the strongest and most cultured Jewish communities in Eastern Europe. Although she was later to denounce her Jewish heritage, the Jewish tradition into which she was born was an important factor both in her coming to revolutionary consciousness and in shaping the ethical content of the socialist ideology she was later to embrace. Descended on her mother's side from an impressive line of rabbinical scholars, Luxemburg was unconsciously molded and formed by the spirit of biblical humanism and social righteousness that was the keynote of her religion.

For any Jewish child growing up in Eastern Europe in the nineteenth century, political awareness came early, a natural product of an oppressive political climate that targeted the Jew as a special object for discrimination. Luxemburg witnessed two pogroms as a child, a brutal ordeal that triggered the radicalization of many Jewish youth. Revolted by such vicious prejudice, systems of segregated schools, and state and social pressures to assimilate themselves within the prevailing national culture, many Eastern European Jews like Luxemburg were attracted to international socialism precisely because they found its supranational claims to brotherhood and solidarity appealing and comforting. The number of Jews in European revolutionary parties was out of all proportion to their numerical representation in the population,[27] a reality certainly attributable to the ruthless oppression they experienced in the Russian Empire and elsewhere.

The values and patterns of the *shtetl*, the Jewish communities in the small towns and villages of Eastern Europe, not only infused Luxemburg with this fighting spirit of radical rebelliousness but also inspired her lifelong commitment to academic and intellectual excellence. The cult of scholarship had a long history within the Jewish tradition. Devotion to learning was not only a source of status within the *shtetl* but was also genuinely admired and praised.

Within Eastern European Jewish culture, however, ritual and learning were honorific occupations for men only. Daughters were not encouraged in advanced study but were left alone to teach themselves from any available source. Traditional Jewish culture laid great emphasis on the strict demarcation of sex roles, symbolized by the pervasive belief that the properly dependent and submissive Jewish woman entered heaven at her husband's feet.[28]

Insofar, however, as Luxemburg's assumption of a political role in later life demonstrated her rejection of this traditional, patriarchal, sex role ideology, what she took from her religious heritage must be clearly differentiated from that which she chose to let fall by the wayside. While very little is known of Luxemburg's early life—she was an intensely private person who left no diaries, autobiographies, or memoirs—the role models with which she was provided in early childhood seem to be important factors in understanding her adoption of an activist female role.

Luxemburg's family was totally assimilated within the Russo-Polish community. Her father had long ago given up the orthodox heritage of his forebearers, scandalizing the rest of the Jewish community by his insistence that his children attend secular schools. Neither he nor any member of his family ever played a part in any specifically Jewish movement or cause. When Rosa was almost three, Elias Luxemburg moved his family to Warsaw. Although he was attracted by the superior educational and business opportunities available in the capital, the move may also have been prompted by his impatience with traditional Jewish life. Rumors quickly spread that the elder Luxemburg could "no longer stand life with the Jews of Zamosc."[29]

Because her parents had rejected the cultural dictates of the Jewish community, Rosa Luxemburg was freed from the traditional sex role ideology of her religious heritage. Even more importantly, her perception of the options available to her as a woman was strongly influenced by the model of equality in personal and political relationships provided by her parents' own lives. Her father, a successful timber merchant, was widely read in both Polish and German literature. Attracted to West European liberalism, he hated the tsarist autocracy and was sympathetic to the revolutionary nationalism of the Poles. Although Rosa did not inherit socialist or even radical views from her father, since he was never an active participant in any revolutionary or political movement, she certainly benefited from the politically conscious atmosphere of her childhood home. Elias Luxemburg regularly received illegal Western newspapers and discussed them with his wife and family. Throughout her life, Rosa Luxemburg always retained a high regard for her father, from whom, wrote Luise Kautsky, the wife of German socialist Karl Kautsky, she inherited "her strong intellect, energy, and sense of the earnest conduct of life."[30]

Luxemburg's mother Lina also provided her young daughter with a strong model of political and cultural consciousness. An intelligent and well-read woman whose education and intellectual interests were far superior to those of the average Jewish woman of the time, she exercised a considerable influence on the intellectual development of her children.[31] Rosa Luxemburg's perception of the companionate, egalitarian nature of her parents' marriage must certainly be considered an important factor in her adoption of a nontraditional sex role ideology.

From all accounts, Luxemburg's childhood was a warm, happy, affectionate, and financially comfortable one, and in later life she nostalgically recalled the idyllic days of her youth. Even though no member of her family shared or understood her political views, Luxemburg tried to keep in close contact with them, frequently lamenting that "accursed politics" all too often kept her away.[32] Because she had been too preoccupied with political events to visit her mother before her death, she continued to suffer the burden of guilt for years to come. In an especially poignant letter to a friend, Luxemburg described how she awoke one night sobbing and calling her mother's name, only to realize that she was "seven years too late."[33] Later, when her father fell seriously ill, Luxemburg let nothing stand in her way of visiting the old man.

Obviously, therefore, neither personal rebellion against her family nor against an oppressive lifestyle was a factor in Luxemburg's entry into revolutionary activity, as had been the case for Alexandra Kollontai. Significantly, however, her adoption of an activist political role may in part be traced to that same childhood sense of specialness common to the other women of this study. Luxemburg was the youngest of five children, three boys and two girls. In addition to receiving the natural pampering usually bestowed on the youngest member of a closely knit family, Luxemburg, as a sickly child, was the object of special care and attention. Shortly after the family's move to Warsaw in 1873, she was stricken with a hip disease that confined her to bed for an entire year. Her ailment was wrongly diagnosed as tuberculosis of the bone, and subsequent treatment caused irreparable damage, leaving her frail and misshapen for the rest of her life. The special consideration and love lavished on the invalid child may have left her not only with a lingering sense of specialness and mission but also with a strong and early perception of the existence of injustice and evil in the world.

During her convalescence, the precocious Luxemburg embarked on a rigorous program of self-education. She could read and write by the time she was five, translated prose and poetry from German into Polish, and sent her first literary efforts to a children's magazine. In 1884, at 13, she wrote a poem to commemorate the visit of Wilhelm 1 to Warsaw. Saluting the Kaiser as "that mighty man of the West," she continued in a much less respectful tone:

> Your honors mean nothing to me,
> I would have you know,
> But I would like to know what
> You're going to chatter about.[34]

While it is difficult to determine whether her sarcastic and irreverent manner really bespoke latent revolutionary sentiments, her chosen subject clearly demonstrated an early political consciousness.

Certainly Luxemburg's experiences under the school system of Russified Poland contributed to her early politicization. Not only was there a quota system for Jews at the high school she attended, but any sentiments of Polish nationalism were brutally repressed. Polish students drew a strong example from student radicals of Russia, and Polish schools came to be known as hotbeds of political conspiracy. For one such as Luxemburg, infected with her parents' hatred of tsarist absolutism, contact with student revolutionaries came early, while still in high school—a natural product of her domestic and educational environments. At graduation she was denied a gold medal for academic excellence because of her "rebellious attitude toward the authorities."[35] By 1887 she was a full-fledged member of the Proletariat Party, that group which laid the foundation for modern Polish socialism.[36]

The Polish gentry's dream for a liberal, united fatherland was shattered after the abortive insurrection of 1863. That seminal defeat not only exposed the bankruptcy of gentry nationalism but also came at a time when economic developments in Poland made a strictly working class revolutionary organization politically feasible and viable. The Crimean War had furthered the growth of industry in the Russian Empire of which the Congress Kingdom of Poland was a part. More importantly, the profound economic changes produced by the emancipation of the Polish peasants in 1864 had created the labor market necessary for the growth and expansion of Polish capitalism.[37] Although utopian socialist currents had entered Poland through émigré groups as early as 1830, specifically Marxist revolutionary ideas came from the East. The leadership of the revolutionary party "Proletariat" consisted overwhelmingly of former students of Russian universities. This linkage of Polish revolutionary socialism to Russian roots was to have profound implications both for the developing Polish socialist movement and for Rosa Luxemburg's role within that movement. From the first, the strategy of the Proletariat Party was to reject the dead nationalistic heritage of the Polish revolutionary past and to join the fortunes of Polish socialism to events in Russia. Blind to the real existence of Polish nationalism as a vital revolutionary force, the Proletariat Party called for the union of the working classes of the whole Russian Empire—of which the Congress Kingdom of Poland was an integral part—against both the tsarist autocracy and the capitalist Russo-Polish middle class.

The Proletariat's agitational and organizational efforts among urban factory workers soon aroused the suspicions of police. By 1889 Luxemburg herself was marked for arrest. Convinced that she must flee Poland, she chose to embark on that familiar route to personal and political emancipation common to radical women of her generation. Like Alexandra Kollontai, she decided to enroll at the University of Zurich and, with that decision, entered the most important center of revolutionary Marxism in Europe at the time. Certainly the rigorous schooling in political economy that Luxemburg received there was vital to the renown she was later to acquire as a Marxist theoretician, but the stimulating radical milieu of Zurich life itself was an even more important factor in her political development. In the city's large émigré colony, Luxemburg met not only the leading Russian radicals of her day but also that person who was to share, influence, and affect her revolutionary activities for the rest of her life.

Leo Jogiches was well cast in the image of the classical revolutionary. Arrogant, obstinate, and domineering, with strong administrative and leadership abilities, he was a Lithuanian socialist with an established radical reputation. The son of a wealthy Jewish family, he was graced with the economic independence necessary to finance a host of revolutionary and conspiratorial endeavors. His conspiratorial temperament was in fact so total that to this day, history records little of his private life. He remains a romantic personage shrouded in myth and mystery, remembered mainly for his romantic involvement with Rosa Luxemburg.

Shared interests and the personal and intellectual intimacy of Zurich radical life soon drew the pair together, and they embarked on an intense personal and political comradeship that was to last for the next 15 years. Since both their homelands had been absorbed by the Russian Empire, both Jogiches and Luxemburg were vitally concerned with the role that nationalist sentiments should and could play in the socialist revolutionary struggle, and with his help she turned her attention to this aspect of the Polish revolutionary question.

Support for an independent Poland was a long-standing component of the Marxist creed.[38] Highly sensitive to the revolutionary potential of oppressed nationalities, Marx and Engels had repeatedly urged the re-creation of a free Polish state, considering it essential for the development of revolutionary sentiment in Germany and necessary as a bulwark against reactionary Russia. Aware both of this tradition and of the fact that the cosmopolitan, international tenor of the Proletariat Party had never touched the wellsprings of nationalist sentiment deeply rooted in the Polish cultural consciousness, scattered Polish socialist groups had long aimed to reunite Polish socialism with its nationalistic heritage. The fruit of their efforts became the Polish Socialist Party (PPS) formed in Paris in 1892, a party that recognized Poland's right to a free and independent existence.

Luxemburg and Jogiches, however, were highly critical of the PPS's bold plan to "liberate itself from Russian tutelage." Luxemburg specifically rejected the cause of Polish independence, terming it a "utopian mirage . . . a delusion of the workers to detract them from the class struggle."[39] Salvation for the workers of Russian Poland, she explained, lay in socialism, not nationalism, in cooperation with Russian revolutionaries, not middle class Polish patriots.

These ideas were expressed in a small paper that appeared in Paris. *Sprawa Robotnicza*, or *The Workers' Cause*, financed by Jogiches and written in large part by Luxemburg, became her entry card into the international socialist movement of the day. For the next five years, Rosa Luxemburg was the major theoretician of the rival Polish socialist movement that evolved from this rebellious journalistic enterprise,[40] an antinationalist movement daring enough to challenge the classical Marxist position on the Polish question.

In her demand for an irrevocable divorce between revolutionary socialism and Polish nationalism, Luxemburg displayed a remarkable flexibility and independence as a socialist theoretician, a sophisticated and subtle understanding of the complicated reasoning processes behind the original Marxist slogans.[41] According to Luxemburg, Marx and Engels had supported the movement for Polish independence not from any absolutist principles of national self-determination but because of the ability of the Polish national movement to prompt revolution in Europe. When Marx supported the cause of Polish independence, Poland was the revolutionary center of Europe, a highly explosive force with great potential to upset the reactionary balance of power. Forty years later, however, the center of revolutionary gravity in Europe had shifted. Russia was no longer the bulwark of European reaction, but on the verge of becoming revolutionary itself. If the final aim remained as always the unleashing of the great European revolution, then the forces of history dictated that that battle be waged alongside of, and not against, the awakening revolutionary potential of Russia.

Luxemburg buttressed this argument with a sophisticated economic analysis that she presented in her doctoral dissertation, *The Industrial Development of Poland*, the first comprehensive economic history of Poland ever published.[42] The key to the unity of the Russo-Polish revolutionary movement, she argued in her imposing study, was the growth of Russo-Polish capitalism itself, a development that Marx could never have foreseen in his own lifetime. Polish industry was the child of the Russian state—encouraged by tsarist investment, dependent on Russian markets, and needing the protection of the Russian government. While the middle classes of both Russia and Poland had benefited from the growth of capitalism within the Empire, the working classes of both had shouldered the burdens of that economic development. If the middle classes of Poland and Russia had been natural allies in capitalism's advance, then the workers of both nations should be natural allies in capitalism's demise.

The second element of Luxemburg's argument was a tactical, strategic one. For the cause of Polish nationalism to triumph, she reasoned, it would have to defeat the three strongest governments of Europe—Austria, Germany, and Russia as the three original partitioning powers—and it would also have to overcome the economic interests of a middle class that, in all three areas, had more to gain by preserving the status quo than by seeking independence. If the working classes could succeed in this colossal, two-pronged mission and dislodge both foreign and domestic oppressors, then in reality they could achieve a social revolution and create a society run by and for their own interests. Polish workers in those parts of the country controlled by Austria and Germany, she concluded, should reject nationalism and join the revolutionary socialist movements of their respective countries.

Luxemburg's ideas became the theoretical backbone of the Social Democracy of the Kingdom of Poland (SDKP), an organization whose nucleus had been formed among Polish émigrés in Switzerland between 1890 and 1893. Centering around Luxemburg and Jogiches, the revolutionary and fiercely antinationalistic SDKP challenged the right of the PPS to present itself as the true representative of the Polish working class. In 1899 the SDKP united with a group of Lithuanian socialists who also rejected nationalism and who aimed instead to work with the Poles for a socialist revolution within the Russian Empire. This new group was known as the Social Democracy of the Kingdom of Poland and Lithuania, SDKPiL for short.

Both groups always remained small. With a leadership centered in Zurich, the SDKPiL had almost no rank and file following in Poland itself. The most important reason for the organization's failure to make an impact on Polish soil was the simple fact that its leaders were all cosmopolitan types, who never understood or appreciated the deep patriotic yearnings of the Polish masses.

Despite these weaknesses, however, the SDKPiL drew its contemporary political importance from the outstanding quality of its leadership. The small group who made up the SDKPiL has been called "perhaps the most remarkable elite of dedicated professional revolutionaries next to the Bolsheviks themselves."[43] Neither a centralized hierarchy nor a rambling mass party, the SDKPiL was characterized by the existence of informal and personal ties of cooperation between its members. No one member dominated or controlled the decision-making processes, or sought personal power and status alone. The SDKPiL's unique organizational structure, appropriately described as a "peer group," was an outstanding factor in Rosa Luxemburg's political socialization.[44] As the only woman in the group, she was provided with a political base that served as a source of strength, self-reliance, and self-assertiveness, an organization that gave her confidence in her abilities to compete in politics on equal terms with men.

Since Rosa Luxemburg remained primarily responsible for the formulation of policy ideas, she was considered the undisputed theoretical leader of the movement. Her articles attacking the PPS appeared in both *Die Neue Zeit* and *Critica Sociale*, the chief theoretical organs of the German and Italian socialist parties. The growth of the SDKPiL itself added to her stature, and the group was an important vehicle for the establishment of her reputation in the Second Socialist International.

When the Polish question was publicly debated at international socialist congresses in the 1890s, Luxemburg's star first appeared on the horizon. At the Zurich Congress of 1893 the 23-year-old woman startled and shocked the assembled heads of international socialism by her defiant and bold attempt to have her group, not the PPS, recognized as the legitimate representative of Polish socialism. Although the group's mandate was denied, Luxemburg's "magnetic" defense of her cause had made a "striking impression." Her opponents, one delegate noted, "had all they could do to hold their ground against her."[45]

While Luxemburg had already begun to establish a name for herself, she had also made enemies. Biting comments soon began to be heard about the "hysterical spinster" and "ambitious intriguer" who had the effrontery to challenge the masters on the question of Polish nationalism. Certainly, the fact that her views were considered important enough to warrant refutation was a significant accomplishment for one so young. Yet the manner and tone in which she was attacked provided a foreboding glimpse of her future treatment at the hands of international socialism.

Naturally, most of the criticism against her was voiced by PPS leaders who felt threatened and challenged by her powerful oratory. While their portrayal of Luxemburg as a fanatical enemy of the Poles may have been unfair, at least that characterization was grounded in the argument at hand. Luxemburg never really understood the genuine national longings of the Poles, and the charge that she was a traitor to the land of her birth is heard to this day.

Other attacks, however, were not so firmly rooted in the essentials of her argument. The Galician leader Ignacy Daszynski lambasted her as that "pedantic and quarrelsome person with a mechanistic interpretation of Marxism."[46] At the London Congress of 1896, PPS members accused her of political opportunism, charging that she was stubbornly seeking revenge on them because her credentials had been denied at Zurich. Her challenge to the PPS was seen as a desperate attempt to come up with anything that could gain her influence and power.[47] Not only was this accusation a totally incorrect assessment of Luxemburg's attitude toward power, but it was also an interesting commentary on the manner in which Polish socialist men perceived the political motivations of their female counterparts.

The most troubling of all denunciations were those that revealed a blatantly anti-Semitic bias. Since the SDKPiL leadership contained a higher proportion of Jews than almost any other socialist group of the time,[48] the group was condemned as a Jewish attempt to destroy

Poland by urging all workers to "hate their fatherland." Luxemburg's role in the SDKPiL drew violent anti-Semitic outbursts:

> The devilish work of destruction carried on by the Jewish excrement under the guise of defending the working class, turns out to be nothing less than the murder of Poland; as all Jews hate non-Jews, so Luxemburg's Social Democrats have a passionate hatred for Poland.[49]

Attacks on Rosa Luxemburg were not limited to her Polish rivals. Her theories especially offended German socialists who had long prided themselves on their doctrinal loyalty to Marx. In the eyes of a German party where age was highly revered and respected,[50] the young Polish woman was seen as a dangerous upstart. SPD theoreticians naturally resented this brash youngster who had the effrontery to engage in public debates with the likes of Wilhelm Liebknecht and Karl Kautsky. Kautsky, the self-proclaimed "Pope of Marxism," charged that Luxemburg's outbursts had actually done more harm than good. The split in the Polish movement, he insisted, had indirectly aided the tsarist reaction.[51] Others less interested in theory bemoaned the quarreling and disunity that Luxemburg's harangues had caused. To August Bebel, the grand old man of the German party, Luxemburg's actions were simply not "sensible."[52]

The Austrians and Russians also joined in the attack on the impudent young woman. "She is trying to do our thinking for us," moaned Victor Adler, the leader of the Austrian socialists.[53] Perhaps had she been a man, independent thinking on Luxemburg's part might have been tolerated. As a woman, however, she was condemned as a "doctrinaire goose."[54] Adler also brought the first traces of xenophobia to the public debate on Luxemburg's role. "The devil should keep all these emigrants!" he wrote to Karl Kautsky.[55] The Russian Georgi Plekhanov also criticized Luxemburg's stand on Polish nationalism. Having had his own quarrels with the arrogant Jogiches in Zurich, he welcomed the opportunity to get back at the "infuriating couple."[56] Plekhanov was convinced that Luxemburg had to be no more than Jogiches' "mouthpiece"—an interesting insight into his view of the political capabilities of women.

Luxemburg, however, was far from being Jogiches' mouthpiece. Disheartened and disgusted by the impotent and seemingly futile infighting between Polish émigré groups, she decided to forsake Zurich for the more challenging atmosphere of German Social Democracy, the most important political arena in the entire socialist world. Jogiches refused to accompany her, reluctant to give up his own conspiratorial activities and associations and already beginning to show some signs that he was jealous of his former pupil. But Luxemburg was determined to go anyway. Rightfully afraid that the separation might ruin their romantic attachment, she was adamant nonetheless that she could no longer afford "to hide under a bed."[57] Her willingness to leave Jogiches not only proved her fierce independence but also demonstrated her supreme confidence in her own political abilities. Leaving her political adolescence behind her in Zurich, Luxemburg departed in 1898, remaining for the next 21 years of her life most closely associated with the powerful socialist movement of Imperial Germany.

III

The party that Rosa Luxemburg came to Berlin to serve was universally recognized as the best organized, best disciplined, and most powerful socialist party in Europe.[58] Hailed as the model party of the Second International, the German Social Democratic Party and its interpretations of classical Marxism were accepted as the definitive voice of the international socialist movement. The status of the SPD was enhanced all the more because it had survived persecution and repression at the hands of Germany's Iron Chancellor, Otto von Bismarck, bouncing back to create an imposing and impressive structure that was the envy of the other socialist parties of Europe. The party was a "colossal machine," employing an immense bureaucracy of 3,500 people and publishing 90 daily papers that were read by 1.4 million subscribers. An elaborate system of cultural organizations—youth sections, workers' cooperatives, and women's groups—all contributed to its "state within a state" character.[59] By 1912 the SPD was the largest single party in the German Reichstag; by 1914 its membership topped 1 million. All in all, the world of German socialism seemed the perfect place for a zealous and talented young woman like Rosa Luxemburg to make her mark.

Even though her reputation as a controversial theoretician had preceded her, Rosa Luxemburg was well aware that the hierarchical structure of the German party would militate against her meteoric ascent. Content to accept an early position on the darkest fringes of party activity, organizing Polish workers in Silesia, she made a striking impression as an orator and agitator, and she soon came to be regarded as the party's leading expert on Polish affairs. Even her position on Polish nationalism became more palatable to the ortho- dox theoreticians of the SPD when they recognized that the separatist activities of Polish nationalists in Prussia were making serious inroads into their own organizational supremacy. Interestingly enough, the party executive soon lost interest in supporting the cause of Polish independence when they realized their own interests were very much at stake in the battle. The party's decision to side with Luxemburg in her stand against the PPS was the only tactical campaign of her life she ever won.

The Polish connection, however, was never destined to secure Luxemburg's fame, place in history, or notoriety even within the German party itself. The real key to the establishment of her reputa- tion was her bold and brilliant involvement in the "revisionist" con- troversy, that bitter doctrinal dispute that wrecked the complacency of the *fin-de-siècle* socialist world.[60] While the majority of SDP theoreticians had hesitated to get involved in the affair, it was the young Polish woman who had both the theoretical wherewithal and confident self-assurance to defend the sanctity of orthodox Marxism against those who sought to revise and revamp its classical doctrines. Her firm resolve to defend the Marxist heritage was all the more astonishing considering the vaunted position that the leading revision- ist, Eduard Bernstein, a personal friend of both Marx and Engels, held not only in the German but also in the entire European socialist world.

Revisionism, the only important challenge to classical Marxism that ever developed within German Social Democracy, cannot be understood apart from the environment in which it grew up. The SPD, with roots in the ancestral homeland of Marx and Engels, had long considered itself the proud guardian of the Marxist tradition, its claims to theoretical superiority buttressed by the existence of per- sonal ties and affections between many of its leaders and the old masters themselves. By the close of the nineteenth century, however, a glaring gap had come to exist between the theory and practice of the German party. Committed to violent revolution in theory, the SPD had become more and more of a reformist party in practice. With its legality assured after the repeal of Bismarck's antisocialist legislation, the party shunned all policies and practices that might trigger resumed repression by the forces of Imperial Germany. Hoping for an eventual parliamentary majority, the party grew to perceive a "revolutionary" society as one in which political democracy, individual liberties, and social equality would be allowed to flourish.

A critical influence on the moderate, reformist tone adopted by the SPD was a powerful German labor movement that identified socialist gains with increasing material and economic prosperity, rising wages, and improved conditions of life and work. In sharp contrast to French, Italian, and Spanish labor movements where strong syndicalist and anarchist currents infused socialism with revolutionary ardor, German unionists shunned both violence and theoretical orthodoxy in exchange for enjoying the economic and material benefits that life in the booming economy of Imperial Germany afforded them.[61]

Acknowledging the contradiction between the theory and practice of the German party, the revisionists sought to "revise" Marxist doctrine by frankly admitting that the aims and needs of the workers could be achieved more effectively by reform than by revolution. In a series of articles written between 1896 and 1898, Eduard Bernstein urged the SPD to free itself from "outdated phraseology" and "to appear as what it really is today, a democratic, socialist reform party."[62] Attempting to "make clear just where Marx was right and where he was wrong," Bernstein explained that Marx's faith in the inevitable economic collapse of capitalism had been a utopian error. Rather than moving inexorably toward collapse, capitalism had actually proven to be amazingly resilient, as evidenced by the remarkable prosperity enjoyed by European economies in the twilight years of the nineteenth century. Even more importantly, the working classes, far from sinking ever deeper into the poverty and despair that was theoretically to trigger their revolutionary consciousness, were coming to share more and more in the fruits of that prosperity. European socialism, therefore, should rid itself of its grandiose revolutionary terminology and concentrate instead on helping the proletariat find a place within the existing system. Bernstein hoped a politically educated working class, organized in trade unions and cooperatives, could pressure the state to achieve social reforms and gradual democratization. This, according to Bernstein and the revisionists, was the essence of socialism in the modern world.

While Rosa Luxemburg was not the first to attack Bernstein, she was his sharpest, strongest, and profoundest critic, and her involvement in the revisionist debate marked her daring foray into the limelight of European socialism. Deep personal considerations attracted Luxemburg to the revisionist controversy. The attempt of the revisionists to strip Marxism of its revolutionary core was heresy to one so steeped in the revolutionary tradition of the East. What Bernstein sought to do destroyed the very essence of the revolutionary spirit that motivated her. At stake in the entire affair, she felt, was the "existence of the Social Democratic movement itself."[63]

Luxemburg characterized the whole revisionist position as one that confused the fundamental relation between social reform and revolution.[64] Reforms were not revolution, and Bernstein was incorrect in making that identification. On the contrary, the movement for reform was only the mundane, prosaic, daily aspect of the workers' struggle. Although the work of achieving reform was and could be a powerful tool in the forging of working class political consciousness, the final goal—the establishment of a socialist society run by and for the interests of the working classes—must never be forgotten.

Luxemburg's attack on Bernstein was marked by a perceptive analysis of the nature of social reform in class society. Reforms and improvements granted from on high in capitalist society were obviously those that served the self-interest of the ruling classes. Magnanimously decreed, they could also be ruthlessly rescinded. Furthermore, the revisionists who hailed the material and economic advances of the proletariat approached the problem from the standpoint of "vulgar political economy" only. What about such intangible factors as working class alienation and exploitation? Wage increases were a far cry from being real control of the productive process. All could not be measured by money alone, at least when the yardstick was Rosa Luxemburg's humane and total perception of socialism.

While Bernstein had glorified the trade unions as the agencies through which gradual social reform was to be made possible, Luxemburg's attack on the unions and their reformist mentality was to haunt her for the rest of her days. Unions, she believed, could be defensive weapons only, securing merely temporary successes for the working classes. Alone they could never abolish exploitation, or alienation, or secure real control over the productive process. Only the seizure of political power by the working class could ensure the future victory of the socialist society. The trade union struggle paled in comparison, remaining forever and for all time only a "labor of Sisyphus" when compared with the real battles at hand.[65]

Finally, Luxemburg attacked as "parliamentary cretinism" the mentality that was at the heart of the revisionist ethos.[66] While she recognized that election campaigns were good opportunities both to disseminate socialist propaganda and to gauge the effect that such propaganda was having on the masses, socialism could never be achieved by a parliamentary vote alone. To believe so, she warned, was a dangerous illusion. A real and vivid perception of the class struggle always remained at the heart of her analysis.

Luxemburg presented her views on reform and revolution before the assembled heads of international socialism at the Stuttgart Congress of the International in 1898, the Amsterdam Congress in 1904, and in a collection of articles entitled *Social Reform or Revolution* published in 1899. Convinced that her interpretations were correct, she was undaunted by her youth, immigrant status, or lack of seniority in the party, or by the fact that she was the only woman attempting to serve the SPD on equal terms with men.

Luxemburg's brilliant articles and orations established her reputation within international socialism but brought her notoriety and opprobrium along with fame and recognition. What was viewed as the brash, brazen tone with which the young "upstart" had attacked Bernstein was never forgotten, and the controversy unleashed a trail of epithets and invective that was to follow her to the grave. She was seen as a dangerous and fanatical firebrand, booed and hooted down at the SPD's Congress in Hanover in 1899. Bebel himself made mention of the "unbelievable animosity"[67] toward Rosa Luxemburg that existed in the party, while others criticized the storm she had stirred up.[68]

Among trade unionists especially, Luxemburg's name became a scorned symbol of hatred. Her unfortunate remark identifying union activities with the "labors of Sisyphus" hurt badly, and she was condemned as an enemy of the unions' cause. Elements of antiintellectualism were also apparent in the unions' attack, in their contempt for "the way Rosa Luxemburg has appeared before us . . . like God from the sky." Her dogmatic and doctrinaire intellectual posturing compared unfavorably to the daily labors of "those of us who have to do the actual fighting and carry the responsibility for it as well."[69]

Luxemburg's age, sex, and foreign status all played a part in the criticism she received. Her arguments against the revisionists were countered with condescension. "You greenhorn," smirked a prominent supporter of Bernstein, "I could be your grandfather."[70] Others complained of the "unpleasant tone in the party press" produced by the "male and female emigration from the East,"[71] while the most biting attacks attributed the rising wave of anti-Semitism in Germany to the volatile effect of Luxemburg's presence and writings.[72]

The most troubling of all attacks were those that sought to link her involvement in the revisionist controversy to her "power complex" and "dirty power-grabbing attitude."[73] As a result of the persistence of such attitudes, Luxemburg never attained real comaraderie or acceptance within the SPD. Although she might be regarded as a prestigious intellectual, she always remained an outsider, estranged from the party hierarchy. Rosa Luxemburg made two attempts to assume roles of limited leadership within the party: one as the editor of the Saxon organ, the *Sächsische Arbeiterzeitung*, in 1898, and the second as the joint editor of the *Leipziger Volkszeitung* in 1901. Both ended in failure because the staffs of the two papers strongly resented the exercise of authority by a woman.[74] Even August Bebel, the enlightened author of *Woman Under Socialism*, was "disillusioned" with Luxemburg. "I am especially annoyed," he wrote, "that she has proven herself too much of a woman and not sufficiently a party comrade."[75] Both affairs confirmed Luxemburg's reputation as a stormy petrel, as a difficult, quarrelsome, and controversial personality.

Although Bebel herself warned Luxemburg against "falling out" with all sides,[76] she was never one to surrender her principles and her fighting spirit for the purpose of securing a niche in the party hierarchy. Luxemburg recognized and accepted her outsider status. She took it with great calm, she wrote to Leo Jogiches. "I always knew it could not be otherwise." Perceptively analyzing the nature of the resentment against her, Luxemburg knew she was distrusted because she was not part of the "ruling clique," but had relied on nothing but her own talents and abilities to make her name in the party.[77] Her age, sex, and foreign status only worsened the situation, because those who expected subservience, meekness, and fawning reticence from her as a young woman got none in return. Naturally those jealous of her abilities sought to narrow her influence through scorning and derisive remarks, yet such tactics, she always insisted, only proved the inability of her opponents to deal with the arguments she raised in a reasoned and rational way.[78]

Despite the attacks, however, acclaim and renown came to Rosa Luxemburg, and in the years before 1905 she reached the height of her influence in the SPD as a speaker, theoretician, and agitator of the first rank. Agitation and propaganda were not revolution, however, and as the winds of revolution began to blow from the East in 1905,[79] Luxemburg felt her outsider status in the stifling bureaucratic atmosphere of the SPD all the more. Her decision to leave Germany to participate in the revolutionary convulsions gripping Russian Poland not only had important implications for her later theoretical work but also served to alienate her even more from a decidedly nonrevolutionary German socialist hierarchy.

All her life, Rosa Luxemburg shared that same mystical faith in the spontaneous revolutionary potential of the masses that also sustained Alexandra Kollontai. The outbreak of revolution in Russia in 1905 strengthened her commitment to that belief. Even more heartening for Luxemburg was the "splendid" effect that the chaos in Russia was having on a heretofore quiescent Polish working class.[80] The Russo-Japanese War had had profound and disturbing effects in Congress Poland. Dislocations in transportation, communications, and economic productivity led to widespread unemployment, and this, in turn, reactivated latent political discontent. A mass demonstration in Warsaw in November 1904 was the first instance of open armed struggle since the abortive insurrection of 1863. A massive wave of strikes erupted in January 1905 and continued throughout most of the year, accompanied by demands for a democratic republic and an eight-hour day. By May the country was on the verge of civil war; in June violent street fighting in Lodz, the largest industrial center of Russian Poland, marked the dramatic entrance of the Polish working class into the political arena.

Life in Warsaw was exciting and exhilarating for Rosa Luxemburg. "The revolution is magnificent," she wrote to a friend, "and everything else is rubbish."[81] As the SDKPiL gained thousands of new recruits, Luxemburg's furious pen unleashed a flood of publications, urging the support of the Russian revolutionary movement as the best and only hope for the Polish working class.[82]

Luxemburg's analysis proved ominously correct. Events in Poland were intimately linked to Russian developments. Encouraged by the tsar's promise of reforms, the Polish middle classes soon withdrew their support from more radical groups. The revolutionary movement in Poland waned, and a vicious tsarist counteroffensive followed. In March 1906 Luxemburg herself was arrested. She languished in a Warsaw prison until July, when prison doctors justified her release on grounds of ill health.

Intellectual maturity was the most important result of Luxemburg's revolutionary interlude. The experiences of 1905 led to the crystallization in her own mind of those revolutionary ideas and tactics that became her hallmark. Convinced by the spontaneous character of the revolution that her faith in the masses had not been misplaced, Luxemburg drew upon the encouraging example of the strike waves of 1904–1906 to develop her theory of the political mass strike as a revolutionary weapon.[83]

The mass strike was a process, a spontaneous outpouring of revolutionary sentiment, the "rallying idea," in Luxemburg's words, of a long, conscious, intense period of class struggle. Social Democrats could hasten the development of things and "endeavor to accelerate events," but they could never create the mass strike or miraculously decree its use. Luxemburg was adamant that the mass strike emerged only from the proper set of economic and political conditions. Arising initially from economic grievances, it gradually assumed political overtones, helped along through the educational and agitational efforts of a revolutionary party. Not only was the mass strike a link in the chain of revolution, but it was also a powerful component in the education of a self-conscious working class. Viewed from this perspective, the role the mass strike played in the implantation of revolutionary consciousness was even more important than its immediate practical results.

The German party that Luxemburg hoped to educate by her writings on the mass strike showed itself to be decidedly hostile to taking its lessons from her. All those things that had alienated Luxemburg from the SPD before her departure from Warsaw—its factional squabbles, parliamentary opportunism, and subservience to trade union reformism—sickened her all the more after her return. The atmosphere in Berlin seemed more stultifying and putrid than ever. "Since my return I feel rather isolated," she wrote to a friend, "I feel the pettiness and the hesitancy of our party regime more clearly and more painfully than ever before. . . ."[84]

Adding to Luxemburg's acute emotional despondency in this period was a traumatic change in her long romantic involvement with Jogiches.[85] He had also been arrested for his revolutionary role in 1905 but had managed to escape from prison and hide for a time in Cracow and Warsaw. While in hiding he was assisted and cared for by a Polish woman comrade named Izolska. The precise nature of his relationship with the woman is not known, shrouded in the same mystery that colored all of his personal and political dealings. What is clear, however, is that Luxemburg's immediate response to the news was to break off relations with Jogiches immediately. Disgusted by compromise and mediocrity of any kind, she demanded absolute loyalty in both her private and political life. Luxemburg and Jogiches remained political associates for the rest of their lives, but they never resumed their earlier romantic involvement. Politically, the most important result of their separation was Luxemburg's declining interest and influence in the Polish socialist movement of which she and Jogiches had both been the creators.

After the Revolution of 1905 Luxemburg also grew increasingly isolated from German affairs. While the events of that year had confirmed her revolutionary ardor and faith, they instilled horror in the hearts of a German party dedicated to crushing the revolutionary specter at all costs. According to her old nemesis, the reformist trade unions, not revolution but "peace and calm" were needed to solidify the advances already made. Their attacks on her were scathing. Of course, they proclaimed, "scribbling literati" like Luxemburg, individuals "who in their youth were graced with a good education and were never hungry," could not hope to comprehend the unionists' concerns.[86]

In debates on the question of adopting the mass strike as a socialist tactic,[87] party leaders also reacted to Luxemburg's fiery speeches with condescending sarcasm and ridicule. August Bebel claimed he had never listened to debates "with so much talk of blood and revolution," and he jokingly laughed that he couldn't help glancing occasionally at his boots "to see if these weren't in fact already wading in blood."[88]

After 1905 the German party lived not for the coming socialist revolution but for the glorious ritual of the Reichstag election campaigns. With its eyes firmly riveted on a parliamentary majority, the SPD was reluctant to weaken its chances at the ballot box through "irresponsible" calls for revolution. "We dare not hazard the destiny of the movement," one party resolution decreed. "We have built too much, and what has been built is too valuable."[89]

While Luxemburg was not opposed to socialist participation in parliament, she was revolted by the prevailing political wisdom that demanded all party decisions be weighed "from the point of view of the ballot slip."[90] She had an entirely different view of the purpose of election campaigns, seeing them as vehicles in the political and revolutionary education of the working class. Again, however, Luxemburg's theoretical differences with party leaders were accorded not respect and toleration but scorn and derision. Again, her foreign status hurt her. Recurrent and renewed attacks on the "foreigner Luxemburg" demonstrated the strength of latent nationalist sentiments within the party, sentiments that would be glaringly unveiled in 1914, when German socialists queued up in droves to wage war for the fatherland. The "Easterner" Luxemburg was called a Russian patriot who sought to bring Russian intrigues and chaos to Germany. Only a foreigner could dare imply that the culturally and politically superior Germans should take revolutionary lessons from the backward Russian barbarians. Her revolutionary proclamations were regarded as "utterly irresponsible."[91] Kautsky criticized her for insisting on the importance of her own "second rate preoccupations" when there was vital party work to be done.[92] The most vicious condemnations came from those who insisted that the real motive behind Luxemburg's incessant criticism was her desire to split the party. The "poisonous bitch" really wanted a small party where she could dominate. "Her only motive," charged Victor Adler, "was an almost perverse desire for self-justification."[93]

Fed by such attacks, Luxemburg's unpopularity in the party mounted. Shouted down at the Magdeburg Congress of 1910, she found it harder and harder to obtain mandates for party gatherings. Of the last five congresses before the war, she attended only three. She also began to experience difficulty in having her writings published by the party press.

In the final analysis, the real reason for Luxemburg's ostracism was not her doctrinal intransigence but the simple fact she was a woman. Her closest political comrades believed this to be so,[94] and her own letters hinted at the possibility. Some socialists, she recognized, could simply "not abide politically active women."[95] Others were amazingly blunt in this regard. "When wise men speak I'm glad I understand what they say . . . ," a leading SPD member admitted. "But I am not glad when wise women talk in such a way that no one can understand them."[96] The German party had survived challenges to its views before, most notably from Bernstein, but former oppositionists had never had to withstand the intense torrent of verbal abuse that was hurled at Luxemburg. While political camaraderie and a network of personal friendships had saved Bernstein from ostracism, Luxemburg was never sustained by such luxuries.

What did sustain her, however, during her years of isolation was her fervent and fervid belief that an irrevocable gulf existed between the leaders of the German party and the masses themselves. Her faith in the intrinsic goodness and revolutionary creativity of the German masses grew in direct proportion to her estrangement from their leaders. Contact with the people themselves, through agitation and propaganda work, became her solution to the problem of organizational impotence. A formidable orator, she was in great demand at local party meetings, for the enthusiasm, euphoria, and passionate conviction she inspired. Her very popularity assured her of the validity of her views. "In any Siberian village you care to name," she came to believe, "there is more humanity than in the whole of German Social Democracy."[97] If the leaders would not heed her words, the masses would.

More important than her agitational efforts among the working classes was the emotional and intellectual fulfillment Luxemburg received from her work as an instructor in the SPD's Central Party School in Berlin, work that sustained her from 1907 to the very outbreak of the war. The SPD had founded its school in 1906 to train an elite corps of agitators, activists, and union leaders. Significantly, however, "the best brain among the scientific heirs of Marx and Engels" was not asked to be an instructor from the outset but came to the school to fill an emergency vacancy, when the arrest and deportation of another instructor necessitated an immediate replacement. Teaching courses in history and political economy, Luxemburg flourished in this atmosphere, reveling in the opportunity to contribute directly to the political education of selected members of the working classes. She was popular with her students, who praised her exuberant teaching style and natural abilities as a teacher.[98]

Luxemburg's work at the school was important for another reason. Teaching enabled her to clarify and refine her political views and resulted in the publication of that work for which she is still best known, *The Accumulation of Capital.*[99]

Luxemburg designed her work to deal with a fatal gap in Marx's *Capital*: the problem of why, almost 30 years after his death, capitalism had not collapsed but really appeared to be growing stronger. Simply put, economic imperialism, or the invasion of primitive economies by economically superior ones, was the key to the process by which capitalism was being kept alive. Imperialist foreign policies gave the economies of capitalist nations a powerful shot in the arm by opening new areas both to investments and to the disposal of surplus products. Marx, she explained, could not have foreseen these possibilities for continued capitalist expansion.

Luxemburg drew two important political conclusions from her detailed economic study. Obviously, since there was a definite economic and territorial limit to capitalism's expansive possibilities, she encouraged the workers to be strengthened in their revolutionary resolve. Second, she emphasized the crucial and immediate need for all socialists to educate themselves in the meaning and character of imperialism itself. Since capitalism would be unable to survive if deprived of its imperialist outlets, socialists everywhere should commit themselves to a firm condemnation of the imperialist practices of their own governments.

This, however, the German Socialist Party was not prepared to do. Preoccupied with the ballot box, the SPD was afraid to take a stand against nationalistic and imperialistic policies that were proving increasingly popular with the electorate. Here again, in her work on imperialism, Luxemburg felt her estrangement from the majority opinion of her adopted party. Reviews of her work were hostile. All challenged the effrontery of the brash Polish woman who dared to treat what Marx had left unfinished.[100]

Luxemburg's battle against imperialism and militarism preoccupied her in the twilight years of old Europe.[101] A modern day Cassandra, she warned socialists to open their eyes, and to face up to the imminent debacle of imperialist war. In this battle, however, destined to be her last with the old SPD, the revisionist, reformist, nationalist tendencies that she had been attacking for so long again proved victorious. Timid vacillation on the question of socialist response to war characterized the behavior of the German party.

The SPD consistently rejected resolutions that urged a general strike by the international proletariat in the event of war.[102] Arguing that a strike "would prove fatal to party activities, and under certain circumstances, to the very existence of the party," it persisted in its staunch commitment to the conservative, static philosophy that Luxemburg had repeatedly challenged.

As the largest, strongest, most powerful socialist party of the Second International, the SPD must certainly bear the brunt of the responsibility for the failure of European socialism to prevent, or at least attempt to prevent, the conflict that erupted in July 1914. While the party's unanimous decision to support the fatherland's war effort shocked and horrified the most orthodox of old socialists, Rosa Luxemburg foremost among them, that decision appears neither incomprehensible nor unexpected when viewed in the light of historical retrospective. Since the turn of the century, all SPD policies had been framed in response to fear: fear of alienating the electorate; fear of jeopardizing the party's legality; and fear of undermining its organizational integrity. Socialist condemnation of the national war effort would have flown in the face of all three considerations.

The SPD justified its support for the fatherland by presenting the war as a life-and-death struggle against Russian reaction. If the German proletariat were enslaved by the Russian colossus, then all European socialism would be doomed. Party theoreticians found powerful support for their views in the writings of Marx and Engels themselves, writings clearly imbued with a current of German cultural superiority and also blatantly anti-Slavic in tone.[103]

Regardless of such doctrinal justifications, however, Rosa Luxemburg blamed the moral bankruptcy and hypocrisy of the German party for the collapse of international Social Democracy. On the very night of August 4 itself, immediately after the SPD's Reichstag delegation unanimously voted to support the government's request for war credits, she resolved to take up the struggle against the war policy of her own party.[104] Her long history of opposition to the SPD made her the natural leader of the small left-wing party group that coalesced to fight against the imperialist war. Over the next few months, Rosa Luxemburg made a desperate attempt to harness and lead oppositionist sentiment, a struggle made more difficult by the imposition of wartime censorship, and by the mounting nationalistic fervor of the German Socialist Party itself.

Her entrance into opposition unleashed a new and furious round of attacks, attacks fueled by old hatreds and fanned by old fears. Luxemburg continued to be haunted by her foreign status. Certainly the German workers' attachment to their fatherland was something that "traitor" could never understand. Judged "clever as a monkey," she was accused of being single-handedly behind the opposition, "feverishly busy trying to split the party" to obtain power for herself.[105]

Because she spent most of the war years in prison, however, Luxemburg was tragically impotent to effect the kinds of changes that the leaders of the SPD so feared. Arrested in 1915 on charges of inciting soldiers to disobedience, she languished in prison while the war she hated so fiercely raged unceasingly around her.

There she spent her time planning and writing, preparing the German proletariat for the debacle she believed to be imminent. The most famous product of her imprisonment was the so-called Junius pamphlet, named for a legendary protestor from a former era.[106] Written for mass propaganda, the illegal pamphlet was a furious, trenchant, bitter indictment of the imperialist war and of the role of German Social Democracy within that war. Luxemburg's anguished condemnation of the horrors of war was matched in its fury only by her revulsion at the treachery of German socialists. By representing "imperialist bestiality" as a defensive war, they were guilty of an "impudent fraud," accomplices in the "suicide of the European working class." Only cowardice could explain the farcical and arbitrary decision of that "stinking corpse," the SPD, to set aside the class struggle for the war's duration. Declaring "war against war," Luxemburg called for a reconstructed Second International, an International purged of the diseased and hypocritical putrefaction that had infected, corrupted, and killed classical European socialism.

At Luxemburg's insistence, a conference of all left wing antiwar radicals was held in Berlin on New Year's Day, 1916. To carry on the struggle against the war and the SPD, a group emerged from the conference that came to be known as the Spartacus League, named for the legendary leader of a Roman slave uprising. From the start, Rosa Luxemburg was the guiding and inspirational spirit of the *Spartakusbund*, the impact of her moving exhortations never blunted even though they came from behind prison bars.

Two others were instrumental in leading the Spartacist battle against the SPD: the ever revolutionary Jogiches, and the antimilitarist Karl Liebknecht, son of one of the original founders of the SPD itself. Together, Luxemburg, Leibknecht, and Jogiches formulated the main themes of Spartacist policy. Their pamphlets and leaflets urged popular revolution as the only effective antidote to war. Only mass action could stop the senseless slaughter.

Isolated in prison, Luxemburg was unaware of similar planning then going on in Switzerland: the Bolshevik dream to foment a revolution in Russia based on the same principles. When the Russian Revolution came, however, she greeted it with cautious optimism, convinced that the German proletariat had to complete the task their Russian brothers had only begun.

Yet Bolshevik victory only accentuated the splits in German Social Democracy.[107] Even though the fall of the tsar robbed the socialist right of the pretense of defensive war against Russian reaction, it continued its support of the war effort, hoping a democratized Germany might be the result. The party's pacifist center, on the other hand, had grown increasingly disgusted with the nationalist fervor of the right. Breaking from the party in January 1917, they formed a new Independent German Social Democratic Party (USPD). Consumed by the desire for peace alone, the USPD languished in impotence and vacillation, caring little for the proletariat's conquest of power. Only the Spartacus League called for the transformation of the war into a social revolution, a war to the death against the imperialist and capitalist world.

Such was the tragedy of German socialism that in the days when real political power was in its grasp, it showed the same lack of revolutionary élan, the same absence of purpose that had characterized its policies in the decades of peace before the war. The German Revolution of 1918, in the words of one historian, came as an "unwanted child." "It just happened," wrote another.[108] Really a military collapse in the guise of a revolution, what occurred in war-torn Germany was of a negative not positive character. The so-called revolution lacked intensity, direction, and will. The old machinery of government simply ceased to function, the victim of a revolutionary situation that, far from being planned, was the catastrophic result of the compounded disasters of war. Years of emotional, physical, and material deprivation had made the German populace keenly aware of the glaring flaws of their imperial fatherland, a fatherland that sucked the life blood from its sons and daughters but gave little, if nothing, in return. Inspired by the twin goddesses of peace and democracy, the revolution in the end was a reaction to the brutal repression of German political life.

The German Republic was born in chaos on November 9, 1918. The collapse of the military front had sparked a three-tiered process of revolutionary ferment. Naval revolts, military mutinies, and massive industrial work stoppages were capped by local democratic upheavals, the spontaneous appearance of workers' and soldiers' councils modeled on the Russian example, and the abdication of the emperor himself. With the proclamation of the Republic, power passed to the men of the SPD, the largest party of the prewar Reichstag, because the SPD, with its cautious program of moderate constitutionalism, seemed to have the best hope of bringing order out of the chaotic situation. Revolution for the leaders of the SPD was not bloody Bolshevik upheaval, but democratic reform, reform enacted as much as possible within the confines of the existing state machine. Thus a strange revolution occurred in postwar Germany, a revolution that preserved almost intact the machinery of the old government—Germany's judiciary, civil service, economic structure, and military command all remained as before.

Like the story of all revolutions, the history of the German Revolution after November 1918 is a history of the contest for power between radical parties, the seemingly inexorable struggle between stagnation and advance in the revolutionary process. In that struggle, the starring role belonged to a frail, white-haired woman, a woman for whom the outbreak of revolution spelled salvation itself. With the coming of the revolution to Breslau, the prison gates were flung open, and Rosa Luxemburg was freed. Years of imprisonment may have taken their physical toll, but they hadn't deadened her fighting spirit.

After her release from prison, Luxemburg embarked on a feverish round of activities. Her letters confirm the hectic pace of these days—a "veritable hell," she called them.[109] Still, she was exhilarated, planning and working for the revolution that had been her lifelong ambition.

Luxemburg and the Spartacus League sought to prepare the proletariat for what they took to be the next stage of the German Revolution—the overthrow of the SPD government and the transformation of the limited political revolution into a genuinely proletarian one. The program of the Spartacus League, drafted by Luxemburg, called for the "abolition of capitalist rule and the creation of a socialist order of society," a society where workers' and soldiers' councils would be the new forces of government, and where the nationalization of the means of production would guarantee a genuine economic transformation.[110]

Tragically, however, the Spartacus League lacked the tactical and organizational means necessary to put its theories into practice. Inspired by Luxemburg's mystical faith in the creative revolutionary potential of the masses, it never assumed the form of a disciplined vanguard party, consciously refusing to obtain political power "over the working masses or through the working masses."[111] Considering itself only the "most conscious part of the proletariat," the *Spartakusbund* suffered from its inability to exert effective control over all those who flocked to its banners. The stirring, revolutionary rhetoric of Spartacus appealed to a variety of criminal hangers-on—

the destitute, desperate, and adventuresome element that has played a part in all revolutionary movements. This was to prove a fatal attraction for Spartacist idealists, hard pressed to distinguish the creative revolutionary consciousness of the proletariat from the rioting, looting, and random acts of destruction carried out by the *Lumpen*.

Spartacist troubles mounted in January 1919. Recognizing the need for a more formalized organizational structure, and anxious to differentiate their more radical position from socialists of both right and center, the leaders of Spartacus reluctantly agreed to merge with a variety of left radical groups to form a new Communist Party of Germany (KPD). The KPD had only a few thousand supporters in all of Germany, and although Luxemburg clearly attempted to separate the new party from the Russian example, the model of Bolshevik chaos loomed large in a German cultural consciousness longing for discipline and order. The provocative, messianic fervor of Luxemburg's messages, announced boldly in the pages of *Die Rote Fahne*, the organ of the Spartacus League, only infuriated and frightened the forces of order all the more.

In her last tragic weeks, Rosa Luxemburg suffered from that same ignominious malignment that had plagued her all her life. Identified as the leader of the radical left, the Jewess Luxemburg was excoriated in an atmosphere that smacked of pogrom, and Spartacist became a synonym for criminal in a vicious hate campaign with a strongly anti-Semitic character. The fact that Spartacus was headed by a man and a woman became grist for the mill of the reactionary press. Scandal sheets spoke of "red orgies," and the public widely believed that Liebknecht and the "she-devil" Luxemburg were lovers. "What will Liebknecht and Co. bring us?" ubiquitous placards demanded. "Famine, death, and the end of Germany," was the inflammatory reply.[112]

Even the SPD joined in the attack on its one-time comrade. "The despicable actions of Liebknecht and Rosa Luxemburg soil the revolution and endanger all its achievements," judged *Vorwärts*, the official party organ. "The masses must not sit by quietly for one minute longer while these brutal beasts and their followers paralyze the activities of the republican government . . . nine-tenths of the population hate and despise their actions."[113]

The final battle of Rosa Luxemburg's life was waged against an SPD government that had become a definite counterrevolutionary force, a government more fearful of the left than of the right. In the wake of increasing repression by the government, a variety of left-wing groups, including the new KDP, planned an insurrection for January 1919, a last, futile attempt to regain lost revolutionary momentum. Despite her doubts about the wisdom of the upheaval, Luxemburg felt she had a moral obligation to support the masses in their heroic struggle against the counterrevolution. True to her worst fears, however, the Spartacist uprising proved a senseless and directionless failure.[114] Suppressed in three days by the combined power of the old German military caste and the antirevolutionary SPD bureaucracy, it was the last gasp of a revolutionary German socialism inspired by Luxemburg's vision.

IV

Rosa Luxemburg, this small, frail, slightly deformed woman with the large bright eyes and probing mind, was much more than the rigorous theoretian historians recall and scholars admire. There was an immensely human side to Red Rosa, a sensitive moral tone to her socialism usually lost sight of in the brilliant rationality of her theoretical arguments. For her, socialism was an all-absorbing emotion "of the head and heart."[115] She was a woman with enough passion "to set a prairie on fire,"[116] a woman who felt and suffered with every living creature, whose love for birds, plants, animals, and life itself nourished and enriched her love for all humanity.

Rosa Luxemburg holds a special place in socialist history because of her unique ability to combine sensitive compassion with rational calculation in a way that none of her contemporaries, male or female, ever could. She "humanized her doctrine," a comrade wrote. "For her, every case of misery, of exploitation, of the people subjugated by a great power, every movement of collective anger, became one more human argument with which to justify revolution."[117] Her vision of the future socialist society was marked by acute morality and humanism, an idealistic, ethical fervor that she shared with Marx and Kollontai. The new socialist society would above all else be a humane society of comrades, an idyllic community of equals where all people could realize their human potential, in peace, free from want and need. Rescued from alienation and oppression, the great laboring mass would cease to be a "dominated mass," but would live their lives as autonomous beings, with dignity and purpose. Socialism promised peace and fraternity, harmony, solidarity, and "respect for everything that bears a human countenance."[118]

Inspired by these ideals, Rosa Luxemburg embraced political life for the sole purpose of being allowed to influence European socialism, molding it in line with her own dreams and desires. Devoted to the "struggle for the rights of workers, poor, and oppressed,"[119] she was revolted and disgusted by the possession of political power for its own sake. In a sense, Luxemburg's entire revolutionary career can be understood in terms of the contest between her own struggle for political influence and simultaneous revulsion against political power. Both her successes and failures must be judged in the context of this struggle. Tragically, Luxemburg never understood—or perhaps refused to understand—that power politics itself was the route to influence in the European socialist world of her day. Because she never agreed to play the political game, a position of real authority always eluded her. In the final analysis, her estrangement from the centers of power in the German party was due as much to her own revulsion at securing a niche in the SPD hierarchy as to the corresponding reluctance of that hierarchy to grant her—a woman, a Jew, and a foreigner—a place within its ranks.

What the SPD had become by the early years of the twentieth century was alien to Luxemburg's notions of revolutionary romanticism, purity, and dynamism. The character of the SPD was ably described by sociologist Max Weber, who saw in the party's immense bureaucracy nothing less than "an increasing army of people who, beyond all else, have an interest in getting ahead."[120] A new line of professional careerists, bureaucrats, functionaries, and parliamentarians had risen to prominence within party ranks, all sober, practical, pragmatic politicians, steeped in revisionist conservatism, with no use for revolutionary theories or practices that might threaten their own privileged positions.

The mark of success in the German party was no longer theoretical brilliance, oratorical exuberance, or agitational expertise, but the simple and glorified act of becoming a Reichstag member. Luxemburg's dislike of parliamentary activity for its own sake was paralleled by her growing contempt for parliamentarians, whom she considered to be poseurs consumed with their own self-importance. "It is laughable," she wrote to a friend, "how being a member of the Reichstag suddenly goes to all those good people's heads."[121]

Parliamentary posts, judged Luxemburg, were only "decorative shams,"[122] egoistic preserves that insulated their holders from the real tasks and challenges ahead. "Politics" itself Luxemburg attacked in even more vituperative terms. "Goddamn politics," she fumed, is "inane Baal worship, driving people—victims of their own obsession, of mental rabies—to sacrifice their entire existence."[123]

Luxemburg's hatred of "spiritually bankrupt"[124] politics and politicians left her isolated, never in a position to influence a party where obedience and line-toeing had become crucial factors in hierarchical approbation and political advancement. She was made to feel that it was some sort of a "disease" to harbor the kinds of ardent emotions she did.[125] By her own admission, she "never felt at home" in party congresses, reluctant even to admit her estrangement for fear she might be accused of "treason to socialism."[126] Alexandra Kollontai analyzed Luxemburg's political impotence more closely. Without obedience, she wrote, it was simply impossible to make a career in the SPD. The disobedient Luxemburg, therefore, was "always kept at a distance."[127]

While Luxemburg's hatred of the "organization man" mentality kept her from real political power in the SPD, her hostility to organization as such became even more important in terms of her future revolutionary role. So total was her disgust with the "organization is everything" ethos of the German party[128] that, in the final analysis, she blinded herself to the vital role that organization and leadership do and must play in revolutionary success. She created an unbridgeable chasm between leaders and led, contrasting what she took to be the complacency, opportunism, and innate conservatism of leaders with the creative revolutionary potential and dynamism of the pure, unsullied masses. For Luxemburg as for Kollontai, the masses and the masses alone became the critical factor—"they are the rock on which the ultimate victory of the revolution will be built."[129] Nothing else—neither party committees, nor the all-powerful and brilliant leader, nor the little circle of conspirators—counted according to Luxemburg's definition of revolutionary success.

She always saw to it that the Spartacus League never became a Bolshevik-type revolutionary cadre. As much as she hated the sterile bureaucracy of the immense German party, she also despised the "Tartar Marxism" of the Bolsheviks.[130] Placing all her faith in the masses, she excoriated those narrow-minded disciplinarians who sought to play "schoolmaster" with the proletariat.[131] An all-powerful Central Committee, she feared, might give way to stultifying and stupefying dictation, manipulating the masses from on high instead of drawing its own revolutionary impulses from them down below.[132] Social Democracy was a mass movement, Luxemburg maintained, not a private club that required blind obedience and mechanical subordination. "The working class demands the right to make its mistakes and learn in the dialectic of history," she insisted. "The errors committed by a truly revolutionary movement are infinitely more fruitful than the infallibility of the cleverest Central Committee."[133]

Luxemburg's statement is a highly significant one, for it reveals her original definition of success in the revolutionary drama. "Success" and "political victory" were not equivalent terms for Rosa Luxemburg. She had nothing but contempt for those who were consumed with the lust for political victory alone, those who would "expect the revolution to triumph at one blow."[134] Revolutionary defeat, according to Luxemburg, was an integral part of the self-education of the working masses. Revolution, she contended, was a "tough, inexhaustible" struggle over a long period of time, a lengthy process of defeat and renewal that brought the working masses ever closer to the day of eventual victory. Success, therefore, was in the attempt itself, in the process of revolutionary education. So-called premature revolutions were not failures but vital elements in the clarification of mass political consciousness.

Most importantly, because Luxemburg staunchly preferred political defeat to "moral collapse," her revulsion to compromise prevented her from being mesmerized by the ostensible success of the Bolshevik Revolution. The essence of the "Russian tragedy," as she defined it,[135] was its surrender to German militarism to selfishly save itself, its betrayal of proletarian internationalism, and its use of terror to keep the revolution alive. Her vision of a spontaneous, majoritarian mass revolution, fed and fomented from below, allowed no room for terror. A truly proletarian revolution "hates and abhors human murder," she believed; only a minority dictatorship needed terror to survive.[136] "The unheard of acts of violence and cruelties of the Bolsheviks do not let me sleep," she wrote in the last months of her life.[137] Vigorously opposing the creation of a new International that might become a vehicle for their domination, she trembled lest the Bolshevik example become a model for the socialist world.[138]

Despite the glowing idealism that isolated Luxemburg both from the centers of power in the socialist world and from practical political successes, the sheer force of her intellectual superiority and theoretical achievements ensured her political survival. One so gifted as she did not need the crutch of organizational acceptance to make her mark on the socialist movements of her day. As a woman, her isolation and impotence could have been doubly painful had it not been for her own supreme confidence in her intellectual abilities, and for the generally, though begrudgingly, recognized nature of those abilities.

Nonetheless, Luxemburg's reluctance to involve herself in the routine tasks of organizational creation and political fence-mending had serious consequences. Not only did her aversion to such concerns weaken the German revolutionary movement when it did come, but her failure to provide a successful model of female political gamesmanship curtailed the possibility that other women, unfortunately all not so gifted as she, might follow in her footsteps.

Even though Luxemburg herself had felt the sting of criticism because of her sex, she never believed that the needs and problems of women as a group deserved special attention. Totally accepting the standard Marxist position on the woman question, she always insisted that the class struggle must remain primary, that the movement's full and complete attention must be devoted to that end alone. With the victory of socialism, she was convinced, all groups oppressed under capitalism—women and others—would be truly free.

Despite the fact that the socialist feminist movement of Imperial Germany was the strongest and most powerful organization of its kind in Europe, Luxemburg always held aloof, maintaining an indifferent if not actually hostile attitude to any separatist campaign for women's rights. From her earliest days in the SPD, she angrily resisted the official and obviously condescending suggestion that work in the women's groups of the party would be a natural field of activity for her. Although she recognized the importance of recruiting women to the socialist cause, she was adamant that the women's battle be linked to the "proletariat's general struggle for liberation,"[139] and equally insistent that she take her rightful place in that larger battle.

Luxemburg's hostility to the feminist movement may be explained by a variety of factors. Graced with a self-confident assurance in her own abilities, she sought to influence matters of—in her perception—*real* substance within international socialism. The women's movement of Imperial Germany, strong as it was, remained—and would always remain, she acutely suspected—a rather peripheral activity. When an editor of *Pravda* asked Luxemburg to write an article about the lot of the German working woman, she refused, confessing to Jogiches that it was simply "not worth the trouble."[140] At times Luxemburg bluntly accused work among women—or "old ladies' nonsense," as she termed it—of being a waste of time, remote from the critical issues facing the SPD.[141] On one occasion she was furious at Clara Zetkin, the leader of the German socialist women's movement, because the feminist had been too busy to participate in the party debates on imperialism, "all tangled up," Luxemburg analyzed, in "old women's affairs."[142] Although Zetkin remained her lifelong personal and political ally, Luxemburg was always skeptical of her friend's real intellectual abilities. Zetkin, she felt, was a "decent, open, and honest person," but an "empty sack" intellectually, with few if any original ideas of her own.[143] Perhaps Luxemburg transferred her lack of respect for Zetkin's intelligence to the women's movement as a whole, seeing it as an arena where the less intellectually gifted might hope to excel.

The increasingly conservative nature of the German socialist women's movement may also have alienated Luxemburg from it. Women's preoccupation with reformist issues after 1908 paralleled the nonrevolutionary ethos of the SPD hierarchy,[144] a hierarchy with which Luxemburg was vehemently at odds. Furthermore, the reformist, if not at times frivolous, tone of the feminist organ *Die Gleichheit* was not about to endear Luxemburg to the women's cause. The paper regularly published articles on fashions and cooking, recipes, dress patterns, and nonpolitical features "for mothers and children." Certainly such prosaic concerns did not appeal to one such as Luxemburg, ever-conscious of the need to prepare the working classes for the larger struggle. The withdrawal of Social Democratic women from important socialist agitation clearly disgusted her.[145]

Finally, Luxemburg's opposition to feminism may be explained by her unhappiness and uneasiness with what she took to be certain basic feminist assumptions. Luxemburg was always convinced that women were different from men, physically, emotionally, and intellectually. While different did not mean inferior, she quickly noted,[146] she was opposed to the intolerance of some feminists, even Zetkin, who sought to mold all women into their own properly conceived images of total and rigid equality. All women were not born to become agitators or stenographers, she chided Zetkin, or to assume other so-called socially useful roles.[147] She was impatient with feminism because it refused to allow gentle and simple women to live their own lives, and because it seemed to deny and degrade the innate beauty of the female spirit.

Luxemburg was convinced of the validity of her views because she had been sustained, in her political isolation, by a caring and loving female support network, a group of basically apolitical women who provided her with the only genuine friendships she ever formed in Germany. The women in this group included Luise Kautsky, the second wife of the German socialist Karl Kautsky; Sonia Liebknecht, the wife of Spartacist Karl Liebknecht; Marta Rosenbaum, a militant socialist and USPD member; and Mathilde Jacob, a journalist who served Luxemburg with utmost devotion as a personal secretary and confidante.

It was to these women that Luxemburg poured out her innermost feelings on the beauty of nature and life, art and literature. With them she felt safe and secure from the trials and traumas of the political arena. While certain of her letters do show that she tried to help her women friends establish a strong independent identity, or free themselves from overly domineering husbands, neither politics nor feminist consciousness was the basis of these friendships. Generosity and devotion, love, comradeship, and spiritual affinity were what Rosa Luxemburg sought—and received—from these women, whose loving, sustaining characteristics she believed to be uniquely female properties.[148]

Female friendships became even more important to Luxemburg after the tragic end of her relationship with Jogiches. "We two know how one loves," she wrote poignantly to Luise Kautsky.[149] Clearly, her experiences with Jogiches had disillusioned her. Yet, despite the feminist implications of her words, Luxemburg was no Kollontai. Always opposed to women who made their private affairs blazing public concerns,[150] she never cared to extrapolate from her own personal problems onto a wider arena. Had she chosen to do so, however, she would have found many similarities between her own personal problems and those of both Kollontai and Marx. With Jogiches, Luxemburg had grappled with that ever-familiar problem common to revolutionary women: the dilemma of combining love, work, and politics.

In the early years of her relationship, she seemed to have succeeded. Jogiches had been her tutor in her salad days in Zurich, days when she was insecure and unsure of her abilities. Because the activist and conspiratorial Jogiches was never self-disciplined enough to write or theorize himself, he took pride in his pupil and lover, molding her arguments and guiding her thoughts. In those idyllic days in Switzerland, Luxemburg appeared to have solved that eternal feminist dilemma, combining her love with her work in a way that Marx or Kollontai never could.

When the student began to surpass the teacher, however, first Jogiches and later Luxemburg grew restive. Although he was proud of her fame and accomplishments, he sensed that he was losing his grip on his former pupil, while Luxemburg, for her part, resented his annoying and pedantic habit of "playing the mentor."[151] Yet the relationship continued. Despite arguments both personal and political, trivial and critical, Luxemburg clung to her comrade and lover. Jogiches brought her strength, she wrote, "joy, support, and the encouragement to go on."[152]

More importantly, he gave her happiness and fulfillment, a life outside the eternally "boring and draining cause."[153] Always insisting on the "sacredness of love in her life,"[154] Luxemburg knew she could never find personal satisfaction in politics alone. "There is a world apart from the Reichstag," she consistently maintained, a world in which she was determined to "haggle for her daily portion of happiness with the stubbornness of a mule."[155] Inspired by this vision of an integrated "perfect life,"[156] she struggled to hold onto her relationship with Jogiches, even when he was no longer prepared to fulfill her needs. For years she begged him to come to Berlin to live openly with her as "man and wife."[157] "No couple on earth has the chance we have," she wrote in an especially touching letter. "We will both work and our life will be perfect!!"[158] Repeatedly she pleaded with him to end their long-distance relationship, held together by an endless trail of letters and tiring rounds of snatched visits and shared vacations. Repeatedly Jogiches refused. Jealous and suspicious of her success, he was reluctant to give up his conspiratorial ways, reluctant to leave Switzerland for Berlin, reluctant to set up the "peaceful and regular" daily life together that she so desired. Eventually the relationship degenerated into one of bickering quarrels and stubborn refusals on both sides to back down. Luxemburg repeatedly scolded Jogiches for his asceticism, for his failure to recognize and partake in the vitality of "real life."[159]

Desperately she yearned for a home of their own, nice furniture, their own library, a small circle of friends, and "perhaps even a little, a very little baby? Will this never be allowed?"[160] So "unbearable" was Luxemburg's painful maternal need that for a time she seriously considered adoption. The end of her relationship with Jogiches, however, quashed these plans as well.

After her falling out with Jogiches, Luxemburg made at least two other attempts to fulfill her lifelong vision of combining love and work, one with Konstantin Zetkin, the son of her friend Clara, and the other with a mild-mannered army physician named Hans Diefenbach. Neither relationship, however, could compare in its emotional and intellectual intensity with the fierce intimacy of her earlier partnership. Despite the great discrepancy in age between Luxemburg and Zetkin—she was 14 years his senior—the relationship, for a time, satisifed her deepest emotional needs. Zetkin gave her the love, respect, attention, and adoration she had always wanted. There was also a maternal side to Luxemburg's affection. She picked out Zetkin's clothes, and helped him with his work and education. The affair, however, died quietly when she grew to suspect that the relationship was "stifling" him. Luxemburg also sensed the silent disapproval of Konstantin's mother Clara. Like so many other socialists of this generation, the German feminist, for all her revolutionary proclamations, also continued to be imprisoned by the mores of the past and never quite accepted the intimacy between her long-time friend and her twenty-two year old son.[161]

Luxemburg's romance with Diefenbach held much greater promise. Although he had been a would-be suitor for years, it was only during the war years that Luxemburg came to appreciate his shy and sensitive nature. The two shared interests in many areas, and friends suspected they would marry after the war's end. They had "a thousand plans for the time after the war," plans to travel, read, enjoy life, and "marvel at spring as never before." In her prison letters to Diefenbach, Luxemburg painted a beautiful picture of the domestic tranquillity of their future lives together.[162] News of his death in action, therefore, came as a terrible blow. In prison, Luxemburg had resolved to live life to its fullest as soon as she was free.[163] She was never able to keep that promise.

V

With the crushing defeat of the Spartacist uprising, the forces of order in postwar Germany sought desperately to consolidate their power, brutally determined to root out all remnants of chaos and mayhem. Counterrevolutionary groups targeted both Liebknecht and Luxemburg as the forces singlehandedly behind the revolutionary maelstrom of the past months, and rumors proliferated that a price had been put on their heads by a number of Berlin's paramilitary organizations. Certainly, there were "men enough willing to shoot them," testified a contemporary observer.[164] While the question of premeditation or complicity on the part of the German government has never been answered, that government certainly did nothing to defuse the murderous climate in which Liebknecht and Luxemburg feared for their lives.

Few crime sagas are as sensational or vicious as the all-too-real account of this pair's last hours. Sleeping in different hotel rooms every night, they refused to leave Germany, loathe to save themselves through an ignominious escape. Hunted down like criminals, the Spartacist leaders were finally discovered in their hiding places in a middle class section of Berlin. Arrested on January 15, 1919, they were taken to the Eden Hotel, the headquarters of one of the counterrevolutionary, paramilitary organizations with which postwar Germany was rife. There, Liebknecht was summarily shot and murdered in cold blood, while a fate even more heinous awaited Red Rosa. Hit in the head with a rifle butt, the semiconscious Luxemburg was dragged into a waiting car and shot, her body then unceremoniously dropped from a bridge into the waters of the Landwehr Canal. Leo Jogiches also met assassination in his heroic attempt to discover and publish the truth about her savage end.

Virtually the entire Berlin press regarded the brutal murders as "having something of divine justice in it." Liebknecht and Luxemburg had gotten their due for leading the workers in senseless revolt. Even *Vorwärts*, the official organ of the SPD, shared these sentiments. The death of Liebknecht and Luxemburg "was the result of their appeal to the lowest passions and violence." "Red Rosa," full of "fire, vigor, and hatred," had "fallen victim to the basest passions which she herself had engendered."[165]

Others, however, saw Luxemburg in a different light. To these she was not a bloodthirsty fury but a heroine, a martyr to that cause to which she had devoted her entire life. "The world brotherhood of workers is the highest and most sacred thing on earth to me," she had once written. "It is my guiding star, my ideal, my fatherland. I would rather lose my life than be untrue to this ideal."[166] Luxemburg sincerely believed self-sacrifice to be an essential part of the socialist creed.[167] Martyrdom had always appealed to her. "I hope to die at my post," she had written while in prison.[168] The murderous hordes of barbarous postwar Germany gave Luxemburg that opportunity.

And so Rosa Luxemburg became a martyr in the socialist pantheon, a tragic heroine like Eleanor Marx. Her picture came to adorn German Communist meeting halls and party offices, even as the party she had reluctantly helped to found moved farther and farther away from the ideals that had been her inspiration.

Luxemburg's death deprived the KPD of the one person who might have stood up to Lenin and prevented the total Bolshevization of the German party. In the last months of her life, she had warned her followers against accepting dictation from Moscow. Her successors in the KPD, however, lacked her courage, idealism, and fierce independence. As the party came under the command of less independent-minded individuals, the few remaining heirs of the Luxemburgist tradition soon fell from grace, and the Russification of the KPD proceeded apace.[169]

The key reason for the Bolshevization of all the parties that comprised the new Third International was that Bolshevik success set the Russians apart from the struggling Communist parties of Europe, the KDP foremost among them. Lenin's revolution had succeeded; Luxemburg's had not. No matter how much Luxemburg might be praised for her valiant, heroic, sacrificial struggle, the revolution she had attempted had failed, and, in the end, its failure was attributed to her refusal to create in Germany an elite vanguard party based on the Russian model.[170] Hailed as a martyr, Luxemburg became a symbol without substance in the Communist world, an "eagle" in Lenin's own words,[171] one deserving of praise in all areas except those in which she had defended a view different from his.[172]

Although Lenin himself had always respected Luxemburg's intellectual ability and revolutionary ardor, he was quick to assail "pompous Rosa" whenever she had the temerity to challenge his ideological authority with her "childish" and "ridiculous" interpretations of Marxism.[173] Upon her death, he eagerly enumerated her errors:

> Rosa Luxemburg was mistaken over the question of Polish independence. She was mistaken in 1903 in her evaluation of Menshevism. She was mistaken in her theory of the accumulation of capital. She was mistaken when . . . she stood for the unification of the Bolsheviks with the

Mensheviks in July 1914. She was mistaken in her writings from prison in 1918.[174]

Most of all, of course, she was mistaken in her "not-to-be-taken-seriously nonsense of organization and tactics as a process."[175] Certainly Lenin's "active" view of revolutionary creation was decidedly superior to Luxemburg's "passive" one. Through her "disastrous" and "gross" mistakes, by her own "disorganized view of organization," she had created a "utopian radical" but not a Marxist party.[176]

As Moscow's influence in the German Communist Party grew throughout the 1920s, Luxemburg's theoretical influence was denounced as a "syphilitic bacillus."[177] With Stalinization, "Luxemburgist" and "Trotskyite" came to be equivalent terms, both denoting deviant and dangerous theoretical heresies. Although an official biography as well as a collection of Luxemburg's works appeared in East Germany in 1951, both carefully annotated her errors. Praising Luxemburg the valiant martyr, her official biographer firmly insisted that "we love her on account of her ruthless struggle on behalf of the workers . . . but we cannot lose sight of her errors."[178]

While assassination made Rosa Luxemburg a martyr and tragic symbol, the posthumous publication of her letters from prison served to foster the legend that "Red Rosa" was not a fierce and committed revolutionary at all, but a gentle and romantic figure. These letters, as well as hagiographic reminiscences by close friends, threatened to create a sentimentalized image of the real Rosa Luxemburg, a picture of a childlike, simple, and passionate woman who loved flowers, nature, and babies, who cried for suffering bison and dead wasps.[179] Recent attempts to emphasize her "feminine" side by calling attention to her romantic involvement with Jogiches have served the same purpose. Neither image, however, suffering martyr or lovelorn saint, must be allowed to mythologize Rosa Luxemburg's real revolutionary achievements or theoretical contributions, her insistence on a humane socialism freed from political corruption and opportunism, or her trenchant criticisms of Bolshevik methods and terror.

The greatest Luxemburgist myth of all, however, is that which persists in saluting her as a full-blown symbol of female achievement in the revolutionary world. She is the greatest token woman of the socialist pantheon, history's best-known example of the accomplished political woman. Yet the isolation, scorn, derision, and loneliness that constantly accompanied her on her road to greatness are, unfortunately, not as well known. No socialist party of her day—least of all the SPD—ever paved the way for her on her path to success, or made that journey easier or less threatening.

Rosa Luxemburg's fame and place in history resulted from her sheer intellectual superiority and immense passion for work. She really lived the words of her favorite motto: "Man must live like a candle, burning at both ends."[180] Tragically, she never held the power or influence within the SPD that her posthumous reputation would seem to warrant. Her contemporary fame always remained a begrudged fame—and it is this facet of Rosa Luxemburg's revolutionary career, not the simple fact of her fame alone, that deserves to be remembered.

Chapter • Four

Angelica Balabanoff

The Female Revolutionary
as Pariah

I

Women embraced revolutionary socialism for a variety of reasons. Although "socialism of the head" may aptly describe Rosa Luxemburg's attraction to the socialist cause, not all women—and certainly not all men—came to the movement propelled by the same lofty intellectual considerations. The stronger emotional appeal of a "socialism of the heart" better explains the motivations of many socialist men and women whose fame and contributions never approached the gigantic dimensions of Luxemburg's.

Angelica Balabanoff took her place among the countless women who adopted revolutionary socialism from purely humanistic inclinations, women who became tireless workers for the cause, doing the thousands of thankless tasks that rendered their names mere footnotes to history. An analysis of her career provides a useful illustration of the kinds of ideals that she, and other women like her, hoped to bring to international socialism—ideals like selflessness, brotherhood, and peace that would prove to be sorely lacking in the socialist world of the early twentieth century.

Curiously, however, Balabanoff's contributions to the international socialist cause make her deserving of a far better treatment than has been accorded her by historians. She was more than a mere footnote to history. A true internationalist, she was among the best-known figures of European socialism in the first two decades of the twentieth century. Active in the Italian Socialist Party (PSI) in the critical prewar period, she became one of the central actors in the PSI's determined search for an international socialist response to the Great War. Bolstered by the support given her by the PSI, she assumed a starring role in the Zimmerwald movement, the ill-fated socialist crusade for peace during the war years. After the Bolshevik Revolution, she returned for a brief time to her Russian homeland where, contemporaries acknowledged, she was the "second most important" woman in the new Russia after Alexandra Kollontai.[1]

Despite these achievements, Balabanoff remains in a strange historiographical position. Due to the wide-ranging nature of her activities, her name appears and reappears in histories of international socialism, but no attempt has yet been made to analyze and isolate the precise nature of her contributions. Although her widely published memoirs and recollections have been used and reused to cast light on both contemporary events and political personalities, no biographer has sought to use her recollections as the starting point for a serious and complete analysis of Balabanoff's own career itself.[2] When she is given fleeting mention by historians, it is usually in a deprecatory tone. She has commonly been depicted as an ugly, dowdy, prudish, and hysterical woman "without a trace of humor," and quick summations of her career are plagued by distortions and generalizations.[3] The most frequent and troubling of these recalls her as Mussolini's "Marxist tutor," the woman who "launched" *Il Duce* on his notorious path to fame[4] —a dubious and undeserved distinction that certainly serves to cast her in a very unfavorable light.

In the face of all these sins of omission and commission both, it is not surprising that no attempt has ever been made to place Balabanoff's career into a larger context, or to demonstrate how she compared with other women who were also attracted to revolutionary socialism in this same period. Commonalities exist, however, and they exist in abundance.

As a woman born in late-nineteenth-century Russia, Balabanoff was bred in the tradition of both Alexandra Kollontai and Rosa Luxemburg, and she followed in the footsteps of hundreds of rebellious, independent-minded nihilist and populist women who made of revolutionary politics a personal statement.[5] For many of these women, and for Balabanoff in particular, the personal freedom obtained through participation in the revolutionary movement was always just as important as the political and revolutionary theories they embraced in the process. Certainly the existence of a heritage of female revolutionary involvement in Russia made it all the easier for Balabanoff to satisfy her need for personal emancipation within that context.

Although she was first inspired by the Russian heritage, the peripatetic Balabanoff chose to work for the achievement of socialism not in Russia but in Italy, for whose spirit and people she felt a kind of "mystical attraction."[6] Her involvement in the Italian Socialist Party was the central, formative, political experience of her life. While the Russian tradition molded, shaped, and formed her earliest perceptions of options available to her as a young woman, Balabanoff flourished in her adopted homeland because the Italian cultural tradition also recognized and encouraged the political involvement of women.[7]

To speak of the existence of such a tradition is not necessarily to challenge the standard depiction of a staunchly and oppressively patriarchal Italian culture where, even in the late nineteenth century, "Arabian oriental" conceptions of women still prevailed.[8] Buttressed by the powerful grip that Roman Catholicism held over the popular imagination, law, customs, and traditions all served to keep Italian women subordinate and suppressed, in sexual ignorance and maternal bliss. Both a notorious sexual double standard and an abysmally low female educational level kept the average Italian woman immersed in the glorious sanctity of family life. In the absence of intellectual and companionate bonds between husband and wife, the "backward" Italian woman became so attached to her children that, in the words of one nineteenth-century observer, "she too often finished by making herself their slave."[9]

Yet the model of the learned, highly intelligent, and astute political woman was also not unknown in the Italian context. Although recent research has begun to discount the familiar notion that men and women did enjoy absolute equality in the heady days of the Italian Renaissance,[10] the image of the respected and admired Renaissance "virago" remains a very real one nonetheless. Ambitious "warrior women," women with "qualities of virility" like Beatrice d'Este, Catarina Sforza, and Vittoria Colonna have endured as central characters in the Italian political tradition.[11] Italian folklore also assigned a high place of honor to one Lucia Rosso, a mystical Joan-of-Arc-type heroine, who saved the day in a rebel insurrection against the Venetian Doge in 1310.[12]

Italian universities were never peremptorily closed to women, and the highly educated upper class woman of the salon tradition always played a major role in Italian intellectual life.[13] The heroes of the *Risorgimento* drew attention to this fact, maintaining that the regeneration of a united Italy could never proceed without women's support. Both Mazzini and Garibaldi excited the female imagination and urged women to work for the cause of unification.[14] Once nationhood was achieved, Italian feminism as a movement was itself born from the recognition that educated women could make significant and much-needed contributions to the future of the new Italy.

Even more important to Angelica Balabanoff's acceptance by the Italian socialist movement were the critical needs faced by that movement itself, a movement in many ways like the Russian, which could not afford the luxury of discriminatory sex barriers. Italian socialism actually rose to prominence due to the weaknesses and failures of the long-awaited *Risorgimento*, which, unfortunately, had not brought the grand and glorious social republic promised by Mazzini and his followers. The glaring inability of the new Italian state to solve the social question provided fertile ground for socialist propagandists championing the need for a second revolution to atone for the sins of the first.

But was this to be a peasant rebellion, a conspiratorial putsch, a millenarian uprising, or a disciplined workers' movement? Because the unevenness of Italian economic development made a strictly proletarian uprising unfeasible if not impossible,[15] self-proclaimed socialists of all stripes argued bitterly as to the form the hoped-for revolution should take. What came to unite all those claiming to be socialists was not theoretical consistency but the ethical fervor of their common creed.[16] From the first, the essence of Italian socialism was its missionary ardor and its religious ethic translated from the Catholic context, its vision of an uplifting sacrificial crusade on behalf of the exploited and inarticulate.

In a nation where the development of primary education was a slow and painful process, a nation with a tragically high illiteracy rate persisting well into the twentieth century, what the socialist movement needed above all else were exciting and enthusiastic orators and agitators, committed and dedicated individuals whose talent lay not in the ethereal realms of abstruse theory but in the passionate preaching of the socialist faith to simple and ill-educated masses badly in need of redemption. Furthermore, the fact that the Italian working classes, from their earliest attempts at self-organization, had shown themselves to be decidedly suspicious of "uncommitted bourgeois intellectuals" served to reinforce the emotional, nontheoretical emphasis of the developing Italian socialist movement.[17] Insofar as Angelica Balabanoff's talent lay in her ability to communicate her own intensely emotional understanding of socialism in simple terms to simple people, she found ready acceptance in a movement greatly in need of such individuals, male or female.

Perceptively analyzing its real needs, the PSI not only devalued theory and theoretical achievements but was content to draw its own revolutionary credo from foreign sources. Foreign influences had long played a critically important role in Italian intellectual life, and both anarchism and socialism came to Italy as imported doctrines. Attracted by the revolutionary potential of Italian nationalism, the Russian anarchist Michael Bakunin spent years there, and his unique brand of socialism exerted a powerful impact on a nation whose embryonic industrialization guaranteed that orthodox Marxism would be slow in taking root.[18] With the defeat of the Paris Commune, battered and disillusioned Communards like Benoît Malon and Paul Brousse took refuge in Italy, bringing with them more developed French notions of revolutionary creation.[19] Malon's intellectual influence proved especially critical, because his emphasis on a "humanitarian socialism" based on considerations of "right and justice" blended nicely with the moral, nontheoretical tenor of Italian socialist thought.[20] German exiles fleeing Bismarck's repressive antisocialist legislation also found solace in Italy, and their influence, coupled with the enormous intellectual prestige enjoyed by the SPD itself, caused the leaders of the PSI consciously to model their infant party on the German example.[21]

Accustomed to accepting revolutionary guidance from foreigners, the tolerance of the Italian Socialist Party extended to women as well. One of the most renowned intellectual figures of the PSI in its early years was Anna Kuliscioff,[22] the Russian-born, German-trained wife of socialist leader Filippo Turati. Together Turati and Kuliscioff founded and edited the review *Critica Sociale*, the highly acclaimed journal whose establishment in 1891 marked the real flowering of Marxist socialism in Italy.

Searching for a role in this context, Angelica Balabanoff was spared the humiliating xenophobia that Rosa Luxemburg experienced in Germany.[23] As a foreigner Balabanoff was not only accepted but also genuinely and highly respected for the contributions it was hoped she could make to an Italian cause much in need of individuals with her sincerity, energy, and vigorous proselytizing fervor.

II

Born to a wealthy Jewish family in the Ukraine in 1878, Angelica Balabanoff reacted early in life against the smothering and overprotected lifestyle characteristic of Russian women of her class in the nineteenth century. Although her childhood evidences many similarities with the lives of the other women considered in this study, especially Kollontai's, what distinguishes her autobiographical recollections from theirs is the centrality of the rebel image, the constant emphasis and reemphasis on her seemingly innate rebellious temperament. To accept her reminiscences at face value is to believe that Angelica Balabanoff was a born revolutionary.[24]

Unlike the case of Rosa Luxemburg, however, it was not Balabanoff's Jewishness that first alerted her to injustice, oppression, and evil in the world. Never having attended public schools, she never faced the sting of prejudice and discrimination that radicalized the young Polish woman. Balabanoff never mentioned her Jewish heritage as having had any effect on her political or revolutionary consciousness, and she never dealt with the question of her Jewishness in any of her writings. Her later rejection of her religious birthright appears to have been simply part and parcel of her rejection of everything having to do with her privileged background. Neither does it appear that she inherited political or political-religious awareness from her parents, both of whom she described as apolitical types.

Balabanoff neglected to consider the many factors possibly responsible for her political consciousness because she was so strong and vehement as to the sole cause of her revolutionary temperament: "the unbridgeable abyss" between her mother and herself. This woman, she wrote, "ruled my life and for me personified all despotism."[25] Her mother assumed such great importance because her father, a prosperous landowner and businessman, was "very absorbed" in his work and died when Balabanoff was ten. While other memories of her father were dim, Balabanoff adamantly insisted that the only quarrels she had ever had with him were those her mother provoked.[26] Because her mother took full charge of her personal development, it was she who suffered the full force of Balabanoff's wrath.

Balabanoff depicted her childhood as lonely and oppressive. As the youngest of 16 children, she was excessively sheltered and fussed over, forbidden to attend public school or to have playmates her own age. Her parents had great hopes for their last unmarried daughter. Groomed to be the "crown of the household," she was educated by a succession of governesses in the fine arts of becoming a "great lady" and was expected to marry well. From an early age, however, Balabanoff greatly resented these efforts to mold her life in a proper and traditional direction. Her recollections of her girlhood were no more than a litany of conflicts and confrontations with her overbearing mother—conflicts over prosaic matters like practicing her piano lessons, drinking milk, and taking cod liver oil, or over weightier ones like being allowed to attend public school. Most of all, she grew to despise her mother's excessive preoccupation with what constituted proper gentility, and her slavish attention to the dictates of public opinion. Her home was a "prison," she decreed, her mother unreasonable and domineering, her governesses "futile," superficial, and unintelligent.

Because of their recurring quarrels, Balabanoff came to identify with all those who were also the victims of her mother's rage: the household servants and laborers on the family's palatial estate. Her coming to social consciousness was in many ways similar to Kollontai's. Angered by her mother's supercilious manner and total lack of regard for "human dignity," the young Balabanoff was puzzled by the chain of obedience and command she saw operating at first hand in her own little world. Why, she wondered, "were some born to command and others to obey?"[27] She cringed with shame when the servants kissed the hem of her parents' clothes, or knelt before them in fawning solicitude.

Remnants of a social conscience were implanted in the young girl not only through her daily dealings with servants but also through regular visits to the local poorhouse, a common philanthropic activity of leisured upper class women. Here she was overjoyed that she could play the role of a young "Lady Bountiful," distributing clothes, gifts, and food to the unfortunates who flocked around her.[28] One of the highlights of Balabanoff's youth was the day she gave a silk scarf to a shivering beggar woman. The only repayment she desired was that she be allowed to kneel before the woman and kiss her hand. In this way, she believed, she was able to establish in a small way a kind of "balance between those who were able to give and those who were compelled to receive."[29]

Impatient and eager to understand why poverty and opulence could coexist side by side, Balabanoff searched for someone able to explain the mysteries of this "terrible injustice," but no one—neither her mother, her governesses, nor the instructors at the elite girls' boarding school she attended—could furnish a satisfactory explanation. As her search grew more restless, the keynotes of her adolescence became a tremendous burden of guilt over her privileged lifestyle and a gnawing sense of duty toward the unfortunate. Anxious to give "meaning" to her life, she came to hate her luxurious and conventional routine, determined to break away from the "futile, egotistical, and parasitic" destiny that her mother had mapped out for her.[30]

Ironically, for all her obsession with traditional femininity, Balabanoff's mother had in a curious way also provided her daughter with an important model of activist female behavior. She was a shrewd and successful businesswoman herself, and Balabanoff often recalled with pride how she had watched her mother bargain with the tenant farmers to whom she rented orchards on the family's large estate. Though Balabanoff was never on good terms with the woman, she also secretly admired her. She admitted that her mother had a "certain sharp intelligence" that was highly attractive, and she always preferred her company to that of her simple-minded governesses.[31]

In this way Balabanoff came to realize that by pursuing some kind of independent career she might be able to accomplish the many goals she had set for herself in life. Although raised to be a leisured lady, she did have one definite marketable skill: a talent and facility with languages. She was fluent in at least five. Trained at a fashionable Swiss language school for young women, she was once told that she might make a good teacher, and from then on the word "teacher" became synonymous for her with her dream of escape.[32] For two years she gave private language lessons to girls preparing to enter universities outside Russia, and slowly, in her own way, she realized that university education might enable her to combine her own very real needs for personal freedom with her burgeoning sense of duty toward the unfortunate.

Although she had never met an anarchist or socialist, she had heard that "there were revolutionary men and women who sacrificed their lives for the liberty and welfare of the poor and oppressed." While she knew that she wanted to live with the poor, she "did not know how to be useful to them," but university life, she was convinced, would reveal this to her. With the decision to pursue her education, Balabanoff embarked on that familiar route to emancipation common to radical women of her generation. Giving up all claims to her inheritance and eager to live "like a working girl," she left Russia in 1897. Her last memory connected with her mother, she bitterly recalled, "was her curse upon me."[33]

Because Balabanoff was the first to recognize that her political ideas were markedly undeveloped, she purposely chose not to enroll at the highly politicized University of Zurich, the alma mater of both Luxemburg and Kollontai. Her choice, instead, was the somewhat bohemian milieu of the New University of Brussels, a recent addition to European intellectual life.[34] Several years earlier, the founders of the New University had broken away from the Free University of Brussels in a controversy over academic freedom, and the young institution was gradually acquiring a reputation as a center of free thought and tolerance for a host of political opinions. In the stimulating cosmopolitan atmosphere of Brussels life, the highly impressionable and somewhat timid Balabanoff flourished, reveling in the personal liberty and freedom she had long been seeking. Befriended by Russian and Italian émigrés—with whom, she claimed, she felt an immediate "mystical bond of sympathy"[35] she also met many prominent figures of the Second International, which was headquartered in Brussels, and of the Belgian socialist and labor movements. Taking courses in labor history and tactics, Balabanoff regarded her education in humanistic, not theoretical, terms, seeing it as an important preparation for her great mission "to defend the have-nots against the haves."[36] By 1898 she already considered herself a Marxist.[37]

After two years of study at Brussels, Balabanoff chose to continue her socialist education at universities in London, Leipzig, and Berlin. The most important educational experience of her life, however, occurred at the University of Rome, where she enrolled on the advice of a fellow Russian émigré. There Balabanoff came under the spell of the eminent Neapolitan philosopher Antonio Labriola,[38] and it was his emotional vision of socialism, not the more rigorous political and economic variant of Marx and Engels, that proved to be the decisive intellectual influence on her life and work.

As a writer, teacher, and lecturer, Labriola sought to reconcile the spontaneity of the Italian revolutionary tradition with Marxism as a political movement. Hoping both to infuse "effete" parliamentary socialism with revolutionary fervor and to inspire Italian intellectuals with his ideals, he instructed his students in the role they, as intellectuals, should play in the achievement of socialism. In his view, the socialist intellectual should assume the part not of awesome leader but of patient teacher, one who always remembered that his primary obligation was to the people he served. Society, he simply explained, was divided into exploited and exploiters, "and those . . . who choose to fight with the former against the latter are fulfilling a generous noble task."[39] Longing to inflame his students with his sense of mission, Labriola routinely concluded his lectures with these stirring words—words that made a profound impact on the idealistic and impressionable Balabanoff. She found in Labriola intellectual justification for the moral fervor that had always been at the core of her radicalization. Throughout her life, her favorite maxim came not from Marx and Engels but from him. His credo—"to put knowledge at the service of the proletariat"[40] —became her watchword.

As a result of her personal friendship with Labriola, Balabanoff found the "great cause" to which she hoped to dedicate her life. Anxious to involve herself in propaganda work, she knew she could never return to Russia, for she had neither talent nor inclination for the underground conspiratorial activities that formed the backbone of the Marxist movement there. Considering her intellectual debt to Labriola, her decision to join the Italian Socialist Party was simply the "next logical step" in her personal development.[41]

Balabanoff easily and quickly realized where her talents could best be put to use. Her eagerness to work among Italian emigrants in Switzerland was motivated by two factors: Labriola's own special interest in the question of emigrant labor and her own personal experiences. On her girlhood travels with her family, Balabanoff had witnessed first hand the plight of the displaced Italian laborer. From unification to World War I, wholesale emigration was one of the most important features of Italian political life. Beginning in the last decades of the nineteenth century, hordes of Italian men and women routinely left Italy for economic reasons, seeking temporary or seasonal employment in burgeoning industrial centers elsewhere in Europe, most commonly in Switzerland.[42] "Despised by everyone," treated as a caste apart, Italian emigrants did the heaviest, most dangerous and degrading work, digging ditches and dynamiting tunnels in the Alpine playground of Europe's rich.[43]

One of the most important centers for Italian emigrants in Switzerland was the area around St. Gall, and it was here that Balabanoff began her earliest agitational efforts. It was a perfect milieu for someone with her inclinations and talents. The fluidity of émigré life demanded agitators whose strength lay elsewhere than in rigorous political and theoretical skills, for emigrants, cut off from a day-to-day political movement, had no clearly defined political status. What was needed were enthusiastic speakers who could explain to this powerful labor reserve army the basic moral tenets of the socialist creed, the ideals of comradeship and fraternity, the need to join unions, and the urgency of solidarity in times of strike. The abysmal living conditions of the emigrants also mandated that the socialist agitator play the role of social worker, instructing audiences in the dangers of alcohol and in the value of proper diet and personal hygiene. Balabanoff's fluency in languages, evangelical fervor, simple oratorical style, and individualistic conception of socialist salvation all contributed to her success as an agitator within this context.[44]

Like Marx and Kollontai before her, Balabanoff also realized the urgent necessity of recruiting women to the socialist cause. Certainly there was much to be done in this area, for after the turn of the century, Swiss industrialists had actively recruited Italian girls to work in their textile, chocolate, shoe, and rag factories. Young women were an especially docile labor force, willing to work longer hours and for lower wages than both native Swiss and Italian men.

Propaganda and organizational work among these emigrant women was Balabanoff's most important contribution to the Swiss labor movement. Along with a socialist schoolteacher named Maria Giudice, the successfully organized a model union in St. Gall and published a special propaganda paper for women. The editors of *Su, Compagne!* sought not only to touch the personal lives of their women readers—Balabanoff, for example, launched a furious crusade against the horrors of the corset—but also attempted to raise their political consciousness by urging them to join forces with their men in the class struggle.

Balabanoff's agitational and journalistic efforts were immensely successful. Her powerful oratory inspired semiliterate women to write poignant reports for *Su, Compagne!*, describing the barbaric conditions under which they labored, and her rigorous exposé of the so-called *Mädchenheime* system prompted an official government inquiry into the oppressive living conditions in these worker-convents run by religious orders.[45]

Her success in these and other areas soon drew her to the attention of the Italian Socialist Party in Switzerland (PSIS). Although affiliated with the PSI, this organization had been formed specifically to deal with the particular problems of political life among Italian emigrants. In 1904 Balabanoff was elected to its Executive Committee; in 1907 and again in 1910 she was delegated its official representative to the Stuttgart and Copenhagen Congresses of the Second Socialist International.

By far, however, the most significant—or notorious—event of Balabanoff's Swiss sojourn was her meeting and resulting friendship with the young Benito Mussolini, then an itinerant adventurer with socialist pretensions who had fled his native Italy to avoid the draft. The pair met in Lausanne in 1903, at a socialist party meeting where Balabanoff was the principal speaker. While her oft-repeated story of how this "wretched and miserable" human being attracted her attention may perhaps be overdrawn,[46] her analysis of their relationship is quite useful for what it reveals both about her personality and about her heartfelt vision of socialist humanitarianism.

The "agitated" manner of the unkempt vagrant who had come to hear her speech aroused Balabanoff's greatest pity and sympathy. Advising him to study the tenets of the socialist creed he professed, she offered to help him in any way she could. When Mussolini expressed amazement and skepticism at her genuine interest in his welfare, Balabanoff explained in simple terms the motivations and yearnings that brought her to socialism. Mussolini, she explained, was "living proof" of what environment did to one who had not had all the advantages she had had. She was actually grateful to him because he gave her an opportunity to test her socialist faith, a chance to atone for the privileges of her youth, "to make up a little for a great injustice." She welcomed the chance to help him, she insisted, because she felt the need "to repay not only the working class but each individual belonging to it." Their lives were similar, she concluded. "I escaped because I had too much. You ran away because you had too little. But now socialism unites our efforts."[47]

Balabanoff began her personal mission of salvation by helping Mussolini translate a copy of Karl Kautsky's *The Coming Revolution*, a job for which he had been offered 50 francs. Interested in both his personal and political development, she lent him socialist books and pamphlets, introduced him to comrades at local socialist clubs, tried to find him employment, and attempted to temper his wild, egotistical, and unfocused anger. There her "tutelage" ended.

While it is true that Balabanoff aided Mussolini at a critical period of his life, the story of their relationship has been distorted and misrepresented on both sides. After Mussolini's fascist triumph, she wrote several accounts of their earlier relationship. In these she probably exaggerated the despondency of the "syphilitic, nervous, and filthy" comrade who exacted her pity so that her "role" in his rise to infamy might be minimized if not justified. Others, however, tilted the scales in the opposite direction. To christen Balabanoff "Mussolini's benefactress," or to single her out as "the woman who more than any other shaped his life"[48] is to shackle her with a kind of guilt by association of which she, in her good faith and boundless idealism, stands undeserved.

Mussolini was eventually expelled from Switzerland when, as a rising—and redeemed—socialist revolutionary, his violent anticlerical and antimilitarist denunciations were termed a threat to peace. He was later to meet and work with Balabanoff again, however, in the Italian Socialist Party, where both were to find their "spiritual home."

III

Angelica Balabanoff left her political adolescence behind her in 1910, when she decided to leave Switzerland and return to Italy. The transfer was necessary she believed, to complete the "intimate fusion" between her work for the Italian proletariat and for the Italian Socialist Party.[49] Actually her interests had really been drawing her more and more toward Italy for some time. Funds had run out for her paper, *Su, Compagne!*, she had had some misunderstandings with the leaders of the PSIS over the responsibilities of her role as delegate to the Stuttgart Congress,[50] and a growing dissatisfaction with the unstable character of émigré political life all may have played a part in convincing her to relocate.

The struggle among party factions was the dominant characteristic of the party Angelica Balabanoff came to join.[51] Factionalism was deeply rooted in Italian political history, and the development of socialism in Italy was no exception to this rule. Diverse strands of revolutionary thinking—Mazzinian republicanism, Bakuninite anarchism, peasant millenarianism, and Labriolan Marxism—had all merged to create a socialist movement in Italy.

The Italian Socialist Party officially considered itself to be a revolutionary party,[52] but from the start it was plagued not only by the diversity of the Italian revolutionary tradition and the unevenness of Italian economic development, but also by the same kinds of battles between reformists and revolutionaries that were already beginning to scar the major socialist parties of Europe. For a time the PSI prospered under the humanitarian leadership of its grand old man, Filippo Turati, and managed to create a spurious unity between its right, left, and center wings. "Neither to the right nor left but straight ahead" was the proud motto of the integralists,[53] for whom party unity was always much more important than rigorous and precise theoretical formulations. Strengthened by this creed, the PSI flourished in its early years. Its growth since 1892 was considered nothing short of "sensational." Ten years after its birth, it was the third largest socialist party in Europe.[54]

By 1908, however, the PSI had begun to lose fire. "It was suffering from a precocious old age," wrote a contemporary observer.[55] Under reformist leadership, the party had moved more and more in the direction of a parliamentary party with ever increasing involvement in Italian political life. As socialism became a respectable political force, it lacked vibrancy and dynamism, losing touch with the restless Italian revolutionary tradition that had always inspired it. Sapped of fresh energy as its membership declined, the party was forced to strike a precarious balance between its revolutionary proclamations and daily reformist activities.

The dilemma faced by the PSI was not unlike that confronted by a similarly fence-straddling SPD. Yet, while ever increasing industrial development strengthened socialist reformism in Germany, the corresponding weakness of economic life in Italy contributed to the growing dissatisfaction with the reformist rationale of the PSI. Turati's brand of evolutionary socialism, much akin to Eduard Bernstein's,[56] demanded for its continued success both a state ever responsive to reformist measures and an economy healthy enough to meet the rising expectations of the working classes. By 1910-1912, Italy had neither. Not only did increased military spending by the government threaten the social-reformist program of the PSI, but the downturn in Italy's always "jerky" economic life effectively quashed working class aspirations for the peaceful but successful extortion of concessions in a healthy economic environment. Furthermore, the bifurcated nature of Italian economic development—the continued existence of an industrialized North and a semifeudal South—had never met the demands of the nation's land-hungry peasant masses. For them, revolution and rebellion, not politics, had long appeared to be a ready answer to the miseries of daily life.[57]

When Angelica Balabanoff arrived on the Italian scene in 1910, the latent strength of the revolutionary wing of the PSI was already making itself manifest. Immediately confronted with the stagnant state of socialist political life, she, by natural inclination, was moved to join forces with the revolutionizers against the reformists. Inspired by Labriola's attacks on stagnant and insipid reformism, her brand of socialism had always had a revolutionary core. Because proselytizing fervor was a central component of Balabanoff's Marxism, her frustration with the reformists was understandable. Italian socialism, she was convinced, had lost that all-important spirit of contact with the masses. Speaking at a party congress in Milan soon after her arrival, she linked her own concrete personalistic conception of socialism to the needs of the PSI. To attract new members it was imperative that the party make clear its staunch opposition to the present regime, that it overcome its "parliamentary myopia," and reach out and "touch the masses in their misery."[58] According to Balabanoff, neither wild revolutionism nor government sponsored reformism was the answer to the crisis of Italian socialism. What was needed was a vigorous and determined educational campaign to bring the masses to the side of the movement. Only with popular support could the party harness and channel the innate revolutionary sentiments of the masses, hoping, in the end, to lead them to a successful socialist conclusion.

For the next two years, Balabanoff remained true to her reputation as an indefatigable crusader on behalf of the socialist cause. Beginning her career as a wandering journalist and propagandist around Umbria and Perugia, she devoted her agitational efforts to bringing the masses of unorganized workers into the party. Tireless in her labors as a lecturer and organizer, she became a regular contributor to the prorevolutionary journal *La Soffitta* and continued her propaganda work among women as acting editor of the socialist women's paper *La Difesa delle lavoratrice*. Her most important contributions to Italian socialism were to come after 1912, when she was a member of the revolutionary, so-called intransigent faction that seized control of the PSI.

The event that solidified Italian socialism's swing to the left was the Libyan War, Italy's imperialistic adventure in Northern Africa in 1911–1912.[59] The war for Tripoli, which Italy had long considered to be its rightful share of the decaying Ottoman Empire, wreaked havoc on the PSI, forcing it to take a stand on the nature of its relationship with the existing "bourgeois" state.

Although there was "huge enthusiasm" for the war in Italy, the official policy of the PSI was militant opposition to imperialism in general and to the Italian government's program of colonial conquest in particular. While the socialist rank and file vehemently opposed the war, the party's right-reformist wing had begun to hedge over the question. Arguing for a policy that allowed nationalism "to retain a monopoly of the national sentiment,"[60] reformists suggested that imperialist expansion into backward communities might actually hasten the coming of socialism in the home country, since imperialism carried in its wake the germs of a more mature capitalist development. On top of this ideological heresy, the flirtations of the right wing with government collaboration effectively sealed the fate of the reformist faction. When the reformist leader Leonida Bissolati did not immediately and vehemently refuse Prime Minister Giolitti's invitation to join him in the government, the PSI could no longer afford to gloss over the dangerous discrepancy that had come to exist between its rhetorical declarations and practical political meanderings.

The war gave a new generation of restless young socialists the opportunity to challenge the staid parliamentarians then at the head of the PSI. While Angelica Balabanoff gained renown with her antiwar articles, it was Benito Mussolini who capitalized on the popular spirit of antimilitarism to gain the party's attention. After his expulsion from Switzerland he had returned to Italy, teaching and serving in the army before attaining a measure of success as a socialist journalist. Bitter in his condemnation of the war, he published vituperative articles in the weekly socialist paper he edited in Forli, and spent five months in prison for his participation in the socialist general strike of September 1911, called to protest the imperialist policies of the government.

The publicity Mussolini received from his violent antiwar activities earned him the privilege of becoming the spokesman for the revolutionary faction at the fateful PSI Congress at Reggio Emilia in

July 1912.[61] His youth, bravado, and passion made him a convenient symbol for the militant direction the intransigents hoped to
bring to the PSI. While a split between revolutionaries and reformists
had long been foreshadowed, the revolutionary faction's bold demand for the expulsion of the reformists was precipitated by the
recent ministerial inclinations of Bissolati and his followers. At
Reggio Emilia, the intransigent contingent of Mussolini, Costantino
Lazzari, Giovanni Lerda, Giacinto Serrati, and Angelica Balabanoff
succeeded in winning support for their resolution from a growingly
impatient and revolutionary rank and file.

Balabanoff's role in the expulsion of the reformists was especially
significant. Searching for someone to place the expulsion resolution
before the Congress, intransigent leaders recognized their need for
someone who enjoyed "great moral prestige," someone whom no
one could suspect of being led by sentiments of "personal rancor or
ambition" alone. Easily the choice fell on Balabanoff.

Hers was a sensitive, idealistic, and in some ways prophetic
speech, completely lacking in the aura of bloodletting and vendetta
that motivated Mussolini's cries for expulsion. Although Balabanoff
praised the reformist leaders for their honorable contributions to the
socialist cause, she reminded them that their actions had betrayed
the masses who formed the bedrock of the workers' movement. By
flirting with personal power, by ignoring the needs of the class struggle, and by losing contact with popular antiwar sentiments, the
reformists had forgotten their most basic responsibilities to the
socialist movement. "When the masses disapprove of us," she intoned
sadly, "we have to go." So magnanimous was Balabanoff's speech
that she was congratulated even by members of the defeated and disgraced minority.[62] For her efforts, she won a place on the newly
elected Executive Committee of the PSI.

With their victory at Reggio Emilia, the intransigent faction also
won the right to editorial control over *Avanti!*, one of the largest
socialist papers in Europe. Why the Executive Committee decided
to entrust the editorship of their official organ to the newcomer
Mussolini has never been convincingly resolved. Balabanoff explained
that the reasons for his election were more symbolic than substantive.
Mussolini's reputation as a radical firebrand blended nicely with the
new militant image the PSI was hoping to create. He also did have
considerable journalistic experience. Furthermore, the editorship of
Avanti! had never been regarded as a one-person operation. Mussolini,

it was thought, would simply carry out the editorial and policy decisions promulgated by the PSI's Executive Committee. Balabanoff encouraged Mussolini to accept the appointment. Moved both by her own perception of duty and by the real needs of the party, she believed him to be a sincere and devoted revolutionary who could help put the PSI back on the right radical track.[63] Actually she had no reason to think otherwise.

Mussolini accepted the position on the condition that Balabanoff be named his editorial assistant. Here again, however, the true details of their association have become mired in distortion and exaggeration. Balabanoff insisted that Mussolini's insecurity and need for an advisor with international prestige dictated his decision, while her detractors charge that she "forced herself upon him." In keeping with her heartfelt sense of mission, Balabanoff attributed her own willingness to accept the appointment to her eagerness to serve the proletariat in whatever capacity she might be allowed.[64]

Mussolini and Balabanoff collaborated on *Avanti!* for about eight months. During that time, although the intellectual level of the paper declined as a result of Mussolini's sensationalistic and lively brand of journalism, sales soared and there was a real improvement in the paper's financial status.[65] Both editors decried socialist collaboration in "bourgeois" governments, attacked an exclusively reformist mentality, and believed that only by adopting a tone of vigorous opposition could socialists extract greater concessions from the state at a faster rate. Despite agreement on these issues, however, their partnership was not a happy one. Balabanoff always had an ambivalent ideological and personal relationship with Mussolini. She never harbored the same restless, impatient, quasi-syndicalist impulses that propelled him, but even more importantly, she disliked his rather callous way of dealing with staff and associates. Mussolini routinely left her with all the most unpleasant tasks—refusing articles, dismissing staff members, and defending controversial editorials.[66] Finally she had enough. When Mussolini's abrupt and unfeeling manner touched her old friend Maria Giudice, Balabanoff resigned from her editorial post.[67]

It was World War I that finally and decisively separated Balabanoff from Mussolini's orbit. With the outbreak of the war, both embarked on different paths. Although the PSI decided to remain true to the antimilitarist, antiimperialist tenor of international socialism,[68] Mussolini—whether from a weak will, a real desire for personal power, revolutionary inclinations, or French money—suddenly and

boldly called the nation "to join the vital forces" in the war effort.[69]
His Judas-like *volte-face* on the question of intervention shocked
Balabanoff and the PSI, and he was expelled from both the Party
Executive and his position on *Avanti!*. Even in the wake of Mussolini's
treachery, however, Balabanoff displayed remarkable sensitivity to
the plight of her one-time associate, requesting that he be given a
temporary allowance by the party to support himself and his family
until he found work.[70]

The war came as a tremendous personal blow to Balabanoff's
international socialist faith. It was a "catastrophe," she wrote, a "terrible conflagration," a "bloody abyss which threatened to engulf us
all."[71] Despite the failure of international socialism to prevent the
war, she drew an immense sense of pride from the fact that her
adopted party, the PSI, had remained true to Marxism's internationalist, antimilitarist stance.[72] Even when Italy entered the war in
April 1915, the PSI's parliamentary delegation refused to support the
government's request for war credits, making it, in Lenin's words, "a
happy exception" among the "social-chauvinist" socialist parties of
Europe.[73] "Neither support nor sabotage" remained the policy of
the PSI for the war's duration.

As a respected member of a party whose doctrinal fidelity lent it
renewed international prestige, Angelica Balabanoff embarked on a
new role during the war years. Her central position in the coordination of international socialist efforts to find a peaceful solution to
the war remains the role for which she is still best known, a role that
was highly in keeping with her firm belief in international socialist
solidarity. From the first, Angelica Balabanoff was intimately involved
in the efforts of international socialism to deal with the Great War.

As a representative of the PSI, Balabanoff was a member of the
International Socialist Bureau (ISB), that group which sought to act
as a kind of executive organ for the Second Socialist International.[74]
As the administrative organ of a federated body, however, it was
weak and ineffective, certainly powerless to deal with the imminence
of war. At a hastily summoned meeting in July 1914, Balabanoff's
impatient pleas for "immediate action" fell on deaf ears, as one by
one she saw the leading socialists of Europe fall away from long-
cherished ideals and scurry to support their fatherlands in the war
effort.[75]

After the outbreak of the war, the ISB was paralyzed. Forced to
move its headquarters from Brussels to a neutral country, it was

unwilling to risk the breakup of the International by urging socialists from belligerent countries to take the kind of "decisive action" that might subject them to treason charges at home or opprobrium at the hands of socialist parties suddenly become fiercely nationalistic in the face of the war fever.

Because the ISB was both reluctant and unable to undertake vigorous international leadership, the task of saving what was left of the international workers' movement fell to socialists from neutral countries. From the start, representatives of both the Swiss and Italian parties were the leaders of this effort. Not only did Balaban-off's staunch belief in socialist internationalism make her ideologically appropriate to assume this new role within the PSI, but more importantly, her earlier working relationship with the leaders of the Swiss Socialist Party specially equipped her to be an effective liaison in bilateral peace efforts. At an informal gathering at Lugano in September 1914, Swiss and Italian representatives issued a joint protest against the war, condemning the conflict as a "result of the imperialist policy of the Great Powers."[76]

This initial action by the Swiss and Italian parties became the backbone of the Zimmerwald movement, the socialist peace crusade in which Alexandra Kollontai had also been active.[77] Angelica Balabanoff served the Zimmerwald movement tirelessly from its inception, attending all its meetings and informal gatherings, handling its correspondence, issuing and circulating appeals, and editing its multilingual *Bulletin*. As the elected secretary of Zimmerwald, she served as a member of its executive organ, the International Socialist Commission (ISC). In the face of the paralysis of the ISB, the ISC, with headquarters in Berne, became the mouthpiece of the international socialist movement, hoping to coordinate the pacifist, antiwar activities of "all parties, workers organizations and groups which had remained true to the old principles of the International."[78] The most important of its activities were three international socialist gatherings, held at the Swiss villages of Zimmerwald and Kienthal in 1915 and 1916, and at Stockholm in 1917. Attracting delegates from both neutral and belligerent countries, the successful convocation of these gatherings was itself a noteworthy achievement in time of war.[79]

The primary goal of the Zimmerwald movement was "to restore the Second International and to work for peace."[80] According to Swiss socialist Robert Grimm, a prominent member of the ISC, Zimmerwald had become a symbolic alternative "to the horrors produced by the disintegration of bourgeois civilization."[81] Certainly it was the symbolic nature of the Zimmerwald spirit, with its emphasis on socialist unity, brotherhood, and solidarity, that most appealed to Angelica Balabanoff. She had a deep faith in what Zimmerwald was all about, hailing it as an "international collectivity that had not abandoned its principles, its traditions, its honors, its duty."[82] Balabanoff's vision of Zimmerwald was most apparent at the Kienthal Conference, which ended its deliberations in the early hours of May 1, 1916. Even though the unity of the Conference had been shattered by bitter dissensions between socialists of left and center, Balabanoff remained optimistic, suggesting that the assembled delegates not disband once the conference had concluded its work, but await together the sunrise of International Labor Day, the symbol of working class unity.[83]

In her euphoria, Balabanoff failed to realize not only that the Second International had been irreparably torn asunder by the hatreds of war, but also that socialist calls for peace alone were inadequate to halt the machinery of that war. While most Zimmerwaldians echoed Balabanoff in their optimism and hope, the Left Zimmerwaldians, led by Lenin, opposed the impotent peace slogans of the majority, calling instead for a socialist revolution to end the capitalist war.[84]

Lenin's "splitting tactics" were naturally offensive to someone with Balabanoff's sensibilities. While her estimate of Zimmerwald's potential emphasized hope, his seemed only to exude despair. Highly sensitive to the human suffering wrought by war, tormented by the vision of a Europe that had become a "gigantic human slaughterhouse,"[85] she could not commit herself to a policy that actively called for more slaughter, more starvation, more misery.

Other factors also colored Balabanoff's resistance to the Left's appeal. Scrupulously conscious of her responsibilities as a member of the ISC, she felt bound to support the decisions of Zimmerwald's affiliated parties, the majority of which were centrist, pacifist, and anti-left in tone. Believing strongly in the values of the old International, she desired only its reconstruction, revival, or rebuilding, never its replacement by the new grouping that the proposals of the Left Zimmerwaldians seemed to foreshadow. Finally, and perhaps most importantly, she simply despised the tactics of Lenin and his followers, a dislike that went back to her student days spent among Russian émigrés in Brussels and Switzerland.[86] Balabanoff had never been able to understand why the Russians always "wasted so much time" in polemics. Impatient and disgusted with their "irrelevant, petty bickerings" and inordinate obsession with the minutiae of theory, she was especially shocked to find them again behaving in such a fashion despite the "overwhelming tragedy of the war," when "our movement was so weakened that the purely theoretical decisions of an insignificant minority of intellectuals seemed of so little importance."[87]

Yet it was the tendency represented by the Bolsheviks of the Zimmerwald Left, not by Balabanoff, that proved historically successful. Soon after the March Revolution in Russia, the Zimmerwald movement began to disintegrate. It had really become an anachronism in a world where revolutionary events in the East, not conferences and diplomacy in the West, seemed to hold the best hopes for peace. As Balabanoff's faith in international socialist solidarity proved to be misplaced, she was heartened by news of events in Russia. Once the process of revolution had begun there, she grew anxious to return to the "revolutionary Holy Land," eager to take her place in the ranks of that revolution for which she had yearned so long.[88]

After her return to her homeland, Balabanoff became increasingly absorbed in Russian affairs. Despite her reservations about the Bolsheviks, she joined their party in the summer of 1917, convinced that the "salvation" of the Russian Revolution lay in the tendencies they represented. Both her physical distance from Italy and Italian worries about her new "pro-Bolshevik" orientation dictated her decision to resign from the Executive Committee of the PSI, a post she had continued to hold throughout the war years. In announcing her resignation, she assured her "inconsolable" Italian comrades that her emotional ties to them and their party would always remain intact.[89]

Balabanoff chose to retain her position on the ISC, but this role became more and more problematic in the face both of the disintegration of Zimmerwald itself and of the unscrupulous efforts of Lenin and the victorious Bolsheviks to use the movement for their own purposes. A critical blow to Zimmerwald came in June 1917, when an "indiscretion" on the part of Swiss leader Robert Grimm seemed to offer conclusive proof that the group had always been working for a German victory.[90] The widespread publication of a telegram Grimm had sent to the Swiss Foreign Minister, asking him to inquire on what terms Germany would be willing to make peace, disgraced Zimmerwald as an organization. Lenin's successful revolution proved to be the death blow for the hapless organization.

Nonetheless, Balabanoff persevered in her attempt to reconcile her dual role as Bolshevik and Zimmerwaldian. In the wake of the Grimm affair, she left Russia to attempt to pick up the pieces of the rapidly decaying ISC. Claiming that the Russian Revolution needed international support to survive, she sought to coordinate Zimmerwald propaganda for peace with Bolshevik aims, urging mass action by the international proletariat both to end the war and to save the revolution in Russia. "Will the revolution kill the war, or will the war kill the revoluution?" became the new slogan of the moribund movement.[91] She spoke enthusiastically and frequently at public meetings in Switzerland and Sweden, the two centers of Zimmerwald strength, praising the Russian Revolution and seeking to mobilize working class opinion throughout Europe in its defense. Only further revolution, she asserted, could destroy militarism and capitalism both.[92]

Yet, despite her efforts, Lenin was determined to crush Zimmerwald as an organization. Angrily he condemned it as a "comedy," a "mire" he could no longer stand.[93] Clearly, any organization that welcomed socialists of both left and center, an organization dedicated to the rebuilding of the old International after the war's end, was contrary to Lenin's purposes, for the revival of the Second International would mean the rebirth of an organization in which he and his Bolsheviks had always represented an impotent minority.

For as long, however, as the fate of the revolution in Russia seemed to hang on Western support, Lenin was willing and eager to use the "rotten" Zimmerwald movement "to gather information."[94] Recognizing that its established machinery of international contacts, information networks, and propaganda channels was well suited to meet his needs, Lenin sought to use Zimmerwald—and its "naive" secretary, Angelica Balabanoff—as "windows to the West." Lenin flattered and courted Balabanoff because he felt her international prestige, knowledge, and connections with socialist movements in the West might help him both to gauge and to stimulate the revolutionary tenor of the international working class movement. After its victory in Russia, the Bolshevik Party appropriated money "for aid to the left internationalist wing of the labor movement of all countries."[95] Since Balabanoff believed that her task at this time was to coordinate international propaganda efforts and to instigate mass action in support both of the Bolsheviks and of international revolution, she was shocked to discover that money, not fervent preaching and propaganda, was to supplement her efforts. "Spend millions, tens of millions," Lenin wrote to Balabanoff in Stockholm, where the headquarters of the ISC had been relocated. "There is plenty of money at our disposal."[96]

Balabanoff herself was unwilling to sanction such methods, and the funds that had been apportioned for her use were channelled through other hands. Convinced that the Bolsheviks could neither manufacture international revolution nor impose a communist apparatus from above, she feared lest such tactics antagonize rather than win the confidence of the European working class. Despite her real, intense opposition to "artificial instigation,"[97] Balabanoff came nonetheless to be feared and suspected by anti-Bolshevik forces across Europe. Condemned as that "damned courier of revolution,"[98] she was denied the international mobility that her work for the ISC required. Expelled from Switzerland in 1918 in the wake of national paranoia over the Swiss general strike,[99] she was denied readmittance to Sweden. Returning to Russia in November 1918, she embarked on what was to be the most disheartening and disillusioning phase of her long revolutionary career.

In the wake of calls by the British Labour Party for the revival of the Second International,[100] Lenin and the Bolsheviks acted swiftly to create the new international alignment that had long been central to their thinking. The Third International, or Comintern, was born at a hastily summoned Moscow Congress in March 1919.[101] According to British journalist Arthur Ransome, the only noncommunist observer in attendance at the gathering, there was a "make believe character to the whole affair."[102] Only one delegate, the Spartacist Hugo Eberlein, held a legitimate mandate from a socialist organization.[103] The others, owing to the difficulties of foreign travel and the speed with which the Congress had been assembled, were hand-picked Bolshevik representatives—"profiteers of revolution," Balabanoff called them—adventurers, ex-prisoners of war who had remained in Russia, or foreigners who had long ago lost all contact with their native countries.[104]

In an effort to impart an air of legitimacy to the Congress, Lenin sought to establish the continuity of his new organization with the decaying Zimmerwald movement. Because Balabanoff was the secretary of Zimmerwald and a prominent member of the ISC, she held a central role in his plans, and the proposal was made that she formally transfer Zimmerwald's functions and documents to the new organization. In what proved to be a fateful decision, Balabanoff refused. While she recognized and acknowledged the temporary character of the Zimmerwald movement, an organization born to deal with the temporary war crisis,[105] she insisted on the absolute right of Zimmerwald's affiliated parties to make their own decisions as to its demise. Alone, she had no "moral right" to make decisions in their name. Visibly annoyed by her "legalistic squeamishness,"[106] Lenin and other former members of the Zimmerwald Left simply decreed the "liquidation" of the old organization. "The Zimmerwald Union has outlived its purpose," the Congress resolved. "All that was really revolutionary in it goes over to the Communist International."[107]

Despite Balabanoff's intransigence, Lenin personally selected her to be the secretary of his new organization. Her international reputation and contacts with both the Swiss and Italian parties seemed to lend an aura of international respectability to the exclusively Russian affair. When Balabanoff appeared reluctant to accept a position that seemed to offer limited prospects for contact with the masses, Lenin insisted she obey his wishes. "Party discipline exists for you too, dear comrade. The Central Committee has decided."[108]

The "fraud" that Angelica Balabanoff had seen perpetrated in March 1919 marked the beginning of her disgust, disappointment, and disillusionment with the "amoral" corruption of Bolshevik methods. Next to Mussolini, she came to consider Gregory Zinoviev, the chairman of the Comintern Executive Committee, to be the "most despicable individual" she had ever met.[109] Soon she discovered that her role as Comintern secretary was to be a mere formality, that real decisions were being made elsewhere than at the meetings she was ceremoniously expected to attend. Blinded by her real faith and hope in the new socialist republic, she persevered in her idealistic internationalism, aspiring to win the respect and allegiance of Europe's socialist parties by legitimate means. Tragically, however, Zinoviev's chosen methods were demonstrably different from hers. If the respect and support of existing parties could not be willingly obtained, then bribery, flattery, and the cooption of "vulgar, power-seeking parvenus" could be tools in the arbitrary creation of affiliated parties and labor groups.

Hoping to gain trust, respectability, and prestige from Balabanoff's presence on the Comintern Executive, the new Soviet government persisted in fêting and flattering her through the bestowal of empty titles. Appointed minister of foreign affairs for the Ukraine, Balabanoff was satisfied for a time with the opportunity to do "real work" in this suffering and war-torn region.[110] Making as many as five propaganda speeches a day to win support for the Bolshevik cause in the civil war, she acquired a reputation as being "soft-hearted" because of her efforts to get the prisons opened and to distribute food to all who asked for help. Here again, however, Balabanoff's idealistic attempts to win support for socialism through speeches and deeds contrasted starkly with Bolshevik methods. "Profoundly shocked" by the Red Terror,[111] the "wholesale slaughter" being used to keep the revolution alive, she was shattered most of all by the so-called Pirro incident,[112] Bolshevik use of *agents provocateurs* in the best tsarist manner. In the summer of 1919, one Count Pirro came to Kiev in the guise of a Brazilian ambassador. Making no secret of his antagonism to the Bolsheviks, he was rumored to be able to secure Brazilian passports for those wishing to escape the new republic. When all those accused of contact with Pirro were rounded up and executed, Balabanoff complained to Lenin that she could not understand why nothing was being done against Pirro himself. His only response to her query was utter amazement at her naiveté. "Comrade Angelica," he was reported to have mused, "what use can life make of you?"[113]

Soon afterward, Balabanoff was shocked to receive an official order from the Party Central Committee ordering her to report to a sanatorium for health reasons. Although she was sick, undernourished, and underweight, she was incensed by privilege of any kind and refused to consider the luxury of such special treatment when "thousands of ordinary citizens" were suffering just as seriously as she from the combined ravages of scarcity, inflation, revolution, and war.[114] When she informed the general secretary of the party that she had no intention of going, she was summarily given a new assignment—heading a propaganda mission to Turkestan. Certainly this was a strange task for one considered ill enough for a stint in a sanatorium. Russia's Asian provinces were riddled with typhus, and Balabanoff would clearly be of little assistance in a region with whose language she was unfamiliar.[115] Yet when she balked at this suggestion as well, she was duly rewarded for her "undisciplined" refusals: she was promptly and unceremoniously removed from her post as secretary of the Comintern.

Although she was pained and disillusioned by her rapid fall from grace, Balabanoff nonetheless felt a tremendous sense of liberty at her removal from an organization with whose tactics, aims, and methods she had never agreed.[116] For a time she still hoped to be able to serve the revolution in that individual, "loner" capacity to which she had always been accustomed, but all bonds of loyalty that tenuously held her to the Bolsheviks were irrevocably snapped when the "amoralism" of their "whole system of lies and intrigues" began to threaten her beloved Italian Socialist Party.

Throughout 1919 and 1920, the PSI had been the chief foreign supporter of the new Russian regime.[117] Italian socialists had long harbored sentimental ties of affection for Russian revolutionists, particularly identifying with the Bolsheviks since their antiwar hostility seemed to match the antimilitarist fervor of the PSI. Furthermore, postwar conditions in Italy, of all countries in Europe, best seemed to approximate those existing in revolutionary Russia. Finding itself in the paradoxical position of a vanquished though victorious nation, Italy after the war was gripped by a series of revolutionary convulsions.[118] Waves of social unrest engulfed the country—wholesale land seizures in the countryside, urban riots against the high cost of living, violent strikes and factory occupations. Hoping to follow in the footsteps of their Russian brothers, Italian socialists applauded the Bolshevik example and eagerly entered the Comintern. The first socialist party to join the Third International, the PSI immediately became its largest Western affiliate.

By the time of the second Comintern Congress in July 1920, however, the Bolsheviks demonstrated that they expected more than glowing admiration from their Western supporters. Citing the "danger of dilution by unstable and irresolute elements" that had not yet "completely discarded the ideology of the Second International,"[119] the Congress decreed that continued affiliation with the Third International would from then on be subject to an assortment of restrictions and preconditions known to history as the 21 Points.[120] These called upon all member parties to remove all "reformists" from responsible positions, and to expel all such persons as the Comintern Executive might designate as "enemies."

The preconditions of the 21 Points crippled the Italian party. Although continuing to profess allegiance to the Comintern, PSI leaders demanded a measure of autonomy, refusing to expel many of the party's oldest and most respected members to satisfy Moscow's whim.

Recognizing that it would be unable to control the PSI, Moscow sought to destroy it, by launching a smear campaign against the highly renowned centrist and former Balabanoff protégé Giacinto Serrati.[121] Although Lenin himself had expressed grave doubts about the potential success of a socialist revolution in Italy, communist tacticians nonetheless sought to shackle Serrati with the blame and opprobrium when a massive postwar mass strike movement in Italy collapsed for lack of decisive and responsible leadership. The collapse of this movement was just the proof Lenin needed to demonstrate the validity of his call for a "real Communist Party to act as a vanguard for the revolutionary workers of Italy."[122] Plagued by internal and external difficulties, the spurious unity of the PSI was shattered at the Congress of Leghorn in January 1921,[123] when, through the direct intervention of the Third International, its secessionist left wing boldly proclaimed itself the new Communist Party of Italy (PCI).

It took the full force of the "Italian tragedy" to remove the gleam from Balabanoff's eyes. This revolution, she poignantly realized, had already begun to devour its own children, its first victims those who had been its dearest friends.[124] When Lenin spoke proudly and brazenly of the "destruction of Turati's party," when he sought to destroy the independence of all parties not subservient to his will, when life in Russia had become so "painful" that each succeeding day made Balabanoff appear more and more of an "accomplice," she knew she had had enough of life in the "revolutionary Holy Land." Four-and-one-half years after she had returned "with such hope and eagerness to participate in the consolidation of the Workers Revolution,"[125] Angelica Balabanoff left Russia forever.

IV

There was no place in Lenin's new Russia for one with the sensibilities and sensitivities of Angelica Balabanoff. For her, the regime in power in the Soviet Republic was a "monstrous caricature," a "perversion" of the Marxist spirit, a vile machine that created nothing but "hatred, horror, and illusions."[126] Depressed and tormented by the use of terror, she was appalled by the cheapness with which human life had come to be regarded. Certainly she expected such behavior from "capitalists" who had never appreciated nor respected the full meaning of human dignity,[127] but the use of such weapons by self-proclaimed Marxists came as a tremendous shock to her idealistic, quasi-religious conception of what socialism was all about. The new socialist society, as Balabanoff had always understood it, was to have been a place where violence would be neither necessary nor possible.[128] In Russia, however, violence had not only become a habit but was justified as a necessity. "If one wants the ends, one must also want the means," Trotsky diagnosed,[129] and the pervasive obeisance paid to that odious Machiavellian maxim repulsed and disgusted her.

The gravest error of the Bolshevik regime, Balabanoff believed, was its treacherous betrayal of the masses themselves, those whom she had always taken to be the "chief protagonist of a collective movement."[130] Having spent virtually her entire adult life preaching and teaching among them, outlining their central role in the advancement of the new socialist society, she feared above all that Bolshevik methods threatened to undo what she had achieved, that the workers, disheartened and disillusioned, would lose faith in the future, in socialism. In her despair, Balabanoff accused the Bolsheviks of more than having simply betrayed the masses. Their demand for blind obedience alone unmasked the ugly truth that they had actually never had any faith in popular revolutionary potential. The Bolshevik Revolution, as she saw it, was an elite affair, made by intellectuals who were not teachers, not even leaders, but manipulators, profiteers who had joined the party for political and material reasons, power seekers who saw the world as a chessboard where they could call all the moves.[131] Only Rosa Luxemburg, Balabanoff recalled with praise and admiration, had foreseen the development of that "pernicious opportunism" that was to result in the "tragedies" of the postwar years.[132]

Like Luxemburg, Marx, and Kollontai before her, Balabanoff directed the full force of her criticism against the ominous development of the leader cult, or what she called the "fetishism of leadership."[133] Despising demagoguery and "hysterical and groveling" adulation, she was vehement in her assessment of the "hypnotic" and corrupting effect of power and success.[134] She always insisted that single individuals could only influence events, never hoping either to create or to control them. If the Russian Revolution had any heroes, she explained, these were not to be looked for among its big names—the Lenins, Trotskys, or even the Balabanoffs—but "they were to be found among the workers who, resisting cold and hunger, went on working in factories and offices throughout this terrible period. ...."[135] These were the men and women whose suffering faces should rightfully have been "immortalized" by the artistic chroniclers of the revolution. When English sculptress Claire Sheridan appeared in Russia to preserve for posterity the heads of Lenin and other Bolshevik leaders, Balabanoff was furnished with one more demonstration of the betrayal of the revolution's proletarian essence.[136]

What most disgusted Balabanoff with life in the new Russia was its tendency to create a new class of privileged, its apparent revival of the "petit-bourgeois" spirit.[137] Since revolt against privilege had played such a major role in Balabanoff's coming to revolutionary consciousness, it was natural that the slow but steady reappearance of the hallmarks of gentility—champagne and caviar at government receptions, lavish displays of silverware and wealth, special food rations and modes of transport for party leaders—all should have upset her. Self-denial was an essential element of Balabanoff's lifestyle. Her steadfast desire to lead a life of self-abnegation was partly a response to the privileged opulence of her youth, and partly an assessment of duties befitting the revolution's leaders, who, she felt, should share in the physical discomforts of the transition period. "When I thought of the women who worked all day in cold factories, returning to unheated rooms and a piece of black bread, it was difficult for me to enjoy my own food."[138] Several of Balabanoff's contemporaries confirmed this picture of her as the suffering and self-sacrificing public servant. Living all her political life in a succession of sparsely furnished "student rooms," she worked to the point of utter exhaustion, "at the beck and call of everybody." Oblivious to her own needs, she "often went without necessaries herself, giving away her own rations, always busy trying to secure medicine or some little delicacy for the sick and suffering."[139]

Balabanoff's conception of socialism was in many ways like that of Eleanor Marx. Love, not hate, a supreme sensitivity to human suffering, had brought her to the movement, and she never ceased to see socialism as a rather sophisticated means by which the rich might help the poor. Her whole approach to socialism always remained primarily ethical. The new society, according to her definition, would not be divided into "bosses and their dependents, exploiters and exploited," but would consist of free and equal human beings, working together for the welfare of all. "None would be a tool for the enrichment of another. The dependence of men on men would disappear."[140]

It was this quasi-religious nature of Balabanoff's socialist creed that, above all else, separated her from the Bolsheviks, and that, most importantly, separated the Bolsheviks from her. Many openly mocked her goodness. She was no more than a "sentimental philanthropist," they said, "always wasting her time trying to procure milk for some sick baby, extra things for a pregnant woman, or old clothes for people of useless age."[141] While Lenin condemned her "inconvenient moralism,"[142] she attacked his "ruthless singleness of purpose" and "all-absorbing, almost fanatical spirit of factionalism."[143] She valued unity, solidarity, and passionate fervor. He reveled in tactical debate and theoretical polemics.

Because of her distaste for theory, Balabanoff was frequently dismissed as vacillating and wishy-washy by theory-conscious socialists.[144] Krupskaya probably echoed Lenin's opinion when she condemned Balabanoff's lack of attention to detail and her inability to grasp the nuances of opposing arguments.[145] There was an unbending, dogmatic tone to her Marxist understanding, an inflexible faith that she defended, in the words of one observer, with "arguments worthy of a sentimental college girl." While her passion and fervor were genuine, contemporaries noted, her oratory powerful, "it takes more than eloquence to rise to the stars."[146] Even in an Italian party where attention to theory was not highly prized, a party that routinely condemned the "sterile and pompous nonsense of doctrinaires and academicians,"[147] speculations were raised about the real range of Balabanoff's intellectual capabilities. Anna Kuliscioff considered her intellectually shallow and was annoyed and embarrassed by her recurrent and bothersome requests for advice and opinions.[148] Turati shared his wife's sentiments, creating a minor furor during the war years by his published admission that Balabanoff "certainly" was "not a woman of genius."[149] In private correspondence he was more blunt. Balabanoff had the "brain of a chicken," he rather viciously concluded.[150]

Although Balabanoff always claimed to have received a doctorate from the New University of Brussels, university records contain no documentation that she ever completed her dissertation or that the degree was ever awarded.[151] Nonetheless, she always used and was accorded the title "Doctor," in a subtle and probably effective attempt to enhance the authority and status with which she was regarded. Perhaps feeling her isolation in a highly theory-conscious movement, Balabanoff clung fiercely to her degree as an emblem of respectability, as visible proof of her long and arduous socialist education.

It is true that Balabanoff never did make a real theoretical contribution to Marxist thought. Two pamphlets, *Marxism as a Philosophy*, and *Marx and Engels as Freethinkers*,[152] were little more than plodding, mechanical summaries of basic Marxist principles. Careful and cautious, both were heavily sprinkled with quotations from her theoretical favorites—Bebel, Labriola, and Plekhanov. To these neatly assembled maxims, she added her own simplistic explanations, interpretations, and illustrations. Her understanding of Marxism was rudimentary at best. The vague and imprecise characterization of Marx and Engels as "freethinkers" would probably have appalled her self-acclaimed Marxist mentors.

Perhaps Angelica Balabanoff was intellectually unable to make a real theoretical contribution to the socialist cause, but perhaps she was simply insecure and needed prodding in this direction. Traditionally, women have automatically assumed their inferiority in certain areas of political activity like theory-making, and have refrained from serious involvement, unless openly and actively encouraged. Often it was a male lover who played the mentor. Forging a sexual and mental bond with his young and timid charge, he introduced the woman to the higher realms of abstruse theorizing and became her paradigm of political authority in the process. Hence the pattern of Luxemburg-Jogiches, Marx-Aveling: Even the brilliant Luxemburg needed encouragement in her early years in the movement; even Karl Marx's daughter sought the security of joint authorship with Aveling. Balabanoff, however, never found such a teacher. A loner, she never had the kind of intimate personal and intellectual relationship that might have helped her to overcome her insecurity or hesitancy to involve herself with theoretical questions. Yet significantly, even though she never derived the benefits from a partnership of this kind, she shared nonetheless in the opprobrium and scorn that have been heaped on the private lives of other political women. Her opponents tried to place her squarely within the radical Russian free-love tradition, labeling her "shamefully ostentatious" in her sexual encounters. Police reports on Balabanoff's activities in Switzerland during the war years hinted that she and prominent PSIS member Francesco Misiano were lovers, and there have been abundant rumors of her possible love affair with the young Benito Mussolini, even charges that she had a child by him.[153] No evidence exists to corroborate any of these claims. While Balabanoff may have had some passing and unimportant love affairs, there was never a Leo Jogiches in her life, never an Edward Aveling with whom she could collaborate, never one individual to encourage and aid her intellectual efforts if, in fact, insecurity was at the root of her theoretical aversion.

Like Eleanor Marx, Angelica Balabanoff spurned theorizing and was content to contribute to the socialist movement by assuming a variety of plodding, supportive, and rather prosaic roles. The linguistic—not theoretical—abilities of both women were the ones that were most valued by European socialism in the best days of its heady internationalism. At socialist congresses, Balabanoff's services as translator and interpreter were routinely applauded and praised. To Bebel she seemed a living incarnation of socialist internationalism.[154] Her painstaking translations of Trotsky's antiwar declarations, appearing in *Avanti!*,[155] contributed to the antimilitarist fervor of the PSI, and it was specifically "in the capacity of interpreter"[156] that she was elected to membership in the ISC. According to official reports, Balabanoff also served as the official interpreter for both the Zimmerwald and Kienthal conferences, a behind-the-scenes role to be sure, but definitely one critical to Zimmerwald's coordination of international socialist peace efforts. As the organization's secretary, it was Balabanoff's administrative and linguistic, not theoretical, skills that proved most valuable.

Perhaps, as her comrades suspected, Angelica Balabanoff was intellectually incapable of making a real theoretical contribution to the socialist cause, a fact that certainly contributed to her isolation in a highly theory-conscious movement. Yet it was never a theorist that she chose to be, and those who assailed her nontheoretical bent unmasked their own implicit assumptions about the importance of theory in the process of revolutionary creation.

Balabanoff always maintained that people, not theories, dictated the course of human events. Because of her opposition to the leader cult, and her sincere belief in the creative revolutionary potential of the masses, education, not theory-making, assumed a place of central importance in Angelica Balabanoff's vision of socialism. The emancipation of the workers themselves, she always insisted, had to proceed from their own initiatives and experiences alone, arising from their intimate understanding of the goal they sought to achieve.[157] In this process of creating class consciousness, the teacher, not the theorist, was all important. It was the teacher, not the theorist, who brought and interpreted the socialist creed to the working classes, those most in need of simple, not sophisticated, propaganda. Not only was oral propaganda the most effective, if not the only, means of socialist agitation in nations like Italy and Russia with high rates of illiteracy, but it was also the best vehicle the socialist had to touch the hearts, minds, and most intimate needs of the masses.[158]

And Angelica Balabanoff, a highly successful and powerful orator herself, did touch those hearts. In her years as an organizer and agitator in Switzerland, Italy, and Russia, she received many tributes from those whose minds she moved, those who felt that she spoke for people like themselves, "for all the oppressed, the unhappy, the down-trodden."[159] "A real spellbinder," she was called, "fiery, vehement, and hypnotic."[160] Perhaps Balabanoff was not "a woman of genius," as her detractors were so quick to admit, but she was a woman of sincerity and feeling, a woman whose inner qualities and deep convictions made a strong and lasting impression on all who heard her speak.

Balabanoff compiled her advice, strategies, and insights on the tasks of the socialist agitator in a pamphlet, *The Education of the Masses to Marxism.*[161] A kind of handbook for would-be agitators based on her own wide-ranging experiences, it remains her most important contribution to socialist thought. The successful agitator, she outlined, must have a key to the psychology of the particular audience that he or she was called upon to address, an ability to anticipate their questions, problems, and needs. This could only be achieved by "projecting oneself" into the minds of one's listeners, and by having a real familiarity with the economic, social, and political situation that formed the fabric of their daily lives. After such psychological preparation, the agitator was ready to make his address. He should speak in simple and readily understandable terms, always remembering that his task was to teach, not to mystify or impress his audience. Only by convincing his listeners that he was "no stranger to them," that he was vitally interested in their destinies, their careers, their sorrows, and their futures, could he win their hearts for socialism.

Buttressed by such a sincere and heartfelt vision of the agitator's task, it was no wonder that Balabanoff felt writing or theorizing to be a waste of time and precious energy better spent on propaganda. Immensely sensitive to the needs of her listeners, she always explained socialist ideals in direct, practical, and nontheoretical terms. In her analysis of the woman question, for example, she eschewed legalistic jargon and egalitarian rhetoric, relating basic feminist issues to the vital concerns of proletarian family life. Because she recognized that "it is hard to make women appreciate ideals when they are cold and hungry,"[162] her agitational activities among women touched them in those two areas that affected them most—in their dual roles as producers and reproducers, workers and mothers. She encouraged women to organize politically and economically, to join unions and socialist organizations, to fight alongside their men against their common enemy: capitalist society. As workers, women had to understand that only the achievement of socialism could bring a "new and saner order," an economic system that would provide for their needs, end "starvation salaries," and guarantee them equal pay for equal work.

Balabanoff's discussion of the woman question was in many ways similar to Kollontai's. In her onslaught against capitalism, she condemned the horrors of a socioeconomic system that ripped proletarian women away from their children, a system that separated the infant child from his "savior and treasure."[163] She always stressed the centrality of the mother's role in the life of her child, emphasizing the child's real physical and psychological need for his mother in the early years. Proletarian motherhood was "martyrdom," she insisted, a time of profound sadness, because the working mother was robbed of the real intimacy of this physical and psychological bonding. Pressured to work by sheer economic necessity, she was often forced to leave her child alone and unattended.

Again like Kollontai, Balabanoff believed that only the achievement of socialism would ensure that the full joys of motherhood could be shared by women of all classes. She also emphasized and extolled the social values of motherhood for working women. Women, she felt, bore a special and unique responsibility to future generations, a responsibility both physical and ideological. Physically, women should struggle to counteract the deleterious effects that the industrial environment and the economic deprivations of working class life had on their developing fetuses.[164] Even more importantly, they should also keep mentally strong, educating themselves so that they could properly educate their children in a true socialist consciousness. According to Balabanoff, women held a special place as the first teachers of the future socialist society.

Balabanoff always remained strongly hostile to "feminism" as she defined it, directing the full force of her fury against "bourgeois feminists" who sought "to ape men."[165] Adopting the standard Marxist position on the woman question, she insisted that her efforts to recruit women to socialism had "nothing to do with feminism," maintaining to the last that there were no separate women's problems or issues that the victory of socialism alone could not solve.

Even during her stay in Soviet Russia, Balabanoff continued her resistance to an organized women's movement. Always giving priority to propaganda and agitation, she was disgusted with the pervasiveness of an organizational mentality, disheartened by the recognition that everything appeared to "end up as a bureaucratic institution."[166] Balabanoff resisted all attempts to recruit her for work at Zhenotdel, the women's bureau, because she probably perceived it as another wasteful and inefficient hierarchical institution.[167] When asked to head the bureau in the wake of Alexandra Kollontai's dismissal, she refused. Openly admitting her lack of interest in the organization, she may have considered the offer to have been another of those empty titles the Bolsheviks were eager to bestow on their foremost "prima donna."[168] Perhaps she was also beginning to sense the similarities between her own precarious position and that of the soon-to-be-disgraced Alexandra Kollontai.

Like Kollontai, Angelica Balabanoff had come to socialism filled with the fervent, sincere desire to spend her life in the service of a great cause. Life lived in behalf of a great cause, she always maintained, was spared its "personal futility," and participation in such a cause, the "opportunity to live for an ideal," was the "greatest joy" any human being could experience.[169] In 1917, burning idealism attracted her to revolutionary Russia; in 1921, crippling realism drove her from it.

V

Considering what service to the socialist movement had always meant to Angelica Balabanoff, her self-imposed exile from the Soviet Union demonstrated great moral integrity and courage. Not only was she deprived of the opportunity to serve that cause to which she had dedicated her life, but she was also to suffer the sting of calumny, insults, and lies from those whose grip she was escaping.

Permission to leave the Soviet Union was not granted without a price. Her expulsion from the Comintern Executive had disgraced the new International in the eyes of the European labor movement, and her staunch and determined resistance to all attempts to woo her back to the communist fold infuriated party leaders. Any hopes Balabanoff had of continuing to serve the Soviet Union in an official diplomatic capacity were quashed when Lenin attached restrictions to such service. She could become a member of the Norwegian embassy staff only on the condition that she write a pamphlet attacking her long-time friend Serrati. Balabanoff refused. Final permission for her to leave Russia came after more than a year of bureaucratic delays, with the explicit stipulation that she was "prohibited to express her opinion, verbally or in writing, on the Italian question."[170] Nonetheless, freedom came to Angelica Balabanoff at a price far less than that which would be demanded of other dissenters in the years ahead.

After Balabanoff's departure, the pain and impotence of exile were worsened by the sting of slander and lies she was forced to endure. Repeatedly spurning offers of money and support made on the condition that she break with the PSI, she was unceremoniously expelled from the Russian Communist Party. In April 1924 *Pravda* carried the expulsion decree, citing her "Menshevik" political approach and condemning her collaboration with a "social fascist" paper.[171] Yet Balabanoff had never been a Menshevik, and the "social fascist" paper for which she continued to write was *Avanti!*, one of the most highly respected organs of European socialism.

Balabanoff's sufferings in exile serve to illuminate the intense conflicts also sustained by the similarly disillusioned Alexandra Kollontai, and they make her entrance into diplomatic service somewhat more understandable. For both women, dedication to the movement had been an all-consuming passion, yet one chose exile and impotence, the other, suffering silence and a modicum of respectability. Balabanoff had once had great personal respect for Kollontai, especially proud that the "first organized opposition to the policies of Lenin and Trotsky was led by a woman."[172] But in later life she grew to resent Kollontai's change of heart, and she was deeply troubled by what appeared to be her apparent reconciliation with Stalin's regime.[173] Unknown to Balabanoff, however, Kollontai suffered greatly from her decision to labor silently in diplomatic exile. Recognizing that she was not strong enough to withstand the "mud-slinging" that Balabanoff somehow endured,[174] she kept her political opinions to herself and quietly persevered in her "work for humanity."

In this way Kollontai at least had the opportunity to serve her beloved revolution in another capacity. Nothing remained to Balabanoff, however, but a host of memories and the profound conviction that she had been strong enough to "swim against the stream."[175] She was the "only socialist," she never tired of reminding herself and others, "to have voluntarily left Russia because of her moral and political disagreements."[176] In her political isolation, this proud and satisfying conviction of personal strength was all that was left to her.

Sometimes, in her moments of disillusionment, Balabanoff speculated on what her later life would have been like had she chosen to remain in Russia. Bitterly yet somewhat wistfully, she was always forced to remind herself that "the Russian Bolsheviks were capable of anything." If she had ever had the slightest doubt of that conviction, her life would not have been "what it is now"—one of wandering exile, political isolation, and personal futility.[177]

After leaving the Soviet Union, Angelica Balabanoff never again had a real home, nor did she ever involve herself in a powerful mass movement that could utilize her talents and energies. As an internationally renowned and somewhat fearsome revolutionary, she found doors closed against her, as conservatives in both Sweden and Italy clamored against her admission to their countries.[178] Finally settling in Vienna, she returned to the only form of gainful employment she had ever known—the teaching of languages—and, despite her poverty, felt happier than at any time in the past few years.

Isolated from the Italian socialist movement, she watched in horror as fascism tightened its grip on the nation she loved. Mussolini's triumph came as a "terrible blow."[179] In 1926 she moved to Paris, which, in the wake of the fascist victory, was a favorite gathering spot for Italian radicals and socialists in exile.[180] There Balabanoff became a well-known figure, seeking to unite all Marxist and "freedom loving" groups in a spirit of determined opposition to fascism, and serving for a time as editor of the Parisian edition of *Avanti!*. Italian socialism in exile, however, always remained weak, plagued by the old battles between revolutionaries and reformists and rocked by new disputes with pro-Moscow communists. Disillusioned and tormented by the never-ending factionalism, Balabanoff pulled away, obsessed by the "anguish" of her own "impotence."[181]

She spent the war years in the United States, living in New York City, where she embarked on a furious one-woman crusade to promote awareness, especially among Italian-Americans, of fascism's full and sinister meaning. Friends with Norman Thomas and Ludwig Lore of the American Socialist Party, she wrote occasionally for the *Socialist Review*, its official organ, but always refrained from joining any formal political group.[182]

With the war's end and Mussolini's overthrow, Balabanoff was finally able to return to Italy. By this time she had become staunchly anticommunist and strongly pro-American in her political sentiments. Hoping American aid could resurrect Italy, she had high praise for the United States. "These are the people who know what communism is and how to fight it."[183] Present at the 1947 founding congress of yet another Italian socialist party, the Italian Workers Socialist Party of Giuseppe Saragat,[184] Balabanoff denounced socialist flirtation with communist collaboration, warning right-wing socialists to safeguard their autonomy and to avoid fusion with other Italian socialist groups that might sooner or later come under communist influence. Undaunted in her demand for a democratic, anticommunist socialism, she continued her agitational work, especially among women, but old age and failing health robbed these efforts of the vibrant militancy of her younger years. She died in Rome in 1965 at the age of 87, just as she had notified the Italian Social Democratic Party that she was ready to embark on yet another lecture tour, a tragic and long-suffering survivor of another era.

The keynote of Angelica Balabanoff's life in exile was tremendous disillusionment, interspersed with valiant, well-meaning, but ineffectual efforts to fight both communism and fascism, those two demons that together had played havoc with her lifelong commitment to socialism. She dedicated her early years in exile to "teaching the truth" about fascism, acquiring some public notoriety as Mussolini's former "tutor" who had now chosen to tell all.[185] During her stay in the United States, she published, at her own expense, a bilingual play depicting the life and rise to power of her former associate [186] and advertised that the entire collection could be obtained for one dollar by writing to her in New York. Tremendously worried about the spread of fascism, Balabanoff again embarked on her familiar role as teacher, seeking to instruct all Americans on the nature and causes of fascist victory. As part of her continuing efforts in this behalf, she wrote and distributed a small pamphlet of poems, *To the Victims of Fascism*, proceeds from which she dedicated to the antifascist resistance in various countries.[187]

Balabanoff also used her exile period to write her memoirs.[188]

Published in three languages, they contained the record of her disillusionment in the USSR, and, with their caustic, biting, and brutal
depiction of Bolshevik methods, were taken to be timely, effective,
and prophetic, a powerful commentary that aided understanding of
contemporary developments in Stalinist Russia.[189] More poignant,
however, than the "Russian tragedy" Balabanoff so passionately and
frankly outlined was the tragedy of this woman's life itself, for
whom the act of writing her memoirs was not so much a scholarly or
even a political endeavor, but a highly personal venture, a touching
monument to the life she had once led in pursuit of a great cause, a
last-ditch attempt to hold on, to remind both herself and others of
her years of service to the revolution, to socialism. The dominant
theme of her memoirs was a kind of "I was there" tone, a repetitive
undercurrent of presence and involvement, an emphasis not to be
regarded as pretentious or self-seeking, but one that can only be
understood in conjunction with an appreciation for what the movement meant to Angelica Balabanoff, a sensitive acknowledgement of
her tremendous need to belong. No longer belonging, her memoirs
bore visible and tangible testimony to the fact that she once had. A
companion volume, *Impressions of Lenin*, reflected this same need,
revealing much more about Balabanoff herself than about her announced subject.

Poetry was another vehicle Balabanoff used to record the emotional outpourings of her own increasingly troubled spirit. Although
critics panned her literary efforts, terming them "admirable in sentiment, but not strongly impressive as poetry,"[190] her poems are
important, bearing strong witness to the ethical, religious, and profoundly moral fervor of her socialist creed. Obviously recognizing the
nonideological tenor of her work, Balabanoff virtually apologized for
her tender sentimentality, assuring her readers in the preface to her
collection that there was "no contradiction" between her "deep
sense of human tragedy" and her "lifelong struggle for socialism."[191]

Appropriately entitled *Tears*, Balabanoff's inspirational volume
contained poems written in five languages, poems of sorrow, pain,
hopelessness and hunger, political martyrdom and political despair.
Depicting life as a "chain of infinite suffering," she sought to capture
the "tears of the underprivileged" in a world where babies die and
children starve, where death, deception, and cruelty thrive, where
"lies are the natural law of life."[192] Many of the poems in the collection were frankly autobiographical, reflecting the compounded

illusions of her lifelong struggle to win "happiness for all." "I have no home," the humane, inspirational voice of the poet intoned, ". . . I am where a man stretches out his hand in despair . . . where there is suffering and fear."[193]

The most touching of all Balabanoff's poetic endeavors, however, was one that captured the essence of her need to belong, of her frantic desire to be remembered for her political services. Aware perhaps that these were not the blazing kind that would ensure her a place in the history books, she became deeply concerned with the question of her reputation after her death, and this poem, a record of her disillusionment, remains her tragic epitaph:

> I searched for Truth
> And I adored it
> To it I sacrificed
> All that I am and all I have been
> But I die forgotten . . .[194]

Neglect, perhaps, but not oblivion has been Angelica Balabanoff's historical legacy. While she has had her share of detractors, her place in the socialist pantheon has been assured by all those not mesmerized by "great" achievements alone, those who recognized that the "rich fount of love"[195] this simple and unassuming woman brought to European socialism was as important, if not more so, than the theoretical strategies and tactical tools of Lenin. "No one needed a communist membership card to Angelica Balabanoff's heart," Emma Goldman once wrote.[196] John Reed called her "the best revolutionist" he had known in Russia.[197] "A woman of great loving kindness,"[198] she tried in her own way to impart something vibrant, gentle, and good to a Russian movement much in need of those qualities. That she failed to do so was not *her* tragedy.

Chapter • Five

Dolores Ibarruri,
"La Pasionaria"

The Female Revolutionary
as Symbol

I

If historical obscurity has been the fate of Angelica Balabanoff, notoriety and renown have been that of Dolores Ibarruri, the fiery heroine of the Spanish Civil War. Continuing the fight against European fascism that Balabanoff had only begun, Ibarruri came to be seen as the very embodiment of democracy in a world moving inexorably toward Armageddon, the greatest symbol of suffering and bleeding Spain, the staunchest advocate of republican resistance. Known worldwide for her mesmerizing oratory and matchless fervor, she became a legend in her own time, a heroine, a warrior, a Spanish St. Joan, celebrated in song and immortalized in prose and poetry. "Goodness and truth shine from her as from a true saint of the people," Hemingway recorded in *For Whom the Bell Tolls*. "Not for nothing is she called La Pasionaria."[1]

Ibarruri has been called the greatest living woman revolutionary of the twentieth century, the most important woman alive, the greatest living figure of the world communist movement,[2] but actually very little is really known about the woman behind the hype, the praise, the headlines.[3] The mystique and the cult of La Pasionaria are repeated if not extolled in every history of the Spanish Civil War, but the exact nature of her role, her influence, her contribution has been lost in the seemingly endless literature of that encounter. Like Balabanoff and the other women of this study, she remains a mystical, almost semidivine creature, as controversial and multifaceted as the war of which she became a symbol. Her name inspires the same kind of conflicting emotions as that great crusade that still engenders passions more than 40 years after its conclusion. Was she saint or witch, bloodthirsty virago, godless Joan, or *mater dolorosa*? Even Hemingway is unclear, as competing images of Pasionaria merge in his pages.[4]

The position of the historian seeking a clear picture of Ibarruri's role is directly hampered by the ambivalent, if not unpleasant, ideological positions she herself adopted. In the view of many, that "great voice, where pity, compassion, and truth were blended,"[5] was one of a poseur, a ruthless fanatic who was both docile and despicable in her unflinching support for Stalinist truth.[6] Her uncritical orthodoxy and fulsome praise for the Soviet leader are jarring, easily resulting in a tendency to dismiss her as no more than a Stalinist apologist or self-serving opportunist. With all we have come to know about Stalinist crimes, La Pasionaria inevitably loses much of her saintly glow.

Finally, there is a third layer of murky confusion that surrounds Ibarruri. Although she occupied positions of prominence in the world political spectrum and in the socialist revolutionary pantheon in particular, it was in Spain itself that her role was played out, a Spain that for centuries has been insufficiently known if not ignored by historians. Seen as a land of cruelty, superstition, and bigotry, Spain had been portrayed as a land where the warm sun of the Reformation never shone and where the seeds of enlightened modernity never took root. Yet the Spanish revolutionary heritage, especially as it involves women, needs to be explored in much greater detail. To include Ibarruri in this study is to attempt to demonstrate how much she, and the Spanish experience in general, do in fact share with the wider European socialist tradition. Pasionaria fit the mold of the other women of this study in many ways; she was heroine and martyr, visionary and, yes, even pariah, all in one. In fact, compared to the other women studied here, the greatest paradox of Ibarruri's career is that she achieved the acceptance, acclaim, and virtual deification she did in a country where, as the twentieth century opened, the position of women was among the most backward and oppressed in Europe. Feminism, of either the socialist or bourgeois variety, was virtually unknown in the nation that proudly boasted of being "the manly man's country," where every Spaniard is a dictator in his own home.[7] Although rich and poor women led vastly different lives, culture, customs, and the laws all worked to ensure that the roles of both would be equally circumscribed. According to an early twentieth-century observer, Spanish men considered women "their inferiors in everything," and looked down upon them "with the disdain of veritable oppressors."[8]

The Spanish civil code relegated married women to the position of minors before the law. Denied all civil and political rights, women were charged simply to obey their husbands in return for the benevolent protection furnished by the married state. Divorce was nonexistent, and even adultery was denied as a legitimate basis for separation if the charge were brought by the wife rather than by the husband. Legally under his protection, a married woman had no authority even over her own children.

While the wealthy women of early twentieth-century Spain were preoccupied with perfecting their French, finding husbands, acquiring Paris trousseaux, or performing obligatory works of charity— all, of course, under the proper supervision of their mothers or governesses[9] —poor women were relegated to the triple oppression of law, family, and workplace. Centuries of prejudice, unequal wage scales, the virtual nonexistence of a spirit of association among women, and the absence of industrial education all worked to reduce poor women to the ranks of unskilled brute labor only. Peasant women carried heavy burdens on their shoulders, tilled the fields, and split wood, while their sisters in the industrial realm worked in the manufacture of cigars and lace, as miners, or domestic servants.[10]

The education women received rendered them unfit for any other kind of work. Girls were seldom taught trades or industrial skills. Even the secondary school curricula included nothing more than singing, dancing, drawing, and needlework. By 1900 only 30 percent of Spanish women were literate.[11] Where girls' schools existed, they were of a uniformly poor quality. It was an exception, several observers wrote, if the schoolmistress herself knew how to read intelligently.[12]

The biggest role of all in shaping and creating the misogynist strain in Spanish culture was played by the Roman Church, which, after the monarchy, had for a millennium been the most important of all Spanish institutions. Liberian theologians fully accepted the patriarchal and antifeminist traditions of Pauline Christianity. Clerical moralists stressed the virtues of the dutiful and submissive wife, urged women to bear their husbands' infidelities uncomplainingly, and counseled them to be content with their subordinate position.[13] Women were told to accept male superiority as a matter of course, for clearly the supremacy of the male was ordained by nature. While not explicitly mandating that women should be kept illiterate, some theologians suggested that the educated woman might be a danger to the hearth. Surely women had no need for book learning, for "the best book is the cushion and the embroidery frame."[14] Others were even more blunt in their hostility. In the view of an Augustinian friar, "Woman is the most monstrous animal in the whole of nature, bad-tempered and worse spoken. To have this animal in the house is asking for trouble."[15] A Jesuit writer agreed: "Different kinds of temptations make war on man in his various ages, some when he is young and others when he is old; but woman threatens him perpetually."[16]

The extremely sexist nature of Spanish society is well documented. Certainly, the pervasiveness of antifeminist beliefs only serves to complicate any attempt to understand or explain the fame achieved by Dolores Ibarruri. Yet an equally powerful component of that same Spanish Catholic tradition provided a historical and cultural vehicle for her adulation. Mariolatry, or the cult of the Virgin, is the excessive, feverish, and fanatical devotion to the mother of God. Growing in magnitude and popularity since the late Middle Ages, it has an especially strong grip in Spain, where every parish church has its favorite virgin.[17] There are countless stories of Mary's miraculous involvement in the Iberian world, both old and new, and the most famous harks back to the very dawn of the Spanish Christian era.

Spain was originally apostalized by St. James the Elder in the first century. Legend and Catholic tradition teach that his work was specially favored by Mary, who is believed to have a particular fondness for things Spanish. One day as he stood on the banks of the Ebro at Saragossa, she is said to have appeared to him, seated at the top of a pillar of jasper, surrounded by a choir of angels. Taking a small wooden statue of herself from the hands of the angels at her service, she commanded him to build a sanctuary on the spot to commemorate his vision. The original chapel housing the pillar with the statue at its top became the site of a grand and famous shrine to *La Virgen del Pilar*, the cradle of the Spanish Church.[18]

The story of the Virgin of the Pillar would remain nothing more than an amusing bit of medieval folklore were it not for the very real role that the cult has played in the Spanish political past. Neither Romans, Goths, Moors, nor Vandals could desecrate or destroy the statue itself because the people of Saragossa defended it with such fierce heroism. The legend of the Virgin is inextricably interwoven with Spanish nationalism, patriotism, and pride. By a peculiar bit of military tradition, images of the Virgin have routinely been appointed to the highest commands of the Spanish army. Sometimes a saint was made a field marshal, as in 1810 when the Cortes of Cadiz gave the supreme command to St. Teresa of Avila, but more commonly it was the Virgin who was so acclaimed.[19] In the Napoleonic wars, the Virgin of Pilar was named Captain General of the army of Aragon, and the common people of Aragon defied the French by singing a popular ditty:

> The Virgin of Pilar says
> She doesn't want to be French
> She's the captain general
> Of the army of Aragon.[20]

In 1898 the Virgin was appointed commander-in-chief of the Spanish army, and by the early twentieth century military insignia were placed near the statue in recognition of her becoming patroness of the armed forces of Spain. During the civil war a parody of the old anti-Napoleonic ballad again became popular, only this time, according to the song, the Virgin had become captain general of the communist column and was proclaiming her antifascist resolve.[21]

In this way an intensely patriarchal culture linked in one popular image the themes of war and womanhood, patriotism and sacrifice. The tradition is an important but neglected one, difficult to reconcile with the concept popularly known as *machismo*, or the familiar and oft-repeated belief that Latin Catholicism and the repression of women have routinely gone hand in hand. It is only recently that students of Iberian culture have begun to examine the "other face" of machismo, or the unique set of attitudes and behavior patterns with which Latin women are regarded.[22] The term *marianismo* has been coined to describe this curious and ostensibly contradictory state in which the Spanish woman finds herself. Far from being victims of sex role stereotyping, women are actually beneficiaries of a cult of feminine spiritual superiority that teaches that women are "semi-divine, morally superior to, and spiritually stronger than men."[23] The spiritual strength of women engenders self-sacrifice, an infinite capacity for humility and suffering, and the emotional stamina needed to sustain the intimacy of family life in the wake of untold horrors.

The saintly and maternal Pasionaria followed directly in this tradition. She became the communist Virgin in a nation where women had routinely participated in periods of national upheaval and war.[24] More importantly, she entered a revolutionary tradition where, even in Spain, the support of women was deemed vital to the cause. European socialist ideas, with their emancipatory rhetoric on the woman question, had crossed the Pyrenees by the mid-nineteenth century. The followers of Marx, Cabet, Fourier, and Saint-Simon were all active, each of whom, as we have seen, vigorously encouraged women's participation in the revolution to come. Women's attendance at early socialist assemblies was noted by contemporaries, who left vivid accounts of the meetings of several socialist clubs. These generally took place in abandoned churches, certainly an environment with which women were familiar. Many were present, one spectator recalled, sitting on the ground, knitting or nursing their children, listening to the socialist credo "as if it were a real sermon."[25]

To Dolores Ibarruri Gomez, who came to revolutionary consciousness in the highly politicized atmosphere of the opening decades of the twentieth century, it was.

II

Like Rosa Luxemburg, Dolores Ibarruri was powerfully molded by the inspirational revolutionary heritage of the region in which she grew up. Born on December 9, 1895, in the mining town of Gallarta in northern Spain, she was nurtured in Vizcaya, that so-called cradle of rebels, the most important of the oppressed Basque provinces. The Basques are an ancient race of mysterious origin who have inhabited a small corner of Spain at the western edge of the Pyrenees since before the dawn of written history. Noted for their religious devotion, fierce spirit of independence, and deep respect for self-government, they were never conquered, even by the Moors, and have struggled for centuries to protect their carefully guarded civil liberties from a succession of Spanish monarchs. While the nationalist victory in the civil war may have brought to an end the ancient tradition of Basque independence, their battle for political autonomy within the Spanish government continues to this day.

Although she was obviously affected by the insurgent climate of her beloved "Euzkadi"—whose ancient liberties she championed during the civil war—it was more than the purely political aspirations of the Basques that shaped Ibarruri's revolutionary inclinations. Even more important were the social and economic grievances of the workers of this region. Because of their mineral wealth, the Basque provinces had become major industrial centers by the early nineteenth century. The coming of the mining railways radically transformed traditional ways of life, bringing with them great factories, blast furnaces, dry docks for shipbuilding, mills of all kinds—and a revolutionary ideology. Socialist doctrines of both the Marxist and anarchist variety had come to Spain by the mid-nineteenth century, and Vizcaya itself was one of the main foci of the burgeoning socialist movement. The first workers' organizations affiliated with the International Workingmen's Association were established here, and Bilbao, the major industrial and commercial center of the Basques, soon boasted a large, well-educated, and overwhelmingly socialist working class.[26]

Ibarruri's own family was part of the Basque underclass to whom revolutionary doctrines might particularly appeal. Her grandfather, father, uncles, and brothers were all miners, as her future husband would also be. Even her mother had worked in the mines before marriage. In her autobiography Ibarruri presented an absorbing, heartrending account of life in the mining towns of Vizcaya, a life so unbearable and subhuman that the breeding of rebels such as herself she believed to be clearly inevitable.[27]

Life in the mining community was "squalid, jammed, and depersonalized," "like a deep pit without horizons, where the light of the sun never reached."[28] Here men came from all parts of Spain to earn their bread in the bowels of the earth. To house these transients, the great mining companies built ramshackle bunkhouses that looked, she recalled, "like a scene from Dante," and stank of "sweat, fermented food, and the odors of the latrine."[29] Both need and debt tied men to the mine, for company officials usually owned both the food and clothing shops in the area, and workers were forced to make their purchases there. Even prostitutes were routinely supplied in an ingenious cycle that ensured that the workers' wages would in one way or another return to their source.

Yet the horrors of the conditions in which the miners lived paled beside the terrors under which they worked. Owners carefully exchanged blacklists of their more rebellious employees and tried to crush the comradeship of the workers in imaginative ways—dividing them into crews and organizing competitions that fomented regional rivalries and prejudices. Accidents were a fact of life, cave-ins frequent, wages low. Ibarruri's own grandfather had been killed in a mining accident, crushed by a block of ore.

Her childhood was a sad one, unrelieved by hope.[30] Although Ibarruri's family appeared to be relatively better off than most, the task of feeding 11 children was never an easy one. As a specialist in explosives, her father earned comparatively good pay, but the family's economic condition worsened as he aged. Left with no alternative but to continue working, those past their prime were routinely given the most painful and unbearable tasks to do. Her father's was to sift through the wastes washed down the embankments by the rain. Standing in a sea of mud with his pants rolled up above his knees, he would shovel the mire containing small pieces of ore into screens, until he emerged from the water, "livid, trembling with cold, exhausted."[31] This made an indelible impression on his sensitive young daughter.

Clearly it was the accumulated sufferings of her own family, rather than their explicitly political convictions, that colored Ibarruri's development. Her parents were not socialists, but staunchly conservative Catholic monarchists, like most Basques. In rejecting their beliefs, however, Ibarruri rebelled not against them as individuals, but against the brutality of their lives. If her family angered her in any way, it was purely because they appeared to have accepted their lot with the docile fatalism and resignation common to the Catholic poor. The adolescent Ibarruri, on the other hand, came to be fueled by a bitter, almost instinctive resentment that made her "lash out against everything and everybody."[32]

She especially grew to resent her mother's repeated reminder that the degree of a woman's success in life was measured solely by her success in marriage. With such traditional ideas, Ibarruri's mother was obviously not a role model for her daughter in the strictest sense, for she was neither well educated nor politically conscious herself. Yet she was strong in the way all the women of the mining region were, raising their children amid incredible poverty and hoping that they might acquire at least a minimal education. From her later speeches, actions, and reminiscences, it is clear that Ibarruri saw strength in these mining women and was proud that she was one of them. Alleviating their daily struggles was the task to which she devoted her life.

Ibarruri came to be impressed by all individuals who gave their lives to a challenging cause, of whatever kind. In her autobiography she paid special tribute to an old teacher of hers, Antonia Izar de la Fuente, who tried, "with apostolic zeal," to combat the ignorance of the miners' children in her classes.[33] Despite her praise for Doña Antonia, however, Ibarruri had little regard for the education she received. Her lessons were monotonous and joyless, geared toward instilling respect for established authority. Even as a child she seemed to have recognized the stark contrast between the lessons of the classroom, with their assurance of the immutable justice of the laws of God, and the lessons of the street, for it was on the streets that the children of miners received their real education. In school they were expected to sing hymns of thanksgiving to God, or ballads that glorified the labor of the mines, but at home they sang songs of the union hall, rousing tunes of rebellion and revolution.[34]

As the twentieth century opened, Spain was a nation badly in need of industrial, social, economic, and political modernization. A virtual relic from Europe's medieval past, it was governed by an effete monarchy, dominated by a narrow and reactionary army caste, and guided by the economic, cultural, and political tyranny of the Church. Its capitalist development was slow and uneven, its economy dictated by the interests of the traditional landowning classes, and its agricultural system characterized by feudal patterns of tenure. Although semifeudal Spain had seen at least five would-be revolutions throughout the nineteenth century, each had been incomplete, and the middle class had yet to wrest power from the old landed aristocracy in a bourgeois revolution on the French pattern. The nominal proclamation of universal manhood suffrage in 1890 had done little to introduce democracy to Spain, for a corrupt system of local political bosses—the notorious *caciques*—terrorized the rural areas and convinced the masses that electoral activities were clearly not meant for them.

Even the burgeoning revolutionary movement had its problems. Although a socialist party, the Socialist Labor Party of Spain (PSOE), had been formally organized by 1879, tracing its origin to no less an emissary than Karl Marx's Spanish-speaking son-in-law Paul Lafargue, the left had, unfortunately, developed in two directions by the early twentieth century. While the center and northern provinces, especially the Basque country, were centers of socialist strength, the east and south, with their teeming masses of landless peasants, were infused with anarchosyndicalist fervor. Both groups organized rival unions to court working class followers, a breach that weakened labor strength and would dash hopes for an imminent and successful revolution in Spain.

Dolores Ibarruri passed her youth during years of intense political activism. The loss of the last remnants of Spain's empire in 1898 cost the regime much needed prestige and stimulated the growth of anarchist and socialist sentiment. Sharply rising prices led to a series of strikes in the late 1890s, with demands for higher wages and an eight-hour day. Food riots, agricultural disturbances, and waves of anarchist violence greeted the new century, and a series of general strikes continued into its opening decade. A wave of unrest following the highly unpopular Moroccan War culminated in the horrors of Barcelona's tragic Bloody Week in 1909, when government repression—highlighted by the execution of celebrated educational reformer Francesco Ferrer—shocked the world.

While the young Ibarruri may not have understood the significance of these events, the reality of the political struggle was a vital part of her girlhood. By a lucky accident her family lived next door to the center where the miners gathered in their free time. These *Casas del Pueblo*, or Workers Houses, originally devised by the Belgian socialists, were adopted by the Spanish and became vital centers of working class culture in the villages where they were located.[35] Their free lending libraries, offering a variety of both Marxist and popular literature, were important educational institutions at a time when Spain itself boasted few public libraries. Other *casas* organized choral societies and theater groups, or housed cheap cafes. This was the social world of the young Pasionaria, a seeming oasis in a desert of despair, and the excitement of the *casa*, with its red flag prominently displayed and the cupboard containing photos from the Paris Commune, clearly impressed her. She enjoyed going there, listening to the speeches and sitting in on meetings, and it was there that her interest in oratory probably had its start. Enthused by the "musical sound of the language, the sonorous phrases, the blistering and sarcastic jibes," she "drank in all the orators said,"[36] and would routinely run home to repeat what she had heard, word for word, for her father's approval.

Among the clearest memories emerging from the haze of her girlhood were events from the spring of 1903, when she was eight. The miners of Vizcaya had called a general strike, and her home town became the center of action and leadership. In a flashback strikingly similar to one of Kollontai's, Ibarruri remembered running into the streets and seeing soldiers everywhere, a terrifying experience for a girl her age.[37] Even more important for her developing political consciousness was her vivid recollection of the women of Vizcaya who, with babies in their arms, desperately implored the soldiers, as sons of the people, to lay down their guns.[38]

Such experiences must certainly have colored her views of women's political potential. In her recollection, the world of her youth was one surprisingly devoid of sex role stereotypes. Accustomed to a hard life, neither boys nor girls were afraid to take risks of any kind. Ibarruri's own pleasures were decidedly tomboyish ones—racing through mine sites, leaping into moving freight cars, hanging from aerial tramcar cables, crawling through tunnels, and exploring railroad trestles.[39]

But the youthful tomboy matured into a frail young woman, whom poor health spared from joining her brothers and sisters in the mines. Good grades, a great ambition to be a teacher, and her parents' willingness to finance her education, at least for a time, enabled her to depart from the normal pattern of young womanhood in Gallarta. She enrolled in the teachers' normal school—certainly a far cry from the educational experiences of Kollontai, Luxemburg, and Balabanoff—but was unable to complete the two-year course when the cost of even this rather modest education became too great for her family to bear.

Over the next few years, Ibarruri's life followed a typical path for a girl of her class—a short stint in a dressmaking academy, followed by a series of odd jobs—domestic servant, laundress, cafe waitress—until her inevitable and expected marriage. This came in 1915, at age 20, when she married an Asturian miner from Somorrostro, Julian Ruiz, who was already quite active in socialist circles. The marriage was not destined to be a happy one. In many ways Ibarruri's opinion of married life echoed Kollontai's, but while both women complained that marriage robbed them of self-fulfillment, stripped them of personal identity, and committed them to sacrifice and abnegation, Ibarruri's laments were compounded by an incredible poverty that Kollontai never knew. Living on Ruiz's salary of four *pesetas*—less than a dollar a day—theirs was a life "worse than animals."[40] Her husband's wretched wages were not enough to pay the rent in the miserable hovel they called home—"without light, without water, freezing in winter, roasting in summer, afloat in a sea of mud."[41] Instead of meat they ate a few potatoes cooked with red peppers to give them color. When her first child was born, Ibarruri was too malnourished to nurse the infant. Only love for her baby kept her alive.[42]

These experiences pushed her inexorably toward a political career. When her rebellion came, it was not an intellectual one like that of Kollontai, the general's daughter who had felt the psychological oppression of a bird in a gilded cage, but the feverish outlash of a woman who could no longer cope with the grim realities of everyday life. Convinced life was not worth living, she rebelled "against the inevitability of such lives as ours . . . against the idea that we were condemned to drag the shackles of poverty and submission through the centuries like beasts of burden."[43] Sometime during the first year of her marriage, Ibarruri seriously embraced the socialist beliefs with which she had long been familiar. The Marxist literature she found in the Somorrostro *Casa del Pueblo* was like a "window opening on life," a life she now regarded not as a "swamp" but as a "battlefield."[44]

Her assessment was an accurate one, for Spain was a battlefield during these years of her socialist awakening. Trotsky, after a visit in 1916, considered Spain, next to Russia, to be the country most likely to experience revolution in the near future.[45] Although Spain's neutrality in the Great War led to a temporary commercial and industrial boom, since it supplied food, equipment, and supplies to both sides, the long-term economic consequences of the war were devastating.[46] Inflation reached new heights in 1916, and the sharp rise in prices wreaked great hardships on the poor. The war also reduced the great currents of migration that had traditionally acted as a safety valve, and led to the gradual contraction of industrial production. Thus, the spread of strikes was rapid by 1916, as workers embarked on national campaigns demanding a reduction in the high cost of living. During the spring of that year, the unrest was of unusual intensity in the Basque provinces and also among the Asturian miners, and it was at this time that Ibarruri made her first foray into the public political realm. During Easter week—*la Semana de Pasion*—she published an article in *El Minero Vizcaino*. Signing herself "Pasionaria," the Passion Flower, to hide her sentiments from her disapproving family, she coined the name by which she would be internationally known for the rest of her life.

During the next few years, Spain seemed continually on the verge of revolution. There were crop burnings in the countryside, rumblings in the army, economic grievances among the workers, and continued hopes for a democratic republic among the middle classes. By August 1917 plans were afoot for a nationwide general strike to culminate in the proclamation of a republic, and Ibarruri, along with other Vizcayans, eagerly prepared for the coming revolution by making crude bombs of tin cans, nails, and dynamite. "The political temperature was rising," she recalled. "We went without sleep, waiting for the call to action at any moment."[47]

The Bolshevik Revolution was the match that set this Spanish powder keg on fire. The enthusiastic reaction of the Spanish workers to the Bolshevik seizure of power was unsurpassed in any other European country.[48] A rash of pro-Bolshevik journals appeared, millenarian excitement mounted among the peasants of the south, and in cities all over Spain, scores, possibly hundreds, of pro-Bolshevik meetings and demonstrations were held. The effect of Lenin's revolution was especially strong in Vizcaya, where revolutionary fervor intensified as economic conditions deteriorated. Ibarruri herself was "electrified" by Russian events. Instinctively she knew that something "immeasurably great" had taken place.[49]

Paradoxically, however, the Russian Revolution was to have a disastrous effect on the Spanish labor movement. While the fear of revolution strengthened and united the forces of the right, doubts about the wisdom of emulating the Russian example hopelessly divided the forces of the left. A violent and embittered debate over the exact nature of the relationship between Spanish socialism and Russian communism was the consuming preoccupation of the PSOE over the next few years. Suspicious of accepting dictation from Russia, the party's reform-minded leadership was convinced that Spain needed first to enter an extended bourgeois phase before rushing headlong into revolutionary adventurism. The question of adherence to the Comintern split the Spanish party as it split the other socialist parties of Europe. When a majority of the PSOE rejected affiliation with the Comintern, the small pro-Bolshevik faction seceded to form the Spanish Communist Party (PCE) in 1921.[50]

There was no question as to where Dolores Ibarruri and the other

Vizcayan militants stood on this issue. Steadily drawing away from the evolutionary socialism of PSOE leaders, and especially disgusted with their weakness and hesitancy during the strike movements of 1917, the entire socialist section of Somorrostro to which she and her husband belonged decided as early as 1920 to affiliate with the Third International, one of the first Spanish sections to do so. Ibarruri had nothing but praise for this decision, and nothing but scorn for the cowardly indecision of socialists unwilling to change the reformist orientation of the PSOE. Mesmerized by the triumph of socialism in the largest country in Europe, she embraced the guidance of the Comintern, which, in her opinion, represented and embodied Marxist socialism and brought Russia's successful experience to the international labor movement.[51]

Ibarruri was clearly attracted by Soviet propaganda of this period, which called for immediate mass action and centered on the need to "smash" the bourgeois state.[52] Her haste was understandable, considering the worsening economic plight of Vizcaya at the time. By mid-1921, as a result of the virtual cessation of exports, some 40 percent of Vizcayan miners were unemployed and the rest restricted to a three-day work week.[53] Caught up in a kind of "revolutionary fever," she and the other Vizcayan militants planned for revolution—stockpiling weapons and explosives in the hope of launching an armed insurrection.

Yet it was precisely tactics like these, which invoked the specter of red revolution, that led to the rightist coup of Primo de Rivera in 1923. Primo was a strongman in the old tradition of Spanish generals, heartily welcomed by a ruling elite who saw the army as the only power capable of creating order out of the general chaos. The coming of his dictatorship virtually destroyed the fledgling PCE. Riddled with dissension in its own ranks, handicapped by its small size, and lacking both leaders and effective propaganda channels, it was barely developed by the time of the civil war.

The 1920s were equally bad years for the woman called La Pasionaria. Her husband was frequently picked up in police raids, arrested, and jailed, so that much of the time she was left alone, taking in sewing and mending to support her family or depending on the charity of friends. She watched four of her six children die during this miserable period, tragedies that only reconfirmed her communist faith. Each time she passed their graves her revolutionary conviction mounted.[54] Her involvement in both local and provincial party activities increased throughout the 1920s, and she also spent time in prison on a variety of charges.[55] By 1930 Ibarruri was a familiar enough figure in the minuscule and illegal party to be elected to the central committee of its national organization.

The five years intervening between the bloodless proclamation of the Spanish Republic in 1931 and the outbreak of the civil war in 1936[56] saw Ibarruri make the final break with her role as wife, mother, and part-time revolutionary. They were the chrysalis stage from which she emerged as a nationally known political leader. Sharing in the hopeful climate of joyous expectancy that gripped Spain following the collapse of the Rivera dictatorship in 1930, she embarked on her first public speaking role, as a communist propagandist for the nationwide elections scheduled for 1931. When a majority of the electorate voted the monarchy out in April of that year, it finally appeared that Spain was on the threshold of a new era of progress and democratic development.

With the coming of the republic, the PCE was legalized, and Ibarruri was able to devote full time to public and constructive party work. Moving to Madrid, she worked on the staff of the party paper, *Mundo Obrero*, and took charge of the organization of women's activities. She also embarked on a series of propaganda campaigns in Toledo and Andalusia, attended the first PCE congress ever held publicly and legally, and—a clear sign of her rising position in the party—was named a delegate to the thirteenth Communist International plenary session held in Moscow in 1933.

By 1934 Dolores Ibarruri was already the unchallenged heroine of the Spanish working class. In that year the early euphoria that had greeted the establishment of the republic began to fade, as the government fell into the hands of a rightist bloc that had never reconciled themselves to the new Spain. To protest this development, and to protect their infant republic against the urgent threat of a full conservative takeover, the workers of the northern mining province of Asturias rose in revolt in an event the likes of which Europe had not seen since the days of the Paris Commune.[57] Although desperately short of arms and ammunition, the partisans of "red Asturias" established a type of soviet government in the area, expropriated large businesses and factories, rationed food and medical services, and struck terror in the hearts of black Spain by lynching civil guards, property owners, and priests.

Undaunted by the wave of vicious reprisals unleashed by the government, Ibarruri traveled to Asturias to aid the families of the imprisoned miners and to evacuate their children to safety in Madrid. She was hailed for these relief activities, and her popularity grew as she came to be increasingly associated with the miners' cause and efforts to pressure the government for their speedy release from prison. She also became one of the most vigorous supporters of the so-called Popular Front program, which urged unity of all democratic parties, not only against the conservative backlash in Spain itself, but also against the ominous tide of fascism in Europe.[58]

In the wake of the defeat of the heroic Asturian miners, and the growing reality of the rightist menace in Spain and elsewhere, all the parties of the Spanish left signed a unity pact to guarantee their triumph in the 1936 elections. Among the 16 communist deputies elected to the Cortes that year was the tall, stately miner's wife from Gallarta, who hoped that her position in the legislature would help both to safeguard the republic and to bring its long-promised socioeconomic reforms to fruition.

But this was not in the cards. The Popular Front victory ushered in the most devastating war in Spanish history, the final climactic encounter that would decisively determine which forces—red or black, revolutionary or traditionalist—would rule Spain.

III

Perhaps the most convincing proof of the mystique of bestial savagery that surrounds La Pasionaria is the fact that official Franquist historiography credits her sharp tongued oratory with precipitating the civil war itself.[59] Most historians agree that the event that triggered the insurrection was the assassination of José Calvo Sotelo, a prominent conservative parliamentarian, former government minister, and highly regarded monarchist closely in touch with military leaders. Although political violence was a marked feature of the troubled period that followed the Popular Front's victory in the 1936 elections, no victim had been so well known, and the death of the foremost spokesman of the rightist National Front was the spark that set the long-advancing plans of army plotters into action.

Throughout the spring and early summer of 1936, Ibarruri, the dominating personality among the tiny flock of communist deputies in the Cortes, had engaged in a series of furious debates with Calvo

Sotelo, whose fierce determination to rescue Spain from anarchy as he defined it was as impassioned as her own firm insistence that the reforming edicts of the republican government be accepted and carried out. After one particularly violent exchange, she is alleged to have made a shrill and true prophecy, warning him that the speech he had just made would be his last. Although credible witnesses deny hearing the remark, and there is no record of her threat in the *Diario de Sesiones*,[60] the speech was Calvo Sotelo's last, and the belief—real or imagined—in Ibarruri's accessory role in the assassination is symptomatic of the confusion and myth that cloud both her own career and the war in general.

To some the Spanish Civil War was the last great cause, the central focus of a generation's youthful idealism, a clear contest between good and evil, right and wrong, progress and reaction, darkness and light. It made no difference that communism and democracy were bedfellows in the struggle against fascism, for to many it seemed that only the communists were really prepared to fight. These were years of naive innocence, before the horrors of Stalin's crimes were fully known, before the Nazi-Soviet pact had exposed his treachery to the world. It was the era before the great communist god had failed, when many intellectuals tended to see communism as twentieth-century Americanism, to salute Lenin as another Jefferson, and to hail the Spanish experience as a long-delayed replay of 1776.[61]

To others, however, the war was and remains a totally different saga, a sacred crusade of religious dimensions, the historic culmination of Spain's providential mission to save and redeem Western civilization from all dark forces threatening to destroy it. Nationalists from the very beginning claimed that they were rescuing Spain from red domination, that their coup forestalled Moscow's desire to turn Spain into a "powerful, red communist state," that the war was a tragic but necessary battle "between those who hold the doctrines of Karl Marx and those who hold the doctrines of Christ."[62]

Such were the beliefs of the army plotters led by Francisco Franco, who rose in rebellion against the republic during the night of July 17, 1936. Ever since the Napoleonic wars, officers of the Spanish army, seeing themselves as the guardians of the "true" Spain, had used force to direct Spanish political life. The conspirators of 1936 were direct heirs of this tradition. From their base in Spanish Morocco, they planned for a quick coup, hoping that their revolt against the civil government would be repeated in all portions of

Spanish territory. Within a few days of the uprising, the battle lines were well defined across the nation. The legally elected government, supported by a diverse coalition of republican forces—liberals, anti-clericals, radicals, socialists, anarchists, communists—struggled to fend off the challenge of a much more unified nationalist bloc, composed of clergy, large landowners, military leaders, and other segments of Spain's traditional ruling elite. It would be three years and almost 600,000 casualties later before all parts of Spain would again proclaim allegiance to one central government.

Ostensibly the contest at hand was one between democracy and fascism, between a legal government and an illegal one, but to summarize the Spanish Civil War in a shorthand phrase is an impossibility. There were too many issues at stake, too many players, too many curious allegiances and alliances. Yet a few facts appear unassailable. Although international issues and controversies came to be embroiled in this tragic curtain raiser that set the stage for World War II, the war was an exclusively internal matter, the result of wounds left festering since the overthrow of the monarchy in 1931. Old hostilities had been exacerbated by the weakness of the fledgling republican government, and new ones created. In a nation with no tradition of parliamentary democracy, there were too many segments of the population predisposed to disregard the dictates of the new government as they had disobeyed the old. Here was a classic case of revolutionary creation: the republic's limited program of socioeconomic reform was not farsighted enough to appease the left while at the same time being radical enough to antagonize the right. The great property owners were angered by government calls for land reform, while the Catholic hierarchy was offended by its loss of influence in a regime that proudly decreed the separation of church and state. Probably the republican government's greatest weakness was its inability to control the waves of violence that continued throughout its five-year existence. Church burnings, illegal land seizures, strikes, uprisings, assassinations, and arson convinced many that the government was incapable of maintaining public order. So the army—with its long tradition of interfering in political affairs and its naturally conservative outlook—acted.

Attempts to understand the real nature of the Spanish Civil War are further complicated because of the role played by the Spanish Communist Party.[63] While the rightist specter of an imminent communist takeover was a clear fabrication, manufactured both to justify and to drum up support for the army coup, the PCE was destined to rise meteorically during the course of the war. Although it was weak and inconspicuous in 1936, the smallest of the revolutionary parties in the republic, with no more than 30,000 members in all of Spain,[64] its membership actually tripled during the war's first year.[65] Eventually it became the strongest political party in the anti-Franco camp, drawing support from army leaders, government officials, intellectuals, peasants, and members of the middle class.[66] Its fabulous rise was due to many factors: the deficiency of the other parties; its own disciplined, efficient, and monolithic organization; and the inevitable prestige it derived from the receipt of much-needed Soviet aid. Heeding the new Comintern policy that urged communists everywhere to put aside their long-term revolutionary goals and deal first with the menace of fascism in Europe, the PCE entered the republican government in September 1936, the first time a communist party anywhere in the world had ever done so. Over the next three years its influence and power grew steadily, as it proclaimed its staunch loyalty to the democratic republic and its vigorous resolve to repulse the fascist threat.

One of the most important reasons for communist ascendancy after 1936 is the fact that, of all groups in loyalist Spain, the PCE was graced with the best, most colorful, and most inspirational leaders. It was the communist deputy La Pasionaria, the insignificant miner's wife, who was destined to become the best known and best loved of all. She made a startling metamorphosis during the war, from flaming revolutionary to patriotic symbol, known worldwide as the most fervid proponent of the republican cause. The war transformed her into a national leader of the first rank and saw the full development of her fantastic oratorical gifts. From the first days of the insurrection, her deep vibrant voice could be heard in every corner of Spain, as she exhorted the masses to defeat the conspirators in any and all ways. These speeches animated a nation, and she seemed the very incarnation of the Spanish will to resist.

Above all else, it is as the heroine of the siege of Madrid in November 1936 that Dolores Ibarruri, this Spanish Joan of Arc, remains best known. The Spanish people's defense of Madrid in the war's first months is a classic story of resistance against incredible odds, a testament to the resilience of the human spirit, and a tribute to the love for liberty that inspired the republicans. Had the beleaguered capital fallen to the insurgents in November, the war would have been over much sooner, but its lessons would have been lost and Pasionaria's inspirational career would have been cut short. The republicans' tenacious defense of Madrid was nothing short of miraculous, besieged as the city was by four heavily armed columns of Franco's finely-honed rebel army. The loyalists' success—as well as Ibarruri's role in that success—is the stuff of which legends are made.[67]

Pasionaria's rousing exhortations kept the resistance alive. She was heard on radio and in person, in mass public meetings and via countless loudspeakers installed on every street corner and public square, her words, burning with passionate intensity, gripping the imagination of the world. Denouncing the "traitorous rebels and villains" who longed to turn democratic Spain "into a hell of terror and torture," she urged every man, woman, and child to block all enemy attempts to reach the capital, for as long as Madrid remained in the hands of the republican government, victory, she reasoned, was assured.[68] It was during the battle for Madrid that she coined the memorable watchwords that would forever be associated with the Spanish struggle. *No pasaran*, they shall not pass, made famous at the French defense of Verdun in 1916, was applied to the Spanish situation, as she pleaded tirelessly with all Madrileños to dig trenches and barricade streets, to make the capital strong and inaccessible. No matter where one went in the besieged city, one saw banners bearing her words. "Madrid will be the tomb of fascism," these proclaimed. "Spain will never be fascist."[69]

Appealing to the patriotism and sense of duty of the city's population, Ibarruri demanded that the war "be felt by all," that an end be put to all frivolous, indifferent, or irresponsible attitudes, that every citizen become a soldier, that all be prepared for action.[70] Many heeded her calls for total mobilization. Thousands rushed to the front, often without rifles, hoping perhaps to pick up the gun of some dead comrade. "Better to die on your feet than to live on your knees," she chanted, in words that have become a legend.

Her nightly broadcasts upheld popular morale sorely in need of uplifting, for nationalist air attacks unprecedented in ferocity were clearly calculated to terrorize the civilian population into submission. With their round-the-clock bombing, the fascists appeared to be "determined to wipe the capital of Spain from the face of the earth." Contemporaries noted the blind fury of the fascists. "What is happening now could destroy the sanity of sane men."[71]

Yet Pasionaria did not let up, promising more artillery, more Russian aid, more food supplies, or denying the many rumors that the enemy had entered this or that district of the city. Hoping to awaken a sense of communal responsibility in the civilian population, she urged the organization of ward committees to give needed assistance to the families of militia fighters, proposed a system of food rationing and distribution to eliminate the food lines, encouraged universal compulsory labor, and suggested that identification cards be issued by the organizations and parties of the Popular Front so that the invidious saboteurs and fifth columnists might be driven out of their hiding places.[72]

The most important result of Pasionaria's speeches was to galvanize the women of Madrid into action. Gearing her addresses specifically to them, she taught women how to back up their husbands and sons at the front by actively participating in the defense of the city. In one especially memorable speech, she encouraged them to fight with knives or any other weapons at their disposal, even to pour boiling oil on their attackers if necessary.[73] The women of Madrid heeded Pasionaria's words, building barricades, digging trenches, organizing collective dining rooms and laundries, running soup kitchens for refugees and first aid stations for victims of fifth-column sniping.[74]

As a result of their efforts and those of thousands of others like them, Generalissimo Franco failed to capture Madrid by direct assault in the fall of 1936. Undoubtedly, the epic defense of the Spanish capital was the most successful republican action of the war. Even the final loyalist defeat and the eventual fall of the city three years later could never dim the glory of a heroic resistance that all had believed to be impossible. It was a victory in which Dolores Ibarruri and the Spanish Communist Party would always share.

Pasionaria's wartime activities were also important for another reason. Throughout the civil war, in Madrid and elsewhere, her feverish appeals swept millions of Spanish women into unprecedented political activity. In the words of a German émigré who had come to fight for republican Spain, Ibarruri became the ideal for fighting antifascist women everywhere,[75] the symbol of the massive and general involvement of Spanish women, suddenly shaken from centuries of quiescence, in the intensely politicized atmosphere of the war. It took the fascist rebellion to bring equality of the sexes to Spain. One woman told a reporter that even if nothing else were to come from the struggle, "the emancipation of our women will turn out to have made it a good thing."[76]

While the women of the nationalist zone also contributed to the defense of their cause, a veritable social revolution occurred in republican Spain. Contemporaries were quick to comment on the changed position of women, especially conspicuous in Madrid, where women by the hundreds appeared in public unchaperoned or wearing trousers, actions that would have been "unthinkable" before.[77] Legalized abortion and the free distribution of information on venereal disease and birth control led, in the words of one female socialist, "to a new sense of human relationships."[78] Observers pointed to the unusual self-assurance of women, who drew confidence and pride from their participation in the war effort, both on and off the front. Front-line involvement of women was a noted feature of the war in its initial stages, but women also contributed in more traditional ways, helping with cooking or first aid, serving as nurses, orderlies, or laundresses. The services of women were vital to the success of the loyalist cause, as women by the thousands took up the jobs vacated by men, working in hospitals, factories, telephone exchanges, or as teachers in the some 2,000 special schools started to reduce illiteracy among army recruits.

Ibarruri's activities among the women of republican Spain were among her most important. Her work took many forms: propagandizing to heighten women's military resistance and resolve, urging women to take up the jobs men had left behind, and raising the feminist consciousness of men and women both, educating them in the new patterns of social relationships that would characterize the victorious republic. She also worked to keep the resistance alive by organizing more than 100,000 women into anti-fascist committees,[79] and by publishing a communist women's magazine, *Companera.* As the Spanish head of the International Women's Committee Against War and Fascism, she continued work she had begun before the war, uniting women from all republican parties into a common antifascist front.

By using images and appealing to sentiments with which they would be familiar, Ibarruri aimed her emotional and inspirational propaganda specifically at women. She centered her appeals on three traits long associated with the cult of Spanish womanhood: their emotional strength, their love for their children, and their indomitable pride. "We women must demand that our men be courageous," she insisted, for the lives and futures of their children were at stake.[80] Yet, for the thousands who had lost sons she also had words of consolation, urging them to be proud of the fact that they had borne heroes.[81] Such exhortations were deeply rooted in the Spanish past, strikingly similar to old military ballads that reminded women that spiritual immortality awaited their dead sons.[82] Of course, in Pasionaria's version it was the promise of freedom and the fascist defeat, not a heavenly reward, that was to comfort grieving mothers. Many of her speeches and writings also praised women who had died while fighting the fascists, given blood to the victims of war, or followed dead husbands and sons to the front. Millions of Spanish women, as they sent their loved ones into battle, repeated another of her famous battle cries: "It is better to be the widow of a hero than the wife of a coward."[83]

Another aim of Pasionaria's propagandizing was to convince women that work in the rear was of no less importance than work at the front. "It is the imperative duty of every communist," she maintained, to work untiringly for the incorporation of women in production, for only in this way could victory be assured.[84] Here she realized she needed to combat the prejudices of women as well as men. Encouraging women to have faith in themselves, she told simple but moving stories of valiant women who had contributed both to their own glory and the glory of the loyalist cause by working in industries that had been traditionally closed to them. In one typical account, a woman employed in a cartridge factory locked horns with a fifth-columnist foreman who tried to sabotage the war effort. By his refusal to repair machines when they broke down, this factory, which could produce hundreds of thousands of cartridges per day, was producing only 80,000. Of course the moral of Pasionaria's tale was that her heroine could learn to repair the machines herself. Production skyrocketed, and the war effort was saved.[85]

Yet, according to Ibarruri, more than a republican victory was at stake in the communists' concerted drive to draw women into industry. The consciousness of women needed to be raised for the sake of the revolution itself, for as Lenin had taught, the success of any revolution depended on the extent to which women took part in it.[86] Routinely accepting the orthodox Marxist belief that the crux of the woman question was primarily economic, Pasionaria preached the gospel of work, the belief that only through work could women emerge from centuries of slavery and seclusion, that they would become free only when they were in a position to earn their own livelihood.[87] Although she admitted that there were real problems with drawing women into industry—basically a need for kindergartens and crèches where women might leave their children during work, and the establishment of public dining rooms to ease the burdens of individual family responsibilities[88]—these were problems of socialist reconstruction that would have to await the war's end for their successful solution. In the meantime, however, she was adamant that the wholesale entrance of women into industrial activity would be triply beneficial: for the war, for the revolution, and for women themselves.

While Ibarruri's approach to the woman question certainly did not have the creative originality or passionate conviction that marked Kollontai's, she was frank and forthright in her assessment of the failings of Spanish communism in this area. The party, in her opinion, hadn't done enough to mobilize women, and its commitment to the cause of women's emancipation had so far proven to be little more than a mere slogan.[89] Women's slow movement into the party was due to two reasons: the PCE's own failure to be sensitive to their very real needs and pressures, and the rather blatant hostility of Spanish men, both in party cells and in trade unions, who had yet to overcome ancient beliefs in female inferiority.[90] Addressing groups of trade unionists, Ibarruri was blunt in her criticism. She actually held communist men responsible for the reactionary and backward condition in which Spanish women found themselves. Although the staunch traditionalism of women was routinely lamented, she challenged all communists to ask themselves what they had done to draw women to the cause. Had they brought their wives to meetings, or encouraged them to join the party?[91] "Those who hold reactionary views on the role of women cannot be called communists," she asserted,[92] as she urged men to abandon petty fears that competition from women would somehow jeopardize their own jobs. "When the war is over," she assured them, "tens of thousands of men and women will be required for the building of the new Spain we desire to create."[93]

Ibarruri's feminist ideals, however routine, limited, or subordinated to larger aims, were in sharp contrast to the image of women unfolding in those areas of Spain under insurgent control. The nationalist position on the woman question was clear. The good state rests on the family, its propaganda decreed. "It will be strong if the woman at home is healthy, fecund, hard working, and happy."[94]

Ibarruri's vision was a decidedly different one. Ensured a "creative, industrious, joyous, and happy life,"[95] women in the new Spain would be more than "mere drudges" waiting patiently on husband and children, but would be the equals, friends, and comrades of their husbands, citizens who in factory, workshop, institute, and laboratory "would work, study, and investigate alongside men, with the same rights and with the same duties."[96] In preparation for that end, she urged that women be promoted to responsible leadership positions in the PCE, and asked Jesús Hernández, the communist minister of education in the republican government, to help women receive a higher education.[97]

Despite her very real interest in women's issues, however, Pasionaria's major preoccupation during these years was military, the need to win the war against a well-trained and well-equipped insurgent army. "Each of us," she recognized, "must place the interests of the war above all others."[98] Her oratory heralded the communists' main theme: the urgent need to organize a disciplined and efficient army in the republican zone. From the very outbreak of the insurrection, the PCE through its major spokesman, Dolores Ibarruri, agitated tirelessly for the organization of a regular army, for the introduction of compulsory military service, for a purge of army ranks to weed out saboteurs, and for the creation of reserves. Pasionaria herself led the recruiting drive that culminated in the establishment of the famous fifth regiment, the PCE's outstanding military achievement. Added to the four regiments normally stationed in Madrid, this force of 8,000 volunteers became the cornerstone of the popular army. Through its fifth regiment, the Communist Party undertook the training of military cadres and the formation of units with technical staffs and specialized departments. All historians agree that it was because of communist pressure that the government, out of the general chaos, was able to create a modern army capable of withstanding for three years the combined forces of Franco, the Moroccan legion, the Spanish Foreign Legion, several Italian divisions, and sections of the German army.[99]

The prestige of the PCE was also heightened through its close association with one of the most romantic chapters to come out of the Spanish Civil War—the story of the International Brigades. While the majority of these volunteers were exiled socialists and communists from countries that the fascists had already overrun, the 40,000 idealists who risked their lives for Spanish liberty came from many nations. Dedicated to the fight against fascism, they caught the imagination of the world for their spirit, their selflessness, and their passion.

Ibarruri was among the most enthusiastic in her repeated praise for the valor of all republican units, the International Brigades in particular. Dividing her time between Madrid and the front, she was a regular visitor to Guadarrama, Aragon, Catalonia, and Estremadura, bolstering army morale, thanking soldiers for their bravery, and convincing them that their steadfastness and courage would compensate for their lack of arms and training.[100]

Her esteem for them, however, was matched if not surmounted by their affection for her. Many contemporary accounts give us a clear and stirring picture of what Pasionaria came to mean to the men in the trenches. She fulfilled their desperate need to be led, spoken to, heartily encouraged. She "electrified us," one civil war veteran recalled. "After hearing her, you'd pick up a rifle or bayonet and go wherever she wanted you to go. You'd find her in the most dangerous places at the most difficult time, comforting us to keep us going."[101] Mess hall barracks and reading rooms were covered with her portraits, and for many men, she was second only to their own wives in importance. One communist militiaman recalled the feelings of his unit. As part of the government's campaign against illiteracy, many recruits were being taught to read and write at the front. They were tremendously excited by their progress, he explained, and when they learned, they invariably wrote two letters, "the first to their wives, the second to La Pasionaria, to inform her of the good news."[102] Among members of the International Brigades, her appeal was especially great. American volunteer Alvah Bessie called her one of the greatest human beings of his generation.[103] Poems were written about her, battalions named after her.[104] For some she became a new saint, a curious fusion of religious and revolutionary beliefs. Her sayings and slogans were repeated like talismans, revolutionary prayers replacing the religious ones of youth. In *For Whom the Bell Tolls*, a peasant warrior thought first of Pasionaria, not of Mary, as he lay dying.[105]

Outside Spain, Ibarruri also came to be hailed as a saintly symbol of idealism and resistance. Her broadcasts informed the world of Spain's furious determination to continue the struggle for the republic—"as long as we have left a single olive tree to defend, a single yard of soil on which to plant our feet, a single stone to serve as a breastwork."[106] Her message was especially strong in other countries menaced by the scourge of fascism, and her speeches paid special tribute to "invaded China," "menaced Czechoslovakia," disappeared Austria, and "shamelessly abandoned" Abyssinia.[107] As the civil war came to be more than an isolated, purely national struggle, Ibarruri took on a new role, that of prophetic Cassandra, emphasizing the international importance of Spain's resistance to fascism. The disappearance of democracy in Spain would herald the inevitable beginning of a new world war, she warned, for the involvement of Germany and Italy had given the war a special character.[108] Pointing to their support of Franco, she appealed to Western democracies to help save the republic.

The failure of the West to protect the beleaguered republic remains one of the most tragic episodes in this tragic tale. Under international law, the Spanish government had every right to buy arms from abroad for the suppression of an internal rising, but the complexities of international politics in the 1930s worked to ensure that the government would be denied that right. In the late summer and early fall of 1936, 27 European nations—including France, Great Britain, the Soviet Union, Italy, and Germany—signed a nonintervention agreement pledging to leave the Spanish to fight it out alone.[109] Although each signatory had its own reasons for the decision, most hoped nonintervention would prevent a wider war. Ironically, however, the pact, with no binding clauses and nothing that could legally be defined as a clear violation, worked inexorably in that direction. While France and Great Britain generally observed and enforced it, German and Italian intervention went unchecked. Italy sent large conscript armies; Germany, munitions, technical aid, and war planes; and both helped blockade republican ports and engaged in piracy on the high seas against vessels carrying arms or supplies to the Spanish republicans.

Dolores Ibarruri came to be the most biting critic of the "farce of nonintervention." As the member of a government-named committee, she made several trips to France during the course of the war, a nation which also had a left-wing Popular Front government and was menaced on both sides of its borders by the fascist threat. Addressing mass meetings to solicit aid for the republican cause, she appealed directly to Prime Minister Leon Blum for the French government to change its mind on the issue of intervention.[110] Her speeches aimed to tell the truth about Spain as she saw it, and to outline what the defeat of the republicans would mean for France. The Spanish war, she insisted, was not a war for communism, as some had tried to depict it, but a war of invasion, a war of conquest. This was a war "for the preservation of our national independence," fought against those who would turn Spain into a colony, divide up its mineral wealth, seize its resources, and use it as a strategic base for the impending world war that loomed so prominently in their plans.[111] Imploring the French workers, with their "heroic traditions," to force their own government to change its policies "so barbaric, so inhuman, so inimical to the interests of the masses of the people,"[112] she painted a touching picture of the horrors of the war in Spain. Hunger raged because of the infamous blockade, the suffering of children was especially acute, and more than 2 million refugees had fled their homes rather than live under fascist rule.

Ibarruri excited the same passions in France that she did elsewhere. While French conservatives feared her trip would incite civil war, and fascists published lurid tales of her revolutionary exploits— claiming she had once slashed a priest's throat with her own teeth[113] — she captured the hearts of the audiences she addressed. "Tears streamed from the eyes of men and women as they listened to Pasionaria," and crowds threw themselves upon her, crying, kneeling in her path.[114]

Yet, despite her popularity, Ibarruri was unable to overturn the nonintervention policy of France or other Western democracies. Her life-long praise for Stalin and the Soviet Union is understandable only in light of this failure, for when it was unable to purchase arms elsewhere, the Spanish republic came increasingly to depend on aid, equipment, and materiel supplied by Russia. Certainly as the leader of the world revolutionary movement, the USSR, for reasons of prestige and credibility, needed to support the republic, but the Soviet people were also genuinely and naturally sympathetic to its cause. From the very beginning of the war, spontaneous collections in factories and farms yielded tons of food, clothing, and medicine for the women and children of Spain.[115] Communist-sponsored organizations throughout the world also collected large sums of money, and the Comintern created a new network of relief organizations solely for Spanish support. When Stalin saw how little the nonintervention agreement was being observed, he sent artillery, tanks, airplanes, pilots, and tank operators to Spain—aid that made the communists the heroes of the republican cause. As one observer put it, every Russian airplane that flew overhead was communist propaganda.[116]

Dolores Ibarruri never forgot that the Soviet Union came to the rescue of her beloved Spain. The socialist fatherland already held her heart for ideological reasons, but her communist faith was only strengthened by Stalin's willingness to furnish much-needed military assistance. For the impressionable Ibarruri, the "generous and unconditional" aid supplied by the Russians was proof of the "international solidarity of socialism." Although deserted by the West, the Spanish people could take heart from the fact that they had not been abandoned by "their Soviet brothers." The USSR, she repeatedly reminded her audiences, was the "inspiration and the hope of the international proletariat . . . the hope of all peoples threatened by fascism . . . the impregnable fortress, the firm pillar of strength," around which all might rally.[117]

Unquestionably, Soviet aid did save the republic for a time, but it forced both the government and the PCE into greater reliance on the Russians. Imprisoned by the desperate need for Soviet assistance, the PCE throughout the war adopted domestic policies that we now clearly see served Soviet rather than Spanish interests. Dependent on Western democracy for his own defense against Hitler, Stalin's main concern in supporting the republic was to keep Spain out of the hands of fascist dictators, thereby saving his ally, France, from the perils of encirclement. His real intent was to protect himself—never actually to promote a communist Spain. In fact the contrary was true. Because the specter of a red Spain would have alienated Britain and France—on whom Stalin relied for his own defense against the mounting threat of fascism in Europe—he instructed the Spanish communists to limit themselves to the defense of the legal republican government against Franco, rather than to work openly for the success of the socialist revolution.[118]

Here, the ever grateful Pasionaria—with her burning oratory, incredible popularity, and Spanish soul—was in a prime position to do Stalin's bidding, and he, dangling the carrot of continued assistance, was in a prime position to dictate terms. Thus throughout the war, she repeated over and over again that what was taking place in Spain was not the proletarian revolution, but the "bourgeois democratic revolution which was achieved over a century ago in other countries."[119] Although she continued to believe that the communists were not abandoning their desire to achieve the victory of socialism "in due time," she insisted that it was simply impossible to discuss the future revolution while the war was still raging.[120]

In this way, the PCE actually became a rather conservative force among Spanish republicans. Its domestic program was both realistic enough for a country besieged by war and moderate enough to appeal to a wide variety of middle class republican groups. Calling for amnesty for revolutionary and political prisoners, improvement in the conditions of life and work, liberation of the oppressed nationalities of Catalonia, Galicia, and Euzkadi, and confiscation of church property, it contained no alarming phrases like destruction of the bourgeois state or collectivization of private property. Actually the PCE came to be a staunch protector of the interests of the rural and urban middle classes, whose hopes for a better life centered in the accumulation, not the abolition, of private property. While it supported the government's policy of confiscating the large landholdings of Franco supporters, it roundly condemned the collectivizations that had taken place in some parts of Spain.

The party's industrial policies were similar. Allowing factories that had been owned by rebels to be expropriated and nationalized, the communists were opposed to their ownership and management by workers. This, in the words of Pasionaria, would be detrimental to the war effort, resulting in disorganization and chaos in production.[120] All nonrebel-owned factories would continue under private ownership and management. These communist positions, made in Moscow, adopted by the PCE, and enunciated by Pasionaria, greatly disillusioned many observers who came to believe that the Spanish communists were working not merely to postpone the revolution "but to make sure it never happened."[121]

Ideological conflicts among the republican forces were further exacerbated by the political priorities of the Soviet Union. One of the main supporters of collectivist revolutionary activity in Catalonia and rural Aragon was a small but vigorous anti-Stalinist party headed by a former secretary to Leon Trotsky. The United Marxist Workers Party (POUM) was not a Trotskyist party, but Moscow had fallen into the habit of pinning that label on all with whom it disagreed. In a clear case of Soviet squabbles being transplanted to Spain, the PCE, despite the pressures of war, moved to destroy this tiny group. This fratricidal civil war within the republican camp came to a head in several days of street fighting in Barcelona in May 1937, as communists and socialists battled anarchists and the POUM.[122]

When socialist Prime Minister Francisco Largo Caballero refused to join in the suppression of the POUM, the communists precipitated a cabinet crisis. Their strength had risen to such heights by this time that they were able to make or break ministries. The ever obedient Pasionaria led the fight against him. Charging that the uprising in Barcelona had been staged under fascist instigation with the aim of starting a civil war in the rear and paralyzing the government, she accused Largo Caballero of treachery and defeatism, claiming that he was protecting the POUM because he saw them as useful in his own power struggle with the communists.[123]

From this brief description, it is clear that the republic was never able to achieve the unity and discipline that Franco created in his part of Spain. By 1938 the republicans were quarreling among themselves, and the war itself had degenerated into the long and bloody agony of a war of attrition. Throughout the republic, revolutionary zeal had begun to subside, food was terribly short, and factory output, because of the lack of raw materials, fell alarmingly.

With the collapse of Catalonia in January 1939, there was little hope that the republic could be saved. In February, Britain and France recognized Franco's government. Although the republicans still held one third of Spain, including Madrid and Valencia, they had almost no supplies, and the army knew further resistance was futile. The communists, on the other hand, preached resistance to the last. Years later, Pasionaria continued to maintain that it would have been possible, that defeat was the result of republican cowardice, not fascist strength.[124] In her opinion, the man to whom Franco "owed" his victory was Colonel Segismundo Casado, a republican officer of long standing known to be very hostile to communism.

Believing that the republicans had become too dependent on aid from Moscow,[125] Casado overthrew the loyalist government in a military coup on March 6, 1939, and established a national defense junta to arrange an end to the fighting. His action was resisted by several units, roused to resistance by communist appeals, and in another tragic episode of this most tragic war, bitter street fighting between one-time republicans continued in Madrid until the end of March.

By that time Pasionaria, along with other government and communist leaders, had already left Spain, departing by plane for France via Alicante. Certain death would have awaited all of them had they remained, and hopes for maintaining a republican government in exile and the tenuous grouping of an underground communist party both would have been lost. Thirty-two months after it had first begun, the war with which Dolores Ibarruri would forever be associated was over.

IV

During the Spanish Civil War, two completely different portraits arose of the woman known universally as La Pasionaria, portraits intimately bound up with one's interpretation of what was ultimately at stake in that conflict. Her supporters loved and worshipped her, and for many she became a sort of living saint who might lead them through their darkest days of trial and tribulation. Wherever she went, a contemporary wrote, the masses reached out to touch her, "to see if she is really made of flesh, or if she is imaginary."[126] There was a profound motherliness about her, someone said, something of a medieval ascetic and religious personality combined.[127] Undoubtedly she was the best-known personality to emerge from the civil war, respected as one of the world's most outstanding women. Heroine, warrior, saint of the new order, symbol of hope, she was a female Don Quixote, more loved by the masses than any other person in Spain.

Yet she worked her magic elsewhere as well, and on others besides her own people. Because of the moderate programs adopted by the PCE, to democrats everywhere she appeared to be a firm proponent of liberal principles: "private property and liberty of conscience."[128] Americans knew her as the communist heroine of the workers,[129] and a British reporter called her the only Spanish politician who had really impressed him as being "a great person."[130] Two American congressmen visiting Spain were deeply moved by her tender love for children, and by her obviously sincere concern for the young orphans of the war.[131] "Men love you, hear you, listen to you, esteem you," wrote a French woman.[132] "You are stalwart, strong . . . good . . . wise," hailed another.[133]

But her image in the nationalist zone was something quite different. Vicious rumors and allegations of all kinds explained the past of this most "unspeakable person." One of the most common was that she was a former nun who had married an unfrocked monk— hence her hatred for all religious orders.[134] Pasionaria and her imaginary love affairs were the favorite target of rebel reporting perversely fascinated with sex and violence.[135] General Queipo de Llano, the commander of the insurgent army in the south, talked nightly on Radio Seville and, in the words of Claude Bowers, the U.S. Ambassador to Spain, ridiculed Ibarruri "with the ribald humor of the barracks and the picturesque phraseology of the fish market."[136] To the nationalists, she seemed to epitomize the unnatural freedom that communist liberation of women, with its doctrines of "free love," was all about. The vulgarity of fascist accounts verged on the burlesque, with their descriptions of naked combats between men and women, "febrile rumbas in hospital orgies," and "Red Amazons," "many of them actually stripped to the waist, carrying modern rifles, and with blood in their eye."[137] Pasionaria became the symbol of all these horrors and abominations. Portrayed as ferocious and bloodthirsty, she was said "to look more like a beast than a man,"[138] and nationalist soldiers were taught to fear the day they would face loyalist brigades that carried the awe-inspiring label, "the Grey Wolves of La Pasionaria."[139]

Clearly Ibarruri, like the war itself, was neither as black nor white as she has been depicted. No one was as ruthless in condemning the "Trotskyite poison" as she, and the rantings of Pasionaria came to be associated with the terror that had become a fact of life in both parts of Spain.[140] But her deep and sincere love for "plain ordinary people" is well documented,[141] and the plight of innocent civilians greatly affected her. Impartial observers confirmed that despite her popular image, Pasionaria was a powerful influence for clemency among communists. Her intervention spared the lives of many, especially women, and "those, however wealthy, who had given generously to charities could count on her protection."[142] Among those she rescued were several communities of nuns, whom she spirited to safety during the war's first desperate days in Madrid, when pent up passions exploded in waves of church burnings and murders of religious. Arranging for their protection in an empty Augustinian convent in Madrid, she saw to it that the building was properly furnished with religious pictures and crucifixes, well stocked with provisions, and guarded by the fifth regiment. She led others to shelter in embassies and helped them to get abroad.[143]

Such stories have about them a certain strange-but-true quality. While Ibarruri herself clung to orthodox Marxist atheism, she upheld the right of religious freedom and spoke out against religious persecution in Nazi Germany and elsewhere.[144] Despite the communists' reputation for being priest-killers, they actually worked to restore religious life in Spain, efforts that won the praise and support of the staunchly Catholic Basques.[145]

Although opinion may forever be divided as to whether Ibarruri was indeed saint or devil, all contemporaries were unanimous in their praise of her extraordinary abilities as an orator. Well over six feet tall, with sharp chiseled features and fiery eyes, she was a stark and impressive figure who moved audiences to tears and tumult. "I have never seen nor heard anything like it," a listener recalled, "never felt, between orators and hearers, such a communication of strength."[146] "Whatever one's politics, it is thrilling to hear her," wrote one reporter.[147] "Hers is a voice one cannot forget."[148]

In her listeners, Pasionaria inspired love, devotion, and ardor, a willingness to believe and act on all she told them. An American caught in Madrid during the siege attested to the incredible power of her oratory. "Everyone who left the theater that night had overcome the fear and despair of the previous week. Everyone went out with firm assurance—*no pasaran*."[149] After listening to her for three and one-half hours, one journalist insisted that he could have "listened for another ten."[150] Often she spoke until she grew hoarse, yet somehow she was always able to draw inner reserves of strength from the deep conviction behind her words. One contemporary described a night she could not continue, totally exhausted, but apologizing effacingly for her failure. "There was not the slightest touch of ostentation in it," he recalled.

> Only regret at being unable to tell the meeting those things she had wanted to tell it. This gesture, in its profound simplicity, sincerity, and its convincing lack of any personal interest in success or failure as an orator, was more touching than her whole speech.[151]

Ibarruri's powerful oratorical talent seems to have been the major reason that she attained the acceptance and acclaim she did within communist party ranks. Not for her was the hostility, opprobrium, and scorn heaped on Luxemburg, Kollontai, and Balabanoff. Serving several vital functions in a nation the Kremlin was anxiously seeking to bring within its orbit, she was flattered, fêted, and extrolled in a Spanish version of the cult of personality rivaling only Stalin's own in its sweeping magnitude.

Ibarruri became the communist virgin in a land where all sides came to have their token female madonnas, useful, of course, for rallying women to the cause but even more understandable within a Catholic Spanish context where the Marian cult and the idolatry of the spiritually stronger woman were deeply rooted. The socialists had deputy Margarita Nelken; the anarchists, libertarian Federica Montseny; while fascist propaganda described the ideal female as a combination of St. Teresa of Avila and Isabella the Catholic.[152] Religious and political images were clearly fused on both sides; rituals were religious and political at once. In Pamplona in 1936, a fascist procession in honor of the Virgin of the Pillar was followed by an execution. With the local clergy in military formation, 60 republican prisoners were shot "for the honor and glory of the Virgin," to the accompaniment of a peal of bells.[153]

Curiously, however, many republicans also adopted the Virgin as their own. During several demonstrations, her image was borne in triumph, and banners carried the bold announcement, "We are communists. Our knives for anyone who touches her."[154] Devotion to Mary was especially strong among the Spanish poor, who could not fail to see revolutionary overtones in basic Catholic teachings. Mary's great song of triumph, the Magnificat, could very well have applied to Pasionaria, who also rejoiced that the mighty had been humbled and the meek exalted, the hungry filled with good things and the rich sent empty away.

Because the policy of the PCE came to be so closely identified with Moscow, because the republic owed its very salvation to Soviet aid and because of the large number of Comintern agents openly active in Spain, it was especially important that Spanish communism develop a uniquely Spanish symbol and spokesman. Pasionaria, "quintessentially Spanish, quintessentially woman, quintessentially proletarian,"[155] fit that bill perfectly. Contemporaries recognized that her strength lay in the fact that she was typical, not exceptional, "a daughter, wife, and mother of the working class."[156] Her rhetoric was Spanish, the examples she used were Spanish, the historical heritage to which she appealed was Spanish. Portraying the civil war as a struggle for national liberation, independence, and freedom, her speeches emphasized the glorious traditions of heroic Spain. Fascist generals, supported by foreign powers, were not men of the people, she explained, but a "caste," the aristocratic sons of those officers who had betrayed Spain during the war of independence in 1808 and delivered it over to Napoleon.[157]

Not only did the communists benefit by having one of the greatest orators of the twentieth century in their camp, but they also profited from the sincere sentiments of devotion and love that Pasionaria inspired in the masses. By all accounts, her appeal to the people was genuine, and her popularity certainly contributed to the fantastic growth of the PCE. With her colorful, fiery personality and emotional, maternal character, she was the strongest leader the communists had. Her speeches were always sure to command large audiences, "and no other voice," a contemporary wrote, could so surely have reached the depths of every mind in the crowds she attracted.[158] Having leaders "so beloved of the masses" seemed to prove the very righteousness of the communist cause,[159] and they were quick to take full advantage of the heroine of Madrid. Propaganda pamphlets proudly touted the fact that she was on their side. "Wherever she went," boasted one, "Dolores was a shining example of what a communist should be."[160]

Certainly a valuable asset because of her popular appeal, Ibarruri was able to rise to the influential position she did because of the absence of any other really strong or charismatic figure within the PCE. Splits and sectarian squabbles in the party in its first decade of existence had eliminated most of its potential leaders, while those who did rise to power had no previous record of leadership and were not destined to become well known even during the civil war itself. According to contemporaries, men like party chiefs José Díaz, Vicente Uribe, and Jesús Hernández were hardly known to the masses, and they certainly did not owe their positions to their personal prestige.[161] Furthermore, Stalin would have been the last to watch them acquire any personal prestige that might have made them independent of his orders. But Pasionaria was different. While she did have an enormous amount of personal influence, she was not a strictly political leader, if leadership implies autonomy in policy setting and decision making.

It was precisely her willingness to toe the Stalinist line on each and every issue that made her so valuable—and accounted for the influence and repute she came to hold within both the PCE and the Comintern. From the very start, there was a conscious aura of conversion in her acceptance of socialism, an explicit recognition that this "new faith" had come to replace the traditional religious devotion of her youth.[162] For one who had been so devoutly religious, the transposition between socialism and Catholicism was easy to make. Both had their cult of saints, both demanded sacrifices, both had tremendous emotional appeal, and both promised comradeship in the larger struggle for the larger cause. While her new faith was "more reasonable and more solid" than her religious faith had been, she embraced it with the same unconditional emotionalism that she accepted the old. The Stalinist credo became her catechism; quotations from his speeches and writings peppered her own. His teachings she repeated over and over again, as if by rote, the memorized watchwords of a profession of faith. Stalin replaced the God she had abandoned. Eternally grateful for Soviet aid, she praised and thanked him repeatedly in paeans of gratitude, like prayers of thanksgiving to a beneficent deity.[163] Praising and honoring the Soviet fatherland she called her "sacred duty."[164]

As she had never challenged the dictates of priests or confessors, so she accepted unquestioningly the rulings of the Soviet hierarchy. A revolutionary party cannot be a debating club, she concluded; its decisions, once made, must be firmly and resolutely carried out by all its members.[165] This belief continued all her life. Having come to socialism in an era when discipline and authoritarianism were the order of the day, her inclination toward passive and uncritical obedience was difficult to shed. Moreover, unlike the other women of this study, Ibarruri adopted socialism just as the Soviet Union was on its way to becoming a reality. It was common for believers of her generation to look with reverence on the socialist mecca, natural for Ibarruri herself to think its teachings and doctrines as infallible as the dogmas of the Catholic creed she had only recently abandoned.

Ibarruri was a good communist as she had been a good Catholic— uncritical and unquestioning in her constant and tireless support for party programs, whether she was analyzing the basic issues at stake in the civil war, condemning the Trotskyists or Social Democrats, or recruiting women to the antifascist cause. She actually had few, if any, original ideas of her own, and when official Soviet policy changed, hers did accordingly.[166] Observers knew she frequently spoke from texts prepared for her in advance,[167] and sometimes she herself admitted that her only task was to popularize and publicize what the PCE had instructed her to say.[168] Perhaps, as one contemporary noted, she simply did not have the theoretical grounding necessary to resist or question official Comintern policy for Spain,[169] or as a woman raised in a staunchly patriarchal culture, perhaps she simply believed she should not. In her speeches, she always paid tribute to the "great theoreticians of socialism," or routinely summarized policies as being in strict conformity with the "Marxist-Leninist-Stalinist" line on a particular issue.[170] Like Balabanoff, her understanding of Marxism was somewhat rote and mechanical. She was impatient with intellectuals, a friend remarked, and she never felt at ease among them.[171] Perhaps conscious of the deficiencies of her own education, she never attempted one purely theoretical undertaking. Those publications she has to her credit were rousing propaganda pamphlets, or reprints of her most popular speeches. While these may have been powerful in delivery, they were disappointing in written form, eclectic, disjointed, and unsophisticated, often filled with the same stock jargon, picturesque phrases, and standard explanations that had made her famous.

Yet, like Balabanoff, it was never a theorist that Ibarruri aimed to be. Publicist, propagandist, and recruiter, she sought with simple and convincing words to bring her message to all who would hear her, and to save, in her opinion, both them and Spain in the process.

Ibarruri's strictly conformist career has blackened her reputation in the noncommunist West, where Stalinism and sincerity are believed to be mutually exclusive. Added to the she-devil image of the civil war are equally unflattering portraits of a woman who, in the view of some, "astutely played the revolutionary saint" to hide her deeper ambitions.[172] Her motives have been questioned, her revolutionary ardor minimized. But, while it may be difficult to see any virtue in her position, it is wrong to judge history by retrospect, to condemn the men and women who embraced communism in those years because of what we now know about the terrors of Stalinism. The world of the 1930s was a very different place from our own; fascism, not communism, was the loathesome enemy of humanists everywhere. Perhaps Pasionaria was either naive or deluded in her effusive praise for Stalin and the Soviet Union, but if so, she found herself in good company in the 1930s and early 1940s.[173] Even socialists markedly hostile to communism came to believe that the Soviet Union must survive, that the great socialist experiment be allowed to continue. Among socialists, Ibarruri in particular, there was immense pride in Soviet achievements and resolute determination to work untiringly so that these might be protected. The Russian people had been the most backward in Europe, she noted, yet had been able to overcome all the difficulties of revolution and achieve victory "in spite of everything." This enheartened her tremendously, especially during the siege of Madrid, when she exhorted the Spanish to follow the example of their "magnificent Russian brothers and sisters" who had demonstrated undeniably that "one people, by acting resolutely, could become the masters of their own country."[174]

Inspired by this faith and impressed by these achievements, Ibarruri regarded the Soviet Union with almost religious devotion, and it is easy to see why she turned a blind eye to any defects she may have seen there. As was the case with her contemporary Kollontai, it would have been incredibly difficult for her to turn her back on an ideal in which she had total faith and for which she had long sacrificed, a nation which at that very moment was aiding her to realize her dreams for republican Spain. Other Spanish communists confirmed that there was a "mystical, almost religious" element in the PCE's attitude toward the Soviets in these years,[175] when Russia alone could be relied on for support against the fascists. The USSR also sheltered and schooled thousands of Spanish children during the chaos of the war, including Ibarruri's own.

Dolores Ibarruri was far from being a vile and self-seeking careerist with a Stalinist bent for deception, pure and simple. As often as contemporaries wrote of her oratorical power, they paid tribute to her unusual sincerity, the genuine conviction behind the words she spoke, her character and passionate candor. American journalist Vincent Sheean summarized this best. Although he realized that her speeches were probably the carefully reasoned work of a trained political committee, they drew their unique power, he explained, from being filtered "through her own exceptional heart and brain. And that text, in that voice, carried the very taste and substance of truth."[176]

Ibarruri was a socialist who chose to become a communist almost two decades before the Spanish Civil War broke out. Therefore, the opportunities for personal power and political ascendancy presented by that war were clearly not the motives that triggered her stalwart loyalty to party and Comintern. While the conformist career of the one-time rebellious revolutionary may rightly raise eyebrows, the nature of her conformism was in sharp contrast to that of many ambitious or blatantly opportunistic careerists who joined the Communist Party during the war itself—individuals impressed by communist efficiency and military discipline who were simply seeking a safe haven or a niche in a sure-to-be-successful regime.[177] Contemporaries noted that it was Ibarruri's very aloofness from the atmosphere of political intrigue that contributed to her popularity. Her "lack of conceit" was obvious, her self-effacement "touching," her "simple, self-sacrificing faith" in sharp contrast to the posings of professional politicians.[178]

Hungarian communist Arthur Koestler once tried to describe the motives of another Spaniard who had also fallen under the spell of Stalin during these years. "It is impossible to be angry with Picasso," he explained, "for believing that Stalin was the greatest benefactor of mankind, for one feels that his error is the result of a naive and warmhearted passion."[179] These words may apply with equal validity to La Pasionaria. Ibarruri believed deeply in an egalitarian society where simple people might occupy a dignified place, and her readiness to sacrifice everything to this end deserves admiration, even though it may at times be hard to understand why she acted as she did.

Throughout her lifetime she fought in the best way she knew how for the "creation of a free human race, a liberated world, a world without poverty or distress, without inequality . . . without exploiters and war makers."[180] While her belief that life in the Soviet Union came nearest to this description may have been grossly misconceived, her desire to relieve human suffering was genuine, pouring forth in both her actions and her words. She loved all with whom she came into contact, not as mere associates, but as individuals—the girl interpreter and secretary assisting in her interviews, the messenger boy with news from the latest workers meetings, the pale wounded youth she welcomed from the front as if she were greeting her own son.[181]

All her efforts during the civil war were geared to establishing and protecting a Spain that would give land to the peasants, nationalize industry for the benefit of the masses, establish much-needed social reforms, protect the liberties of national minorities, and solve the economic problems that lie at the heart of all revolutions.[182] There was a profoundly human tone to her speeches, as she detailed the indescribable villainies wrought by war, the exigencies of grief, starvation, homelessness, and death. Her moral outrage at the fate of Spain was moving, fervid, and real. Humaneness was her most endearing quality, a contemporary wrote.[183] No hateful word she uttered seemed to have been inspired "by anything save love."[184] Dolores Ibarruri was a "warm, dignified, uncomplicated human being."[185] If she had a Stalinist head, she did not have a Stalinist heart.[186]

V

After the civil war, the Spanish Communist Party was declared illegal in Spain and became the target of a furious campaign of brutal repression unleashed by the Franco government. Spanish communists by the thousands retreated to underground activity or exile, and Dolores Ibarruri took her place among the more than 10,000 Spaniards who sought refuge in the Soviet Union.[187]

Ibarruri's Soviet sojourn lasted almost 40 years. As a reward for her fierce loyalty to the USSR, she was rescued from the life of wandering and impotence that other loyalist émigrés were forced to endure. More importantly, she was in the position to keep the PCE alive, albeit as an illegal party in exile, for the Spanish party was afforded the unique privilege of being the only foreign communist party allowed to operate from Moscow. Pasionaria's status in the international communist hierarchy also grew during these years, and she performed a variety of services for the communist cause worldwide. During the period of her exile she actually played a dual role: as an international communist emissary ever loyal and grateful to the Soviet fatherland, and as titular leader of the Spanish Communist Party. It would not always be easy to reconcile both.

As Ibarruri had predicted, Franco's victory in Spain presaged a worldwide confrontation between fascism and democracy. Five months after Spanish resistance was crushed, World War II broke out in all its tragic fury. During the war she turned her propaganda and oratorical talents to bolstering the Soviet cause against Hitler. Addressing many of her speeches to women the world over, she repeated the themes she had developed during the civil war, only this time she augmented her authority by speaking as a Spaniard who truly knew the meaning of fascism's new order. Aiming to educate the women of the world to "the real nature of Hitlerism before it was too late," she warned of the denigration and subservience that Nazism aimed to impose on all women.[188] The women of Britain, America, and the invaded countries of Europe must shake off their passivity, she cried, be worthy of their men, fight day and night, at the front and in the rear, "without rest, without respite," for the defeat of fascism.[189] Pasionaria also took her place among those women who gave "all that was most precious to them" in that fight. Her only surviving son Ruben met his death at Stalingrad, as commander of a machine gun company in the Red Army.

It is difficult to determine how much Ibarruri really knew about what was taking place in Russia during these years. A hard-line Stalinist uncomfortable in a non-Stalinist world, she never discussed them in any detail, and she was loathe to criticize her Soviet hosts even after her Russian exile had ended. Visibly annoyed at journalists' attempts to press her for information, she insisted that she knew nothing about Stalin's crimes more than what she read in the newspapers or saw superficially.[190] Only once is she known to have protested, when the Stalinist reign of terror threatened her long-time companion and personal secretary Irene Falcon. When Falcon's safety was jeopardized because of her association with a Czech executed as a traitor, Pasionaria pleaded with the Central Committee of the Soviet party, begging that her friend be allowed to leave the country. Her request was granted, and Falcon was sent to China to work in the Spanish department of Radio Peking.[191]

Whether her immediate godhead was Stalin, Khrushchev, or Brezhnev, Ibarruri was a loyal supporter of the Soviet Union, and, as a result, was afforded fame and recognition all over the communist world. She acted as vice-president of the communist-sponsored Women's International Democratic Federation, attended Soviet party functions as an honored guest, and represented the PCE at Kremlin congresses. Traveling extensively to China, Rumania, and Yugoslavia, she consulted with communist leaders worldwide, Castro and Mao among them, and is even said to have influenced Castro to stay in the Soviet camp after Moscow's rift with Peking. For all these achievements she was duly praised, honored with the Lenin Peace Prize, the Order of Lenin, the Order of the October Revolution, and the Yugoslavian Victory of Socialism award. Her portrait hangs in Leningrad's Museum of the Revolution, and observers claimed that she came to be even more renowned and loved in the USSR than in Spain itself.[192]

Alongside her growing international reputation, Pasionaria retained her position as the most celebrated of the Spanish communist leaders who had settled in Russia after the war. Unfortunately, however, the frustrations of impotent exile caused Spanish communists to fall upon each other in an orgy of recrimination and backbiting, which gave the world the impression that they were more concerned with fighting among themselves than with toppling the Franquist dictatorship. From the very first years of exile, a bitter power struggle arose among PCE leaders, a struggle that compounded the mythology and confusion that surround Pasionaria. While she had heretofore been condemned only by fascists and fascist sympathizers, this time she was assailed by former communist comrades who accused her of a multitude of sins.

The dispute that came to rock Spanish communism in exile— actually a dispute that continues to this day—was fought over the degree of independence that could and should be maintained by the PCE, and, conversely, the degree of loyalty the party owed to its Soviet host. Two factions soon emerged: one staunchly Stalinist, centered around Ibarruri; the other rival group focused around Jesús Hernández, former Minister of Education in the republican government and a close collaborator of ailing party Secretary General José Díaz.

While the issue of Stalinist orthodoxy was a valid bone of contention between the two, the men around Hernández tried to discredit Stalinism by challenging its symbol, Ibarruri, striking first where the political woman remains most vulnerable—at her private life. Their charges are significant, not only for what they might reveal about Ibarruri herself but also for their similarities with the innuendoes, barbs, and condemnations leveled against the other women of this study. It is the pattern and kind of these accusations, therefore, rather than their truth or falsity that is the real issue.

Pasionaria had walked away from her disappointing marriage sometime during the civil war. Although she once hinted at some possible reasons for the breakup—the pressures of her rising fame, her husband's desire for a typical domestic arrangement and rather traditional view of woman's role, his rather "timid" revolutionism[193]—the exact cause is unclear. Certainly it was not political. Ruiz remained a communist who fought valiantly for the loyalists during the civil war and followed his wife into exile in Russia.

After the failure of her marriage, Ibarruri fell in love with Francisco Anton Sáenz, a party member 17 years her junior, who served as secretary of the Madrid Provisional Committee of the PCE. The pair shared a house in Madrid during the war and lived together in Moscow during her early years in exile.

While party leaders were clearly displeased with the liaison and tried to keep it quiet, the infighting among Spanish émigrés in Moscow exposed its details to the world. Ibarruri's rivals used it to impugn her moral character, and to attempt to prevent her rise to secretary general of the PCE. Possibly out of resentment at his own failure to secure the post of secretary general after the death of José

Díaz in 1942, Jesús Hernández publicized Ibarruri's affair with Anton and, in so doing, assailed her credibility in a number of ways. He presented her as a silly and laughable middle-aged woman who had thrown herself "shamelessly and unreservedly" at a man who might have been her son. Anton, on the other hand, was portrayed as an unscrupulous opportunist who attached himself to her only to secure a position of influence in the party, a cowardly dandy who lounged all day in silk pyjamas while the workers whom the "hypocritical" Pasionaria had roused to action risked their lives at the front.[194]

Pasionaria's private life had provoked discussion in party circles during the civil war, and Anton's rather rapid rise in the hierarchy was credited to her influence. According to Hernández, she "hated" party secretary José Díaz because he had dared chastize her conduct, reminding her that she had both a husband at the front and an image to uphold. From that day on, according to his account, the "cold and scornful" Ibarruri vowed to get her revenge. When Díaz died mysteriously in a Tiflis sanatorium in 1942, Hernández actually accused her of "bringing about his death,"[195] not only to seize power for herself but to avenge his wartime criticisms of her affair.

Hernández's portrait of Pasionaria as the "high priestess of the Stalinist temple" was confirmed by other dissidents like Enrique Castro Delgado, a former Politburo member, and Valentin González, the peasant commander "El Campesino" of civil war fame. In their opinion, Pasionaria was a "typical Stalinist" who always put Russia first and Spain second—"or perhaps nowhere."[196] Calling her a "hysterical woman" and "lickspittle" with no ideas of her own, González repeated several of Hernández's charges. A cruel and thoughtless woman who totally neglected her husband and son, she was consumed only by her own interests and those of her lover Anton. While many Spanish communists with good service records were rotting as prisoners in France and North Africa, her opponents charged that she contrived Anton's release from a concentration camp in occupied France and arranged for his transfer to Moscow in a Nazi plane.[197] In Moscow, according to them, Pasionaria and Anton sought to dominate the lives of the Spanish refugees under their control. Fawning obedience to the Soviet Union and threatening condemnation of all who dared to disagree marked—they claimed—her behavior in exile.

Hypocrite, fool, murderer, bad mother, bad wife—these were the epithets hurled at Pasionaria. That they came, however, from three men who grew completely disillusioned with Stalinist Russia and broke with the party complicates attempts to get a true picture of the real Ibarruri and her actions during these years. Moreover, each of them had personal reasons for disliking her. González openly called her his "personal enemy," while Hernández may indeed have resented her own rise in the party hierarchy at what he believed to be his expense. Castro Delgado's dislike for Pasionaria went back to the civil war, when the pair quarreled—rather significantly—over the role women should play in the republican ranks. While Pasionaria supported the formation of women's companies, Delgado questioned her preference for "whores over combatants." Later he blamed his own fall from favor in military circles on her intervention.[198]

Despite the charges of these men, Ibarruri did become secretary general of the PCE in 1942, a post she continued to hold until 1960. Under her leadership the party continued its struggle against Franco by supporting guerrilla activity in Spain and by encouraging the communist underground to penetrate his bureaucracy, labor syndicates, youth, and intellectual circles.[199] She also solicited international support for the struggle, urging antifascist forces worldwide to work together to root out the last remnants of Hitlerism in Europe. In a widely published pamphlet, she asked the world's workers to boycott the goods and ships of fascist Spain, and begged democratic governments to break off economic and diplomatic relations with her homeland.[200] These appeals continued throughout the 1940s and 1950s. Calling Spain "one large prison," she repeatedly entreated all democratic parties opposed to Franco to unite in a renewed effort to restore the republic.[201] The PCE hoped that a nonviolent uprising of workers, students, peasants, and the petty bourgeoisie would force a change of regime, and this message was beamed to Spain through clandestine *Radio España Independiente*, with the fiery Pasionaria herself giving no less than four to five speeches weekly throughout the 1960s.

With Ibarruri at the helm, the PCE continued its close ties with Moscow, echoing the Soviet line on all major issues. Yet such knee-jerk loyalty could prove dangerous, for when Soviet policy abruptly changed, PCE tactics also did. Pasionaria herself became a victim of the move toward destalinization that followed the dictator's death in 1953. Subsequent PCE resolutions admitted that the party had embraced the cult of personality to some extent, and that "excessive emphasis" had been placed on Ibarruri in particular.[202] Significantly, the man who outlined these errors before the Central Committee was destined to succeed Pasionaria as secretary general of the Spanish party.

Santiago Carrillo, who had organized youth brigades during the civil war, assumed leadership of the PCE in 1960. At that time, Ibarruri accepted the purely honorary post of party president, a role created specifically for her. While her advanced age was cited as the official reason for the change, to some it seemed she had been "kicked upstairs,"[203] a hoary vestige from another era.

Ibarruri's passing was a watershed in Spanish communist politics. Although she would continue to remain a valued asset, popular orator, and historic link with the party's past, she had by the late 1950s been increasingly shunted aside by newer and younger leaders like Carrillo, men whose visions of both Spain and the Soviet Union were different from her own. Many of these new leaders had spent their exiles in the more liberalizing atmosphere of the West, especially in France, and Carrillo for one never hid his anti-Soviet line. His coming to power marked a change in PCE policies, as the party began to strengthen its ties with Europe's more independent-minded communist parties.

The event that abruptly sharpened the PCE's growing split with the USSR was the Soviet invasion of Czechoslovakia in 1968. This, in Carrillo's words, was "the straw that broke the camel's back," the "culminating point in winning our independence."[204] In the spring of 1968 an official PCE resolution voiced "profound sympathy" with the process of renewal and reform then taking place in Czechoslovakia, a process that party leaders hoped Spain itself might follow in its own future evolution to democracy.[205] The PCE, therefore, was understandably shocked and angered by the invasion. It was even more rankled, however, by the fact that the Kremlin had made its decision without advising anyone. Both Carrillo and Ibarruri were on vacation near Moscow at the time but learned of the invasion only after it had taken place. Upon demanding an explanation, however, they were further embittered by the imperious Soviet reply. Surely they could not have expected to be consulted, because "after all, you're only a small party," they were told.[206]

Ibarruri herself formally delivered her party's protest in Moscow that summer. From then on, the PCE strengthened its belief that "no party has the right to impose its views on another,"[207] and it moved dramatically to a position of autonomy in the international communist movement. While Carrillo's dislike for Moscow was well known, it was Pasionaria's stance during these years that was significant. In 1970 she was credited with playing a decisive role in quashing what potentially might have been a much larger revolt by a pro-Soviet wing within the PCE.[208] After the party's condemnation of the Czech debacle, Moscow had retaliated by throwing its support and financial assistance to the so-called Spanish Communist Workers Party of veteran civil war commander Enrique Lister, and launched a blistering attack on the party of Ibarruri and Carrillo in the process. Obviously, once she had outlived her usefulness, the former civil war heroine was no longer beyond reproach. Nonetheless, she continued to emphasize her party's independence from Soviet domination. In a 1973 interview she insisted that although there were no differences between the Spanish and Russian parties on broad policy issues, in those specific instances where the Kremlin seemed mistaken, "we say so."[209]

One of the major reasons for the PCE's increasingly independent stance was the rising expectation that the party might soon be able to return to open and legal activity in Spain. As the death of the long-lived Franco appeared imminent, all parties, including the communists, planned for the post-Franco era. With that end in mind, the PCE was especially anxious to stress its commitment to parliamentary democracy, its belief in a peaceful transition to socialism, and its independence from the Soviet Union.

Franco's 36-year authoritarian reign finally ended with his death in 1975. Ibarruri was ecstatic. Probably filled with a sense of personal vindication that she had outlived her former rival, she was also confident that his passing would create new conditions for the democratic development of Spain.[210] Tremendously heartened by the gradual introduction of reforms under the restored monarchy of King Juan Carlos, the former PCE underground cautiously came out into the open after decades of clandestine activity. Even before the party's official legalization, communists appeared at news conferences, organized strikes and work stoppages, met with leaders of other parties, and published their views in the nation's press.

However, the status of Party President Pasionaria continued to be problematic, a real stumbling block to formal and final legalization. Such was her continuing magic and mystique that the government feared the return of the 81-year-old grandmother might rekindle the passions of the civil war. Most anxious that the party be legalized, Moscow even suggested changing the leadership of the PCE if that might hasten legalization—another callous demonstration of its willingness to thrust her aside when she no longer served Soviet interests.[211]

Nothing, however, came of this suggestion. Formal permission for Ibarruri to return to her homeland came in May 1977, one month after the PCE's final legalization. The government agreed to issue her passport only if the Spanish party would promise to forego a tumultuous reception upon her arrival, for the still-insecure regime dared not antagonize entrenched Francoists in the bureaucracy and military. On these terms the venerable Pasionaria slipped quietly back to her beloved Spain after 38 years of exile.[212]

One month after her return, Ibarruri headed the communist ticket in Spain's first free elections in 41 years, and she was elected to the same seat in the Spanish lower house from which she had risen to prominence in 1936. As the oldest member of Spain's governing body, she was celebrated even by her opponents and occupied a place of honor in the Cortes.[213] In a curious way, the very return of this woman who had once exemplified Spain's deepest wounds seemed to provide the greatest assurance that those wounds had indeed healed, that the democratic Spain for which she had struggled so ferociously during the civil war had finally arrived.

In post-Franco Spain, Dolores Ibarruri became the elder statesman of a party that continued to revere its most famous member but was troubled and discomfitted by her fiery past. Aspiring to be a democratic Marxist party neither Social Democratic nor Stalinist, the PCE is probably the most anti-Soviet in Europe,[214] a vigorous proponent of the doctrine of Eurocommunism that stresses independence from Moscow and the right of each national party "to chart its own road to socialism."[215] Ibarruri was frankly an embarrassment to such a party, for the memories she conjured up and for the Soviet-dominated legacy she evoked. Following her return to Spain, there were persistent reports that Carrillo and PCE leaders made every attempt to keep her out of the national limelight to avoid charges that the Spanish communists were really covert Stalinists.[216] Ibarruri was a relic of an epoch long past, and in the words of one journalist, Eurocommunism "left her out in the cold."[217] On this issue the once-fiery orator fell strangely silent, often refusing to speak at party rallies or simply voicing curt and enigmatic remarks about the birth of democracy and socialism in Spain.[218]

In private she dismissed Eurocommunism as "a lot of foolishness." Carrillo, she once told an interviewer, "has his opinions and we have ours."[219] There were also discreet displays of hostility, like withholding applause after certain speeches. Nor did she ever join Carrillo in his attacks on the USSR, to which in her first emotional public address after her return in 1977 she continued to refer as "the great Soviet nation."[220] Such remarks even prompted rumors that the Soviets might again choose to utilize her by making her the focus of a new pro-Soviet party.[221] Perhaps in sensitive deference to the ailing octogenarian they did not.

Yet there were also other indications that Ibarruri had indeed come to a kind of accommodation with her party. In June 1977 the PCE proudly noted that she was one of nine noted leaders who proposed a resolution condemning Moscow's repeated attacks on Eurocommunist "deviations." The line adopted by the Spanish party is "realistic and correct," she brusquely decreed, as she urged Moscow to end its use of weapons of "anathema and excommunication" against political opponents.[222]

Dolores Ibarruri has been hailed, flattered, and fêted perhaps more than any other political woman of modern times, but there has been a tragic component to her adulation. Extolled and exalted for her usefulness to several causes, she was just as readily shunted aside whenever that usefulness ceased. Although her role had long been a symbolic one, never did she play the "captive saint"[223] more than since her return to Spain.

According to reports, the PCE guarded her every move, restricted her public appearances, and limited her access to journalists—all, it appeared, because party leaders feared what she might truly say, because her pro-Soviet views or fiery revolutionism would harm the image they were striving to project. Yet, even in her silence she remained useful. Because her popularity and personal magic endured, her portrait adorned red satin scarves and matchboxes, keychains and political buttons.[224] While she had always been a kind of female *caudillo* in a nation long mesmerized by the cult of personality— religious, fascist, communist, or otherwise—her amazing longevity made her a celebrity in an age of conspicuous consumption, and subjected her to a kind of popular packaging that the other women of this study—all also symbols in their own right—were quite fortunately spared.

A recent observer may have gone quite far in solving the riddle that is Ibarruri. Perhaps she herself agreed to this last silent but symbolic role, resolved to keep her real opinions to herself, to support correctly but unenthusiastically the decisions her party reached.[225] Years earlier, Pasionaria had insisted that parties were not debating clubs, that individual opinions must cease to matter when the larger cause was at stake. Whatever the party decided about the coming of democracy to Spain and the PCE's role in that democratic Spain must, therefore, be more important than her own personal beliefs. Ibarruri had learned her lessons well, and her lifetime of loyal subservience was a testament to that education. In the interests of her revolutionary faith, she would do what she was told—that phrase might become her epitaph.

Dolores Ibarruri has been the subject of more controversy, more confusion, more mythmaking than any other woman of this study. Known almost exclusively as La Pasionaria, the reality of her life and role, even her personal identity, has been obscured behind the legend that grew up around her. Was she "Red Queen" or red martyr, blindly loyal party hack or blindly idealistic true believer? Did she simply act the revolutionary saint, or become one in the eyes of many? Perhaps the greatest tribute to her success is the fact that commentators will probably never agree, that she will remain as controversial as the cause she championed. Undoubtedly, she was a vividly dramatic figure, a symbol of women's continuing involvement in the struggle for a better world, in the crusade against poverty, injustice, oppression, and despair in which all these women shared.

Conclusion:
Toward a General Theory of
the Female Revolutionary

For the most part, the real essence of the lives of the women who make up this study has remained hidden from history. Faceless names to historians, romanticized symbols to the movements they came to serve, "she-devils" to the societies they spurned, they have rarely been sensitively or clearly portrayed as the women they really were. More recently, efforts to present them as blazing feminists fighting for recognition in a man's world cheapen and distort the real core of what they hoped to do. Driven by an ideology, they sought, each in her own way, to bring that ideological dream to fruition. In the process they suffered scorn and pain, disappointment and tragedy, and any attempt to analyze their lives in a critical fashion should never trivialize, minimize, or forget the immense heroism that was the price of their revolutionary contributions.

Why did they become revolutionaries? Each had her own reasons, but all were moved by conflicting mixtures of hope and despair, idealism and utopianism tinged with quasi-religious fervor. Dissatisfied with their societies, they came to believe that only revolution could bring the fundamental changes for which they longed.

Clearly, the process by which they all became revolutionaries was a much more complicated one than the established models of revolutionary behavior would have us believe. With the rich texture of their lives and the complexity of their socialization experiences, it seems grossly misconceived to attribute their revolutionary impulses to psychoanalytic causes, to a simple conflict with authority or with their fathers as authority figures. None of these women was a female version of the male revolutionary, or, more precisely, a female version of the established model of male revolutionary behavior.

According to that model, the future revolutionary is one who has "unfinished business with his parental generation."[1] He is a man who had an "unusually ambivalent" relationship with his father, a

243

relationship that was exacerbated during the critical period of adolescence, that time when "each youth must forge for himself some central perspective and direction."[2] Because he is never able to resolve his relationship with his father during these years, the revolutionary transfers his personal hostility to authority from the private to the public realm. The existence of a public political conflict, in which the state and its leadership assume the character of a universal father figure or father substitute, enable him to come to grips with his relationship to his father by aspiring to be the father, or the leader, himself. It is out of the identity crisis of adolescence that the revolutionary is born. Political authority becomes a kind of surrogate father in his troubled mental picture, and his personal hatred of his father becomes a revolt against the social system in general. Only as the leader of a new nation can the revolutionary finally assert the "prerogatives of fatherhood." Only then can he come to the final realization of his "manhood."[3]

This admittedly simplified description of the established picture of revolutionary socialization leaves no doubt that this is an exclusively male model. Not only are women revolutionaries totally ignored in the standard literature on revolutionary behavior, but even more importantly, the Freudian psychoanalytic base on which the existing literature relies is also problematic when an attempt is made to apply the standard model to them. Although it has become a commonplace to point out the biases and prejudices of the Freudian psychology of women,[4] the traditional literature on the revolutionary as a type either ignores women totally or relates to them in Freudian and immensely value-laden terms.

According to traditional Freudian theory, the psychosexual growth of women hinges on the presence of an appropriate Oedipal relationship between father and daughter. The path to normal womanhood begins with the little girl's pre-Oedipal recognition that she lacks that organ necessary for any love relationship with her mother, the parent who is the first focus of love for both boys and girls. When the little girl transfers her love from mother to father, she has taken the first correct step on the road to normal development. According to Freud, however, this event also gives a "special stamp to the character of females as social beings." Little girls have no fear of castration, since it is an already accepted fact of life, and this, he continues, eliminates a powerful motive for seeking independence from the father and other authority figures. Deprived of a penis, the female has no incentive to abandon the Oedipal position. Passive and submissive, the "normal" woman is said to have less of a superego than the normal man, to be less capable of sublimation, and to be less interested in social issues and problems. A woman's conscience is never as thoroughly developed as a man's, since she lacks the powerful motivating force of castration fear. Her overriding concerns remain on an affective level only, that is, her dominant preoccupations remain the wish to be loved and the fear of loss of love. From such concerns arise other feminine personality characteristics, notably jealousy and vanity.[5]

Extrapolating from Freud, then, and from those theoreticians who have chosen to base their work on him, a female revolutionary, by definition, would not be a normal woman. Certainly any traits necessary for her political success, such as assertiveness, self-confidence, and independence, would not be those of a normal or "well adjusted" woman. According to the model, these are essentially "male" traits that, along with others like industry, energy, determination, willpower, and decisiveness, arise in boys due to their identification with Oedipal authority. A woman who followed this model of revolutionary motivation would clearly not have adhered to the Freudian outline of proper father-daughter relations. For a woman to become a revolutionary according to this schema, she would have to go completely counter to the normal pattern of psychosexual development of most daughters vis-à-vis their fathers, at least as the Freudian view describes it.

This is the most important reason that the established model of the revolutionary personality cannot be applied to women. Based as it is on Freudian psychology, it immediately brands the independent and assertive female political actor as abnormal. Moreover, the very method employed is one that is especially damaging to women. While psychohistory can be challenged on many grounds, psychoanalytic explanations of political behavior are even more problematic when applied to women than to men. Because politics, and especially revolutionary politics, has traditionally been regarded as a male affair, the historian has never really had to "explain" why an individual man chose to enter political activity. In the case of certain famous revolutionaries, psychohistorical interpretations of political motivation have been welcomed as simply one more explanation of the obvious. E. Victor Wolfenstein, for example, the most famous of the revolutionary personality theorists, once insisted that it was never his purpose to deny the importance of other than psychological motivations in explaining the behavior of revolutionaries. "It doesn't often happen," he explained, "that psychoanalysis contests anything which is maintained in other quarters; as a rule, psychoanalysis only adds something new to what has been said."[6]

As applied to women, however, all explanations of political behavior that hinge on unconscious, subconscious, or deep-seated conflicts are especially dangerous, simply because—in contrast to men—so very little about women's political past has thus far "been said." Because political involvement has not been the common historical experience of women, an exclusive reliance on psychoanalytic models to explain female political behavior would seem to imply that women, throughout history, could not have chosen to enter political or revolutionary activity for conscious, deliberate, rational, or sincere reasons. In certain studies, women's assumption of traditional male roles has been attributed to a strong father identification, a hatred of men, an "enormous masculine complex," or a constant fear of being subordinated to a man. The assertiveness of the "abnormal" female has been portrayed as nothing less than the sign of a desire to be male, a classic case of "penis envy" in Freudian terms.[7] It has also been fairly commonplace to assume or even assert that a woman's "unfulfilled and loveless life" pointed her in a revolutionary direction.[8] Unfortunately, interpretations like this one still abound in the attempt to understand why women might adopt atypical, even revolutionary, behavior. Only a few years ago, in fact, an interviewer asked Dolores Ibarruri if her unhappy marriage had been the catalyst that transformed her into a revolutionary fighter.[9]

While factors like personal tragedies, conflicts with authority, the relationship with the father, a rebellious temperament, and the causes of that rebellious temperament may certainly have been important in forging women's revolutionary consciousness, such factors, at least as demonstrated by this study, have not been central to female revolutionary development. In any analysis of the socialization of female revolutionaries, the initial and most important question to be raised is how these women came first to develop an activist sex role ideology, a feeling that they should and could adopt and embark on other than traditional female roles. The most important generalization that can be drawn from the socialization experiences common to the women of this study is that all, in childhood, for a variety of reasons, were treated with a sense of specialness, a treatment that they perceived and in turn acted upon. Feeling that they were somehow different from ordinary women, they were endowed with the confidence necessary to embark on careers markedly distinct from those usually defined as typically or traditionally feminine. Balabanoff and Kollontai even went so far as to consider themselves mystically or even divinely chosen, graced with a unique mission to fulfill in life. Certainly this sense of specialness was important to their decision to become politically active, since successive studies of politics and personality have repeatedly identified self-esteem to be a personality trait with special significance for politics.[10]

The sources of this sense of specialness were varied: birth order, severe sickness in early childhood, or other exceptional circumstances. Eleanor Marx, Rosa Luxemburg, and Angelica Balabanoff were the youngest children in large families. Marx, because her sisters were so much older than she, actually came to assume the position of an only child in the household. A large age difference with her brother and sisters also put Alexandra Kollontai in the same position, but in her case the sense of specialness was magnified by her status as the love child in the scandalous union between her parents. While Ibarruri's position as the eighth of eleven children did not mark her out for special treatment, frail health did. It separated her from her brothers and sisters, spared her from work in the mines, and may have convinced her that she had a unique role to play in life. The cases of Marx and Luxemburg were similar. Poor health in infancy and girlhood heightened the fawning adulation, love, and excessive attention they received.[11]

In the process by which they broke from a traditional sex role ideology, these revolutionary women were all provided at close range with models of strong and independent female behavior, women who were politically conscious, had strong personalities, important work of their own, or were partners in egalitarian and companionate marriages. Although Freud ignored the role that could be played by an active mother, or other strong female figure, in the development of the girl child, recent works have highlighted the mother's importance to the process of political socialization.[12]

For the most part, the mothers of these five revolutionaries were women of independence, achievement, and competence, women who inspired respect for a variety of reasons. Lina Luxemburg and Jenny Marx were both politically conscious, intelligent, literary women, while the mothers of both Kollontai and Balabanoff were assertive and successful businesswomen. Ibarruri's mother had worked in the mines and shared equally in the struggle for survival waged by all Vizcayan mining families. Other women—Helene Demuth, Lizzy Burns, Maria Strakhova, Antonia Izar de la Fuente—served as important role models for Marx, Ibarruri, and Kollontai, positive demonstrations of strong and fulfilling female roles.

Such evidence of positive political and personal socialization seems to have been more important for these women's future careers than purely negative ones such as ambivalent or rebellious relationships with their fathers. In the case of four of these five women—except for Balabanoff, whose father died while she was young and was decidedly nonpolitical nonetheless—their fathers were politically active and conscious themselves, and encouraged their daughters' interests in this direction.

Where rebellion or resentment did exist, it was of a markedly different kind than that described by the established model. Marx's relationship with her famous father was at times ambivalent. Resenting the demands of her role as dutiful daughter, she sought to assert her independence through her long-lived attachment to Lissagaray. If this was "rebellion," however, it was certainly rooted in a very traditional area. Karl Marx's role in his daughter's political development was immensely more important for its positive, rather than negative, character.

Elements of rebellion may also be identified in the lives of the remaining four women. Kollontai and Balabanoff sought to escape from the smothering and overprotective lifestyles characteristic of Russian women of their class in the nineteenth century, while Luxemburg rebelled not against her family but against the oppression and discrimination that she, as a Polish Jew, was forced to endure in the Russian Empire. Ibarruri rejected the resigned and fatalistic Catholicity of her parents, which she believed condemned them to lives of inevitable despair, but she never rejected them as individuals. As her own political involvement increased, their relationship actually warmed and improved, as she depended on them more and more to care for her children during her frequent absences.

Ibarruri's case is most instructive here. Coming from the lowest social class of all five women, she rebelled against a life that, in her opinion, was not worth living. Her coming to revolutionary consciousness is most clear, and it uncovers one of the major problems with established revolutionary personality theories that minimize and overlook the social setting in which the revolutionary activity occurred.

Neither parental conflict nor rebellion, but a craving for freedom and independence, a need to act on their ingrained sense of specialness and mission, and a sincere desire to better the human condition as they perceived it, brought each of these women to revolution. All except Balabanoff were born and bred in politically conscious households, and three learned of class differences and social injustice through their dealings with servants. Marx and Ibarruri had even better teachers. As university graduates, Kollontai, Luxemburg, and Balabanoff were highly educated in social and political theory. In this way, all were taught or came to see the social and political evils of the system in which they lived. Their revolutionary contempt and hostility, therefore, must be viewed against the backdrop of the societies they sought to change, not merely in terms of personal or family conflicts suffered in isolation.

All five women embraced socialism because as an ideology it welcomed them and seemed to offer them a ready place. For Marx it was an inheritance; for Pasionaria, a real answer to a poverty she could no longer bear; for the others, an intellectual attachment. Most importantly, all adopted socialism because its emotional, millenarian vision appealed to them in a remarkably similar way. While an idealistic, utopian core was part of the socialist tradition of this period, and male radicals also spoke of the cause in similar terms, the attraction of socialism's romantic underside was repeatedly and consistently emphasized by all these women, both in their initial decision to join the movement and in the course of their political careers. The vision they all spoke of was the same. Love, not hate, brought all of them to socialism and colored their definitions, goals, and dreams. Even Eleanor Marx, who might have been expected to see socialism in a more precise economic and political way, explained her attraction in ethical, quasi-religious terms. "Socialism means happiness," she simply proclaimed.[13] Moral fervor was always the essence of Ibarruri's socialist faith, while to Balabanoff socialism meant self-sacrifice, devotion to the poor, and the destruction of injustice. Above all it meant "community" to Alexandra Kollontai. The socialist society would be a "big happy family" where the needs of all would be taken care of.[14] Even Luxemburg, who demonstrated the highest theoretical understanding of all, described the future socialist society in highly moral terms: "Highest idealism in the interest of the commonweal, strictest self-discipline, a true civic spirit of the masses, these constitute the moral basis of socialist society."[15]

Hoping to actualize this shared vision, all came to socialism seeking above all else to serve. Service and self-sacrifice became the keynote of their careers; for all, work for the movement became their life. Luxemburg died in its service; Kollontai endured ridicule, disgrace, and political impotence rather than give it up. An aged and weary fighter long past her prime, the 87-year-old Balabanoff died just as she had informed her party that she was ready to embark on yet another lecture tour. Despite heart and circulatory problems, the long-lived Pasionaria persevered in her political role well into her eighties. Eleanor Marx may not have committed suicide had she felt more successful politically, more centrally involved in the movement that had been her life.[16]

The motivations all five women had in entering political activity were thus glaringly different from those defined by established models of male revolutionary behavior. According to the model, the search for power is a key ingredient in revolutionary motivation. Called the revolutionary's distinguishing characteristic, the "ruthless pursuit of absolute power" flows naturally from his quest for political fatherhood.[17] The yearning for power and the need to control are two sides of the same coin. As the surrogate father, the revolutionary leader assumes the right to exercise omnipotent control over followers viewed as having childlike weaknesses.[18]

This restless drive has an even darker underside. Desiring to become the authority figure himself, the revolutionary leader gains strength and a sense of his own power and authority through personal identification with his cause, an identification that often leads to the dogmatic conviction that he and he alone not only understands but also represents the unique dynamic of the revolution he is making. The typical revolutionary is vain, egotistical, and narcissistic. Convinced of his own infallibility, he is "capable of an instrumentalism which rejects all moral limitations on what he may do."[19] If he is to be the sole leader of the movement, he must eliminate any other person who might also strive to occupy that position. Thus, the freewheeling use of terror, the ruthless extermination of all rivals, real or imagined, is, according to the familiar paradigm, an inevitable part of the revolutionary process.[20]

Having destroyed the obsolete power or authority principle, revolutionary leaders have historically wielded a vindictive and equally dreadful form of power in the name of popular revenge. The revolutionary views his world in simplistic terms. Focusing all evil in one object, he focuses all feelings of good in another. To relieve his own guilt over his personal revolt against authority, he displaces his conflicts, seeing himself as the agent of all the poor and oppressed who were abused by authority and on whose behalf he has voluntarily chosen to act.[21] The masses, in other words, become faceless abstractions in the revolutionary's highly developed system of rationalization.

Proclaiming to the last that "the people" as an abstraction are good, he is willing to sacrifice the lives of individuals if revolutionary necessity requires it. The recalcitrant nonbeliever, in the words of Rousseau, would be "forced to be free." Decreeing virtue to be powerless "without intimidation,"[22] Robespierre ordered the slaughter of thousands in its name. What has come to be considered the standard position of the classical revolutionary personality on the question of human importance was ably summed up by the nineteenth-century Russian *intelligent* Vissarion Belinsky. "I am beginning to love mankind *à la* Marat," he confessed. "To make the least part of it happy I believe I could destroy the rest of it with fire and sword."[23]

Again it must be emphasized that the model of the power-seeking true believer, based as it is on male examples, totally ignores female political behavior. This model of political motivation applies to none of these women. None consciously defined political success in terms of the attainment of personal power, nor were her real sentiments on the subject belied by her actions. On the contrary, the careers, ideologies, and actions of each were marked by a supreme hostility to personal power and its manifestations. None equated success in the revolutionary cause with the attainment of power or with political victory, either for themselves as individuals, or for the movement as a whole. They saw it, rather, as the opportunity to serve, gauging it not by the ends attained, but by the work done in the process, in the attempt itself.

Self-effacement seemed to be their special characteristic. "What I have done is nothing out of the ordinary," Ibarruri once remarked. "Hundreds of women have done the same. Why am I pushed into the foreground?"[24] Balabanoff also decried her celebrity status. She was so hostile to "personal advertising" of any kind that she often declined even to be introduced at socialist gatherings where she was to be the principal speaker. Her message, she maintained, was all that was important.[25] When nominated for the presidency of the Gas Workers Union, Eleanor Marx announced she would refuse to serve.[26] Kollontai was reluctant to accept a position even at the Ministry of Social Welfare, fearing that if she did, she would become "just as stupid as all other ministers."[27] Angelica Balabanoff shied away from all positions that would have diminished her contact with her beloved masses. Those positions she did accept, she accepted reluctantly, claiming to the last that the only achievement of which she was proud was that she was a socialist.[28] In one of the most revealing examples of this apparently shared hostility to leadership, Rosa Luxemburg for years refused to attend conventions of the SDKPiL or even be elected to its Central Committee, yet she remained one of the party's de facto leaders, principal policy maker, and its main public voice.[29]

Their common hostility toward power politics was clearly demonstrated by their common conception of the ideology they all shared. Disgusted with power and its political manifestations, all firmly separated their vision of the socialist movement from "bourgeois politics." According to Ibarruri, socialism and self-sacrifice were synonymous. There was a real difference, she believed, between those who entered public life to work for and better the lot of the people and those who merely sought to "play politics" for their own gain,[30] between conscientious revolutionaries of long standing and those ambitious and power-seeking "peacock politicians" who surfaced during all revolutions, their appetites stimulated by the prospect of seizing power.

The sentiments of Eleanor Marx on power, politics, and ambitious politicians were remarkably similar. Her break from the Social Democratic Federation was itself occasioned by her disgust with the spirit of "opportunism, reformism, and electioneering" that had come to characterize the organization. So great was her opposition to Hyndman and the leader cult that the new Socialist League she helped to form announced its hostility to "leaders" from the very beginning. To carry out its aims, its manifesto decreed, "no overshadowing and indispensable leader is required." Founded on the principle of rotating leadership, the lack of one real head always remained its greatest weakness. Eleanor Marx, for her part, consistently refused to assume leadership herself.

Kollontai, Luxemburg, and Balabanoff all continued in the attack on the "vile disease" of careerism that had come to afflict the socialist parties of Europe. All condemned power politics, the "fetishism of leadership," and the idea of a "managed" revolution.

In the single-minded unanimity of their violent and vicious onslaught on power-seeking socialists, these women clearly demonstrated that a craving to attain power for themselves was not among the motivations that brought them to socialism. Faith in the masses themselves, not in the potential of the individual leader, was the linchpin of their socialist creed—a faith that always remained much more than a rotely parroted slogan of their adopted ideology. All their actions—their errors and their strengths—revolved around this admittedly romanticized vision of the innate goodness of the masses and the potential of their revolutionary capabilities. All shared the idea that the masses were somehow purer than their leaders, and that the movement's only chance for true success lay in following the tendencies that they represented. Over and over again, all used different words to repeat the same idea: the socialist movement was a mass movement; the "people" must achieve their own emancipation; the masses were the "ultimate source" of the revolution, the "rock" on which the victory of the revolution would be built.

When their respective socialist organizations failed them, when socialist leaders showed themselves to be a "handful of dictators" seduced by power, the response of all five women was again the same. Their disgust with institutions and politics simply heightened their faith in the purity and superior moral goodness of the masses. All retreated from institutional intrigues to renew contacts with the people themselves. Although Pasionaria's fame is greatest in this area, all these women found fulfillment as orators and agitators spreading the socialist gospel. After their battles with the socialist hierarchy, Balabanoff, Kollontai, and Luxemburg each found solace in propaganda and agitational work—work that exemplified their grass-roots conception of socialism, allowed them a niche in the movement, and shielded them from factional and political disputes for which they had no taste. The response of Eleanor Marx was clearest of all. Disgusted with the institutional impotence of both the SDF and the Socialist League, she broke entirely from all political organizations to work among the masses themselves. The New Unionism in which she was involved was a labor movement without a political base, a movement with no contacts to any existing socialist organization. Here she found the opportunity to do what she considered to be fulfilling work.

Contact with the people themselves made each of these women acutely aware of personal suffering on a practical, nontheoretical level. There was a strong and genuine ethical component to the socialism of each of them. Even though socialists frowned on charity work, regarding such ameliorative efforts as harmful to socialism's future revolutionary goals, Eleanor Marx defied theory to work among the poor of London. She knew the masses of London's East End as individuals, not merely as characters in socialism's theoretical creed. After one of these visits she wrote poignantly to her sister: "I can't tell you the horrors I have seen. Children are little skeletons . . . naked, starving, pitiable."[31] Kollontai was also scrupulously interested in the practical, seemingly prosaic details of social welfare work, while Balabanoff's propaganda tours during the Russian Civil War brought home to her the reality of suffering and cold, hunger and need. Something was innately wrong, she recognized, with an economic and social system that reduced the peasants in the countryside to barter, to trading eggs for cloth.[32] Moreso than any of the others, Ibarruri described her devotion to socialism in explicit reference to the sufferings of the families she knew. The lives of all children in Vizcaya were singularly joyless ones, and she watched many die of disease and malnutrition. When one of her own children died, she had to borrow money for the coffin; another was buried in a fruit crate. "It's horrible to see your children die and not be able to stop it," she cried.[33] As she explained it, it was not surprising that she became a revolutionary.

From its theoretical beginnings in the nineteenth century, the socialist creed had insisted that the "people" as an abstraction were good. Yet to these women, the "people" always existed as much more than a theoretical abstraction. All showed a desire to relate to individuals on concrete, not abstract, terms, a real interest in one-to-one personal relationships with the masses. Perhaps the individualistic conception of socialist salvation demonstrated and held by all of them was, in fact, rooted in their female psychological makeup itself, and if so, supports the conclusion that men and women have brought different values and priorities to the process of making a revolution.

Studies of female personality structure assert it is a "pan-cultural fact" that male and female personalities differ from each other in the dimension of what is termed "relative concreteness vs. relative abstractness." The feminine personality tends to be involved with concrete feelings, things, and people, rather than with abstract entities; it tends toward personalism and particularism.[34] This is accounted for by the quality and type of social arrangements encountered in early childhood. In modern industrial societies, the mother and her work are seen in concrete terms by both male and female children. The father and his work are identified in the abstract. What the father does when he leaves home in the early morning hours remains a mystery. The female child is taught to identify with the concrete mother figure, and the mother, in turn, enjoys a special sense of identification with her female child.[35] The son's case is different. Not only is he treated differently by his mother, but he is also taught to identify with the abstract cluster of traits associated with his father and his father's role. Cognitive psychologists have established that this process is complete by age three, and that by that age boys and girls have a irreversible conception of what their gender is.[36] This process is continued and expanded upon as the girl grows older. She learns from her mother what it means to be a woman, that is, to be that figure whose life revolves around the active physical care and concern for other concrete human beings.[37]

Recent studies analyzing the effect that women's primary involvement with family and child care has on their subconscious mental attitudes and beliefs suggest that innate to all women is a sacred sense of human value and importance. This, claims Dorothy Dinnerstein in *The Mermaid and the Minotaur*, is common to all women because of their socially mandated task of "maintaining the intimate bridge between generations." Women, she writes,

> feel in a peculiarly primitive and intimate way what it is to be human: to be knowingly part, that is, of a process that started before we were born and continues after we die. Humanness itself, then, is in this particular sense more firmly forced on woman than on man. . . .[38]

Others have echoed Dinnerstein's speculations. "An innately greater level of inherent sociability, of attunement to others, and of interpersonal sensitivity . . . may be part of the female's biological heritage." Because women are the primary socializers, "a quality of embeddedness in social interaction and personal relationships characterizes women's life relative to men's."[39]

The careers and concerns of the women of this study suggest that this innately feminine characteristic might in fact have political ramifications. The profound and sensitive humaneness that they brought to the socialist struggle may demonstrate the fact that women in general are more conscious and aware of injustices in the social system than men, because of their day-to-day contact with the intimate realities of life. Although the established model of revolutionary behavior blindly assumes that all political figures are dominated in their quest for power by a primeval desire to replace the father as an authority figure, shouldn't it make sense to ask how women's capacity to be mothers has affected their public roles and political concerns? While men and women do differ from each other anatomically, hormonally, and genetically, the most important fact about gender differences is this: In every society it is women—and only women—who bear children. No researcher, however, has ever examined the political effects either of the mother's role in the socialization process, or of every woman's physical capacity to be a mother herself.

Significantly, Dolores Ibarruri did deal with this question. Recognizing that in her own life it had been love for her children, above all else, that had brought her to revolution, she came explicitly to feel that women's "natural, human, and maternal belief in the sacredness of life" should draw them to politics even more than men. While poor women, cursed to bring more children into the world, should be especially anxious to alleviate poverty, all women, she believed, possessed an instinctive feeling for the preservation of life, an innate recognition that "people are the most valuable capital the world possesses." Since women the world over shared these concerns, women had a special capacity to work for peace, and the international sisterhood could and might guarantee that children would "grow up without the dread phantom of war constantly hovering above them."[40] In the 1960s Ibarruri looked to women worldwide to join together to work for peace, to combat the spread of atomic weapons, and to protect the future of their children—all astonishingly current themes.[41]

Perhaps women's sense of intergenerational connectedness and individual human importance has caused them both to adopt essentially different kinds of concerns in the making of revolutionary policy and also to relate differently to the role of the individual in the revolutionary dynamic. Significantly, it was Rosa Luxemburg, probably the most renowned and successful female revolutionary of all, who launched a biting attack on the ruthless mentality of the true believer. "Each tear that flows, when it could have been spared, is an accusation," she once wrote, "and he commits a crime who with brutal inadvertency crushes a poor earthworm.'"[42] Although Lenin mocked their expectation that "one can make a revolution in white gloves,"[43] Luxemburg, Balabanoff, and Kollontai were all horrified and appalled by the use of terror in the process of consolidating the revolution. Success and victory alone were anathema to them if the price of that victory and success was human suffering and bloodshed. Their common conviction of individual human importance never allowed them to accept Machiavellian notions like "revolutionary necessity" or "human expendability." Luxemburg stated unequivocally that Bolshevik defeat was preferable to their moral collapse. Even the fiery Pasionaria was not really as merciless and cruel as her detractors would have us believe.

A passionate desire to relieve individual suffering is conspicuous in all accounts of what drew these women to socialism. Their real interest in socialism's effect on people as individuals manifested itself in the importance that each assigned to the job of teacher, long identified as a naturally female role. Each of these women, despite her break with traditional social and cultural norms of proper female behavior, chose this position in the socialist party she joined. Balabanoff was the supreme teacher, consciously choosing this role and staunchly defending its importance. Although cynics might argue that Balabanoff came to teaching because she was unable to make real theoretical contributions, even Rosa Luxemburg, the much-vaunted "male revolutionary," also found solace and fulfillment here. Embracing personal contact with the masses when she found herself on the outs with the SPD, she regarded her work at the Central Party School in Berlin as one of the most exhilarating experiences of her revolutionary career. At the founding congress of the Spartacus League, Luxemburg's primary concern was not to lead or create a successful revolution but how best to educate the masses in their revolutionary role.

Alexandra Kollontai believed her greatest political task to be the education of women to political consciousness, and Ibarruri, who had once longed to be a schoolteacher, also shared this goal. The interests of Eleanor Marx were the same. Anxious to reach future workers while they were still young, she worked at a socialist Sunday school in Battersea, where she taught socialist principles in the language of traditional Christian ethics and ethical idealism. Under the auspices of the Social Democratic Federation she also held language and debating classes for workers.

This spirit of sensitive humaneness, of painstaking individual attention, devotion, and concern, is again in sharp contrast to the established model of the revolutionary personality. In the "true" revolutionary, it has been said, "all tender, effeminizing feelings of kinship, friendship, love, gratitude and even of honor . . ." are suppressed by a "total cold passion for the revolutionary cause."[44] The paradigmatic revolutionary is a "doomed man," with no interests, feelings, habits, belongings, or causes of his own,[45] a man marked by the same kind of blind fanatical obsession of which Angelica Balabanoff accused Lenin. Placing his entire life and entire being at the service of the revolution, he allows himself no private life or personal pleasures since these would channel time, energy, and effort away from the all important cause. Self-denial is his special mark. Although Lenin, by his own admission, longed to listen to Beethoven's sonatas, he refused himself even this simple release. "I can't listen to music too often," he confessed. "It affects your nerves, makes you want to say stupid nice things and stroke the heads of people who could create such beauty while living in this vile hell. And now you mustn't stroke anyone's head—you might get your hand bitten off."[46]

Lenin's rather callous but certainly revealing remark lends credence to the belief that the revolutionary's relationships with people are cold and impersonal and characterized by a "lack of fellow feeling." Love, especially, is regarded as a "psychosomatic activity which consumes energy and wastes time."[47] The true revolutionary, like Lenin, is a ruthless professional, one who "for 24 hours of the day is taken up with the revolution, has no thoughts but thought of revolution, and even in his sleep dreams of nothing but revolution."[48]

This model of the "revolutionary ascetic" is also drawn from Freud, who, in "Group Psychology and the Analysis of the Ego," described the primeval leader as one who had "few libidinal ties." The leader of the group—clearly identified as male—was different from its members in that "he loved no one but himself." Other people were important to him only insofar as they served his needs. While the ordinary members of the group needed the security of the illusion that they were loved by the leader, the leader had no need either to give or receive love. He had a "masterful nature, and was absolutely narcissistic, self-confident, and independent."[49] Adopting this Freudian view of the leader, theorists have categorized the real revolutionary as one who combines traditional ascetic traits with a "displaced libido." The true revolutionary has few, if any, loving ties to individuals because he has displaced them on the revolution.[50]

Although the model makers never bothered to apply their hypotheses to women, the image of the revolutionary ascetic appears to be totally inapplicable to the five studied here. A satisfying, ful-filling, and happy personal life was immensely important to all of them. Rosa Luxemburg specifically attacked the whole concept of "revolutionary asceticism," chastizing Leo Jogiches for his obsessive preoccupation with the eternally "boring and draining cause."[51] "My whole nature craves for love," Eleanor Marx wrote to a friend.[52] Alexandra Kollontai called love "a great creative force," that enlarges and enriches the souls of the one who feels it and the one to whom it is given.[53]

All these women felt the need for a shared companion in arms, a partner and comrade with whom they could share both their per-sonal and political lives. Hence the importance of Edward Aveling, Pavel Dybenko, Alexander Shlyapnikov, Leo Jogiches, Konstantin Zetkin, Hans Diefenbach, Francisco Anton, and possibly many others destined to remain unknown. The whole concept of the revo-lutionary ascetic with few libidinal ties is belied by these women's deep love, concern, and need for other people. Nurturing and loving seemed to be their special gift. Although only Kollontai and Ibarruri ever became mothers themselves, both Luxemburg and Marx felt motherhood was essential to their personal happiness. Both yearned for a child neither was ever to have.

Yet all five women fulfilled their need to give and receive love in other ways. One striking similarity that emerges from this study is that Luxemburg, Ibarruri, and Kollontai all took much younger lovers at some point in their lives. Balabanoff's relationship with the young Mussolini also had much of a maternal quality about it, while Marx's passionate attachment to Aveling exhibited its most tender, self-sacrificing, and altruistic side as his health waned. Perhaps there was a compensatory side to all these relationships; perhaps young and dependent lovers served as substitutes for children these women had never had, or for children who, unfortunately, had grown up all too quickly. Both Kollontai and Ibarruri, at initial stages of their careers, sacrificed their children to their revolutionary activities. They may have regretted this as they aged, and as they saw the ideals to which they had dedicated their lives grow tarnished and dulled. Perhaps taking a young lover became one means to recapture their lost youth—a youth spent in service to a cause that grew increasingly disillusioning and disappointing as the years passed.

Personal friendship was also immensely important to each of them. Balabanoff resigned from *Avanti!* out of loyalty to Maria Giudice. Ibarruri challenged the Stalinist machine out of affection for a long-time friend. During the height of the German revolutionary fever, Rosa Luxemburg wrote to a friend, "I feel a desperate need to see you, to put my arms round you and to talk with you."[54]

Historians are only beginning to examine the role that loving and caring female support networks played in the lives of many political women—Marx, Luxemburg, Ibarruri, and Balabanoff among them. Often, nurturing and supportive female friendships were the only source of strength that enabled independent and nontraditional women to survive in political movements dominated by men.[55] Marx's friendship with Olive Schreiner gave her "courage and strength." "Write me a line . . . just one line," she begged in an especially poignant letter.

> Say you love me. That will be such a joy; it will help me get through the long, miserable days, and longer, more miserable nights, with less heavy a heart. . . . I have such a terror of losing your love. . . . I keep wanting to hear you say you love me just a little.[56]

Similarly, Rosa Luxemburg was also sustained in her political isolation by a small group of basically apolitical women who provided her with the only genuine friendships she ever formed in Germany.

Perhaps the similarity between the needs and concerns of all these women was indeed rooted in their common femaleness. Most women, psychologists tell us, have a greater need for affiliation with other people than do men. "It is in terms of highly invested and extraordinarily important loving attachments that most women's secret self-assessments and interior appraisals of self-worth seem to be made."[57] For women, the need to acquire and give love is always primary in importance. Achievement motives remain secondary until woman's primary affiliational needs are met.[58] Whether this is an accurate or reasonable explanation for the behavior of the five women of this study is, however, not as important as a clear understanding of what resulted politically from their common priorities. Their frank admission that other things—love, friends, children, happiness—were just as important to them as the success of the revolutionary cause became an easy way for them to be dismissed as less-than-devoted revolutionaries, preoccupied with frivolous, even trivial concerns. Luxemburg summed this up best when she confided to a friend that she would be accused of "treason" to socialism if her real preferences and priorities—her love for nature, art, literature, and animals—were ever made known.[59] Kollontai was ridiculed and abused for her private life, becoming a target of Lenin's special scorn for all women who sought to combine "their love affairs with politics."[60] Because she specifically yearned for a fulfilling and happy personal life of her own, she was accused of wasting her time, both personal and theoretical, on concerns thought to be unimportant, even harmful, to the cause of the revolution.

Historically, women who chose to act in public have had to redefine both their private and personal lives, something that men have not had to do. While it is now a commonplace to say that the private lives of political women have long been open to public censure and comment, the incredible demands of revolutionary life appear to highlight the truth of this dictum all the more. Each of these women confronted real problems in her attempt to carve out both a public and private life for herself, and all suffered in the attempt to combine the two. There was much tittering in Bolshevik party circles over Kollontai's celebrated love affairs. Because she was widely—and inaccurately—regarded as a sexual wanton, her theorizing on women's need for sexual freedom was grossly misunderstood, revealing, it was claimed, her "disgusting obsession" with sex and free love alone. Luxemburg's relationship with the young Konstantin Zetkin—a man 14 years her junior—also raised eyebrows, while Marx's persistent devotion to "that disreputable dog Aveling" definitely caused her to lose both friends and political opportunities. Notably, when Pasionaria's rivals sought to discredit her, it was to her private, not her public, life that they looked. Although Angelica Balabanoff's contributions to revolutionary socialism have never been completely documented by historians, it is significant that the story of her friendship and possible love affair with the young Benito Mussolini remains the best-known and consistently repeated detail of her unheralded career.[61]

Clearly, the model of the revolutionary ascetic with few libidinal ties is neither descriptive of these women's lives nor useful in highlighting what their contributions to revolutionary socialism were all about. While all were ascetics if the term is used to describe hard work, tireless service, and self-denial for the sake of the revolutionary cause, the self-sacrificing nature of their careers was of a markedly different caliber than the model of revolutionary asceticism defines. As applied to men, the model describes how the adoption of ascetic traits actually stems from self-centered, self-propelled, and self-perfecting motives. Hard work, tireless effort, and a distaste for luxury, in other words, lead to the perfection of oneself as a revolutionary and the eventual success of the cause.

In women, however, asceticism has stemmed from other roots. Women have been traditionally socialized to sacrifice for family and children, and it appears that the female revolutionary, for all her nontraditional, exceptional qualities, has also followed in this pattern. The most important result of this self-sacrificing behavior is that the female revolutionary has above all else been honored, recognized, and praised precisely for the same kind of labor and service for which she would also have been honored in nonpolitical life, in the traditional, private, domestic sphere. Common to the lives of all revolutionary women is the image of heroine or saint, the inspirational and glorified symbol of the goodness and righteousness of the revolutionary cause. While very few political men have ever been called "saints," many political women have,[62] a description which devalues the political character of women's revolutionary activity. Although feminists have long recognized the intimate relationship between sexist language and women's oppression, historians are only beginning to understand how the very words we use can trivialize or marginalize the achievements of women.[63]

As symbols of the idealism and hope latent in the best of all revolutionary movements, women's posthumous deification has often meant the dilution or the obliteration of what they really hoped to achieve in the service of the revolutionary cause. Kollontai has been presented as a blazing symbol of female achievement and potential in the Soviet world. Luxemburg is recalled as the moral heroine, "the selfless fighter for an idea to which she had dedicated her whole being."[64] The gadfly nature of both women's political careers has, however, often been conveniently forgotten.

Traditionally serving the function of powerful rallying and inspirational symbols, token women have become highly touted examples of how revolutionary movements fulfilled their promises to women as a group. Yet the underlying reality of women's revolutionary experiences has often been quite different. The "prima donna" function that Angelica Balabanoff was called upon to serve was the one she resented most of all.[65] She knew she was considered naive, laughed at, and exploited. Eleanor Marx found "doors closed against her" because of her personal life.[66] Kollontai and Luxemburg were specifically and viciously attacked as women. Ibarruri's case is the most glaring of all. She was doubly used. Hailed when she championed the party line, she was shunted aside by the Soviets whenever she showed signs of independence, silenced by the men of the PCE whenever her fiery image was not to their liking. All these women suffered personal tragedies in the course of their service to the revolutionary cause—loneliness, disgrace, suicide, murder, and oblivion—but this symbolic exploitation, the movement's token use of their names without a corresponding commitment to women's real needs, has been the greatest tragedy of all.

It is wrong to say that these women do not fit the established model of the revolutionary personality; rather, one should say that the model does not even begin to fit the reality of their lives. Women's historians have always believed that two factors were responsible for women's absence from the history books: their sex, and the very timelessness of their lives, lives preoccupied with children and family and the prosaic details of daily life down through the centuries. Compensatory history, it was always assumed, would rescue those women worthies who did manage to distinguish themselves in other areas. Yet the continued absence of the overwhelming majority of socialist women from the historical record belies the truth of this neat assumption. Significantly, those political women who have been most written about have been those who acted most like men. Rosa Luxemburg, the master theoretician and tactician, is the woman revolutionary who remains the best known, whose contributions and achievements have been the most thoroughly documented. She stood out from all these women—and probably from most of the men of her day—in her sheer intellectual superiority and inordinate capacity for work. The fame she has achieved may simply demonstrate the truth of the old adage that success for women has demanded that they be superior, intellectually and otherwise, to the average man.

The other women of this study led no successful revolutions, left no master treatises. Their greatest strength was their personal conception of socialist salvation, their desire to live the words of the creed they professed, to reach out and touch the masses in their misery. The services they performed most successfully for the socialist cause—agitation, organization, the raising of consciousness—are precisely those that are most difficult for historians to capture. Perhaps the main reason that they and other women like them have remained in historical obscurity is rooted in the nature of the discipline itself, in historians' own implicit assumptions about the nature of historical success and historical importance. How can historians measure the effect one human being has had on another? And what of all those inspirational orators and teachers who paved the way for Lenin, who lifted spirits and raised minds to believe in the socialist future?

As long as historians' measure of success continues to be Lenin's revolution, their achievements will pale in comparison, but in many ways their two-fold battles—against personal and political oppression—were all the greater. Each of these women, including Luxemburg, knew and sensed in her own way that the crux of socialism was much more than organization—"as Lenin never tired of repeating"[67] — or the seizure of political power, pure and simple, but that it was about sacrifice and spirit, caring and sensitive passion, touching people's lives as people. Years before Yugoslavian communist Milovan Djilas reaped fame and renown for his condemnation of the new communist class and the movement's degeneration at the hands of bureaucrats and careerists,[68] these women knew and sensed this in their hearts. They knew that socialism meant the creation of a truly new and truly revolutionary human society, not the mere appearance of the old under a new label.

Historians' perceptions of truth have been shaped by the victors of the past. Their sense of importance has been influenced by the causes that triumphed. In 1917, when Trotsky condemned his Menshevik rivals as "miserable, isolated, and bankrupt individuals" who deserved to be relegated "to the dustbin of history,"[69] he inadvertently but accurately summarized our usual approach to history and historical truth. Because Lenin's revolution emerged victorious, we have identified classical revolutionary behavior with his. Because he succeeded, social science cast the typical revolutionary in his mold, that of the hard-nosed and driven power-seeker, forceful, competitive, rational, unsentimental, and occasionally violent, rather than in the image of Balabanoff or Eleanor Marx, Kollontai, Luxemburg, or Ibarruri. The humanizing element that these women brought to the socialist movement, their tender kindness, passionate fervor, and sensitive reluctance to utilize power for destructive ends have all, unfortunately, been drastically devalued. Mesmerized by success as commonly defined, the established model of revolutionary behavior fails above all in its failure to realize that human idealism and hopeful striving have held any place in revolutionary creation.

The standard literature on revolutionary behavior has been accused of a multitude of sins—some warranted, others not. It seems, however, that the established model's biggest weakness is neither its tendency to generalize, nor its reductionist nature, nor even its value-laden Freudian base. Neglecting to treat the reality of the female revolutionary experience, both its triumphs and its tragedies, it has deprived history of a humane and sensitizing undercurrent, an alternative vision of revolutionary creation from which we might all stand to learn.

Epilogue:
Beyond Revolution

In 1977, folk singer Joan Baez appeared on Spanish national television and dedicated a song to Dolores Ibarruri. Having vowed never to visit Spain while it was under Franco, she returned after his death to honor the woman most associated with the antifascist cause.[1]

Baez's appearance revealed more than her admiration and esteem for the venerable Pasionaria. It was an important reminder of the continuing legacy these revolutionary women bequeathed to today's world, symbolic but convincing evidence that the fight they waged and the ideals they struggled for are with us in the present. We can learn from these revolutionary women, in many ways. Certain of the problems and issues that they confronted are still central to the lives of political women today. Certainly their treatment at the hands of the socialist hierarchy presaged the real extent of women's emancipation in the modern communist world. Although there is no disputing that more women, percentagewise, are employed in communist countries than anywhere else in the world, their participation in public life is not coterminous with status and power. It has been almost 100 years since Eleanor Marx first joined her father's cause, more than 60 since communism became a fact of modern political life, but in that time women have not entered the upper echelons of communist party structures, and they are still virtually absent from the top policy- and decision-making organs of every communist country.[2]

Each of these five women came to serve a movement that promised women equality and true emancipation but that, in reality, was rather ambivalent about their presence. Two factors were critical in determining the type of acceptance and degree of responsibility given them by the socialist parties they joined: the tradition of female revolutionary involvement within their particular culture, and the political development and maturity of the socialist organizations they entered. Clearly, different socialist organizations at different stages of institutional development had different needs, and the maturity, character, scope, and hope of each particular revolutionary party affected the degree and type of acceptance granted to women participants.

Of course no socialist would dare deny a place to the last and favorite daughter of Karl Marx, but in her case the needs of the infant movement itself also dictated her ready acceptance. Organizationally weak, British socialism in its early years was characterized by a religious ethical spirit and fervor, a tone of moral condemnation of capitalist evils, not reasoned economic and political argumentation. The emotional tone of early English socialism not only served to attract Eleanor Marx to the cause but also ensured that she would be accepted. Fervent evangelists, not rigorous theoreticians, were what the movement most needed and valued at that stage of its development.

The career of Alexandra Kollontai also illustrates this relationship. In Russia, because the struggle against the tsarist autocracy seemed to be so overwhelming, all willing participants, male and female, were eagerly welcomed into the ranks of the revolution. Kollontai shared in a long tradition of female revolutionary involvement. Once that revolution was victorious, however, the needs of the movement changed. Although she had been praised by Lenin for her staunch support of his programs in the months immediately preceding the Bolshevik takeover,[3] she quickly fell from favor when her concerns and priorities showed themselves to be glaringly different from those considered necessary for the revolution's consolidation.

The importance of the cultural revolutionary tradition is further highlighted in the case of Rosa Luxemburg. With roots in the Russo-Polish movement, Luxemburg was bred in the same environment as Kollontai, a tradition that welcomed and accepted the aid of women because the needs and aims of the movement were so great. Because she came to political consciousness in an atmosphere so repressive that there was no possibility of socialism's being or becoming a reformist political movement, preparing the revolution became her "only ambition."[4] Since she chose to serve the German movement, however, the tradition in which she had been schooled clashed dramatically with the heritage, aims, and values of the movement she came to join. As German socialism matured, developed, and prospered, it grew to value electioneering and organizational skills, tasks for which Luxemburg had neither talent nor inclination.

"Germany," she condemned, "was the classical land of organization and to an even higher degree, of organizational fanaticism, even of organizational arrogance."[5] In the rigid, hierarchical structure of the SPD, a rebel with the antiorganization ethos of Rosa Luxemburg could not hope to find a place.

In sharp contrast to the SPD was the nonhierarchical nature of the Italian Socialist Party. Characterized by a fluid and loose organizational structure, the PSI was most impressed by one's ability to attract new members to the socialist cause.[6] Attaching a high premium to evangelical fervor, linguistic skills, and oratorical ability, the party extended a ready welcome to Angelica Balabanoff because her talents and skills closely paralleled its most basic needs. After 1917, however, when she sought acceptance in a Russian party whose needs, values, and organizational development were quite different, Balabanoff's welcome was neither as warm nor as enthusiastic.

Similarly, Dolores Ibarruri rose to prominence in a party so organizationally weak that the talents of all comers were heartily welcomed. She would be a great asset to a movement whose potential had been seriously hampered by a lack of activists and propagandists. It was also a movement of almost wholly proletarian character, with an antiintellectual bias and a simple, emotional faith in the moral superiority of the working class.[7] Here she would also be comfortable. Yet acceptance and real power, even in her case, were two glaringly different things. In many ways like Kollontai, Ibarruri's status and renown hinged almost totally on her willingness to toe the party line.

Significantly, a willingness to shoulder certain kinds of peripheral tasks, like translating and clerical duties, was the easiest path to acceptance and respectability in the socialist organizations these women joined. With the exception of Ibarruri, whose language talents were minimal, all were useful to their respective movements as linguists, translators, and interpreters. While language skills were highly necessary and important to the socialist movement in the best days of its heady internationalism, there was a plodding, behind-the-scenes, noncreative character to such tasks. It is difficult to determine whether these women came to such chores willingly, seeing them as a way to put their talents to use in the service of the movement in whatever way they could, or whether such subsidiary and supportive roles were automatically and perfunctorily assigned to them as women. Certainly insecurity played a part, as each of these women, for all her revolutionary inclinations, struggled to shed traditional patterns of feminine sacrifice and silent subservience inherited from the ages.

Even the brilliant Luxemburg, in her early days in the movement, was plagued by self doubt and managed to convince herself that she could never hope to create "ideas—original, genuine ideas."[8] Although both she and Kollontai were eventually able to conquer these fears, the other women of this study were not. Neither Marx, Balabanoff, nor Ibarruri ever attempted to make a real impact on the socialist movements of their day via original theoretical contributions. Whether their reluctance came from personal insecurity or from the conviction—a convenient rationalization or not—that such work was simply not important, respectability and acceptance in their respective movements came to them from their cheerful willingness to do whatever prosaic tasks were assigned to them. From the very start of her career, when party leaders asked Ibarruri to spend her time recruiting women to the cause, she agreed. Pasionaria was no Luxemburg in this regard, never feeling that this request was a condescending attempt to pigeonhole her into an appropriate field of activity. Wherever the party said she was needed, she went.

Those who were not so willing, however, or who had theoretical hopes of their own, were ridiculed, challenged, spurned, and scorned. Lenin was sharply critical of Kollontai's independent theorizing, and during the height of World War I he specifically requested that she put her linguistic talents to use to spread Bolshevik propaganda. Even the brilliant Luxemburg was useful to the socialist movement as a translator and interpreter, but she was smart, savvy, and confident enough of her own abilities to put up a fight when attempts were made to limit her activities to such prosaic areas. She was "nobody's fool," she wrote to Leo Jogiches, angrily refusing Karl Kautsky's request to help organize and publish Marx's unfinished fourth volume of *Capital*. Her "help," she bitterly suspected, would consist in transcribing or in taking Kautsky's dictation, and this she had no intention of doing. Knowing full well that neither her contemporaries nor posterity would ever learn about her "silent" contributions to Marxism, she smugly advised Kautsky "to buy a Remington typewriter and teach his wife to type!"[9]

Revolutionary socialism, for all its emancipatory pretensions, clearly developed its own brand of sex role stereotyping. All five women played a symbolic and inspirational role within their movements. Lauded for their self-sacrificing devotion and dedication, they served a kind of primping function, necessary and useful to attract women as a group to the side of the revolution. Problems of tokenism are with us yet.

The fact that these women were also struggling for acceptance in male-dominated organizations may also partly explain why, except for Kollontai, the revolutionary energies of none of them extended in a truly radical feminist direction. Only Kollontai came to recognize that sexism is fundamental, that it may exist within any type of economic system, and that the Marxist analysis of women's oppression was neither deep, adequate, nor thorough enough to explain the multifaceted nature of women's situation. The others all adopted the standard Marxist line on the woman question: that women remain eternally separated from each other by class interests, and that only socialism, which welcomed the political participation of both men and women, was the true answer to female oppression. Even though each woman, in different ways, had felt the sting of prejudice because of her sex, all remained eternal optimists, insisting that the female condition would inevitably improve with the consolidation of the new socialist society.

In reality, for a woman to have adopted a more radical or aggressive line on this issue would have endangered her own acceptance, position, and impact within a movement that always insisted that the woman question was one of class and economics, not gender itself. Kollontai's experience is clearly illustrative here. Speaking her mind on the real kinds of psychological and socioeconomic changes that would be necessary if the new socialist society were truly to become a paradise for women, she rapidly fell from grace in the Bolshevik party. Correspondingly, however, her fall also guaranteed that she would be unable to influence the centers of power in even a small way on the real needs and desires of women. Women's ability to achieve feminist ends demanded first that they attain positions of some authority in the parties they joined. This in turn, however, required that they be accepted by the socialist hierarchy, but often, if not always, that acceptance hinged on their willingness and readiness to champion the orthodox party line on this and all issues.

This feminist dilemma continues. On a secondary level, this book is a study of the kinds of leaders that women have developed to defend their needs and desires. All of these women were among the most prominent women of their day, as well as being the foremost women socialists of the period. All were exceptional women, yet all, with the possible exception of Alexandra Kollontai, staunchly resisted the label "feminist," insisting that their efforts to encourage women to participate in public life were neither "separatist," nor "feminist," nor "harmful" to the socialist cause. In assigning priorities to their labors, all, even Kollontai, placed the political needs of the socialist movement first, women's issues second. All saw feminism as a middle class concept and believed women's rights were only part of a wider struggle. How can this ambivalence be explained? Did it arise from some common psychological or character trait they all shared, or from a shrewd recognition of the real limits to which the socialist movements of the time were really prepared to go in their championing of women and women's issues?

Psychologically, the resistance many exceptional women have felt toward the label "feminist" may be related to the phenomenon of "self-hatred," which has a parallel in other underprivileged groups.[10] Many Jewish socialists, for example, came to revolutionary socialism and denied that there was any specific Jewish question or problem that the movement alone could not solve. Similarly, many women socialists denied the existence of a specific woman question. Having broken from a stereotypical female role in their own lives, these revolutionary women feared perhaps that their future success would be threatened or endangered through their identification with the group from which they had managed to escape. Any reminder of their origins in a traditionally apolitical or "out" group might disturb, irritate, or worry them, causing them to deny or minimize any alliance or allegiance. Contemporary feminist thought is acutely aware that achieving, so-called loophole women are often curiously resistant to feminism and feminist movements.[11] Significantly, it was Rosa Luxemburg, the woman who achieved the most success and renown as a revolutionary, who was the most hostile of all to feminism and feminist issues. This question of the quality and character of female leadership is critical to understanding both the weakness of the female political tradition and its prospects for the future. If the best women opt out of the feminist struggle, who remains to lead the fight? Clara Zetkin, the leading socialist feminist of Europe in this period, was clearly regarded as an intellectual lightweight, laughed at even by Rosa Luxemburg, used and exploited.

Curiously, however, the problems that each of these women confronted were precisely those for which contemporary feminists are still struggling for solutions. The burden of combining their personal and political lives was immensely heavy for all of them. There were personal tragedies here, failed marriages and love affairs turned sour over the competing demands of the public and private realm. Ibarruri painfully realized how difficult it is for mothers to devote themselves to politics and revolution.[12] Both she and Kollontai were forced to send their children elsewhere for schooling and care when the juggling of family and politics became too much to handle. Certainly today's achieving women are poignantly conscious of how complicated it is to combine children, lasting marriages, and trail-blazing careers.

For women, American feminist Robin Morgan once said, "the personal is political,"[13] and the lives of the women of this study demonstrate the truth of this observation all the more. Their search for political freedom included a search for freedom in personal life-style as well, and the problems they faced are still with us today: problems like the "moral" reputation of the political woman, her sexual preferences and personal priorities, and her need for the comfort and support of women friends—be that trumpeted as "lesbianism" or not.

Angelica Balabanoff once told American journalist Louise Bryant that freedom is much more precious to women than it is to men, "because women have to go through such a tremendous struggle before they are free in their own minds."[14] Not only was freedom in personal lifestyles important to each of these women, but at least four of them transferred their attitudes on freedom and personal autonomy to the revolutionary arena itself. Once within the revolutionary movement, Marx, Kollontai, Luxemburg and Balabanoff, in a remarkably similar way, refused to play the political "game," so to speak. All were averse to becoming "organization men" and strongly hostile to organizational needs in the process of making a revolution, even if this meant that their own chances of advancing in the revolutionary hierarchy would be threatened. Significantly, it is Rosa Luxemburg's condemnation of the "tartar Marxism" of the Bolsheviks that remains to this day the most trenchant indictment ever made of disciplined, unyielding control of the revolutionary process. "The revolution is magnificent," she judged, "and everything else is rubbish."[15] "Everything else," however, was far from being rubbish if the essential question was in fact that of how and by whom the successful revolution was to be made and consolidated. Only Pasionaria seemed to have learned that lesson well, and only she, significantly, reaped the corresponding benefits, acclaim, and rewards that went with it.

The others, however, displayed such a strong animosity to the disciplined, organizational, and hierarchical side of revolutionary creation that the historian is left with the nagging metahistorical question of whether something innate to them as women formed and molded their common perspectives. The cynic might attribute their hostility to a kind of sour-grapes mentality, a veiled recognition on their part that they, as women, could never quite belong or even hope to belong. While this remains one possible explanation, it skirts the very real fact that resistance to power and organization was consistently apparent throughout the whole course of their lives. Resistance to authority or dictation of any kind, from either the omnipotent leader or the hierarchical group, may simply have been part of their own great personal struggle to escape the authority and dictation of their own cultures, families, and societies, even of their own inner guilt and confusion at the nontraditional roles they had adopted. After breaking so painfully from traditional social expectations of their roles as women, they may have been reluctant to succumb to the strictures of a new organization and its accompanying behavioral norms.

What do their careers teach us about women's future prospects for acceptance into traditionally male arenas like politics? Was their inability to function in political organizations a result of women's lack of training in the art of politics, an example of women's victimization by men, or was it, as biosocial anthropologists like Lionel Tiger would have us believe, a result of bonding traits that men share but women lack, an underlying biologically transmitted propensity to work and function in groups that has its roots deep in human evolutionary history?[16]

More complicated psychological issues might be involved. Albert Camus in *The Rebel* wrote of the tragic dilemma faced by all revolutionaries. Sustained and propelled by a spirit of rebellion, the successful revolutionary must deny that spirit to consolidate the regime his revolution created.[17] This only Pasionaria learned to do. Significantly, the others may have believed and recognized that a true revolution required new and different styles of leadership and authority from the old, nonhierarchical styles that women may have found more comfortable and that would have enabled them to receive the training in leadership roles that they had been denied for centuries. Lenin condemned both Luxemburg and Kollontai for their "not-to-be-taken-seriously nonsense of organization and tactics as a process,"[18] but humane and novel methods of personnel administration and leadership styles might have been among their most promising contributions to the new society. Significantly, the principle of rotating leadership adopted by Eleanor Marx's Socialist League has also consistently been a feature of modern-day feminist organizations.

The way we judge these women and their contributions depends on the glasses we put on to approach them. If success and power as traditionally defined are one's standards for fame and acclaim, then one can legitimately chastise Marx, Balabanoff, Kollontai, and even Luxemburg for their impracticality, their idealism, and their reluctance to compromise. We can laugh at Marx's attempt to appropriate a traditional festival like Christmas to celebrate the "death of darkness and the birth of light" represented by socialism,[19] or snicker at Balabanoff's romantic and perhaps simple-minded emphasis on socialist brotherhood, unity, and solidarity. But if the spirit of socialism is the issue, and one's fidelity to that spirit becomes the measure of true success, then they, not Lenin, were the real revolutionaries.

Notes

NOTES TO INTRODUCTION

1. Recent studies of female group activity in revolutionary movements include Jane Abray, "Feminism in the French Revolution," *American Historical Review* 80 (1975): 43–62; Barbara Engel, "Women as Revolutionaries: The Case of the Russian Populists," in *Becoming Visible: Women in European History*, ed. Renate Bridenthal and Claudia Koonz (Boston: Houghton Mifflin, 1977), pp. 346–369; Ruth Graham, "Loaves and Liberty: Women in the French Revolution," also in Bridenthal and Koonz, pp. 236–254; Olwen Hufton, "Women in Revolution, 1789–1796," *Past and Present*, no. 53 (1971), pp. 90–108; Robert McNeal, "Women and the Russian Revolutionary Movement," *Journal of Social History* 5 (1971–1972): 143–163; and Janet W. Salaff and Judith Merkle, "Women in Revolution: The Lessons of the Soviet Union and China," in *Taking State Power*, ed. John C. Leggett (New York: Harper and Row, 1973), pp. 500–517.

2. See William T. Daly, *The Revolutionary: A Review and Synthesis* (Beverly Hills, Calif.: Sage Publications, 1972); Eric Hoffer, *The True Believer* (New York: Harper and Bros., 1951); Harold D. Lasswell, *Power and Personality* (New York: W. W. Norton, 1948), *Psychopathology and Politics* (Chicago: University of Chicago Press, 1930), and "Types of Political Personalities," in *Personality and the Social Group*, ed. Ernest W. Burgess (Chicago: University of Chicago Press, 1929), pp. 151–161; Nathan Leites, *A Study of Bolshevism* (Glencoe, Ill.: Free Press, 1953); Bruce Mazlish, *The Revolutionary Ascetic: Evolution of a Political Type* (New York: Basic Books, 1976); Stefan T. Possony, *Lenin: The Compulsive Revolutionary* (Chicago: Henry Regnery, 1964); Philip B. Springer and Marcello Truzzi, eds., *Revolutionaries on Revolution* (Pacific Palisades, Calif.: Goodyear, 1973), pp. 184–188; E. Victor Wolfenstein, *Personality and Politics* (Belmont, Calif.: Dickenson, 1969), and *The Revolutionary Personality* (Princeton, N.J.: Princeton University Press, 1967).

3. For criticisms of the model, see Ronald Berman, "I'll Play My Father," *Kenyon Review* 29 (1967): 550–555; Fred I. Greenstein, "Personality and Politics: Problems of Evidence, Inference, and Conceptualization," *American Behavioral Scientist* 11 (1967): 38–39; Peter Loewenberg, review of *The Revolutionary Ascetic*, by Bruce Mazlish, in *American Historical Review* 82 (1977): 336–337; Bruce Mazlish, "Clio on the Couch," *Encounter* 30 (September 1968): 46–54; "Ids of Revolution," *Times Literary Supplement* 66 (October 19, 1967): 975; Mostafa Rejai, with Kay Phillips, *Leaders of Revolution* (Beverly Hills, Calif.: Sage Publications, 1979); Joseph I. Shulim, "Robespierre and the French Revolution: A Review Article," *American Historical Review* 82 (1977): 20–38;

and Zebulon C. Taintor, "Assessing the Revolutionary Personality," in *Revolution and Political Change*, ed. Claude E. Welch, Jr. and Mavis Bunker Taintor (Belmont, Calif.: Duxbury, 1972), pp. 239-249.

4. See, for example, Judith M. Bardwick, *Psychology of Women* (New York: Harper and Row, 1971), pp. 5-20; Jean Baker Miller, ed., *Psychoanalysis and Women* (Baltimore: Penguin, 1973); Ronald V. Sampson, *The Psychology of Power* (New York: Pantheon, 1966), pp. 45-50, 55; and Roy Schaffer, "Problems in Freud's Psychology of Women," *Journal of the American Psychoanalytic Association* 22 (1974): 459-485.

5. Sex role ideology is a woman's "system of beliefs regarding the appropriate behavior of women with respect to men." See Jean Lipman-Blumen, "How Ideology Shapes Women's Lives," *Scientific American* 226 (January 1972): 34. Recent studies by political scientists have examined the variety of active, positive influences that have motivated women to undertake political roles. See Rita Mae Kelly and Mary Boutilier, *The Making of Political Women: A Study of Socialization and Role Conflict* (Chicago: Nelson Hall, 1978).

6. On the heightened visibility of women in the public sphere during this period, see Pat Branca and Peter N. Stearns, *The Modernization of Women in the Nineteenth Century* (St. Charles, Mo.: Forum, 1973); Ivy Pinchbeck, *Women Workers and the Industrial Revolution* (London: Crofts, 1930); Barbara Corrado Pope, "Angels in the Devil's Workshop: Leisured and Charitable Women in Nineteenth Century England and France," in Bridenthal and Koonz, pp. 296-324; and Kaethe Schirmacher, *The Modern Woman's Rights Movement: A Historical Survey*, trans. Carl Conrad Eckhardt (New York: Macmillan, 1912).

7. See Schirmacher, and Theodore Stanton, ed., *The Woman Question in Europe* (New York: G. P. Putnam's Sons, 1884).

8. This literature is extensive and will be discussed in greater detail in subsequent chapters. See, for example, Charles Fourier, *Oeuvres Complètes* (Paris: Librairie Sociétaire, 1841-1846), 1: 130-144, 147, 150; 2: 212-129; 5: 1-7, 258-260; 6: 166-170, 225-244; Etienne Cabet, *La Femme* (Paris: Le Populaire, 1848); August Bebel, *Woman Under Socialism*, trans. Daniel DeLeon (New York: Labor News Press, 1904); Eleanor Marx Aveling and Edward Aveling, "The Woman Question: From a Socialist Point of View," *Westminster Review*, N.S. 69 (1886): 207-222; and V. I. Lenin, *The Emancipation of Women* (New York: International, 1934). For a general discussion of the relationship between socialism and the woman question, see Sheila Rowbotham, *Women, Resistance, and Revolution: A History of Women and Revolution in the Modern World* (New York: Vintage, 1974); and Hilda Scott, *Does Socialism Liberate Women?* (Boston: Beacon Press, 1974).

9. Charles Fourier, *Théorie des Quatre Mouvements* (Paris: Librairie Sociétaire, 1846), pp. 132-133. Usually stingy in his praise for other theorists, Marx praised Fourier's observations. See *The Economic and Philosophic Manuscripts of 1844*, ed. Dirk J. Struik (New York: International, 1964), p. 134, and

The Holy Family, trans. R. Dixon (Moscow: Foreign Languages Publishing House, 1956), pp. 259-265.

10. Marx never composed one complete essay on the woman question, a fact that in itself reveals his real attitude on its importance. His views must be gleaned from a variety of his works. See, for example, *Capital* (New York: Modern Library, n.d.), 1: 405-556; *The Communist Manifesto* in *Marx and Engels: Basic Writings on Politics and Philosophy*, ed. Lewis S. Feuer (Garden City, N.Y.: Anchor, 1959), pp. 25, 29; *Critique of the Gotha Program*, ed. C. P. Dutt (New York: International, 1973), pp. 21-22; "Englische Humanitat und Amerika," *Marx-Engels Werke* (Berlin: Dietz, 1961-1968), 15: 509; and *The German Ideology* (New York: International, 1970), p. 51.

11. See Frederick Engels, *The Condition of the Working Class in England in 1844*, ed. and trans. W. O. Henderson and W. H. Chaloner (Stanford, Calif.: Stanford University Press, 1968), esp. pp. 161-166, and *The Origin of the Family, Private Property, and the State*, ed. Eleanor Burke Leacock (New York: International, 1975).

12. For Bebel's work, see note 8. For his impact on women, see, for example, Adelheid Popp, *The Autobiography of a Working Woman*, trans. E. C. Harvey (London: T. Fisher Unwin, 1912), p. 106.

13. See Dorothy Dinnerstein, *The Mermaid and the Minotaur: Sexual Arrangements and the Human Malaise* (New York: Harper and Row, 1977), p. 267n.

14. See, for example, Erik H. Erikson, "Womanhood and the Inner Space," in *Women and Analysis*, ed. Jean Strouse (New York: Grossman, 1974), pp. 291-319; Erich Fromm, "Sex and Character," in *The Family: Its Function and Destiny*, ed. Ruth Nanda Anshen (New York: Harper and Row, 1959), pp. 399-419; Valerie Saiving, "The Human Situation: A Feminine View," in *Womanspirit Rising: A Feminist Leader in Religion*, ed. Carol P. Christ and Judith Plaskow (San Francisco: Harper and Row, 1979), pp. 25-42; and Lionel Tiger, *Men In Groups* (New York: Vintage, 1970).

15. Carolyn G. Heilbrun, *Toward A Recognition of Androgyny* (New York: Alfred A. Knopf, 1973), pp. x-xix.

NOTES TO CHAPTER 1

1. On women's agitational activity in the English Civil War, see Ellen A. McArthur, "Women Petitioners and the Long Parliament," *English Historical Review* 24 (1909): 698-709.

2. See Joseph Frank, *The Levellers* (Cambridge, Mass.: Harvard University Press, 1955), pp. 105, 199; Mildred A. Gibb, *John Lilburne the Leveller* (London: L. Drummond, 1947), p. 174; Keith Thomas, "Women and the Civil War Sects," *Past and Present*, no. 13 (1958): 42-62; and Michael Walzer, *The Revo-*

lution of the Saints: A Study in the Origins of Radical Politics (New York: Atheneum, 1974), pp. 192-193.

3. See Mary Wollstonecraft, *A Vindication of the Rights of Woman* (London: Joseph Johnson, 1792).

4. See Robert Owen, *The Marriage System of the New Moral World* (Leeds: J. Hobson, 1839), and "Address of Robert Owen to the People of the United States," New York *Daily Tribune*, September 24, 1844. For a general discussion of Owenism and female emancipation, see G. D. H. Cole, *The Life of Robert Owen* (London: Frank Cass, 1925), p. 297; Margaret Cole, *Robert Owen of New Lanark* (New York: Oxford University Press, 1953), p. 208; J. F. C. Harrison, *Robert Owen and the Owenites in Britain and America* (London: Routledge and Kegan Paul, 1969), pp. 60-62, 86, 121, 157; Constance Rover, *Love, Morals, and the Feminists* (London: Routledge and Kegan Paul, 1970), pp. 23-27; and Barbara Taylor, "'The Men Are As Bad as Their Masters . . .': Socialism, Feminism, and Sexual Antagonism in the London Tailoring Trade in the Early 1830s," *Feminist Studies* 5 (1979): 7-40.

5. See, for example, "Woman and the Social System," *Fraser's Magazine* 21 (1840): 689-702.

6. On Fourierist and Saint-Simonian missionary activity in England, see Richard K. P. Pankhurst, "Saint-Simonism in England," *Twentieth Century* 152 (1952): 499-512, and 153 (1953): 47-58, and "Fourierism in Britain," *International Review of Social History* 1 (1956): 398-432.

7. See, for example, R. J. Richardson's "The Rights of Women," and "Address of the Female Political Union of Newcastle upon Tyne to their Fellow Countrywomen," both reprinted in Dorothy Thompson, *The Early Chartists* (Columbia: University of South Carolina Press, 1971), pp. 115-130.

8. See, for example, William Lovett, *Life and Struggles of William Lovett in Pursuit of Bread, Knowledge, and Freedom* (New York: Alfred A. Knopf, 1920), 1: 174n.

9. For a general discussion of the relationship between Chartism and feminism, see J. L. Hammond and Barbara Hammond, *The Age of the Chartists, 1832-1854* (Hamden, Conn.: Archon, 1962); and Ray Strachey, *"The Cause": A Short History of the Women's Movement in Great Britain* (Port Washington, N.Y.: Kennikat Press, 1969), pp. 30-32.

10. Collections of biographical sketches of outstanding Chartists contain no women. See, for example, G. D. H. Cole, *Chartist Portraits* (London: Macmillan, 1965); and Margaret Cole, *Makers of the Labour Movement* (London: Longmans, Green, 1948).

11. Joan Fiss, "The Theory and Non-Practice of British Socialism" (Ph.D. diss., New York University, 1968), p. 38.

12. Neither Jenny (1844-1883) nor Laura (1845-1911) has been the subject of a full-length biography in English, while Eleanor's life has been recorded in two. See Yvonne Kapp, *Eleanor Marx* (New York: Pantheon, 1972-1976), 2

vols.; and Chushichi Tsuzuki, *The Life of Eleanor Marx (1855-1898): A Socialist Tragedy* (Oxford: Clarendon Press, 1967).

13. Marx was so gravely affected by Edgar's death that it was feared he might "jump after the coffin" at the funeral. See Wilhelm Liebknecht, *Karl Marx: Biographical Memoirs*, trans. Ernest Untermann (Chicago: Charles H. Kerr, 1908), pp. 132-134. Marx expressed his tremendous grief to Engels, April 12, 1855 in *Marx-Engels Briefwechsel* (Berlin: Dietz, 1949-1950), 2: 111.

14. Eleanor Marx to Olive Schreiner, June 16, 1885 in Havelock Ellis, "Eleanor Marx," *Adelphi* 10 (1935): 348-349. Also see Paul Lafargue's reminiscences in Institut Marksizma-Leninizma, *Reminiscences of Marx and Engels* (Moscow: Foreign Languages Publishing House, 1961), p. 82.

15. Jenny Marx, "Short Sketch of an Eventful Life," in *Reminiscences*, p. 229.

16. Liebknecht, pp. 134-135.

17. Eduard Bernstein, *My Years of Exile: Reminiscences of a Socialist*, trans. Bernard Miall (New York: Harcourt, Brace, and Howe, 1921), p. 167; Franzisca Kugelmann, "Small Traits of Marx's Great Character," and Jenny Marx to Luise Weydemeyer, March 11, 1861 in *Reminiscences*, pp. 243-248, 285.

18. For a description of Marx's library, see "Portrait of a Bibliophile XIV: Karl Marx and Friedrich Engels," *The Book Collector* 18 (1969): 189-198.

19. Kapp. 1: 82.

20. By all accounts, Marx was a good but demanding teacher. See Bernstein, p. 167; Liebknecht, pp. 79-86.

21. See Eleanor's reminiscences of her father in *Reminiscences*, pp. 250-253.

22. Eleanor Marx to Lion Philips, December 1863 in W. Blumenberg, "Ein Unbekanntes Kapitel aus Marx' Leben," *International Review of Social History* 1 (1956): 94-95.

23. Marx to Philips, June 25, 1864, ibid., pp. 103-104.

24. Eleanor Marx, "Karl Marx," in *Reminiscences*, pp. 252-253.

25. Kapp, 1: 138.

26. Reminiscences by Eleanor Marx in Liebknecht, pp. 156-157.

27. See "Briefe von Eleanor Marx-Aveling an Wilhelm Liebknecht," in *Wilhelm Liebknecht Briefwechsel mit Karl Marx und Friedrich Engels*, ed. Georg Eckert (The Hague: Mouton, 1963), pp. 401-465.

28. Kapp, 1: 107.

29. Eleanor Marx, "Reminiscences of Frederick Engels," in *Reminiscences*, p. 186.

30. Liebknecht, p. 162.

31. Eleanor Marx, "Karl Marx," and "Remarks on a Letter by the Young Marx," in *Reminiscences*, pp. 254, 256-257.

32. Jenny Marx to Wilhelm Liebknecht, May 26, 1872 in *Marx-Engels Werke* (Berlin: Dietz, 1961-1968), 33: 702-703 (hereinafter cited as *MEW*).

33. Jenny Marx, "Short Sketch," pp. 221-235.

34. See, for example, Jenny's letters to Adolf Cluss, October 28, 1852; to Johann Philipp Becker, October 5, 1867; and to Ludwig Kugelmann, December 24, 1867 in *MEW*, 28: 640, 31: 594-595.

35. John Spargo, *Karl Marx: His Life and Work* (New York: B. W. Huebsch, 1910), p. 316.

36. *Reminiscences*, pp. 81-86, 189-190. Various other socialists praised the personal qualities and political acumen of Jenny Marx. See Frederick Lessner, *Sixty Years in the Social-Democratic Movement* (London: Twentieth Century Press, 1907), pp. 55-58; Liebknecht, *Karl Marx*, pp. 53, 117-118, and "A Bad Quarter of an Hour," *The Social-Democrat* 1 (1897): 48.

37. Jenny Marx's article about the actor Henry Irving was published in the *Frankfurter Zeitung*, November 21, 1875. See Eleanor Marx to Karl Hirsch, October 25, 1875 in Chushichi Tsuzuki, "Japanese Archives Relating to British Labour History (2): Eleanor Marx," *Bulletin of the Society for the Study of Labour History*, no. 8 (Spring 1964): 19.

38. Lafargue in *Reminiscences*, p. 81.

39. Eleanor Marx, "Karl Marx," and "Remarks," in *Reminiscences*, pp. 254-257.

40. Eleanor Marx, "Engels," and Lafargue in *Reminiscences*, pp. 191, 82-83.

41. Ibid., p. 191.

42. Ibid., pp. 189-191.

43. See Marx and Engels, *Ireland and the Irish Question* (New York: International, 1972).

44. The Fenians were a secret, armed revolutionary brotherhood dedicated to securing Ireland's independence from Britain. On Lizzie and the Fenians, see Lafargue in *Reminiscences*, p. 88; Gustav Mayer, *Friedrich Engels: A Biography*, trans. Gilbert and Helen Highet (New York: Alfred A. Knopf, 1936), pp. 202-203. Engels was proud of Lizzie's "passionate" feelings of class solidarity. See Engels to Julie Bebel, March 8, 1892 in *August Bebels Briefwechsel mit Friedrich Engels*, ed. Werner Blumenberg (The Hague: Mouton, 1965), pp. 521-522.

45. Kapp, 1: 89. Eleanor's interest in Ireland was noted with pride by both Marx and Engels. See Engels to Marx, September 27, 1869, and Marx to Engels, November 6, 1869 in *Briefwechsel*, 4: 273-275, 281-282. Also see Marx to Paul and Laura Lafargue, March 5, 1870 in *MEW*, 32: 655-659. Eleanor's interest in Ireland continued in later life. See her article, "The Irish Dynamiters," *Progress* 3 (May 1884): 282-291.

46. On the Commune, see Samuel Bernstein, "The Paris Commune," *Science and Society* 5 (1941): 117-147; Georges Bourgin, "The Commune of Paris," *Encyclopedia of the Social Sciences* (New York: Macmillan, 1937), 4: 63-66; D. W. Brogan, *The Development of Modern France* (London: Hamish Hamilton, 1959), pp. 55-72; Stewart Edwards, *The Paris Commune, 1871* (New York: Quadrangle, 1971), and *The Communards of Paris, 1871* (Ithaca: Cornell University Press, 1973); Frank Jellinek, *The Paris Commune of 1871* (New

York: Grosset and Dunlap, 1965); and Edward S. Mason, *The Paris Commune* (New York: Macmillan, 1930).

47. See Helmut Hirsch, "Marx sous l'oeil de la police parisienne," *La Revue Socialiste*, no. 42 (1950): 531-535; and Maximilien Rubel, "Deux Interviews de Karl Marx sur la Commune," *Le Mouvement social*, no. 38 (1962): 3-27. For Marx's views on the Commune, see Marx and Engels, *Writings on the Paris Commune*, ed. Hal Draper (New York: Monthly Review Press, 1971), and *Notebooks on the Paris Commune*, ed. Hal Draper (Berkeley, Calif.: Independent Socialist Press, 1971).

48. See Jenny Marx's letters of April 18, 1871 and May 12, 1871 to Ludwig Kugelmann in *Lettres de Communards et de militants de la Première Internationale à Marx, Engels et autres dans les journées de la Commune de Paris en 1871*, ed. Jules Rocher (Paris: Bureau d'Editions, 1934), pp. 35, 41.

49. On Eleanor's interest in the Commune, see Eleanor Marx, "Record of the International Popular Movement," *To-Day* 1 (April 1884): 307-313; and Allen Hutt, ed., "March 18: The Paris Commune: A Letter of Eleanor Marx," *The Labour Monthly* 22 (March 1940): 158-161. For accounts of her appearance at memorial services honoring the old Communards, see *Commonweal*, April 1885, April 1886, March 10, 1888, March 17, 1888, March 24, 1888, March 9, 1889, March 15, 1890, and March 29, 1890.

50. See the letters of both Marx and his daughter Jenny to the editor of *Woodhull and Claflin's Weekly*, October 21, 1871. For Eleanor's account of the episode, see her letter of December 29, 1871 to Liebknecht in *Liebknecht Briefwechsel*, pp. 413-415.

51. Ibid., p. 415.

52. See Engels to Laura Lafargue, March 11, 1872 in *Friedrich Engels-Paul et Laura Lafargue: Correspondance*, ed. Emile Bottigelli (Paris: Editions Sociales, 1956-1959), 1: 29.

53. Perhaps Marx had had his fill of French sons-in-law. See Marx to Engels, November 11, 1882, *Briefwechsel*, 4: 678-679. He voiced his disapproval of Lissagaray to Engels, May 23 and 31, 1873 in *Briefwechsel*, 4: 473, 478-480.

54. Marx to Engels, May 31, 1873, ibid.

55. Hippolyte-Prosper-Olivier Lissagaray, *History of the Commune of 1871*, trans. Eleanor Marx Aveling (London: Reeves and Turner, 1886).

56. See Marx's letter of August 4, 1874 to Ludwig Kugelmann in *MEW*, 33: 637; to F. A. Sorge, August 4, 1874 in Marx and Engels, *Letters to Americans, 1848-1895*, trans. Leonard E. Mins (New York: International, 1953), pp. 112-113; and to Engels, August 14, 1874 in *Briefwechsel*, 4: 501-502.

57. See Eleanor Marx to Karl Hirsch, November 25, 1876 in Tsuzuki, "Japanese Archives," pp. 20-21.

58. See, for example, her review of Stepniak's *Underground Russia* in *Progress* 2 (1883): 106, 110, 172-176.

59. See, for example, Eleanor's comments on the absence of revolutionary

sentiments among the English working classes in two letters to Natalie Lieb-knecht, October 23, 1874 and January 1, 1875 in *Liebknecht Briefwechsel*, pp. 417-419, 421-423.

60. Eleanor inherited her love for the theater from her parents, both of whom were avid admirers of Shakespeare and the popular Victorian actor Henry Irving. See Lafargue, *Reminiscences* pp. 74-75; Liebknecht, *Karl Marx*, pp. 77, 130-131; Marx to Engels, February 27, 1861 in *Briefwechsel*, 3: 18-20; Eleanor Marx to Karl Hirsch, October 25, 1875 in Tsuzuki, "Japanese Archives," p. 19; and the reminiscences of Eleanor's friend Marian Skinner Comyn, "My Recollections of Karl Marx," *The Nineteenth Century and After* 91 (1922): 161-169.

61. Comyn, p. 167.

62. Ibid., pp. 167-168.

63. On Eleanor's literary activities, see Comyn, p. 166; and Eleanor Marx to Karl Hirsch, June 8, 1878 in Tsuzuki, "Japanese Archives," pp. 21-22.

64. See Christopher St. John's introduction to *Ellen Terry and Bernard Shaw: A Correspondence* (New York: G. P. Putnam's Sons, 1931), pp. vii-xii.

65. Eleanor Marx to Olive Schreiner, June 16, 1885 in Ellis, pp. 348-349.

66. Marx to Engels, January 12, 1882 in *Briefwechsel*, 4: 619-621.

67. See John Eros, "The Rise of Organized Freethought in Mid-Victorian England," *Sociological Review* 2, N.S. (1954): 98-120; and John Edwin McGee, *A History of the British Secular Movement* (Girard, Kans.: Haldeman-Julius, 1948).

68. See Eleanor Marx, "Karl Marx: A Biography," *Progress* 1 (May 1883): 288-294, reprinted in *The Social-Democrat* 1 (1897): 163-168.

69. Eleanor Marx quoted in Aaron Rosebury, "Eleanor, Daughter of Karl Marx: Personal Reminiscences," *Monthly Review* 24 (1973): 45-46.

70. See Eleanor Marx to Dollie Radford, June 30, 1884; to J. L. Mahon, August 1, 1884, both reprinted in E. P. Thompson, *William Morris: Romantic to Revolutionary* (London: Lawrence and Wishart, 1955), pp. 432, 859-860. Also see Bernstein, p. 161.

71. William Morris to John Glasse, September 23, 1887 in R. Page Arnot, *William Morris: The Man and the Myth* (New York: Monthly Review Press, 1964), p. 86.

72. George Bernard Shaw, quoted in E. P. Thompson, p. 429.

73. Contemporary accounts condemning Aveling's moral character are extensive. See, for example, Ernest Belfort Bax, *Reminiscences and Reflexions of a Mid and Late Victorian* (London: George Allen and Unwin, 1918), pp. 55, 109-110; William Collison, *The Apostle of Free Labour* (London: Hurst and Blackett, 1913), p. 82; Thomas Okey, *A Basketful of Memories: An Autobiographical Sketch* (London: J. M. Dent and Sons, 1930), pp. 62-63; John Paton, *Proletarian Pilgrimage: An Autobiography* (London: George Routledge and Sons, 1935), p. 118; Frederick Rogers, *Labour, Life, and Literature: Some Memories of Sixty Years* (London: Smith, Elder, 1913), p. 176; and George Bernard Shaw, *Pen Portraits and Reviews* (London: Constable, 1931), p. 206.

74. Henry Mayers Hyndman, *Further Reminiscences* (London: Macmillan, 1912), p. 142.

75. See Edward Aveling, "Charles Darwin and Karl Marx: A Comparison," *New Century Review* 1 (1897): 321-322; and "Engels at Home," in *Reminiscences*, pp. 309-310.

76. Marx's respect for Darwin was well known. See Liebknecht, *Karl Marx*, pp. 91-92. Also: Marx to Engels, December 19, 1860, *Briefwechsel*, 2: 647-649, and to Ferdinand Lassalle, January 16, 1861 in Marx and Engels, *Selected Correspondence, 1846-1895*, ed. and trans. Dona Torr (New York: International, 1936), p. 125. Aveling called Darwin and Marx his "twin masters." See his "Scientific Socialism," in *Commonweal*, April 1885, and his introduction to *The Student's Marx* (London: Swan Sonnenschein, 1892).

77. See William Stephen Sanders, *Early Socialist Days* (London: Hogarth Press, 1927), p. 32. The anarchist Peter Kropotkin wrote in his memoirs that he was firmly convinced "a revolution was impossible in England." See *Memoirs of a Revolutionist* (Boston: Houghton Mifflin, 1899), p. 493.

78. On the most prominent of the London exiles, see James W. Hulse, *Revolutionists in London* (Oxford: Clarendon Press, 1970).

79. On Hyndman, see his autobiography, *The Record of an Adventurous Life* (New York: Macmillan, 1911), and its sequel, *Further Reminiscences*, previously cited. Also see the memoirs of his wife, Rosalind Travers Hyndman, *The Last Years of H. M. Hyndman* (New York: Brentano's, 1924).

80. Hyndman discussed his relationship with Marx in *Economics of Socialism* (Boston: Small, Maynard, 1921), pp. xiv-xv.

81. See Marx to his daughter Jenny, April 11, 1881, and to F. A. Sorge, December 15, 1881 in *Selected Correspondence*, pp. 389, 397. On Engels' dislike and distrust of Hyndman, see his letters: to Bernstein, May 3, 1882 in Marx and Engels, *On Britain* (Moscow: Foreign Languages Publishing House, 1953), p. 514; to Bernstein, October 27, 1882; to Bebel, August 30, 1883; and to Kautsky, June 22, 1884 in "Marx and Engels on the British Working Class Movement, 1879-1895," *The Labour Monthly* 15 (1933): 582-583, 645.

82. On the formation of the Democratic Federation, see M. S. Wilkins, "The Non-Socialist Origins of England's First Important Socialist Organization," *International Review of Social History* 4 (1959): 199-207.

83. H. M. Hyndman, *England for All* (London: Gilbert and Rivington, 1881), p. vi. Hyndman believed Marx "had no ground for complaint." See his version of the incident in *Record*, p. 261.

84. E. J. Hobsbawm, "Hyndman and the S.D.F.," in *Labouring Men: Studies in the History of Labour* (London: Weidenfeld and Nicolson, 1964), p. 231. The name "Social Democratic Federation" was adopted at its fourth annual conference in August 1884.

85. For the program of the SDF, see E. J. Hobsbawm, ed., *Labour's Turning Point, 1880-1900* (Cranbury, N.J.: Associated University Presses, 1974), pp. 46-

47. On the philosophy of the SDF, see Henry Collins, "The Marxism of the S.D.F.," in *Essays in Labour History, 1886-1923*, ed. Asa Briggs and John Saville (London: Archon, 1971), pp. 47-69.

86. On the Fabians, see M. Beer, *A History of British Socialism* (London: George Allen and Unwin, 1953), 2: 275-294; Joseph Clayton, *The Rise and Decline of Socialism in Great Britain, 1884-1924* (London: Faber and Gwyer, 1926), pp. 40-48; and Edward R. Pease, *The History of the Fabian Society* (London: Frank Cass, 1963).

87. On Hyndman's dictatorial leadership style, see Clayton, p. 12; William Morris to Mrs. Burne-Jones, August 1883; to Andreas Scheu, August 28, 1884, December 18, 1884; and to Robert Thompson, January 1, 1885 in *The Letters of William Morris to his Family and Friends*, ed. Philip Henderson (London: Longmans, Green, 1950), pp. 180-181, 212-213, 221, 228. George Bernard Shaw called Hyndman "the worst leader that ever drove his followers into every other camp . . . to escape from his leadership." See his *Pen Portraits*, pp. 126, 131. As one example of Hyndman's egotism, see his letter to Karl Kautsky, May 11, 1911 in the appendix to R. T. Hyndman, pp. 297-298.

88. See the "Manifesto of the Socialist League," in *Commonweal: The Official Journal of the Socialist League*, February 1885.

89. Eleanor Marx to Wilhelm Liebknecht, January 12, 1885 in *Liebknecht Briefwechsel*, pp. 433-434.

90. Clayton, pp. 34-35.

91. On the weaknesses of the Socialist League, see G. D. H. Cole, *A History of Socialist Thought* (New York: St. Martin's Press, 1953-1960), 2: 414-415.

92. Engels to Paul Lafargue, March 20, 1886 in *Engels-Lafargue Correspondance*, 1: 348-350.

93. On Hyndman's suspicions of Engels, see *Record*, pp. 230-231, 253, 256.

94. On the American labor movement at the time of Eleanor's visit, see Philip S. Foner, *History of the Labor Movement in the United States*, vol. 2: *From the Founding of the American Federation of Labor to the Emergence of American Imperialism* (New York: International, 1955); and Oakley C. Johnson, *Marxism in United States History Before the Russian Revolution, 1876-1917* (New York: Humanities Press, 1974).

95. See "A Woman's Plea for Mercy: An Interview with Karl Marx's Daughter," *Pall Mall Gazette* (London), November 8, 1887; Eleanor Marx and Edward Aveling, "The Chicago Anarchists," *To-Day* 8, N.S. (1887): 142-149.

96. New York *Herald*, September 21, 1886.

97. Ibid.; Chicago *Tribune*, November 6, 1886.

98. For reports of several of the Avelings' lectures, see New York *Herald*, September 14, 1886, September 20, 1886, September 21, 1886, September 23, 1886; Brooklyn *Daily Eagle*, September 24, 1886; Newark *Evening News*, September 27, 1886; Chicago *Tribune*, November 5, 1886, November 7, 1886, November 9, 1886.

99. See Eleanor Marx and Edward Aveling, "The Labour Movement in America," *Time* 5, N.S. (1887): 298-304, 431-446, 554-563, 705-713, published as *The Working Class Movement in America* (London: Swan Sonnenschein, Lowrey, 1888); Edward Aveling, *An American Journey* (New York: John W. Lovell, 1887).

100. See, for example, Paul Lafargue to Engels, September 30, 1886, and Engels to Laura Lafargue, November 24, 1886 in *Engels-Lafargue Correspondance*, 1: 389-390, 407-410.

101. See the New York *Herald*, December 30, 1886, and the New York *Daily Tribune*, December 31, 1886. For Aveling's denial of the charges, see the New York *Herald*, January 10 and 15, 1887; also "Editorial Notes," *To-Day* 8 (1887): 33-34.

102. New York *Daily Tribune*, December 31, 1886; New York *Herald*, January 10, 1887; and the Avelings, *Working Class Movement*, pp. 147-148.

103. See Engels to Laura Lafargue, November 24, 1886, *Engels-Lafargue Correspondance*, 1: 407-410; Engels to Florence Wischnewetzky, December 28, 1886 and February 22, 1888; to F. A. Sorge, August 8, 1887, and December 2, 1893 in *Letters to Americans*, pp. 165-167, 196-197, 189-190, 257-258. Also see his preface to the American edition of *The Condition of the Working Class in England*, trans. Florence Kelley Wischnewetzky (New York: Lovell, 1887), pp. i-vi.

104. Engels defended Aveling widely. See his letters: to Laura Lafargue, February 24, 1887, April 26, 1887, and May 21, 1887; to Paul Lafargue, April 13, 1887 in *Engels-Lafargue Correspondance*, 2: 16-17, 33-35, 40-41, 28-29; to Sorge, February 12, 1887, March 16, 1887, April 6, 1887, April 9, 1887, and April 23, 1887 in *Letters to Americans*, pp. 174-176, 178-184. See especially his vitriolic correspondence with the English translator of the American edition of *Condition*: Dorothy Rose Blumberg, "Dear Mr. Engels: Unpublished Letters, 1884-1894, of Florence Kelley to Friedrich Engels," *Labor History* 5 (1964): 103-133.

105. Engels to Florence Kelley Wischnewetzky, February 9, 1887 in *Letters to Americans*, pp. 169-174.

106. The growing power of the anarchists in the Socialist League was evidenced by the tone of *Commonweal*. By December 1890 it was subtitled, "A Journal of Revolutionary Socialism," and by May 1891, "A Revolutionary Journal of Anarchist Communism." After that its appearance became erratic. Plagued by financial troubles, it discontinued publication May 12, 1894.

107. Eleanor Marx and Edward Aveling, *The Factory Hell* (London: Socialist League, 1885), p. 54.

108. Eleanor Marx to Natalie Liebknecht, January 1, 1875, *Liebknecht Briefwechsel*, p. 422.

109. On the New Unionism, see H. A. Clegg, Alan Fox, and A. F. Thompson, *A History of British Trade Unions Since 1889* (London: Oxford University Press, 1964), 1: 55-96.

110. See Eleanor Marx, "The Liverpool Congress," *Time* 2, N.S. (October 1890): 1088-1097; also New York *Herald*, September 23, 1886.

111. On Thorne, see Giles and Lisanne Radice, *Will Thorne: Constructive Militant* (London: George Allen and Unwin, 1974); and his autobiography, *My Life's Battles* (London: George Newnes, 1925).

112. Radice, pp. 30-31.

113. Thorne, pp. 47, 117.

114. Radice, p. 40.

115. Kapp, 2: 483.

116. For the Gasworkers' Statement of Aims, see Hobsbawm, *Turning Point*, pp. 99-101.

117. Engels to Sorge, April 30, 1890, *MEW*, 37: 398.

118. Radice, p. 37.

119. For an account of Eleanor's activities, see Engels to Natalie Liebknecht, December 24, 1889 in *Liebknecht Briefwechsel*, pp. 355-357.

120. Laura Lafargue to Engels, November 14, 1889, *Engels-Lafargue Correspondance*, 2: 352.

121. *Commonweal*, April 1886.

122. *Commonweal*, August 1885.

123. Engels to Bebel, May 9, 1890, *Bebels Briefwechsel*, p. 390.

124. For an account of the first British May Day, see the extract from *The Star*, May 5, 1890 reprinted in Hobsbawm, *Turning Point*, p. 111; also *Commonweal*, May 17, 1890.

125. Engels to Bebel, May 9, 1890, *Bebels Briefwechsel*, pp. 389-392.

126. Engels to Laura Lafargue, May 10, 1890 in *Engels-Lafargue Correspondance*, 2: 395-397.

127. On the eight hours movement, see Edward Aveling, "The Eight Hours Working Day," *Time* 1, N.S. (June 1890): 632-638.

128. Cole, *History*, 2: 443.

129. On the ILP, see Beer, *History*, 2: 298-326; Clayton, pp. 65-84; and Henry Pelling, *A Short History of the Labour Party* (London: Macmillan, 1972).

130. Kapp, 2: 527.

131. Eleanor edited these works by her father: *Revolution and Counter-Revolution* (London: George Allen and Unwin, 1891); *The Eastern Question* (with Edward Aveling) (London: Swan Sonnenschein, 1897); *Value, Price, and Profit* (London: Swan Sonnenschein, 1898); *The Story of the Life of Lord Palmerston* (London: Swan Sonnenschein, 1899); and *The Secret Diplomatic History of the Eighteenth Century* (London: Swan Sonnenschein, 1899).

132. Eleanor translated Georgi Plechanoff's *Anarchism and Socialism* (London: Twentieth Century Press, 1895); and Eduard Bernstein's *Ferdinand Lassalle as a Social Reformer* (London: Swan Sonnenschein, 1893).

133. For a detailed discussion of the production and publication of various translations of *Capital*, see Anna Uroyeva, *For All Time and All Men*, trans. David Fidlon (Moscow: Progress Publishing, 1969).

134. Engels to Laura Lafargue, April 18, 1884 in *Engels-Lafargue Correspondance*, 1: 194.

135. Engels was at first skeptical of Aveling's ability as a translator. See his letter to Bernstein, January 1, 1884, *MEW*, 36: 78–80. Engels discussed Aveling's contributions in his preface to the first English edition of *Capital* (London: Swan Sonnenschein, Lowrey, 1887), 1: ix–x.

136. See, for example, her essay, "The Rev. W. Lansdell, D. D.," *Progress* 1 (May 1883): 302–304.

137. "The Record of the International Popular Movement" appeared monthly in *To-Day*, January 1884–July 1884. "The Record of the Revolutionary International Movement" appeared monthly in *Commonweal*, February 1885–April 1886. The column appeared twice in May 1886 after *Commonweal* became a weekly. Eleanor's last column appeared May 15, 1886.

138. Wilhelm Liebknecht, "Eleanor Marx," *The Social-Democrat* 2 (1898): 263.

139. May Morris's column appeared under a variety of titles, among them "International Notes" and "International Socialist and Labour Notes." Her first column appeared in *Commonweal* May 8, 1886, and it became a regular feature after June 12, 1886.

140. Marx and Aveling, *The Factory Hell* and *The Working Class Movement in America*, previously cited; *The Woman Question* (London: Swan Sonnenschein and Lowrey, 1886); and *Shelley's Socialism: Two Lectures* (London: printed for private distribution, 1888).

141. Eleanor Marx Aveling, *The Working Class Movement in England: A Brief Historical Sketch* (London: Twentieth Century Press, 1896).

142. Engels to Karl Kautsky, September 29, 1892, *MEW*, 38: 483–484.

143. See her prefaces to *The Eastern Question, Revolution and Counter-Revolution*, and *Value, Price, and Profit*; also, Eleanor Marx, "Marx's Theory of Value," *Progress* 1 (June 1883): 362–366.

144. Eleanor Marx to Karl Kautsky, December 28, 1896 quoted in Tsuzuki, *Eleanor Marx*, p. 55. Eleanor was insecure both personally and politically. Worried that people wouldn't like her, she was often amazed and surprised when she found out they did. See her letters to Olive Schreiner, reprinted in Havelock Ellis, "Eleanor Marx," *Adelphi* 10 (1935): 351, and "Eleanor Marx," *The Modern Monthly* 9 (1935): 287.

145. Hyndman, *Further Reminiscences*, p. 139.

146. Eleanor Marx to Jenny Longuet, January 15, 1882 quoted in Kapp, 1: 227.

147. Liebknecht called her the "soul and interpreter of international congresses." See his "Eleanor Marx," p. 263. Others also praised her ability as a translator. See the *Labour Leader*, April 9, 1898; and Morris Winchevsky [Leopold Benedict], *Stories of the Struggle* (Chicago: Charles H. Kerr, 1908), p. 156.

148. Natalie Liebknecht to Engels, November 26, 1891 in *Liebknecht Briefwechsel*, p. 383.

149. Cunninghame Graham, writing for the *Labour Leader*, July 27, 1889.

150. "Eleanor Marx: Erinnerungen von Eduard Bernstein," *Die Neue Zeit* 16, Bd. II, no. 30 (1897-1898): 120-121.

151. Rosebury, p. 35.

152. See, for example, Bax, *Reminiscences*, pp. 162-165, 197-198, 269-273, and "No Misogyny but True Equality," *To-Day* 8 (October 1887): 114-121; and Hyndman, *Further Reminiscences*, pp. 285-303.

153. Sanders, p. 85.

154. See, for example, Tom Mann, *Tom Mann's Memoirs* (London: Labour Publishing, 1923), pp. 91-92; and Ben Tillett, *Memories and Reflections* (London: John Long, 1931), p. 134.

155. Kapp, 2: 72.

156. Rosebury, p. 34.

157. August Bebel, Victor Adler, and Karl Kautsky's first wife, Luise Strasser Freyberger, were all involved in the affair. See Bebel to Adler, December 20, 1890 in *Victor Adler Briefwechsel mit August Bebel und Karl Kautsky* (Vienna: Wiener Volksbuchhandlung, 1954), pp. 66-67. For a detailed account of the episode, see Kapp, 2: 552-599; Mayer, p. 326; and Tsuzuki, *Eleanor Marx*, pp. 256-267.

158. See Engels to Kautsky, November 3, 1893, in which he admitted that he rarely saw Eleanor anymore: *MEW*, 39: 162.

159. See Engels' discussion of the terms of his will in a joint letter to Laura and Eleanor, November 14, 1894 in *Engels-Lafargue Correspondance*, 3: 370-371.

160. See "Alec Nelson" and Eleanor Marx Aveling, "Dramatic Notes," which appeared monthly in *Time*, January 1890-March 1891. Also see Eleanor Marx Aveling, "Literature Notes," *Time*, December 1890, January 1891, and March 1891.

161. See, for example, Marx and Aveling, "Shelley and Socialism," *To-Day*, 9, N.S. (April 1888): 103-116.

162. Eleanor Marx to Havelock Ellis, December 1884, quoted in Ellis, "Eleanor Marx," *Adelphi* 11 (1935): 35. Eleanor also expressed her high regard for Ibsen in *Time* 1, N.S. (1890): 323-328, and 2, N.S. (1890): 1342-1344.

163. See Eleanor's English translations of Ibsen's works: *An Enemy of Society* (London: Camelot Classics, 1888); *The Wild Duck* (Boston: Walter H. Baker, 1890); and *The Lady from the Sea* (London: T. Fisher Unwin, 1890).

164. Israel Zangwill and Eleanor Marx Aveling, "'A Doll's House' Repaired," *Time* 3, N.S. (March 1891): 239-253.

165. Eleanor Marx Aveling, translator's preface to Gustave Flaubert, *Madame Bovary* (London: W. W. Gibblings, 1901), p. xx.

166. The Avelings' pamphlet, previously cited, first appeared as an essay, "The Woman Question: From a Socialist Point of View," *The Westminster Review* 69, N.S. (1886): 207-222.

167. See the Chicago *Tribune*, November 9, 1886 and November 14, 1886; also Caroline Fairfield Corbin, *One Woman's Experience of Emancipation* (Chicago: Illinois Assn. Opposed to the Extension of Suffrage to Women, c. 1886).

168. On the British feminist movement, see Arthur Arnold, "The Political Enfranchisement of Women," *Fortnightly Review* 11, N.S. (1872): 204-214; Roger Fulford, *Votes for Women* (London: Faber and Faber, 1957); Elie Halévy, *A History of the English People in the Nineteenth Century*, trans. E. I. Watkin (New York: Peter Smith, 1952), 6, bk. 2: 486-527; William L. O'Neill, *The Woman Movement* (London: George Allen and Unwin, 1969); Constance Rover, *Women's Suffrage and Party Politics in Britain, 1866-1914* (London: Routledge and Kegan Paul, 1967); and Strachey, previously cited.

169. Engels to Gertrud Guillaume-Schack, July 5, 1885, *MEW*, 36: 341; to Laura Lafargue, October 2, 1891 in *Engels-Lafargue Correspondance*, 3: 100-101.

170. Eleanor Marx to Dollie Radford, April 14, 1891 quoted in E. P. Thompson, p. 433.

171. See *Commonweal*, December 1885 and May 15, 1886. Thorne called attention to Eleanor's love for children in *My Life's Battles*, p. 148.

172. See Eleanor's comments to Max Beer, quoted in his *Fifty Years of International Socialism* (New York: Macmillan, 1935), p. 74.

173. See Lloyd P. Gartner, "Notes on the Statistics of Jewish Immigration to England, 1870-1914," *Jewish Social Studies* 22 (1960): 97-102.

174. See Edmund Silberner, "British Socialism and the Jews," *Historia Judaica* 14 (1952): 27-52.

175. See Karl Marx, "On the Jewish Question," in *Writings of the Young Marx on Philosophy and Society*, eds. and trans. Loyd D. Easton and Kurt H. Guddat (Garden City, N.Y.: Anchor, 1967), pp. 216-248; also Shlomo Avineri, "Marx and Jewish Emancipation," *Journal of the History of Ideas* 25 (1964): 445-450.

176. Quoted in Beer, *Fifty Years*, p. 71; Eduard Bernstein also recalled her sense of Jewish pride; see his "Erinnerungen," p. 122.

177. See Abraham Cahan, *The Education of Abraham Cahan*, trans. Leon Stein, Abraham P. Conan, and Lynn Davison (Philadelphia: Jewish Publication Society of America, 1969), p. 337; Rosebury, pp. 29-49; Winchevsky, pp. 152-156.

178. Dorothy Dinnerstein, *The Mermaid and the Minotaur: Sexual Arrangements and the Human Malaise* (New York: Harper and Row, 1977), p. 275.

179. Eleanor Marx to Olive Schreiner, June 16, 1885 in Ellis, *Adelphi*, 10: 348-349.

180. See Eleanor's poignant letters to her sister, quoted in Ronald Florence, *Marx's Daughters* (New York: Dial Press, 1975), p. 67.

181. At least Eleanor seemed to imply this much in a letter to a friend. See Rosebury, p. 45.

182. Eleanor Marx to Freddy Demuth, February 3, 1898, reprinted in the *Labour Leader*, July 30, 1898.

183. Bernstein, *Exile*, p. 162.

184. Ibid., p. 202; also see Engels to Laura Lafargue, June 7, 11, 1887 in *Engels-Lafargue Correspondance*, 2: 43–49.

185. Quoted in Mayer, p. 294.

186. Hyndman quoted in Rosebury, p. 36.

187. Bernstein, *Exile*, pp. 202–204.

188. See Hyndman, *Record*, pp. 262, 388–389; and *Further Reminiscences*, pp. 140–144; H. W. Lee and E. Archbold, *Social-Democracy in Britain* (London: Social Democratic Federation, 1935), p. 87; William Morris to Andreas Scheu, September 8 and 13, 1884 in E. P. Thompson, pp. 400–401; George Bernard Shaw to Ellen Terry, January 5, 1898, in *Bernard Shaw: Collected Letters, 1874-1897*, ed. Dan H. Laurence (New York: Dodd, Mead, 1965), 2: 7–8; May Morris, *William Morris: Artist, Writer, Socialist* (New York: Russell and Russell, 1966), 2: 226; Olive Schreiner to Havelock Ellis, August 2, 1884, July 6, 1889, and April 28, 1890 in *The Letters of Olive Schreiner, 1876-1920*, ed. S. C. Cronwright-Schreiner (London: T. Fisher Unwin, 1924), pp. 36–37, 165, 185.

189. Lee and Archbold, p. 87.

190. Eleanor Marx to J. L. Mahon, August 1, 1884 reprinted in E. P. Thompson, pp. 859–860.

191. Beer, *Fifty Years*, p. 74.

192. Rosebury, p. 46.

193. Marx fathered an illegitimate son by his housekeeper, Helene Demuth. Friends and family went along with the fiction that Freddy had been sired by the dashing bachelor Engels, and Engels, out of friendship to Marx, went along with the ruse. Eleanor herself found out the truth only on Engels's deathbed. Disconsolate at first, she later became a close friend of her half-brother. See her poignant letters to Freddy in the *Labour Leader*, July 30, 1898.

194. Rosebury, p. 46.

195. Ibid., p. 37.

196. Ibid., p. 45.

197. See Hyndman, *Further Reminiscences*, p. 144.

198. Eleanor Marx to Freddy Demuth, February 7, 1898 reprinted in the *Labour Leader*, July 30, 1898.

199. The exact sequence of events leading up to and culminating in Eleanor's suicide is still shrouded in controversy. For a detailed account of the known facts, see the *Labour Leader*, April 30, 1898, and the London *Times*, April 4, 1898.

200. See the *Clarion*, April 9, 1898; the *Labour Leader* April 9, 1898 and April 16, 1898, July 30, 1898; *The Social-Democrat* 2 (1898): 227–228; Collison, p. 81; Liebknecht, "Eleanor Marx," p. 264; May Morris, 2: 183; Rogers, p. 177; Thorne, p. 148; and Tillett, pp. 134–135.

201. Contemporaries were shocked by Aveling's callousness. See Bernstein's

comments in *Justice*, July 30, 1898, and his letter to Adler, April 5, 1898 in *Adler Briefwechsel*, pp. 243–244.

202. See Collison, p. 83; Hyndman, *Further Reminiscences*, pp. 145–148; the London *Times*, April 4, 1898; the *Labour Leader*, April 30, 1898, May 7, 1898, and July 30, 1898. Bernstein was determined to take legal action against Aveling. See his letter to Adler, *supra*, and his article, "Was Eleanor Marx in den Tod trieb," *Die Neue Zeit* 16, Bd. II, no. 42 (1897–1898): 481–491. On the lack of evidence to indict Aveling, see Alexander Karley Donald to J. L. Mahon, June 4, 1898 reprinted in E. P. Thompson, p. 874.

203. Aveling was universally praised for his intellectual abilities. See Beer, *Fifty Years*, p. 74; Bernstein, *Exile*, p. 160; Hyndman, *Further Reminiscences*, p. 142; Okey, pp. 62–63; Rogers, p. 175; William Morris to Andreas Scheu, December 6, 1884, December 17, 1884, and December 28, 1884, and to May Morris, February 20, 1885 in *Morris Letters*, pp. 218–220, 224–226, 230. The list of Aveling's writings, both socialist and scientific, is extensive. A complete listing is given in the bibliography.

204. See George Bernard Shaw, *The Doctor's Dilemma* (New York: Brentano's, 1931).

205. See Judith Cherniak, *The Daughter: A Novel Based on the Life of Eleanor Marx* (New York: Harper and Row, 1979); Michael Hastings, *Tussy Is Me: A Novel of Fact* (New York: Delacorte Press, 1971); and Piers Paul Read, *Game in Heaven with Tussy Marx* (New York: McGraw-Hill, 1966).

206. This dubious distinction belongs to Hastings. As for Eleanor's "opium addiction," Havelock Ellis wrote that her abortive suicide attempt in 1887 was caused by an opium overdose, but there is no real evidence that she was addicted. See Ellis, *Adelphi*, 11: 36, and *The Modern Monthly*, p. 292. Upon meeting Eleanor for the first time, Beatrice Potter (later Mrs. Sidney Webb) wrote in her diary for May 24, 1883 that Eleanor's complexion showed "the signs of an unhealthy excited life, kept up with stimulants and tempered by narcotics." See Beatrice Webb, *My Apprenticeship* (London: Longmans, Green, 1926), pp. 291–292n.

207. See Hyndman, *Record*, pp. 388–389.

208. Lee and Archbold, p. 88; Hyndman, *Further Reminiscences*, pp. 140, 147; Thorne, p. 149; and Tillett, p. 135.

209. Beer, *Fifty Years*, p. 71.

210. Arthur Field, *The Social-Democrat* 2 (1898): 264; the *Labour Leader*, April 16, 1898 and May 14, 1898.

NOTES TO CHAPTER 2

1. Alexandra Kollontai, *Love and Friendship*, quoted in Isabel de Palencia, *Alexandra Kollontay: Ambassadress from Russia* (New York: Longmans, Green, 1947), p. 137.

2. Ibid.

3. On the influence of utopian socialism in Russia, see Martin Malia, *Alexander Herzen and the Birth of Russian Socialism* (New York: Grosset and Dunlap, 1965), esp. pp. 99-133; Nicholas V. Riasanovsky, "Fourierism in Russia: An Estimate of the Petraševcy," *American Slavic and East European Review* 12 (1953): 289-302; and Georges Sourine, *Le fouriérisme en Russie: contribution à l'historie du socialisme russe* (Paris: Dupont, 1936).

4. See Richard Stites, "M. L. Mikhailov and the Emergence of the Woman Question in Russia," *Canadian Slavic Studies* 3 (1969): 178-199, and *The Women's Liberation Movement in Russia: Feminism, Nihilism and Bolshevism, 1860-1930* (Princeton, N.J.: Princeton University Press, 1978), pp. 29-63.

5. For a discussion of the role of women in Russian Populism, see Vera Broido, *Apostles into Terrorists: Women and the Revolutionary Movement in the Russia of Alexander II* (New York: Viking Press, 1977); Barbara Alpern Engel, "From Feminism to Populism: A Study of Changing Attitudes of Women of the Russian Intelligentsia: 1855-1881" (Ph.D. diss., Columbia University, 1974), and "Women as Revolutionaries: The Case of the Russian Populists," in *Becoming Visible: Women in European History*, ed. Renate Bridenthal and Claudia Koonz (Boston: Houghton Mifflin, 1977), pp. 346-369; Barbara Alpern Engel and Clifford N. Rosenthal, ed. and trans., *Five Sisters: Women Against the Tsar* (New York: Schocken, 1977); Vera Figner, *Memoirs of a Revolutionist* (New York: International, 1927); Amy Knight, "The Fritschi: A Study of Female Radicals in the Russian Populist Movement," *Canadian-American Slavic Studies* 9 (1975): 1-17; Robert H. McNeal, "Women in the Russian Radical Movement," *Journal of Social History* 5 (1971-1972): 143-163; Cathy Porter, *Fathers and Daughters: Russian Women in Revolution* (London: Virago, 1976); and Stites, *Women's Liberation*, pp. 115-154.

6. Quoted in Peter Kropotkin, *Memoirs of a Revolutionist* (Boston: Houghton Mifflin, 1899), p. 318.

7. Engel, "Revolutionaries," pp. 359-360.

8. Stepniak [Sergei Kravchinsky], *Underground Russia* (New York: Charles Scribner's Sons, 1883), p. 127.

9. Alice Stone Blackwell, ed., *The Little Grandmother of the Russian Revolution: Reminiscences and Letters of Catherine Breshkovsky* (Boston: Little, Brown, 1917), p. 179.

10. Engel, "Revolutionaries," p. 367; Knight, p. 1; McNeal, pp. 153-160; and Richard Stites, "Women and the Russian Intelligentsia: Three Perspectives," in *Women In Russia*, ed. Dorothy Atkinson, Alexander Dallin, and Gail Warshofsky Lapidus (Stanford, Calif.: Stanford University Press, 1977), p. 50.

11. Stites, "Mikhailov," pp. 190-198; "Women and Intelligentsia," pp. 51-53; and Avrahm Yarmolinsky, *Road to Revolution: A Century of Russian Radicalism* (New York: Collier, 1962).

12. Stepniak, p. 8.

13. Figner, p. 112.

14. Memoirs of Vera Zasulich in Engel and Rosenthal, p. 69.

15. Blackwell, p. 28.

16. See Kollontai's short autobiography in *Makers of the Russian Revolution*, ed. Georges Haupt and Jean-Jacques Marie, trans. C. I. P. Ferdinard (Ithaca, N.Y.: Cornell University Press, 1974), p. 353; Alexandra Kollontai, *The Autobiography of a Sexually Emancipated Communist Woman*, trans. Salvator Attanasio (New York: Schocken, 1975), pp. 4, 9; quotations from Kollontai in Palencia, p. 137; and Katharine Anthony, "Alexandra Kollontay: The World's One Woman Ambassador," *North American Review* 230 (1930): 277.

17. Quoted in Palencia, p. 8.

18. Ibid., p. 9.

19. Kollontai, *Autobiography*, pp. 9, 107; Anthony, p. 282; and Margaret Henderson Pertzoff, "'Lady in Red': A Study of the Early Career of Alexandra Mikhailovna Kollontai" (Ph.D. diss., University of Virginia, 1968), p. 3.

20. See, for example, Barbara Corrado Pope, "Angels in the Devil's Workshop: Leisured and Charitable Women in 19th Century England and France," in Bridenthal and Koonz, pp. 296-324.

21. Kollontai, *Autobiography*, p. 9.

22. Quoted in Barbara Evans Clements, *Bolshevik Feminist: The Life of Aleksandra Kollontai* (Bloomington: Indiana University Press, 1979), p. 5.

23. Palencia, pp. 14-15.

24. Kollontai, *Autobiography*, p. 10; Clements, p. 12; Pertzoff, p. 4.

25. On the education available to Russian women during this period, see A. S. Rappoport, *Home Life in Russia* (New York: Macmillan, 1913), pp. 223-237; Sophie Satina, *Education of Women in Pre-Revolutionary Russia*, trans. Alexandra F. Poustchine (New York: n.p., 1966); and Phyllis Stock, *Better than Rubies: A History of Women's Education* (New York: G. P. Putnam's Sons, 1978), pp. 143-152.

26. Kollontai, *Autobiography*, p. 11.

27. Quoted in Kaare Hauge, "Alexandra Mikhailovna Kollontai: The Scandinavian Period, 1922-1945" (Ph.D. diss., University of Minnesota, 1971), p. 10.

28. Ibid.; Kollontai in Haupt and Marie, p. 353.

29. Quoted in Cathy Porter, *Alexandra Kollontai: The Lonely Struggle of the Woman Who Defied Lenin* (New York: Dial Press, 1980), p. 32.

30. Kollontai, *Autobiography*, p. 11.

31. Ibid., p. 11; Kollontai in Haupt and Marie, p. 353; Porter, *Kollontai*, p. 49.

32. Kollontai in Haupt and Marie, pp. 353-354.

33. See J. M. Meijer, *Knowledge and Revolution: The Russian Colony in Zuerich (1870-1873)* (Assen, The Netherlands: Van Gorcum, 1955); and Stock, pp. 141-152.

34. See Elna Malin [Alexandra Kollontai], "Die Arbeiterbewegung in Finn-

land und die russische Regierung," *Die Neue Zeit* 22, Bd. I, no. 24 (1903-1904): 749-757.

35. On the development of Marxism in Russia, see Samuel H. Baron, "The First Decade of Russian Marxism," *American Slavic and East European Review* 14 (1955): 315-330, and "Plekhanov and the Origins of Russian Marxism," *Russian Review* 13 (1954): 38-51; G. D. H. Cole, *A History of Socialist Thought* (New York: St. Martin's Press, 1953-1960), 3, bk. 1: 392-485; Leopold H. Haimson, *The Russian Marxists and the Origins of Bolshevism* (Cambridge, Mass.: Harvard University Press, 1967); and J. L. Keep, *The Rise of Social Democracy in Russia* (Oxford: Clarendon Press, 1963).

36. Kollontai in Haupt and Marie, p. 357; *Autobiography*, p. 15.

37. On the rise of Russian feminism during this period, see Linda Edmonson, "Russian Feminists and the First All-Russian Congress of Women," *Russian History* 3 (1976): 123-149; Richard J. Evans, *The Feminists* (London: Croom Helm, 1977), pp. 112-124; Kaethe Schirmacher, *The Modern Woman's Rights Movement: A Historical Survey*, trans. Carl Conrad Eckhardt (New York: Macmillan, 1912), pp. 215-229; and Stites, *Women's Liberation*, pp. 191-232.

38. See Alexandra Kollontai, "Excerpts from *Around Workers' Europe*," in *Selected Writings of Alexandra Kollontai*, ed. and trans. Alix Holt (Westport, Conn.: Lawrence Hill, 1977), pp. 88-98; *Women Workers Struggle for Their Rights*, trans. Celia Britton (Bristol: Falling Wall Press, 1971).

39. Alexandra Kollontai, "The Social Bases of the Woman Question," in appendix to Stites, *Women's Liberation*, p. 423.

40. Ibid., p. 425.

41. Kollontai, *Autobiography*, pp. 13-19; *Women Workers*, p. 31.

42. Kollontai, quoted in Anne Bobroff, "The Bolsheviks and Working Women, 1905-1920," *Soviet Studies* 26 (1974): 542.

43. Clements, p. 46; Pertzoff, pp. 26-27.

44. On the reasons for the Bolsheviks' changed attitude, see Bobroff, pp. 549-556.

45. Stites, *Women's Liberation*, p. 423. For a discussion of Lenin's relationship with Inessa Armand, see Bertram D. Wolfe, "Lenin and Inessa Armand," *Slavic Review*, no. 1 (1963): 96-114; also Stefan T. Possony, *Lenin: The Compulsive Revolutionary* (Chicago: Henry Regnery, 1964), pp. 123-125.

46. Kollontai, *Autobiography*, p. 23.

47. Ibid.; also see "Excerpts from a Diary," in Holt, pp. 81-87.

48. See Lenin's letter of October 27, 1914 to Alexander Shlyapnikov, in V. I. Lenin, *Collected Works* (Moscow: Progress Publishers, 1963-1970), 35: 167-169.

49. See Michael Futrell, *Northern Underground: Episodes of Russian Revolutionary Transport and Communications Through Scandinavia and Finland, 1863-1917* (London: Faber and Faber, 1963).

50. For Lenin's instructions to, criticisms of, and plans for Kollontai, see

his letters to her: December 1914; May 22, 1915; July 11, 1915; July 26, 1915; August 4, 1915; November 9, 1915; February 17, 1917; March 5, 1917; March 16, 1917; and March 17, 1917; in *Works*, 35: 177-178, 189-190, 193-194, 198-199, 200-201, 210-211, 285-287, 290-293, 295-296, and 297-299.

51. On Kollontai's American trip, see Theodore Draper, *The Roots of American Communism* (New York: Viking Press, 1957), pp. 74-82; the New York *Call*, January 16, 1916; February 13 and 14, 1916; the New York *Times*, October 11, 1915; and her writings in American periodicals: "The Attitude of the Russian Socialists," *New Review* 4 (March 1916): 60-61; "Do Internationalists Want a Split?" *International Socialist Review* 16 (January 1916): 394-396; "The Third International," *American Socialist*, October 23, 1915; "Für die International!" *New Yorker Volkszeitung*, November 8, 1915; "Der zweite Frauentag im Sturme des Weltkriege," *New Yorker Volkszeitung*, March 4, 1916; and her letter to the editor of the *New Review* 4 (1916): 21. Also see Kollontai, "Les Internationalistes d'Amérique," and "Exclusion des Zimmerwaldiens—Le Nouveau Parti Socialiste," *Demain, Pages et Documents* 2 (1917): 34-39, 46-48.

52. Kollontai, *Autobiography*, p. 28.

53. Ibid., p. 35.

54. Leon Trotsky, *The History of the Russian Revolution*, trans. Max Eastman (London: Victor Gollancz, 1934), pp. 361, 926, 1150. Lenin's sentiments were revealed by his wife Krupskaya. See Nadezhda K. Krupskaya, *Memories of Lenin*, trans. E. Verney (New York: International, 1930), 2: 205, and *Reminiscences of Lenin* (Moscow: Foreign Languages Publishing House, 1959), p. 349.

55. Quoted in Clements, p. 121. Kollontai's emotional reaction to the new Bolshevik government was described by John Reed; see his classic *Ten Days That Shook the World* (New York: International, 1919), p. 132.

56. Louise Bryant, *Six Red Months in Russia* (New York: George H. Doran, 1918), p. 131.

57. Palencia, p. 93.

58. Bryant, pp. 131-134.

59. See Alexandra Kollontai, *The Activity of the Russian People's Commissariat for Social Welfare* (London: People's Russian Information Bureau, 1919).

60. See V. I. Lenin, "The Tasks of the Proletariat in Our Revolution," and "Speech at the First All-Russia Congress of Working Women," in *The Emancipation of Women* (New York: International, 1975), pp. 46, 59; "The Tasks of the Working Women's Movement in the Soviet Republic," and "Soviet Power and the Status of Women," in *Works*, 30: 40-43, 120-123.

61. On the legal benefits the Bolshevik Revolution brought to women, see William M. Mandel, *Soviet Women* (Garden City, N.Y.: Anchor Press, 1975), pp. 55-58; Bernice Glatzer Rosenthal, "Love on the Tractor: Women in the Russian Revolution and After," in Bridenthal and Koonz, pp. 378-382; Hilda

Scott, *Does Socialism Liberate Women?* (Boston: Beacon Press, 1974), pp. 63–71; and Stites, *Women's Liberation*, pp. 317–345.

62. Kollontai, *Autobiography*, p. 43.

63. Lenin, "To the Bureau of the Women's Congress in Petrograd Gubernia," *Works*, 30: 299.

64. Kollontai, *Autobiography*, pp. 37–38.

65. Frederick Engels, *The Condition of the Working Class in England in 1844*, ed. and trans. W. O. Henderson and W. H. Chaloner (Stanford, Calif.: Stanford University Press, 1968), pp. 161–166.

66. See Kollontai, "Working Woman and Mother," in Holt, pp. 127–139.

67. Ibid., p. 134.

68. Ibid., p. 138; also see Alexandra Kollontai, *Communism and the Family* (San Francisco: Richmond Record, 1918); "Directive from the Commissariat of Social Welfare," and "The Labour of Women in the Revolution of the Economy," in Holt, pp. 140–149.

69. Kollontai, "Labour of Women," p. 145; *Communism*, p. 14.

70. Lenin, "A Great Beginning," in *Emancipation*, pp. 63–64.

71. Kollontai, *Communism*; also see her utopian description of the new society, "Soon," in Holt, pp. 232–236.

72. Kollontai, quoted in Thornton Anderson, *Masters of Russian Marxism* (New York: Appleton-Century-Crofts, 1963), p. 167.

73. Fears that Bolshevik victory would lead to the "nationalization of women" and the abolition of the family were voiced even in the United States. See journalist Louise Bryant's testimony before the U.S. Senate: U.S. Congress, Senate, Subcommittee on the Judiciary, *Brewing and Liquor Interests and German and Bolshevik Propaganda*, 66th Cong., 1st sess., 1919, 3: 466–561. Feminist organizations in the United States were accused of being agents of the Bolsheviks and charged specifically with advancing the work of the "infamous Madame Kollontay." See F. C. Bursch, "Who is Madame Kollontai?" *Woman Voter's Bulletin* 6 (May 1926): 5–7; J. Stanley Lemons, *The Woman Citizen: Social Feminism in the 1920s* (Urbana: University of Illinois Press, 1973), pp. 193, 209–215; and Edward A. Ross, *The Russian Soviet Republic* (New York: Century, 1923), pp. 280–282.

74. Kollontai, *Autobiography*, p. 35.

75. Quoted in Clements, p. 130.

76. Leon Trotsky, *Stalin: An Appraisal of the Man and His Influence*, trans. Charles Malamuth (New York: Harper and Bros., 1941), pp. 243–244.

77. See Louise Bryant, *Mirrors of Moscow* (New York: Thomas Seltzer, 1923), p. 115; Walter Duranty, *I Write As I Please* (New York: Simon and Schuster, 1935), pp. 240–241; New York *Times*, April 22, 1918; Jacques Sadoul, *Notes sur la Révolution Bolchévique* (Paris: Editions de la Sirène, 1920), pp. 315–316, and *Notes sur la Révolution Bolchévique: Quarante Lettres de Jacques Sadoul* (Paris: Edition de la Librairie de l'Humanité, 1922), p. 81; and Albert

Rhys Williams, *Journey Into Revolution: Petrograd, 1917-1918*, ed. Lucita Williams (Chicago: Quadrangle, 1969), pp. 200-201, and *Lenin: The Man and His Work* (New York: Scott and Seltzer, 1919), pp. 58-59.

78. Lenin, "An Interview on the Woman Question," in *Emancipation*, p. 107.

79. On the Dybenko affair, see Evan Mawdsley, *The Russian Revolution and the Baltic Fleet* (New York: Barnes and Noble, 1978); and Norman E. Saul, *Sailors in Revolt* (Lawrence: Regents Press of Kansas, 1978).

80. Kollontai, *Autobiography*, p. 40.

81. Clements, p. 142; Pertzoff, pp. 107-108.

82. Quoted in John W. Wheeler-Bennett, *The Forgotten Peace: Brest-Litovsk, March 1918* (New York: William Morrow, 1939), pp. 259-260.

83. Sadoul, *Quarante Lettres*, p. 81.

84. On Zhenotdel, see Carol Eubanks Hayden, "The Zhenotdel and the Bolshevik Party," *Russian History* 3 (1976): 150-173; Bette Stavrakis, "Women and the Communist Party in the Soviet Union, 1918-1935" (Ph.D. diss., Case Western Reserve University, 1961); and Richard Stites, "Zhenotdel: Bolshevism and Russian Women, 1917-1930," *Russian History* 3 (1976): 174-193. For Kollontai's work among peasant women, see Alexandra Kollontai, *The Peasant and Working Woman in Soviet Russia* (Moscow: International Secretariat on Work Amongst Women of the Executive Committee of the Communist International, 1921).

85. See the New York *Times*, November 21, 1921; Kollontai, *Peasant*, p. 8; and her remarks to Louise Bryant in *Mirrors*, p. 120.

86. On her work among Moslem women, see Fannina Halle, *Women in the Soviet East* (New York: E. P. Dutton, 1938); Kollontai, *Peasant*, p. 17; Gregory J. Massell, *The Surrogate Proletariat: Moslem Women and Revolutionary Strategies in Soviet Central Asia, 1919-1929* (Princeton, N.J.: Princeton University Press, 1974); and Stites, "Zhenotdel," p. 186.

87. See Lenin, "Draft Regulations on Workers' Control," *Works*, 26: 264-265.

88. On the failures of workers' control, see Paul H. Avrich, "The Bolshevik Revolution and Workers' Control in Russian Industry," *Slavic Review* 22 (1963): 47-63; and "Russian Factory Committees in 1917," *Jahrbücher für Geschichte Osteuropas* 11 (1963): 161-182.

89. Leonard Schapiro, *The Origin of the Communist Autocracy* (London: London School of Economics and Political Science, 1955), p. 290. For a full description of the Workers Opposition, see Robert V. Daniels, *The Conscience of the Revolution: Communist Opposition in Soviet Russia* (Cambridge, Mass.: Harvard University Press, 1960), pp. 119-154.

90. Alexandra Kollontai, *The Workers Opposition in Russia* (Chicago: International Workers of the World, 1921), p. 5.

91. Ibid., p. 9.

92. On the Kronstadt rebellion, see Paul Avrich, *The Russian Anarchists* (Princeton, N.J.: Princeton University Press, 1967), pp. 228-233; Alexander Berkman, *The Bolshevik Myth* (New York: Boni and Liveright, 1925), pp. 291-303; Robert V. Daniels, "The Kronstadt Revolt of 1921: A Study in the Dynamics of Revolution," *American Slavic and East European Review* 10 (1951): 241-254; Daniel Dimitri Fedotoff-White, *The Growth of the Red Army* (Princeton, N.J.: Princeton University Press, 1944), pp. 136-139; George Katkov, "The Kronstadt Rising," *Soviet Affairs*, no. 2 (1959), pp. 9-74; and Schapiro, pp. 296-313.

93. Quoted in Clements, p. 195.

94. Angelica Balabanoff, *Impressions of Lenin*, trans. Isotta Cesari (Ann Arbor: University of Michigan Press, 1964), p. 98, and *My Life as a Rebel* (New York: Harper and Bros., 1938; reprint, Bloomington: Indiana University Press, 1973), p. 252.

95. See Clements, p. 201; Schapiro, pp. 291-292.

96. Balabanoff, *Impressions*, pp. 96-99.

97. See Kollontai's statements to Jacques Sadoul, quoted in *Notes*, pp. 95-96.

98. See Kollontai's comments to Louise Bryant in *Six Months*, pp. 130-134.

99. Kollontai, "Why Was the German Proletariat Silent during the July Days?" in Holt, pp. 99-103.

100. Kollontai, "Excerpts from a Diary," in Holt, pp. 85-86. Rosa Luxemburg's criticisms of the German party echoed Kollontai's and will be discussed in detail in Chapter 3 of this volume. Kollontai admired Luxemburg, but there is no evidence that any great intimacy or friendship ever developed between the two women.

101. Kollontai to Bessie Beatty, quoted in Beatty, *The Red Heart of Russia* (New York: Century, 1918), p. 379; also see Kollontai, *Autobiography*, p. 18.

102. Kollontai to Bryant in *Mirrors*, p. 114. Interestingly enough, the Russian revolutionary terrorist Maria Spirodonova also attributed women's failure to attain positions of political power to their greater integrity and sincerity. "Politicians are usually not very fine," she told journalist Louise Bryant. "They accept political positions when they are elected to them, not because they are especially fitted for them. I think women are more conscientious. Men are used to overlooking their consciences—women are not." See Bryant, *Six Months*, p. 169.

103. Quoted in Beatty, p. 380.

104. Alexandra Kollontai, *La juventud comunista y la moral sexual* (Madrid: J. Pueyo, 1933), pp. 28-29.

105. For a full discussion of Kollontai's role in the marriage law debate, see Beatrice Brodsky Farnsworth, "Bolshevism, the Woman Question, and Aleksandra Kollontai," *American Historical Review* 81 (1976): 302-310, and "Bolshevik

Alternatives and the Soviet Family: The 1926 Marriage Law Debate," in Atkinson et al., pp. 139-165; also see Kollontai's discussion, "Marriage and Everyday Life," in Holt, pp. 300-311.

106. For the opposition to Kollontai's plan, see Fannina Halle, *Woman in Soviet Russia* (New York: Viking Press, 1935), pp. 122-125.

107. Alexandra Kollontai, *Sexual Relations and the Class Struggle*, trans. Alix Holt (Bristol: Falling Wall Press, 1972), pp. 9, 12; "La Crise de la Famille," in *Alexandra Kollontai: Marxisme et Révolution Sexuelle*, ed. Judith Stora-Sandor (Paris: François Maspero, 1973), pp. 94-95; and "Theses on Communist Morality in the Sphere of Marital Relations," in Holt, pp. 225-236.

108. Kollontai, "The New Woman," reprinted in *Autobiography*, pp. 51, 95-98.

109. Kollontai, *Autobiography*, p. 22.

110. Quoted in Clements, p. 272.

111. See Alexandra Kollontai, *A Great Love*, trans. Lily Lore (New York: Vanguard Press, 1929); *Red Love* (New York: Seven Arts, 1927); and *Love of Worker Bees*, trans. Cathy Porter (London: Virago, 1977).

112. See especially her story, "The Loves of Three Generations," in *Love of Bees*, pp. 182-211.

113. Kollontai, *Great Love*, p. 4.

114. Kollontai, *Sexual Relations*, p. 26.

115. Ibid., pp. 8-9; "New Woman," pp. 90-92.

116. Kollontai, "New Woman," p. 92.

117. Kollontai, "Make Way for Winged Eros: A Letter to Working Youth," in Holt, p. 289; *Sexual Relations*, pp. 18-19, 24.

118. Kollontai, "Crise," pp. 80-85; *Sexual Relations*, p. 21; "New Woman," p. 54.

119. Kollontai, *Sexual Relations*, p. 25.

120. Kollontai, "Winged Eros," p. 277.

121. Ibid., pp. 285-292.

122. Kollontai, *Sexual Relations*, p. 4.

123. Holt, p. 205.

124. Quoted in Nathan Leites, *A Study of Bolshevism* (Glencoe, Ill.: Free Press, 1953), p. 269.

125. Ibid., p. 270.

126. Ibid., p. 274.

127. Lenin, "Interview," pp. 101, 108; on his opposition to free love, see his letters of January 17 and 24, 1915 to Inessa Armand in *Works*, 35: 180-185.

128. On "sexual anarchy" in Russia during the civil war, see Halle, *Woman in Russia*, pp. 109-110; Maurice Hindus, *Humanity Uprooted* (New York: Jonathan Cape and Harrison Smith, 1929), pp. 84-100; and Wilhelm Reich, *The Sexual Revolution*, trans. Thérèse Pol (New York: Farrar, Straus and Giroux, 1974), pp. 162-183.

129. See Edward Hallett Carr, *Socialism in One Country, 1924-1926* (New York: Macmillan, 1958-1964), 1: 32-34.

130. For attacks on Kollontai's views, see Kendall E. Bailes, "Alexandra Kollontai et la Nouvelle Morale," *Cahiers du Monde Russe et Soviétique* 6 (1965): 471-496; H. Kent Geiger, *The Family in Soviet Russia* (Cambridge, Mass.: Harvard University Press, 1968), pp. 81-153; Rudolf Schlesinger, ed., *The Family in the USSR* (London: Routledge and Kegan Paul, 1949), pp. 280-347; Jessica Smith, *Woman in Soviet Russia* (New York: Vanguard Press, 1928), pp. 123-144; and Ella Winter, *Red Virtue: Human Relationships in the New Russia* (New York: Harcourt, Brace, 1933), pp. 118-126.

131. Quoted in Bailes, p. 483.

132. Kollontai, *Autobiography*, p. 7.

133. For a full discussion of Kollontai's diplomatic career, see dissertation by Hauge, previously cited.

134. New York *Times*, October 31, 1946.

135. I. Pavlov-Nilskii, quoted in Pertzoff, p. 208.

136. Angelica Balabanoff, quoted in Hauge, p. 52.

137. Alexander Barmine, *One Who Survived* (New York: G. P. Putnam's Sons, 1945), p. 92n.

138. Emma Goldman, *My Disillusionment in Russia* (New York: Thomas Y. Crowell, 1970), p. v.

139. See Kollontai's comments to Marcel Body, quoted in his article, "Alexandra Kollontai," *Preuves*, no. 14 (1952): 17, 23; Ruth Fischer, *Stalin and German Communism* (Cambridge, Mass.: Harvard University Press, 1948), p. 160n.

140. Body, pp. 17, 19.

141. Ibid., p. 24.

142. Ibid., p. 23.

143. Quoted in Hauge, p. 196.

144. See Vladimir and Evdokia Petrov, *Empire of Fear* (New York: Praeger, 1956), pp. 188-194.

145. Roy Medvedev, quoted in Beatrice Brodsky Farnsworth, *Aleksandra Kollontai: Socialism, Feminism, and the Bolshevik Revolution* (Stanford, Calif.: Stanford University Press, 1980), p. 396.

146. Body, p. 12; Pertzoff, p. 220.

147. Pitirim A. Sorokin, *Leaves from a Russian Diary* (Boston: Beacon Press, 1950), p. 59.

148. Marguerite E. Harrison, *Marooned in Moscow* (New York: George H. Doran, 1921), p. 86.

149. Duranty, pp. 239-240.

150. Barmine, pp. 91-92; Bryant, *Mirrors*, pp. 116, 123; Julio Alvarez del Vayo, *The Last Optimist* (New York: Viking Press, 1950), p. 132; Harrison, p. 78; Sadoul, *Notes*, p. 95, and *Quarante Lettres*, p. 81; and "Madame Ambassador," *Time* 43 (March 13, 1944): 24.

151. Kollontai's tale, *A Great Love*, is generally considered to be an autobiographical account of this relationship. See Richard Stites, "Kollontai, Inessa, and Krupskaia," *Canadian-American Slavic Studies* 9 (1975): 88-90.

152. Victor Serge, *Memoirs of a Revolutionary, 1901-1941*, ed. and trans. Peter Sedgwick (London: Oxford University Press, 1963), p. 205. Kollontai's obituary in the London *Times*, March 12, 1952, repeated the fiction that she subscribed to this flippant view of sexual relations.

153. Leonard Schapiro, *The Communist Party of the Soviet Union* (New York: Vintage, 1971), pp. 205, 351; William Henry Chamberlin, *The Russian Revolution, 1917-1921* (New York: Macmillan, 1935), 1: 373; and Carr, *Socialism*, 1: 31.

154. Adam B. Ulam, *The Bolsheviks* (Toronto: Collier, 1968), p. 470; Theodore H. Von Laue, *Why Lenin? Why Stalin? A Reappraisal of the Russian Revolution, 1900-1930* (Philadelphia: J. B. Lippincott, 1964), pp. 158, 217; Louis Fischer, *The Life of Lenin* (New York: Harper & Row, 1964), pp. 438-439; and Georg von Rauch, *A History of Soviet Russia*, trans. Peter and Annette Jacobsohn (New York: Praeger, 1962), p. 140.

155. Ulam, p. 469; Daniels, *Conscience*, p. 127; Avrich, *Anarchists*, p. 224.

156. Pertzoff, pp. 220-221; Holt, pp. 24-25.

157. Compare Alexandra Kollontai, "Ziel und Wert meines Lebens," in *Führende Frauen Europas*, ed. Elga Kern (Munich: Ernst Reinhardt, 1928), pp. 258-286. A new German edition published in 1970 was the first to appear with a more provocative title: *Autobiographie einer sexuell emanzipierten Kommunistin* (Munich: Rogner und Bernhard, 1970).

158. See Kollontai, "Labour of Women," pp. 144-149; *Women Workers*, p. 16; "Révolution des moeurs," in Stora-Sandor, p. 242; and "Critique of the Feminist Movement," in Schlesinger, pp. 47-48.

159. Galina Serebriakova, quoted in Pertzoff, p. 113.

NOTES TO CHAPTER 3

1. *The Economist* 218 (March 19, 1966): 1139.

2. Comment by Edward Fitzgerald, English translator of Paul Frolich, *Rosa Luxemburg: Her Life and Work* (New York: Howard Fertig, 1969), p. 9.

3. Comment by Bruno Schönlank, repeated in Luxemburg to Leo Jogiches, September 4, 1898 in Rosa Luxemburg, *Lettres à Léon Jogichès*, ed. Felix Tych and Victor Fay (Paris: Denoël Gonthier, 1971), 1: 215.

4. Franz Mehring, "Historisch-materialistische Literatur," *Die Neue Zeit* 25, Bd. II, no. 41 (July 17, 1907): 507.

5. See, for example, J. P. Nettl, *Rosa Luxemburg* (London: Oxford University Press, 1966), 1: 138-139; and Michael Dulany Richards, "Reform or Revolution: Rosa Luxemburg and the Marxist Movement, 1893-1919" (Ph.D. diss., Duke University, 1969), p. 39.

6. See *Comrade and Lover: Rosa Luxemburg's Letters to Leo Jogiches*, ed. and trans. Elzbieta Ettinger (Cambridge, Mass.: MIT Press, 1979); and these reviews: *Library Journal* 104 (October 1, 1979): 2091; and Neal Ascherson, "Love and Revolution," *New York Review of Books* 27 (March 6, 1980): 14-16.

7. Kaethe Schirmacher, *The Modern Woman's Rights Movement: A Historical Survey*, trans. Carl Conrad Eckhardt (New York: Macmillan, 1912), p. 232.

8. Kawecka, an important club woman and contributor to *Le Journal des Citoyennes de la Commune*, fought for the defense of Gare Montparnasse. The better known Paule Minck (Paulina Mekarska) founded the Société Fraternelle de l'Ouvrière. In 1875 official French sources reported that 110 Poles had been involved in the Commune. Modern estimates place the number somewhere between 250 and 443. On the role of Poles and Polish women in the Commune, see Hélène Gosset, "Les Polonais Dans la Commune de Paris," *Europe* 29 (1951): 147-156; Woodford McClellan, *Revolutionary Exiles: The Russians in the First International and the Paris Commune* (London: Frank Cass, 1979), esp. pp. 167-169; Apollo Mlochkowski, *Les Polonais et la Commune de Paris* (Paris: Librairie générale, 1871); and Edith Thomas, *The Women Incendiaries*, trans. James and Starr Atkinson (New York: George Braziller, 1966). For the development of feminism in Poland, see Schirmacher, pp. 232-235; and Theodore Stanton, ed., *The Woman Question in Europe* (New York: G. P. Putnam's Sons, 1884), pp. 424-445.

9. Stanton, p. 432.

10. See G. P. Gooch, *Germany and the French Revolution* (New York: Russell and Russell, 1966), esp. pp. 353-366.

11. On the cult of the Saint-Simonians in Germany, see E. M. Butler, *The Saint-Simonian Religion in Germany* (New York: Howard Fertig, 1968); Richard W. Reichard, *Crippled From Birth: German Social Democracy, 1844-1870* (Ames: Iowa State University Press, 1969), pp. 23-24, 37; Constance Rover, *Love, Morals, and the Feminists* (London: Routledge and Kegan Paul, 1970), pp. 10-11; and Jutta Schroers Sanford, "The Origins of German Feminism: German Women 1789-1870" (Ph.D. diss., Ohio State University, 1976), pp. 105-106, 181. SPD leader August Bebel himself testified to the importance of Saint-Simonian influence in his own intellectual development. See his *Aus meinem Leben* (Stuttgart: J. H. W. Dietz, 1911), 2: 259-264.

12. On the young German movement, see Hans Bloesch, *Das Junge Deutschland in seinen Beziehungen zu Frankreich* (Bern: Buchler, 1903); Karen Honeycutt, "Clara Zetkin: A Left-Wing Socialist and Feminist in Wilhelmian Germany" (Ph.D. diss., Columbia University, 1975), p. 19; Hugh Wiley Puckett, *Germany's Women Go Forward* (New York: AMS Press, 1967), pp. 104-109; Sanford, pp. 117-118; and Jacqueline Strain, "Feminism and Political Radicalism in the German Social Democratic Movement, 1890-1914" (Ph.D. diss., University of California, Berkeley, 1964), p. 7.

13. On the role of German women in 1848, see Richard J. Evans, *The Feminists* (London: Croom Helm, 1977), p. 103; Puckett, pp. 116-130; Reichard, pp. 69, 94; Sanford, pp. 132-135, 181-182; Schirmacher, pp. 143-145; and Stanton, pp. 139-160.

14. "The theory of 'what is becoming to a woman' had special binding power in Germany," wrote feminist Clara Zetkin. See her *Zur Geschichte der proletarischen Frauenbewegung Deutschlands* (Berlin: Dietz, 1958), p. 22. On this point, also see Richard J. Evans, *The Feminist Movement in Germany, 1894-1933* (Beverly Hills, Calif.: Sage Publications, 1976), pp. 22-26; Gooch, pp. 365-366; Amy Hackett, "The German Women's Movement and Suffrage, 1890-1914: A Study in National Feminism," in *Modern European Social History*, ed. Robert J. Bezucha (Lexington, Mass.: D. C. Heath, 1972), p. 363; and Talcott Parsons, "Democracy and Social Structure in Pre-Nazi Germany," *Journal of Legal and Political Sociology* 1 (1942): 106.

15. Clara Zetkin, quoted in Honeycutt, p. 338.

16. August Bebel, *Woman Under Socialism*, trans. Daniel DeLeon (New York: Labor News Press, 1904), pp. 114, 121, 231.

17. August Bebel, *Unsere Ziele* (Liepzig: F. Thiele, 1870), p. 15.

18. Bebel, *Woman*, pp. 110-111. On this point, also see Robert Paul Neuman, "Socialism, the Family, and Sexuality: The Marxist Tradition and German Social Democracy Before 1914" (Ph.D. diss., Northwestern University, 1972), and "The Sexual Question and Social Democracy in Imperial Germany," *Journal of Social History* 7 (1973-1974): 271-286.

19. Bebel, *Leben*, 1: 186.

20. Karl Kautsky, "Julie Bebel," *Die Neue Zeit* 29, Bd. I, no. 9 (December 2, 1910): 276-278.

21. Werner Thönnessen, *The Emancipation of Women: The Rise and Decline of the Women's Movement in German Social Democracy, 1863-1933*, trans. Joris de Bres (London: Pluto Press, 1973), pp. 13-14.

22. On the early history of the German labor movement, see Roger Morgan, *The German Social Democrats and the First International, 1864-1872* (London: Cambridge University Press, 1965); Koppel S. Pinson, *Modern Germany*, 2d ed. (New York: Macmillan, 1966), pp. 195-203; John Plamenatz, *German Marxism and Russian Communism* (London: Longmans, Green, 1954), pp. 3-187. For the Lassallean view of women, see Katharine Anthony, *Feminism in Germany and Scandinavia* (New York: Henry Holt, 1915), pp. 174-177; Hilde Lion, *Zur Sociologie der Frauenbewegung* (Berlin: Herbig, 1926), p. 26; Reichard, pp. 212-215; Strain, p. 18; and Thönnessen, p. 16.

23. Neuman, "Socialism," pp. 290, 317-318. On the position of women in the SPD, see Evans, *Feminists*, pp. 163-165; Honeycutt, pp. 338-341; Jean Helen Quataert, "The German Socialist Women's Movement 1890-1918: Issues, Internal Conflicts, and the Main Personages" (Ph.D. diss., University of California, Los Angeles, 1974), pp. 141-148, 417; Strain, pp. 67-70; and Thönnessen, pp. 66-78.

24. Lily Braun, *Memoiren einer Sozialistin* (Munich: Albert Langen, 1922), 2: 177.

25. Clara Zetkin, quoted in Honeycutt, p. 341.

26. Ibid., p. 62; Alfred G. Meyer, "Marxism and the Women's Movement," in *Women in Russia*, ed. Dorothy Atkinson, Alexander Dallin, and Gail Warshofsky Lapidus (Stanford, Calif.: Stanford University Press, 1977), p. 110.

27. See Max Beer, *Fifty Years of International Socialism* (New York: Macmillan, 1935), pp. 105-105; Eduard Bernstein, "Jews and German Social Democracy," in Paul W. Massing, *Rehearsal for Destruction: A Study of Political Anti-Semitism in Imperial Germany* (New York: Harper and Bros., 1949), pp. 322-330; William J. Fishman, *Jewish Radicals: From Czarist Stetl to London Ghetto* (New York: Pantheon, 1974); Leopold H. Haimson, *The Russian Marxists and the Origins of Bolshevism* (Cambridge, Mass.: Harvard University Press, 1967), pp. 60-61; Robert Michels, *Political Parties*, trans. Eden and Cedar Paul (New York: Dover, 1959), pp. 258-263; Leonard Schapiro, "The Role of the Jews in the Russian Revolutionary Movement," *Slavonic and East European Review* 40 (1961): 148-167; and Robert S. Wistrich, *Revolutionary Jews from Marx to Trotsky* (New York: Barnes and Noble, 1976).

28. On the values of the *shtetl*, see Ruth Landes and Mark Zborowski, "Hypotheses Concerning the Eastern European Jewish Family," *Psychiatry* 13 (1950): 447-464; and Mark Zborowski, "The Place of Book-Learning in Traditional Jewish Culture," *Harvard Educational Review* 19 (1949): 87-109.

29. Quoted in Judd L. Teller, *Scapegoat of Revolution* (New York: Charles Scribner's Sons, 1954), p. 164.

30. Luise Kautsky, Introduction to Rosa Luxemburg, *Letters to Karl and Luise Kautsky from 1896 to 1918*, ed. Luise Kautsky, trans. Louis P. Lochner (New York: Gordon Press, 1975), pp. 4-5.

31. Frolich, p. 16; Henriette Roland-Holst, *Rosa Luxemburg: Ihr Leben und Wirken* (Zurich: Jean Christophe, 1937), p. 5.

32. Many of Luxemburg's letters record her constant concern for, and contact with, her family. See her letters to Jogiches: September 2, 1898, June 3, 1899, October 20, 1905, and November 25, 1905 in Ettinger, pp. 59, 80, 152, 157; March 18, 1895, June 9, 1898, July 12-20, 1898, August 3, 1898; December 1, 1898; and July 7, 1900 in *Lettres à Jogichès*, 1: 87, 169, 195-196, 200, 221; 2: 50; and to Hans Diefenbach, August 27, 1917 in Rosa Luxemburg, *Briefe an Freunde*, ed. Benedikt Kautsky (Hamburg: Europäische Verlagsanstalt, 1950), pp. 129-132.

33. Luxemburg to Jogiches, October 4, 1904 in Ettinger, p. 140.

34. Luise Kautsky, *Rosa Luxemburg: ein Gedenkbuch* (Berlin: E. Laubsche, 1929), p. 26; Roland-Holst, p. 10.

35. Frolich, p. 18; Kautsky, *Gedenkbuch*, p. 26. For Luxemburg's academic record at the Russian Gymnasium for girls in Warsaw, see Ralph H. Lutz, "Rosa Luxemburg's Unpublished Prison Letters 1916-1918," *Journal of Central European Affairs* 23 (1963): 306n.

36. For the early history of Polish socialism, see Lucjan Blit, *The Origins of Polish Socialism: The History and Ideas of the First Polish Socialist Party 1878-1886* (London: Cambridge University Press, 1971); and M. K. Dziewanowski, *The Communist Party of Poland: An Outline of History* (Cambridge, Mass.: Harvard University Press, 1959).

37. See Stefan Kieniewicz, *The Emancipation of the Polish Peasantry* (Chicago: University of Chicago Press, 1969), esp. pp. 140-189.

38. For Marx's and Engels' views on the Polish question, see their article, "Poles, Czechs, and Germans," New York *Daily Tribune*, March 5, 1852; Engels' letters of September 29 and October 24, 1891 to August Bebel in *August Bebels Briefwechsel mit Friedrich Engels*, ed. Werner Blumenberg (The Hague: Mouton, 1965), pp. 437-441, 461-465; H. Malcolm MacDonald, "Marx, Engels, and the Polish National Movement," *Journal of Modern History* 13 (1941): 321-334; and N. Rjasanoff, "Karl Marx und Friedrich Engels über die Polenfrage," *Archiv für die Geschichte des Sozialismus und der Arbeiterbewegung* 6 (1961): 174-221.

39. Quoted in Nettl, 1: 76.

40. On the split in the Polish movement, see M. K. Dziewanowski, "Social Democrats versus 'Social Patriots': The Origins of the Split of the Marxist Movement in Poland," *American Slavic and East European Review* 10 (1951): 14-25.

41. See Rosa Luxemburg, "Der Sozial-patriotismus in Polen," *Die Neue Zeit* 14, Bd. II, no. 41 (July 1, 1896): 462-463; "Von Stufe zu Stufe: Zur Geschichte der bürgerlichen Klassen Polen," *Die Neue Zeit* 14, Bd. I, no. 6 (October 27, 1897): 165-175; "Neue Strömungen in der polnischen Sozialistischen Bewegung in Deutschland und Oesterreich," *Die Neue Zeit* 14, Bd. II, nos. 32-33 (April 19, May 6, 1898): 181, 207-211; "The Polish Question at the International Congress in London," and "The Polish Question and the Socialist Movement," in Rosa Luxemburg, *The National Question: Selected Writings*, ed. Horace B. Davis (New York: Monthly Review Press, 1976), pp. 49-98.

42. See Rosa Luxemburg, *The Industrial Development of Poland*, trans. Tessa DeCarlo (New York: Campaigner, 1977).

43. Dziewanowski, *Communist Party*, p. 32.

44. Nettl, 1: 22, 167.

45. Belgian socialist Emile Vandervelde, quoted in Frolich, pp. 51-52.

46. Ibid., p. 53; also see enclosure to Luxemburg's letter to the editors of *Die Neue Zeit*, May 24, 1896 in *Kautsky Letters*, p. 48.

47. Richards, p. 35n.

48. Nettl, 1: 86.

49. Ibid.

50. Michels, p. 170.

51. Karl Kautsky, "Finis Poloniae?" *Die Neue Zeit* 14, Bd. II, nos. 42-43 (July 8, 15, 1896): 484-491, 513-522.

52. August Bebel to Victor Adler, September 29, 1898, in Victor Adler, *Briefwechsel mit August Bebel und Karl Kautsky*, ed. Friedrich Adler (Vienna: Wiener Volksbuchhandlung, 1954), p. 252.

53. Adler to Kautsky, May 13, 1896, Ibid., p. 207.

54. Ibid.

55. Ibid.

56. See Nettl, 1: 71, 82.

57. Luxemburg to Jogiches, July 12, 1896, September 24, 1898, in *Lettres à Jogichès*, 1: 117, 216.

58. On the SPD in these years, see Peter Nettl, "The German Social Democratic Party 1890-1914 as a Political Model," *Past and Present*, no. 30 (1965): 65-95; Arthur Rosenberg, *Imperial Germany*, trans. Ian F. D. Morrow (Boston: Beacon Press, 1964), pp. 33-72; and Guenther Roth, *The Social Democrats in Imperial Germany* (Totowa, N.J.: Bedminster Press, 1963).

59. Michels, p. 274; Mary-Alice Waters, ed., Introduction to *Rosa Luxemburg Speaks* (New York: Pathfinder Press, 1970), pp. 5-6.

60. On revisionism, see Peter Gay, *The Dilemma of Democratic Socialism: Eduard Bernstein's Challenge to Marx* (New York: Collier, 1970); Leopold Labedz, ed., *Revisionism: Essays on the History of Marxist Ideas* (New York: Praeger, 1962); Harry J. Marks, "The Sources of Reformism in the Social Democratic Party of Germany, 1890-1914," *Journal of Modern History* 11 (1939): 334-356; and Roth, pp. 183-192.

61. On the conservative role of the labour unions, see Gay, pp. 137-140; and Roth, pp. 193-211.

62. See Bernstein's series of articles entitled "Probleme des Sozialismus," *Die Neue Zeit* 15, Bd. I (1896-1897), pp. 164-171, 204-213, 303-311, 772-783; "Die Sozialpolitische Bedeutung von Raum und Zahl," *Die Neue Zeit* 15, Bd. II, no. 30 (April 21, 1897): 100-107; and "Das realistische und ideologische Moment im Sozialismus," *Die Neue Zeit* 16, Bd. II, nos. 34, 39 (May 18, June 22, 1898): 225-232, 388-395.

63. Rosa Luxemburg, Introduction to *Reform or Revolution* (New York: Three Arrows Press, 1937), p. 4.

64. Luxemburg's speeches and writings on revisionism include: *Reform or Revolution*; "Speeches to the Stuttgart Congress" and "Speech to the Hanover Congress," in *Selected Political Writings of Rosa Luxemburg*, ed. Dick Howard (New York: Monthly Review Press, 1971), pp. 38-51; "Opportunism and the Art of the Possible," and "Social Democracy and Parliamentarianism," in Rosa Luxemburg, *Selected Political Writings*, ed. Robert Looker, trans. William D. Graf (London: Jonathan Cape, 1972), pp. 72-75, 106-116.

65. Luxemburg, *Reform or Revolution*, p. 37; "Démocratie industrielle et Démocratie politique," *Le mouvement socialiste*, no. 11 (June 15, 1899): 647.

66. Rosa Luxemburg, "The National Assembly," in Looker, p. 265; *The Russian Revolution* (Ann Arbor: University of Michigan Press, 1961), p. 39.

67. Bebel to Karl Kautsky, September 4, 1901 in *August Bebels Briefwechsel mit Karl Kautsky*, ed. Karl Kautsky, Jr. (Assen: Van Gorcum, 1971), p. 139. Kautsky shared Bebel's sentiments. After Luxemburg's death he recalled her

"unbelievable intrepidity and lack of respect that spared no one . . . she aroused the most bitter hate." See Karl Kaustky, *Rosa Luxemburg, Karl Liebknecht, Leo Jogiches: Ihre Bedeutung für die Sozialdemokratie* (Berlin: Freiheit, 1921), p. 14.

68. See Ignaz Auer's letters of June 11 and December 9, 1901 to Karl Kautsky in "Einige Briefe Rosa Luxemburgs und Andere Dokumente," ed. Werner Blumenberg, *Bulletin of the International Institute for Social History*, 8 (1952): 27-28.

69. Quoted in Nettl, *Luxemburg*, 1: 153.

70. Luxemburg mentioned this attack in a speech to the Stuttgart Congress; see Howard, p. 40.

71. Quoted in Nettl, *Luxemburg*, 1: 187.

72. Although in theory socialism proclaimed to be opposed to anti-Semitism, sections of the German party were riddled with prejudice against "Jewish intellectuals." See Frolich, p. 209; Michels, pp. 258-263; Gustav Noske, *Erlebtes aus Aufstieg und Niedergang einer Demokratie* (Offenbach-am-Main: Bollwerk, 1947), p. 27; Roth, p. 261; and Wistrich, pp. 89-90.

73. Quoted in Nettl, *Luxemburg*, 1: 188.

74. See Luxemburg to Bebel, October 31, 1898 in "Einige Briefe," pp. 14-14.

75. Bebel to Bruno Schönlank, November 3, 1898, Ibid., p. 16.

76. For Luxemburg's reply to Bebel, see her letter of October 11, 1902, Ibid., pp. 34-35.

77. Luxemburg to Jogiches, May 1, 1899 in *Lettres à Jogichès*, 1: 196.

78. Luxemburg to Konrad Haenisch, December 2, 1911 in *Freunde*, pp. 28-30.

79. For Luxemburg's analysis of the Russian Revolution of 1905, see "Die Revolution in Russland," *Die Neue Zeit* 23, Bd. I, no. 1 (January 25, 1905): 572-577; and "Nach dem ersten Akt," *Die Neue Zeit* 23, Bd. I, no. 19 (February 1, 1905): 610-614.

80. For the effects of the revolution in Russian Poland, see M. K. Dziewanowski, "The Polish Revolutionary Movement and Russia, 1904-1907," *Harvard Slavic Studies* 4 (1957): 375-394, and "The Revolution of 1904-1905 and the Marxist Movement of Poland," *Journal of Central European Affairs* 12 (1952): 259-275.

81. Luxemburg to Emanuel and Mathilde Wurm, July 18, 1906 in *Freunde*, pp. 42-44.

82. For Luxemburg's activities in 1905-1906, see H. Schurer, "The Russian Revolution of 1905 and the Origins of German Communism," *Slavonic and East European Review* 39 (1961): 495-471.

83. For Luxemburg's writings on the mass strike, see "The Mass Strike, the Political Party, and the Trade Unions," in Waters, pp. 155-218; "Die Theorie und Die Praxis," *Die Neue Zeit* 28, Bd. II, nos. 43-44 (July 22, 29, 1910): 564-

578, 626-642; "The Next Step," and "The Political Mass Strike," in Looker, pp. 148-159, 179-185; her speeches to the Jena Congress on the question in Rosa Luxemburg, *Gesammelte Werke* (Berlin: Dietz, 1974), 1, bk. 2: 595-604; and "Ermattung oder Kampf?" *Werke*, 2: 344-377.

84. Luxemburg to Clara Zetkin, March 20, 1907 in *Illustrierte Geschichte der Deutschen Revolution* (Berlin: Internationaler Arbeiter-Verlag, 1929), p. 62.

85. The breach was reflected in the tone of Luxemburg's letters to Jogiches after 1907. They were strictly business, without personal references or even salutations. See Ettinger and *Lettres à Jogichès, passim.*

86. See Nettl, *Luxemburg*, 1: 311; Roth, pp. 278-279; Carl E. Schorske, *German Social Democracy, 1905-1917* (New York: Russell and Russell, 1970), p. 39. Compare the antiintellectualism displayed by Philip Scheidemann in his *Memoirs of a Social Democrat*, trans. J. E. Mitchell (London: Hodder and Stroughton, 1929), 1: 99-100.

87. On the mass strike debate in the German party, see Richard W. Reichard, "The German Working Class and the Russian Revolution of 1905," *Journal of Central European Affairs* 13 (1953): 136-153; and Schorske, pp. 28-58. Bebel's correspondence makes it clear that he felt the need to restrain revolutionary exuberance among some sectors of the party in the wake of the events of 1905. See Bebel to Adler, September 16, 1905 in *Adler Briefwechsel*, pp. 467-469.

88. Quoted in Ronald Florence, *Marx's Daughters* (New York: Dial Press, 1975), p. 106.

89. Quoted in Roth, p. 281.

90. Rosa Luxemburg, "Concerning Morocco," in Looker, p. 167.

91. Konrad Haenisch, September 18, 1911 in Rudolf Franz, ed., "Aus den Briefen Konrad Haenischs," *Archiv für die Geschichte des Sozialismus und der Arbeiterbewegung* 14 (1929): 470.

92. Karl Kautsky, "Zwischen Baden und Luxemburg," *Die Neue Zeit* 18, Bd. II, no. 45 (August 5, 1910): 652-667.

93. Adler to Bebel, August 5, 1910 in *Adler Briefwechsel*, p. 510.

94. Mehring, p. 507.

95. Luxemburg to Hans Diefenbach, June 23, 1917 in "Letters From Prison," *Partisan Review* 10 (1943): 370.

96. Scheidemann, 1: 100.

97. Quoted in Nettl, *Luxemburg*, 1: 387.

98. Luise Kautsky, *Gedenkbuch*, pp. 36-38; preface to *Kautsky Letters*, pp. 13-14; Angelica Balabanoff, *My Life as a Rebel* (Bloomington: Indiana University Press, 1973), p. 22.

99. Rosa Luxemburg, *The Accumulation of Capital*, trans. Agnes Schwarzschild (New Haven, Conn.: Yale University Press, 1951).

100. Luxemburg was neither the first nor the only socialist to develop a theory of imperialism, but her approach was different in both spirit and content from that of other writers on the subject, Lenin, Hobson, and Hilferding among

them. Lenin accused Luxemburg of economic errors and sentimentalized "non-Marxist" descriptions of the human evils wrought by imperialism. For a detailed analysis of the arguments of both Luxemburg and her critics, see Raya Dunayevskaya, *State Capitalism and Marx's Humanism* (Detroit: News and Letters, 1967); George Lee, "Rosa Luxemburg and the Impact of Imperialism," *Economic Journal* 81 (1971): 847-862; Paul Sweezy, "Rosa Luxemburg's *The Accumulation of Capital*," *Science and Society* 31 (1967): 474-485; and Kenneth J. Tarbuck, ed., *Imperialism and the Accumulation of Capital* (London: Penguin Press, 1972).

101. For Luxemburg's writings on militarism and war, see *Rosa Luxemburg im Kampf Gegen den deutschen Militarismus* (Berlin: Dietz, 1960).

102. For the debate over socialist use of a general strike as an antiwar weapon, see Sinclair W. Armstrong, "The Internationalism of the Early Social Democrats of Germany," *American Historical Review* 47 (1942): 245-258; Richard Hostetter, "The SPD and the General Strike as an Anti-War Weapon, 1905-1914," *The Historian* 13 (1950-1951): 27-51; James Joll, *The Second International, 1889-1914* (New York: Praeger, 1956), pp. 106-157; and Schorske, pp. 59-87. Also see Luxemburg's speech, "On a General Strike Against War," in Olga Hess Gankin and H. H. Fisher, *The Bolsheviks and the World War* (Stanford, Calif.: Stanford University Press, 1940), pp. 56-57.

103. On this point, see William Maehl, "The Role of Russia in German Socialist Policy, 1914-1918," *International Review of Social History* 4 (1959): 177-198, and "The Triumph of Nationalism in the German Socialist Party on the Eve of the First World War," *Journal of Modern History* 24 (1952): 15-41; H. Malcolm MacDonald, "Karl Marx, Friedrich Engels, and the South Slavic Problem in 1848-1849," *University of Toronto Quarterly* 8 (1939): 452-460; and Hermann Wendel, "Marxism and the South Slav Question," *Slavonic Review* 2 (1923-1924): 289-307.

104. Luise Kautsky reported that Luxemburg was suicidal upon the outbreak of the war. See her recollections in Maurice Berger, *Germany After the Armistice*, trans. William L. McPherson (New York: G. P. Putnam's Sons, 1920), pp. 257-258. See Luxemburg's letters to Franz Mehring announcing the organization of a protest movement against the war: September 10 and 13, 1914 in Gilbert Badia, *Le Spartakisme* (Paris: L'Arche, 1967), pp. 321-324, and August 31, 1915 in Rosa Luxemburg, *J'Etais, Je Suis, Je Serai!: Correspondance, 1914-1919*, ed. Georges Haupt (Paris: François Maspero, 1977), p. 90. Also see her letter to the editor of the *Labour Leader*, December 31, 1914.

105. Adler to Bebel, August 5, 1910, and Kautsky to Adler, November 28, 1914 in *Adler Briefwechsel*, pp. 510, 606-607.

106. See Rosa Luxemburg, *The Crisis in German Social Democracy* (New York: Howard Fertig, 1969). "Junius" was the pseudonym of an eighteenth century protestor against the government of Britain's George III.

107. On the divisions in the German party, see Abraham Joseph Berlau, *The*

German Social Democratic Party, 1914-1921 (New York: Columbia University Press, 1949); Edwyn Bevan, *German Social Democracy During the War* (New York: E. P. Dutton, 1919); G. D. H. Cole, *A History of Socialist Thought* (New York: St. Martin's Press, 1953-1960), 4, bk. 1: 135; Lenore O'Boyle, "The German Independent Socialists during the First World War," *American Historical Review* 56 (1950-1951): 824-831; John L. Snell, "The Russian Revolution and the German Social Democratic Party in 1917," *American Slavic and East European Review* 15 (1956): 339-350, and "Socialist Unions and Socialist Patriotism in Germany, 1914-1918," *American Historical Review* 59 (1953-1954): 66-76.

108. On the German Revolution, see Rudolf Coper, *Failure of a Revolution: Germany in 1918-1919* (Cambridge: Cambridge University Press, 1955); Sebastian Haffner, *Failure of a Revolution: Germany 1918-1919*, trans. Georg Rapp (New York: Library Press, 1972); William S. Halperin, *Germany Tried Democracy* (Hamden, Conn.: Archon, 1963), pp. 79-136; Ralph Haswell Lutz, *The German Revolution, 1918-1919* (Stanford, Calif.: Stanford University Press, 1922); Rosenberg, pp. 232-274; Reinhard Rurup, "Problems of the German Revolution 1918-1919," *Journal of Contemporary History* 3 (1968): 109-135; A. J. Ryder, *The German Revolution of 1918* (Cambridge: Cambridge University Press, 1967); and Heinrich Ströbel, *The German Revolution and After*, trans. H. J. Stenning (New York: Thomas Seltzer, 1923).

109. See Luxemburg's letters to Mehring, November 18, 1918 in *The Letters of Rosa Luxemburg*, ed. Stephen Eric Bronner (Boulder, Colo.: Westview Press, 1978), p. 257; to Clara Zetkin, November 18, 24, 29, December 22, 1918, and January 11, 1919 in Badia, pp. 299-300; and to Clara Zetkin, December 25, 1918 in Haupt, pp. 367-369.

110. See Rosa Luxemburg, *On the Spartacus Program*, trans. Eden and Cedar Paul (Colombo, Ceylon: Young Socialist Publications, 1966).

111. Luxemburg, "What Does the Spartacus League Want?" in Howard, pp. 370-375.

112. For accounts of the hate campaign waged against Spartacus, see Badia, pp. 235-245; Princess Evelyn Blücher, *An English Wife in Berlin* (New York: E. P. Dutton, 1920), pp. 289-290, 305-306, 312; Coper, pp. 223, 231; Scheidemann, 2: 594-595; and Ströbel, p. 93. Luxemburg herself recognized that the explicit purpose behind the organized rumor campaign was to create a climate of panic and pogrom. See her "Das Alte Spiel," *Die Rote Fahne*, November 18, 1918, reprinted in Rosa Luxemburg, *Ausgewählte Reden und Schriften* (Berlin: Dietz, 1951), 2: 599-602.

113. Quoted in *Illustrierte Geschichte*, p. 269.

114. On the Spartacist uprising, see Badia, *Spartakisme*, and *Les Spartakistes: 1918: l'Allemagne en révolution* (Paris: René Julliard, 1966); Gerhard P. Bassler, "The Communist Movement in the German Revolution, 1918-1919: A Problem of Historical Typology?" *Central European History* 6 (1973): 233-277; and Eric Waldman, *The Spartacist Uprising of 1919* (Milwaukee: Marquette University Press, 1958).

115. Clara Zetkin, quoted in Charles Easton Rothwell, "Rosa Luxemburg and the German Social Democratic Party" (Ph.D. diss., Stanford University, 1938), p. 19.

116. Luxemburg to Hans Diefenbach, January 7, 1917, in "Letters from Prison," p. 363.

117. Julio Alvarez del Vayo, *Give Me Combat: The Memoirs of Julio Alvarez del Vayo*, trans. Donald D. Walsh (Boston: Little, Brown, 1973), p. 35.

118. See Luxemburg, "To the Proletarians of All Countries," and "What Does Spartacus Want?" in Howard, pp. 352-356, 367-369; "What Is Socialism?" in *Rosa Luxemburg: Selections from Her Works*, ed. Virgil J. Vogel (Chicago: Young People's Socialist League, 1946), pp. 20-22.

119. Luise Kautsky, Introduction to *Kautsky Letters*, p. 7.

120. Max Weber quoted in Marks, p. 349.

121. Quoted in Nettl, *Luxemburg*, 2: 457-458.

122. Rosa Luxemburg, "What Now?" in Looker, p. 174.

123. Luxemburg to Jogiches, October 20, 1905 in Ettinger, p. 153.

124. Luxemburg to Sonia Liebknecht, May 2, 1917 in Rosa Luxemburg, *Letters from Prison*, trans. Eden and Cedar Paul (London: Socialist Book Centre, 1946), p. 16.

125. Ibid.

126. Ibid.

127. Alexandra Kollontai, "Excerpts from a Diary," in *Selected Writings of Alexandra Kollontai*, ed. Alix Holt (Westport, Conn.: Lawrence Hill, 1977), p. 85.

128. "Socialism is organization," the SPD proudly proclaimed in *Vorwärts*, its official organ. See Pinson, p. 374.

129. Rosa Luxemburg, "Order Reigns in Berlin," in Howard, p. 415; "The Next Step," in Looker, p. 159.

130. For Luxemburg's displeasure with the Bolsheviks, see her pamphlet on the Russian Revolution, previously cited, and her letters: to Jogiches, June 24, 1898 in Ettinger, p. 48; to Jogiches, August 10, 1909, in Bronner, pp. 126-127; and to Luise Kautsky, November 24, 1917 and December 19, 1917 in *Kautsky Letters*, pp. 207, 214-215.

131. Luxemburg, "Mass Strike," in Waters, p. 198; "The Next Step," and "Political Mass Strike," in Looker, pp. 154, 181-185.

132. Luxemburg's famous critique of Lenin's organizational methods first appeared in *Die Neue Zeit*. See "Organisationfragen der russischen Sozialdemokraten," 22, Bd. II, nos. 42-43 (July 13, 20, 1904): 484-492, 529-535; reprinted as "Organizational Questions of Social Democracy," in Waters, pp. 114-130.

133. "Organizational Questions," in Waters, p. 130.

134. Luxemburg, "Mass Strike," in Waters, pp. 172-173, 182-183; and "The Revolution in Russia," in Looker, p. 117.

135. See Luxemburg, "The Russian Tragedy," in Looker, pp. 235-243.

136. For Luxemburg's opposition to the use of terror in revolutionary situations, see the statement of Karl Radek in Otto-Ernst Schüddekopf, "Karl Radek in Berlin, Ein Kapitel deutsch-russischer Beziehungen im Jahre 1919," *Archiv für Sozialgeschichte* 2 (1962): 133. Also Luxemburg, *Russian Revolution*, pp. 70-72; "What Does Spartacus Want?" in Howard, p. 370; and her letter of November-December 1918 to Adolf Warski in Bronner, p. 258.

137. Luxemburg quoted in Ryder, p. 277.

138. See the personal reminiscences of Hugo Eberlein in his "The Foundation of the Comintern and the Spartakusbund," *The Communist International* 6 (1929): 437-439.

139. Luxemburg's correspondence indicates that she was interested in propaganda work among women. See her letters to Clara Zetkin, November 18, 24, 29, 1918 in Haupt, pp. 361-365; to Jogiches, April 22, 1899 in *Lettres à Jogichès*, 1: 287; and to Luise Kautsky, Easter 1907 and August 1911 in *Kautsky Letters*, pp. 138, 164. Nonetheless, Luxemburg always insisted that work among women be joined to the proletariat's general struggle for liberation. See "Women's Suffrage and Class Struggle," in Howard, pp. 216-222.

140. Luxemburg to Jogiches, February 1913 in *Lettres à Jogichès*, 2: 290.

141. Luxemburg to Jogiches, September 18, 1900 in Rosa Luxemburg, *Listy do Leona Jogichesa-Tyszki*, ed. Feliks Tych (Warsaw: Książka i Wiedza, 1968-1971), 2: 107; and February 1, 1902 in *Lettres à Jogichès*, 2: 85.

142. Luxemburg to Jogiches, September 18, 1900 in *Listy*, 2: 107.

143. Luxemburg to Jogiches: April 27, 30, 1899, and July 23, 1899 in Haupt, 1: 290, 294, 300; February 2, 1899, May 1, 1899, January 3, 14, 28, 1902, June 27, 1905, and September 17, 24, 1905 in *Lettres à Jogichès*, 1: 255, 296; 2: 62, 74, 82, 123, 133, 135; also see Roland-Holst, p. 117.

144. On the conservative, reformist mood of the women's movement after 1908, see Evans, *Feminists*, pp. 161-165 and *Feminist Movement*, pp. 108, 185-186; Honeycutt, p. 298; and Strain, pp. 241-262.

145. See Luxemburg, "Rebuilding the International," in Looker, p. 199.

146. Luxemburg to Zetkin, quoted in Florence, p. 97.

147. See Luxemburg to Sonia Leibknecht, February 18, 1917 in Haupt, p. 184. The complete version of the letter contained in this collection yields important insights into Luxemburg's views on feminism—sections usually omitted from the standard version contained in *Prison Letters*, pp. 11-13.

148. Luxemburg's correspondence reveals the strong support she drew from women friends. See her letters to Luise Kautsky, undated 1904; January 26, 1917, and undated prison letter from Wronke in *Kautsky Letters*, pp. 84, 191, 197; her letter to Sonia Liebknecht, April 19, 1917 in *Prison Letters*, p. 14; to Mathilde Jacob, May 22, 1915; and to Marta Rosenbaum, in Haupt, pp. 82, 176; to Marta Rosenbaum, January 4, 1919 in *Freunde*, pp. 168-169; and to Jogiches, June 1, 1900 in *Lettres à Jogichès*, 2: 43. Also see Luise Kautsky's reminiscences on this point, quoted in Dominique Desanti, *Visages de Femmes* (Paris: Editions Sociales, 1955), p. 86.

149. Luxemburg to Luise Kautsky, January 26, 1917 in *Kautsky Letters*, p. 191.

150. Luxemburg to Mathilde Jacob, November 10, 1915, quoted in Gilbert Badia, *Rosa Luxemburg: Journaliste, Polémiste, Révolutionnaire* (Paris: Editions Sociales, 1975), p. 780.

151. Luxemburg to Jogiches, January 13, 1900 in Ettinger, pp. 88-89; and July 12, 1896 in *Lettres à Jogichès*, 1: 117.

152. Luxemburg to Jogiches, March 6, 1899 in Ettinger, p. 73.

153. Luxemburg to Jogiches, March 25, 1894; March 21, 1895 in Ettinger, pp. 8, 17-18.

154. Luxemburg to Sonia Liebknecht, November 24, 1917 in Haupt, p. 306.

155. Luxemburg to Jogiches, May 17, 1898 in Ettinger, p. 33; to Hans Diefenbach, March 1917 in "Letters from Prison," p. 367.

156. Ibid.

157. See Luxemburg's letters to Jogiches: March 28, 1895, and March 6, 1899 in Ettinger, pp. 19-21, 72-74; March 29, 1900 in Bronner, p. 80; and May 4, 11, 12, 1900 in *Lettres à Jogichès*, 2: 31-39.

158. Luxemburg to Jogiches, March 6, 1899 in Ettinger, p. 73.

159. Luxemburg to Jogiches, September 23, 1904 in Ettinger, p. 139; and to Sonia Liebknecht, mid-December 1917 in *Prison Letters*, pp. 37-40.

160. See Luxemburg's letters to Jogiches: March 6, 1899, May 27, 1899, December 17, 1899, and January 3, 1902 in Ettinger, pp. 73, 79, 87, 109; and December 17, 1899, and January 3, 1902 in *Lettres à Jogichès*, 1: 341, 2: 64.

161. On Luxemburg's relationship with Zetkin, see Badia, *Luxemburg*, p. 795. On Clara Zetkin's disapproval of the affair, see Luxemburg to Hans Diefenbach, January 7, 1917 in *Freunde*, pp. 77-78.

162. Luxemburg to Diefenbach, March 1917 in "Letters from Prison," p. 367; January 7, 1917 in *Freunde*, pp. 75-79.

163. See, for example, Luxemburg to Sonia Liebknecht, January 15, 1917 in *Prison Letters*, p. 10; and to Luise Kautsky, November 15, 1917 in *Kautsky Letters*, p. 205.

164. Blücher, p. 312.

165. See the London *Times*, January 18, 1919; the New York *Times*, January 18 and 19, 1919; the New York *World*, January 18 and 19, 1919; and the comments by Philip Scheidemann in *Memoirs*, 1: 280, and *Der Zusammenbruch* (Berlin: Verlag für sozialwissenschaft, 1921), p. 238.

166. Luxemburg, "Either/Or," in Howard, p. 344.

167. Luxemburg to Walter Stocker, March 11, 1914 in *Ausgewählte Reden*, 2: 304.

168. Luxemburg to Sonia Liebknecht, May 2, 1917 in *Prison Letters*, p. 16.

169. On the history of the KPD after Luxemburg's death, see Werner T. Angress, *Stillborn Revolution: The Communist Bid for Power in Germany, 1921-1923* (Princeton, N.J.: Princeton University Press, 1963); and Richard

Lowenthal, "The Bolshevization of the Spartacus League," in *International Communism*, ed. David Footman (London: Chatto and Windus, 1960), pp. 23-71.

170. See Walter Held, "The German Left and Bolshevism," *The New International* 5 (1939): 46-48, and "Once Again—Lenin and Luxemburg," *Fourth International* 1 (1940): 47-52; and Max Shachtman, "Lenin and Rosa Luxemburg," *The New International* 2 (1935): 60-64.

171. V. I. Lenin, "Catching Foxes: Levi and Serrati," *Collected Works* (Moscow: Progress Publishers, 1963-1970), 33: 207-211.

172. Ernst Thälmann, *Der revolutionäre Ausweg und die KPD* (Berlin: Schneller, 1932), pp. 71-72.

173. Adam B. Ulam, *The Bolsheviks* (Toronto: Collier, 1968), p. 292; Nadezhda K. Krupskaya, *Memoirs of Lenin*, trans. E. Verney (New York: International, 1930), 1: 161-162, 226, 327.

174. Lenin, "Foxes," p. 210.

175. Lenin quoted in Waters, p. 22. Also see his "Réponse à Rosa Luxemburg," in Daniel Guérin, *Rosa Luxemburg et la spontanéité révolutionnaire* (Paris: Flammarion, 1971), pp. 123-127; and *"Left" Communism: An Infantile Disorder* (London: The Toiler, 1920), pp. 23-25.

176. Held, "German Left," pp. 46-48.

177. See Lelio Basso, *Rosa Luxemburg: A Reappraisal*, trans. Douglas Parmée (New York: Praeger, 1975), p. 137n.; Eberlein, p. 441; Ruth Fischer, *Stalin and German Communism* (Cambridge, Mass.: Harvard University Press, 1948), pp. 21-27; and Joseph Stalin, "Some Questions Concerning the History of Bolshevism," in *Leninism: Selected Writings* (New York: International, 1942), pp. 222-233.

178. Fred Oelssner, *Rosa Luxemburg: Eine kritische biographische Skizze* (East Berlin: Dietz, 1951), pp. 7-8.

179. The most powerful impression of the romantic, sentimental Luxemburg was created by the publication of a letter to Sonia Liebknecht in which Luxemburg poignantly recounted and described the sufferings of the water buffalo that hauled wagons into the prison yard. See *Prison Letters*, pp. 37-40. Also see the hagiographic recollections by Luise Kautsky in Berger, pp. 253-275, in her introduction to *Kautsky Letters*, esp. p. 30, and in *Gedenkbuch*, p. 86; Roland-Holst, esp. p. 88; and Clara Zetkin's obituary tribute to Luxemburg reprinted in Frolich, pp. 219-220.

180. Frolich, p. 221.

NOTES TO CHAPTER 4

1. Jacques Sadoul, *Notes Sur la Révolution Bolchévique: Quarante Lettres de Jacques Sadoul* (Paris: Edition de la Librairie de l'Humanité, 1922), p. 87.

2. A recent doctoral dissertation deals only with Balabanoff's Italian career. See Nancy Gorman Eshelman, "Angelica Balabanoff and the Italian Socialist Movement: From the Second International to Zimmerwald" (Ph.D. diss., University of Rochester, 1977). A biographical sketch also appears in Ronald Florence, *Marx's Daughters* (New York: Dial Press, 1975), but lacks documentation and appears to be based on secondary sources only.

3. See, for example, the poor images of Balabanoff contained in Ivone Kirkpatrick, *Mussolini: Study of a Demagogue* (London: Odhams, 1964), p. 39; Margherita G. Sarfatti, *The Life of Benito Mussolini*, trans. Frederic Whyte (London: Thornton Butterworth, 1925), p. 117; and Bertram D. Wolfe, *Strange Communists I Have Known* (New York: Stein and Day, 1965), p. 81.

4. See Charles F. Delzell, "Benito Mussolini: A Guide to the Biographical Literature," *Journal of Modern History* 35 (1963): 344; Louis Fischer, *The Life of Lenin* (New York: Harper and Row, 1964), p. 367; and Ernst Nolte, *Three Faces of Fascism*, trans. Leila Vennewitz (New York: New American Library, 1969), p. 230.

5. Balabanoff has been called "an almost archetypal radical Russian woman." See Richard Stites, *The Women's Liberation Movement in Russia: Feminism, Nihilism, and Bolshevism, 1860-1930* (Princeton, N.J.: Princeton University Press, 1978), p. 324.

6. Angelica Balabanoff, *My Life As a Rebel* (New York: Harper and Bros., 1938; reprint, Bloomington: Indiana University Press, 1973), p. 14.

7. Although Italian socialism's commitment to women has been described as "ambivalent," contemporaries testified that socialists sought female support, recognizing the party could not survive without it. See Claire LaVigna, "The Marxist Ambivalence Toward Women: Between Socialism and Feminism in the Italian Socialist Party," in *Socialist Women*, ed. Marilyn J. Boxer and Jean H. Quataert (New York: Elsevier, 1978), pp. 146-181. Also see Emilia Mariani, "Le Mouvement Féministe en Italie," *Revue Politique et Parlémentaire* 13 (1897): 494.

8. See Federico Garlanda, *The New Italy*, trans. M. E. Wood (New York: G. P. Putnam's Sons, 1911), pp. 380-394; E. Rodocanachi, *La Femme Italienne* (Paris: Hachette, 1922), pp. 291-294; and Kaethe Schirmacher, *The Modern Woman's Rights Movement: A Historical Survey*, trans. Carl Conrad Eckhardt (New York: Macmillan, 1912), pp. 196-199.

9. Garlanda, pp. 380-389; Rodocanachi, pp. 304-305.

10. The traditional view of the equality of Renaissance women with men, put forth by Jacob Burckhardt in his classic *The Civilization of the Renaissance in Italy* (1860), has been challenged by Joan Kelly-Gadol. See her article, "Did Women Have a Renaissance?" in *Becoming Visible: Women in European History*, ed. Renate Bridenthal and Claudia Koonz (Boston: Houghton Mifflin, 1977), pp. 137-164. Compare Jacob Burckhardt, *The Civilization of the Renaissance in Italy* (Vienna: Phaidon, n.d.), pp. 203-206.

11. Catherine Sforza (1463-1509), daughter of the Duke of Milan, married the Prince of Forli and gallantly defended his hereditary lands against his murderers, then against Cesare Borgia. Beatrice d'Este (1475-1497), Duchess of Milan, was considered one of the most beautiful and accomplished princesses of the Italian Renaissance. She presided over one of the most splendid courts in Italy, and in 1492 visited Venice as an ambassador for her husband. Vittoria Colonna (1490-1547) was the wife of the Marquis of Pescara and wrote poetry in imitation of Petrarch. She too was widely renowned for her literary talents. On the Renaissance "virago," see Marian Andrews [Christopher Hare], *The Most Illustrious Ladies of the Italian Renaissance* (London: Harper and Bros., 1911), pp. 36, 105, 229-256; William Boulting, *Woman in Italy* (New York: Brentano's, 1910), pp. 331-336; Emily James Putnam, *The Lady* (Chicago: University of Chicago Press, 1910), pp. 158-210; Rodocanachi, pp. 266-267, 286-287; and Theodore Stanton, ed., *The Woman Question in Europe* (New York: G. P. Putnam's Sons, 1884), pp. 320-329.

12. Andrews, pp. 36-37; Boulting, pp. 331-332; and Carlo Sforza, *Contemporary Italy: Its Intellectual and Moral Origins*, trans. Drake and Denise DeKay (New York: E. P. Dutton, 1944), p. 61.

13. Andrews, p. 9; Boulting, pp. 317-319; Putnam, p. 185; Schirmacher, p. 201; and Stanton, p. 312.

14. Mariani, pp. 483-486. On the rise of feminism in Italy, see Richard J. Evans, *The Feminists* (London: Croom Helm, 1977), pp. 124, 136; and Schirmacher, pp. 196-206.

15. Marx himself doubted the possibility of a socialist revolution in Italy. See his letter of March 14, 1869 to Engels in *Marx-Engels Briefwechsel* (Berlin: Dietz, 1949-1950), 4: 201-202. On the backwardness of Italian economic development, see Jon S. Cohen, "Economic Growth," in Edward R. Tannenbaum and Emiliana P. Noether, *Modern Italy: A Topical History Since 1861* (New York: New York University Press, 1974), pp. 171-196; John A. B. Faggi, "The Beginnings of the Italian Socialist Party (1890-1900)" (Ph.D. diss., Columbia University, 1954), pp. 33-34; Alexander Gerschenkron, "Notes on the Rate of Industrial Growth in Italy, 1881-1913," *Journal of Economic History* 15 (1955): 360-375; and Ernest Lemonon, *L'Italie Economique et Sociale* (Paris: Félix Alcan, 1913), Chapters II-IV.

16. Robert Michels, *Le Prolétariat et la Bourgeoisie dans le mouvement socialiste italien*, trans. Georges Bourgin (Paris: Giard, 1921), pp. 51-67, 224, 230-237; Sforza, p. 153; Cecil J. S. Sprigge, *The Development of Modern Italy* (New Haven, Conn.: Yale University Press, 1944), p. 69; and John A. Thayer, *Italy and the Great War: Politics and Culture, 1870-1915* (Madison: University of Wisconsin Press, 1964), pp. 86-90.

17. The first actual Italian labor party, the Italian Workers Party, excluded all "bourgeois elements" from membership. See Faggi, p. 26; Michels, p. 266;

and Robert Michels, *Political Parties*, trans. Eden and Cedar Paul (New York: Dover, 1959), pp. 322–324.

18. For Bakunin's influence on Italian socialism, see E. H. Carr, *Michael Bakunin* (London: Macmillan, 1937), pp. 300–344; Faggi, pp. 16–18; Humbert L. Gualtieri, *The Labor Movement in Italy* (New York: S. F. Vanni, 1946), pp. 54–70; W. Hilton-Young, *The Italian Left: A Short History of Political Socialism in Italy* (London: Longmans, Green, 1949), pp. 8–14; Daniel L. Horowitz, *The Italian Labor Movement* (Cambridge, Mass.: Harvard University Press, 1963), pp. 17–23; Richard Hostetter, *The Italian Socialist Movement: Origins (1860–1882)* (Princeton, N.J.: D. Van Nostrand, 1958), pp. 72–121; James Joll, *The Anarchists* (London: Eyre and Spottiswoode, 1964), pp. 88–91; Lemonon, pp. 256–263; Maurice F. Neufeld, *Italy: School for Awakening Countries* (Ithaca, N.Y.: Cayuga Press, 1961), pp. 91–102; and Armand Italo Patrucco, "The Critics of the Italian Parliamentary System, 1860–1915" (Ph.D. diss., Columbia University, 1969), pp. 97–99.

19. On the influence of the ex-Communards in Italy, see Gualtieri, pp. 83–100; and George Woodcock, *Anarchism* (Cleveland: World, 1962), pp. 327–355.

20. On Malon, see Francis W. Coker, *Recent Political Thought* (New York: D. Appleton-Century, 1934), p. 115; G. D. H. Cole, *A History of Socialist Thought* (New York: St. Martin's Press, 1953–1960), 3, bk. 2: 713; Gualtieri, p. 18; Hilton-Young, p. 15. Also see Malon's *Le Socialisme intégrale* (Paris: Félix Alcan, 1890).

21. See Emiliana P. Noether, "Italian Intellectuals," and Rosario Romeo, "Germany and Italian Intellectual Life From Unification to the First World War," both in Tannenbaum and Noether, pp. 278, 292–310.

22. On Kuliscioff, see Faggi, pp. 47–49; and Claire LaVigna, "Anna Kuliscioff: From Russian Populism to Italian Reformism, 1873–1913" (Ph.D. diss., University of Rochester, 1971).

23. Christopher Seton-Watson, *Italy From Liberalism to Fascism, 1870–1925* (London: Methuen, 1967), p. 160, specifically mentions the lack of xenophobia in pre-World War I Italy.

24. Balabanoff's autobiographical memoirs used for this study include *My Life As a Rebel; Erinnerungen und Erlebnisse* (Berlin: E. Laub, 1927); and a typewritten autobiographical sketch in New York Public Library Archives, Schwimmer-Lloyd Collection, Lola Maverick Lloyd Papers, General Correspondence, January 1936 (hereinafter cited as AB-SLC).

25. Balabanoff, *Life*, p. 4; AB-SLC, p. 10.

26. Balabanoff, *Life*, p. 5; AB-SLC, p. 9.

27. Balabanoff, *Life*, p. 4; AB-SLC, p. 5.

28. Balabanoff, *Life*, p. 5; AB-SLC, pp. 5–6.

29. Balabanoff, *Life*, p. 5.

30. Ibid., pp. 2–4; AB-SLC, p. 14.

31. Balabanoff, *Life*, p. 7; AB-SLC, p. 5.

32. Balabanoff, *Life*, pp. 9-10.

33. Ibid., p. 11; AB-SLC, p. 14.

34. On the New University of Brussels, see Cole, 3, bk. 2: 631-632; Andrée Despy-Meyer, *Inventaire des Archives de l'Université Nouvelle de Bruxelles (1894-1919)* (Brussels: l'Empereur, 1973), pp. 7-9; Gary S. Dunbar, *Elisée Reclus: Historian of Nature* (Hamden, Conn.: Archon, 1978), pp. 96-100; E. F. A. Goblet d'Alviella, *L'Université de Bruxelles pendant son troisième quart de siècle, 1884-1909* (Brussels: M. Weissenbruch, 1909), pp. 17-37; Odon Por, "The New University of Brussels," *International Socialist Review* 7 (1906): 209-220; and Emile Vandervelde, *Souvenirs d'un Militant Socialiste* (Paris: Editions Denoël, 1939), pp. 32-37.

35. Balabanoff, *Life*, p. 14.

36. Ibid., p. 17.

37. Ibid., p. 18.

38. On Labriola, see Cole, 3, bk. 2: 738; Faggi, p. 46; Hilton-Young, pp. 21-23. Also see Labriola's own work, *Essays on the Materialistic Conception of History*, trans. Charles H. Kerr (Chicago: Charles H. Kerr, 1908).

39. Quoted in Balabanoff, *Life*, p. 26.

40. See Balabanoff's references to Labriola in her *Erziehung der Massen zum Marxismus* (Berlin: E. Laubsche, 1927), p. 9, and *Impressions of Lenin*, trans. Isotta Cesari (Ann Arbor: University of Michigan Press, 1964), p. 21.

41. Balabanoff, *Life*, p. 31.

42. On the political importance of emigration from Italy during this period, see Robert F. Foerster, *The Italian Emigration of Our Times* (Cambridge, Mass.: Harvard University Press, 1919), pp. 171-188; Bolton King and Thomas Okey, *Italy To-Day* (London: James Nisbet, 1901), pp. 311-321; and Elizabeth Wiskemann, *Italy* (London: Oxford University Press, 1947), pp. 31-33.

43. Balabanoff, *Life*, p. 32; AB-SLC, pp. 15-17.

44. See Eshelman, pp. 100-149, for a good account of Balabanoff's work among Italian emigrants during this period.

45. On the *Mädchenheime* system, see Balabanoff, *Life*, pp. 38-40; and Eshelman, pp. 174-177.

46. For Balabanoff's reminiscences of Mussolini from this period see *Life*, pp. 42-52; AB-SLC, pp. 20-24; "Benito Mussolini: Souvenirs sur l'Homme," *Europe* 18 (1928): 544-556; *The Traitor: Benito Mussolini and His "Conquest" of Power* (New York: Giuseppe Popolizio, 1942-1943); and the New York *Times*, December 27, 1925.

47. Balabanoff, *Traitor*, pp. 27-28.

48. Kirkpatrick, p. 40; George Seldes, *Sawdust Caesar: The Untold Story of Mussolini and Fascism* (New York: Harper and Bros., 1935), p. 39. Mussolini didn't mention Balabanoff in his autobiography. See Benito Mussolini, *My Autobiography* (New York: Charles Scribner's Sons, 1928).

49. Quoted in Eshelman, p. 302.

50. Leaders of the PSIS accused Balabanoff of betraying her mandate and of voting against the party's wishes on the issues of emigration and antimilitarism. See Eshelman, pp. 289-292.

51. Faggi, p. 51; Margot Hentze, *Pre-Fascist Italy* (New York: W. W. Norton, 1939), p. 36.

52. Faggi, p. 57; Hilton-Young, pp. 29-30.

53. Seton-Watson, p. 267.

54. In terms of its membership, the PSI was the third largest socialist party in Europe, behind only the German and the Belgian. See Benedetto Croce, *A History of Italy, 1871-1915*, trans. Cecilia M. Ady (Oxford: Clarendon Press, 1929), p. 148; Hilton-Young, p. 21; King and Okey, p. 61; and Seton-Watson, p. 160.

55. Anna Kuliscioff, quoted in Seton-Watson, p. 270.

56. For the similarities between Turati's brand of revisionist socialism and Eduard Bernstein's, see Spencer Michael DiScala, "Filippo Turati and Factional Strife in the Italian Socialist Party, 1892-1912" (Ph.D. diss., Columbia University, 1969), pp. 22-35; and James Edward Miller, "The Italian Socialist Party, 1900-1914: An Organizational Study" (Ph.D. diss., University of Illinois at Urbana-Champaign, 1974), pp. 81-87.

57. On the economic, political, and psychological division of Italy between North and South, see Shepard B. Clough, *The Economic History of Modern Italy* (New York: Columbia University Press, 1964), pp. 163-169; Shepard B. Clough and Carlo Livi, "Economic Growth in Italy: An Analysis of the Uneven Development of North and South," *Journal of Economic History* 16 (1956): 334-349; Richard Eckaus, "The North-South Differential in Italian Economic Development," *Journal of Economic History* 15 (1961): 285-317; King and Okey, pp. 111-123; Sforza, pp. 94-99; Thayer, pp. 173-191; and Wiskemann, pp. 28-29.

58. Eshelman, p. 317.

59. On the Libyan War and its influence on Italian socialism, see René Albrecht-Carrié, "Italian Colonial Policy, 1914-1918," *Journal of Modern History* 18 (1946): 123-147, and *Italy from Napoleon to Mussolini* (New York: Columbia University Press, 1950), pp. 87-80; William C. Askew, *Europe and Italy's Acquisition of Libya, 1911-1912* (Durham, N.C.: Duke University Press, 1942); Ronald S. Cunsolo, "Libya, Italian Nationalism, and the Revolt against Giolitti," *Journal of Modern History* 37 (1965): 186-207; Giovanni Giolitti, *Memoirs of My Life*, trans. Edward Storer (London: Chapman and Dodd, 1923), pp. 249-352; Hentze, pp. 287-293; Ignotus, "Italian Nationalism and the War with Turkey," *Fortnightly Review* 90 (1911): 1084-1096; C. J. Lowe and F. Marzari, *Italian Foreign Policy, 1870-1940* (London: Routledge and Kegan Paul, 1975), pp. 114-119; Denis Mack Smith, *Italy: A Modern History* (Ann Arbor: University of Michigan Press, 1959), pp. 272-281; A. William Salomone, *Italy in*

the Giolittian Era (Philadelphia: University of Pennsylvania Press, 1960), pp. 97–101; and Seton-Watson, pp. 366-381.

60. Quoted in Cunsolo, p. 200.

61. On the Congress of Reggio Emilia, see DiScala, pp. 336-348; Hilton-Young, pp. 67-77; and Miller, pp. 304-316.

62. For Balabanoff's speech, see *Life*, pp. 96-98.

63. Ibid., pp. 98-99; Balabanoff, *The Traitor*, pp. 60-63.

64. Balabanoff, *Life*, p. 99; Sarfatti, p. 116.

65. Miller, p. 339.

66. Balabanoff, *Life*, p. 100.

67. Balabanoff resigned out of loyalty to her old friend Maria Giudice, who had been fired from her job as a schoolteacher on a vague morals charge. Mussolini angered Balabanoff by publishing an article written by Giudice's accusers. See Balabanoff, *The Traitor*, pp. 124-126; "Benito Mussolini," pp. 552-553.

68. See William English Walling, *The Socialists and the War* (New York: Henry Holt, 1915), pp. 200-201; René Albrecht-Carrié, "Italian Foreign Policy, 1914-1922," *Journal of Modern History* 20 (1948): 329-331; and Lowe and Marzari, pp. 133-159.

69. For explanations of Mussolini's sudden change of heart, see Balabanoff, *The Traitor*, pp. 144-154; Jules Destrée, *En Italie Avant la Guerre, 1914-1915* (Brussels: G. Van Oest, 1915), pp. 31-35; Kirkpatrick, pp. 64-73; Julien Luchaire, *Confession d'un Français Moyen* (Florence: Leo S. Olschke, 1965), 2: 36-38; William A. Renzi, "Mussolini's Sources of Financial Support, 1914-1915," *History* 56 (1971): 189-206; Alfred Rosmer, *Le mouvement ouvrier pendant la première guerre mondiale* (Paris: Librairie du Travail, 1936), 1: 327-333; Gaetano Salvemini, *The Origins of Fascism in Italy*, ed. Roberto Vivarelli (New York: Harper and Row, 1973), pp. 100-102, 108-118; Seldes, pp. 390-395; and Thayer, pp. 266-267. For Mussolini's own explanation, see his *Autobiography*, pp. 35-38.

70. Balabanoff, *Life*, p. 126.

71. Balabanoff, "La Troisième Conférence de Zimmerwald," *Demain, Pages et Documents* 2 (1917): 97. Also see the antiwar poems in her volume *Tears* (New York: E. Laub, 1943), pp. 72-75, 121-122.

72. Balabanoff, "Italian Socialists and the Crisis," *The Socialist Review* 12 (1915): 625-632.

73. Quoted in Eshelman, p. 410. Also see V. I. Lenin, "Greetings to the Italian Socialist Party Congress," *Collected Works* (Moscow: Progress, 1963-1970), 23: 90-93.

74. On the International Socialist Bureau, see Helmut Gruber, ed., *International Communism in the Era of Lenin: A Documentary History* (Ithaca, N.Y.: Cornell University Press, 1967), p. 64n.; and Georges Haupt, *Socialism and the Great War: The Collapse of the Second International* (Oxford: Clarendon Press, 1972), pp. 15-17.

75. See Balabanoff, *Erinnerungen*, p. 55, *Life*, pp. 114-115; Merle Fainsod, *International Socialism and the World War* (Cambridge, Mass.: Harvard University Press, 1935), pp. 22-23; Georges Haupt, *Le Congrès manqué: l'internationale à la veille de la première guerre mondiale* (Paris: François Maspero, 1965), pp. 101-117; James Joll, *The Second International, 1889-1914* (New York: Praeger, 1956), p. 164; Rosmer, 1: 90.

76. On the Lugano Conference, see Balabanoff, *Life*, pp. 123, 130-131; Yves Collart, *Le Parti Socialiste Suisse et l'Internationale* (Geneva: Graduate Institute of International Studies, 1969), pp. 97-195; Fainsod, pp. 46-47; Olga Hess Gankin and H. H. Fisher, *The Bolsheviks and the World War* (Stanford, Calif.: Stanford University Press, 1940), pp. 262-263; Horst Lademacher, ed., *Die Zimmerwalder Bewegung: Protokolle und Korrespondenz* (The Hague: Mouton, 1967), 1: 3-27; and Rosmer, 1: 182-185.

77. On Zimmerwald, see Balabanoff, *Die Zimmerwalder Bewegung 1914-1919* (Leipzig: C. L. Hirschfeld, 1928); Cole, 4, bk. 1: 27-62; Fainsod, pp. 42-164; Gankin and Fisher, pp. 309-703; and Carl Landauer, *European Socialism* (Berkeley: University of California Press, 1959), 1: 530-540.

78. Cole, 4, bk. 1: 31-32.

79. On the first Zimmerwald Conference, see Balabanoff, *Zimmerwalder*, pp. 9-21; Fainsod, pp. 61-74; Lademacher, 1: 43-180; and Rosmer, 1: 368-419. On Kienthal, see Balabanoff, *Zimmerwalder*, pp. 21-56; Lademacher, 1: 263-390; Rosmer, 2: 70-100, 233-236; and Alfred Erich Senn, *The Russian Revolution in Switzerland, 1914-1917* (Madison: University of Wisconsin Press, 1971), pp. 156-166. On the third and last Zimmerwald Conference at Stockholm see Balabanoff, *Zimmerwalder*, pp. 56-107; Gankin and Fisher, pp. 582-703; Lademacher, 1: 445-484; and Landauer, 1: 598-619.

80. Robert Craig Nation, "The Zimmerwald Left: The Roots of International Communism in the First World War" (Ph.D. diss., Duke University, 1975), p. 125.

81. Quoted in Ibid., p. 206.

82. Balabanoff, "La Troisième Conférence," p. 97.

83. Balabanoff, *Life*, pp. 140-141.

84. On the Left Zimmerwald movement, see Fainsod, pp. 96-123; Gankin and Fisher, pp. 479-581; and dissertation by Nation, previously cited.

85. See "Manifesto of the International Socialist Conference at Zimmerwald," in Gruber, p. 62.

86. Balabanoff, *Life*, pp. 67, 71-73, 132-133.

87. Ibid., p. 132; Balabanoff, *Impressions*, pp. 19, 43.

88. Balabanoff, *Life*, pp. 143, 147.

89. Ibid., p. 146; Eshelman, pp. 506-515.

90. On the Grimm affair, see Balabanoff, *Erinnerungen*, pp. 117-162; *Life*, pp. 157-159; and *Zimmerwalder*, pp. 60-63; Fainsod, pp. 154-155; Gankin and Fisher, pp. 613-629; and Lademacher, 1: 573-644.

91. Balabanoff, "La Troisième Conférence," p. 94.

92. Alfred Erich Senn, *Diplomacy and Revolution: The Soviet Mission to Switzerland, 1918* (Notre Dame, Ind.: University of Notre Dame Press, 1974), p. 155.

93. Lenin, "On Zimmerwald," *Works*, 25: 303; also Lenin to Karl Radek, May 29, 1917, *Works*, 43: 632.

94. Lenin, "On Zimmerwald," *Works*, 25: 303.

95. Quoted in William Henry Chamberlin, *The Russian Revolution, 1917–1921* (New York: Macmillan, 1935), 2: 380.

96. Balabanoff, *Impressions*, p. 29; "Lénine et la Création du Comintern," in *Contributions à l'Historie du Comintern*, ed. Jacques Freymond (Geneva: Droz, 1965), p. 35; and *Life*, pp. 175–177.

97. Balabanoff, *Life*, p. 175.

98. Balabanoff, *Erinnerungen*, pp. 190–212; *Life*, p. 192; and Senn, *Diplomacy*, p. 152.

99. On the Swiss general strike of November 1918, see Senn, *Diplomacy*, pp. 169–172. On Balabanoff's work during this period, see Balabanoff, *Zimmerwalder*, pp. 134–159.

100. See Landauer, 1: 790–791.

101. On the founding of the Comintern, see Balabanoff, *Erinnerungen*, pp. 225–226; "Lénine et Comintern,"; Franz Borkenau, *European Communism* (London: Faber and Faber, 1953), pp. 25–49, and *World Communism: A History of the Communist International* (Ann Arbor: University of Michigan Press, 1962), pp. 161–170; Cole, 4, bk. 1: 287–342; R. Palme Dutt, *The Two Internationals* (London: George Allen and Unwin, 1920), pp. 22–29, 68–83; Fainsod, pp. 201–211; and Branko Lazitch and Milorad M. Drachkovitch, *Lenin and the Comintern* (Stanford, Calif.: Hoover Institution Press, 1972), pp. 129–134.

102. Arthur Ransome, *Russia in 1919* (New York: B. W. Huebsch, 1919), pp. 156–157.

103. See Hugo Eberlein, "The Foundation of the Comintern and the Spartakusbund," *The Communist International* 6 (1929): 436–442.

104. Balabanoff, *Erinnerungen*, pp. 239–240; "Lénine et Comintern," pp. 30–35; *Life*, p. 213; and Cole, 4, bk. 1: 301.

105. Balabanoff, *Life*, p. 215.

106. Ibid., pp. 215–217; "Lénine et Comintern," p. 37.

107. Balabanoff, *Life*, p. 215; *Zimmerwalder*, pp. 159–160; Edward H. Carr, *The Bolshevik Revolution, 1917–1923* (New York: Macmillan, 1950–1953), 3: 570. Also see "Report on the Liquidation of the Zimmerwald Organization," in Dutt, pp. 26–27.

108. Balabanoff, *Life*, p. 218.

109. Ibid., pp. 220–222.

110. Ibid., p. 228.

111. Ibid., pp. 179–181, 228–229; *Impressions*, pp. 30–31.

112. On the Pirro incident, see Balabanoff, *Impressions*, pp. 108-109; *Life*, pp. 233-235; Alexander Berkman, *The Bolshevik Myth* (New York: Boni and Liveright, 1925), pp. 240-242; and Landauer, 1: 722.

113. Balabanoff, *Life*, p. 235.

114. Ibid., p. 237; "Lénine et Comintern," p. 36.

115. Balabanoff, *Life*, pp. 238-239; "Lénine et Comintern," p. 36.

116. Balabanoff, *Life*, p. 245.

117. Borkenau, *World Communism*, p. 169.

118. On the revolutionary climate of postwar Italy, see John M. Cammett, *Antonio Gramsci and the Origins of Italian Communism* (Stanford, Calif.: Stanford University Press, 1967), pp. 111-122; Martin Clark, *Antonio Gramsci and the Revolution That Failed* (New Haven, Conn.: Yale University Press, 1977), pp. 148-180; Hilton-Young, pp. 84-117; Landauer, 1: 865-911; A. Rossi, *The Rise of Italian Fascism, 1918-1922*, trans. Peter and Dorothy Wait (New York: Howard Fertig, 1966), pp. 66-81; Salvemini, pp. 265-281; and Adolf Sturmthal, *The Tragedy of European Labor, 1918-1939* (New York: Columbia University Press, 1943), pp. 179-184.

119. Quoted in R. Palme Dutt, *The Internationale* (London: Lawrence and Wishart, 1964), p. 161.

120. See "Conditions of Admission into the Communist International," in Gruber, pp. 287-292.

121. For Lenin's attacks on Serrati and the PSI, see "Catching Foxes: Levi and Serrati," *Collected Works*, 33: 207-211, and *"Left" Communism: An Infantile Disorder* (London: The Toiler, 1920), pp. 89-91. Also see Salvemini, pp. 163-166.

122. Quoted in Florence, p. 226.

123. On the Italian Communist Party, see Cammett, pp. 141-155; "The Constitution of the I.C.P.," in Shepard B. Clough and Salvatore Saladino, *A History of Modern Italy* (New York: Columbia University Press, 1968), pp. 385-388; Earlene Joyce Craver, "The Crisis of Italian Socialism and the Origins of the Italian Communist Party, 1912-1921" (Ph.D. diss., University of Southern California, 1972); Alastair Davidson, "The Russian Revolution and the Formation of the Italian Communist Party," *The Australian Journal of Politics and History* 10 (1964): 355-370; Aldo Garosci, "The Italian Communist Party," in *Communism in Western Europe*, ed. Mario Einaudi, Jean-Marie Domenach, and Aldo Garosci (Ithaca, N.Y.: Cornell University Press, 1951), pp. 153-218; and Landauer, 1: 886.

124. Balabanoff, *Life*, pp. 162, 210-211, 268-269, 275, 287.

125. Ibid., p. 294.

126. Ibid., pp. 184-185, 271-272; *Impressions*, pp. 30-31, 34-35.

127. Balabanoff, *Life*, p. 183; *Impressions*, p. 11.

128. Balabanoff, *Life*, p. 183.

129. Ibid., p. 188; Balabanoff, *Impressions*, pp. 7, 30-31; "Lénine et Comintern," p. 34. Also see Fischer, p. 480.

130. Balabanoff, *Impressions*, p. 119.

131. According to Balabanoff, Lenin used individuals who were the "scum of humanity" to do his bidding. See *Impressions*, pp. 20-21, 28-29, 37, 102-103, 120; "Lénine et Comintern," p. 34; and *Life*, pp. 222-223.

132. Balabanoff, *Life*, p. 198.

133. Ibid., p. 203.

134. Ibid., pp. 84, 165-166; AB-SLC, p. 1; and the New York *Times*, December 27, 1925.

135. Balabanoff, *Life*, pp. 204-205.

136. Ibid., pp. 290-291.

137. Ibid., pp. 200-203, 219. Balabanoff's disillusionment with the corruption of the revolution's proletarian nature was recorded by Emma Goldman. See her *My Disillusionment in Russia* (Garden City, N.Y.: Doubleday, Page, 1923), p. 226, and *My Further Disillusionment in Russia* (Garden City, N.Y.: Doubleday, Page, 1924), p. 99.

138. Balabanoff, *Life*, p. 202.

139. See reminiscences by Goldman, *Disillusionment*, pp. 39, 90; Marguerite Harrison, *Marooned in Moscow* (New York: George H. Doran, 1921), p. 82; Seldes, p. 40; Victor Serge, *Memoirs of a Revolutionary, 1901-1941*, trans. Peter Sedgwick (London: Oxford University Press, 1963), pp. 184-186; and Wolfe, pp. 83-84.

140. Balabanoff, *The Traitor*, p. 21.

141. Emma Goldman, *Living My Life* (New York: AMS Press, 1970), p. 763.

142. *Le Monde*, November 28-29, 1965.

143. Balabanoff, *Life*, p. 70.

144. Goldman, *Disillusionment*, pp. 39-40.

145. Krupskaya quoted in Senn, *Revolution in Switzerland*, p. 122.

146. Max Nomad, *Dreamers, Dynamiters, and Demagogues* (New York: Waldon Press, 1964), p. 212.

147. LaVigna, "Kuliscioff," p. 169.

148. Ibid., p. 344n.

149. Interviewed by a reporter for a nonsocialist paper, Turati was asked whether or not, in the wake of her growing involvement in Russian affairs, Balabanoff was still qualified to speak for the PSI Executive. His published comments on Balabanoff's intelligence were, he claimed, twisted and distorted. See Eshelman, p. 513.

150. Jane Slaughter, "Humanism versus Feminism in the Socialist Movement: The Life of Angelica Balabanoff," in *European Women on the Left*, ed. Jane Slaughter and Robert Kern (Westport, Conn.: Greenwood Press, 1981), p. 186.

151. Eshelman, pp. 53-54, 60n.

152. See Angelica Balabanoff, *Sozialismus als Weltanschauung* (Berlin: Deutscher Freidenkerverband, 1932), and *Marx und Engels als Freidenker in ihren Schriften* (Jena: Urania-Freidenker-Verlag, 1931).

153. On these points, see Eshelman, pp. 495–496; Laura Fermi, *Mussolini* (Chicago: University of Chicago Press, 1961), p. 59; Sarfatti, pp. 115–116.

154. Balabanoff, *Life*, p. 87; Sadoul, pp. 87–88.

155. In his autobiography, Trotsky wrote that the PSI was acquainted with his views "thanks to the many translations by Balabanoff." See Leon Trotsky, *My Life* (New York: Charles Scribner's Sons, 1930), p. 250. Also see Isaac Deutscher, *The Prophet Armed: Trotsky, 1879–1921* (New York: Oxford University Press, 1954), p. 222.

156. For mention of Balabanoff's familiar role as translator and interpreter, see Balabanoff, *Life*, p. 139; Collart, pp. 121, 253; Edmondo Peluso, "Notes et impressions d'un délégué," *Demain, Pages et Documents*, no. 5 (1916): 343; Rosmer, 1: 383, 2: 87; Senn, *Revolution in Switzerland*, p. 92; and "Report of the Proceedings of the Zimmerwald Conference," in Gankin and Fisher, p. 326.

157. Balabanoff, *Life*, pp. 140, 175.

158. Balabanoff, *Impressions*, p. 27.

159. See the tribute to Balabanoff recorded in *Life*, p. 37.

160. Harrison, pp. 80–81; Nomad, p. 210; Sarfatti, p. 115.

161. Balabanoff, *Erziehung der Massen zum Marxismus*. Also see AB-SLC, pp. 18–19, and *Sozialismus*, pp. 18–19, 27–32.

162. Quoted in Harrison, p. 81.

163. For Balabanoff's views on motherhood, see *Erziehung*, pp. 106–118, and *Tears*, pp. 43–45, 118, esp. her poem "Mothers," pp. 26–28.

164. Eshelman, pp. 182–185.

165. Ibid., p. 182; Balabanoff, *Life*, pp. 34–35.

166. Balabanoff, *Impressions*, p. 74.

167. Stites, pp. 333–334.

168. Balabanoff, *Life*, p. 239.

169. Ibid., p. 3; AB-SLC, p. 12; *Tears*, p. 11.

170. Balabanoff, *Life*, p. 294.

171. Ibid., p. 301; New York *Times*, May 4, 1924.

172. Balabanoff, *Life*, p. 25.

173. Ibid., p. 252.

174. Marcel Body, "Alexandra Kollontai," *Preuves*, no. 14 (1952): 17, 19, 24.

175. Balabanoff, *Life*, p. 290.

176. Balabanoff, *Impressions*, p. 1; Balabanoff to Norman Thomas, December 31, 1936 in Scrapbooks, References to Rosika Schwimmer's Associates, Angelica Balabanoff Folder, Schwimmer Lloyd Collection, New York Public Library Archives.

177. Ibid.

178. As late as 1950, Balabanoff continued to be the target of anti-Red hysteria. She was detained, without official explanation, at Ellis Island in New York for three days, even though she had a valid visa and had been living in the United States for years. See the New York *Times*, July 8, 9, 11, 12, 1950.

179. Balabanoff, *Life*, pp. 302, 307–308.

180. On the regrouping of Italian socialists abroad, see Charles Delzell, "The Italian Anti-Fascist Emigration, 1922–1943," *Journal of Central European Affairs* 12 (1952): 20–55 and *Mussolini's Enemies: The Italian Anti-Fascist Resistance* (Princeton, N.J.: Princeton University Press, 1961).

181. See Balabanoff, *Tears*, pp. 123–124.

182. See Balabanoff, "Anti-Semitism in Italy," *Socialist Review* 6 (1838): 7–8, 18, and "Mussolini's Past and Present," *Socialist Review* 6 (1939): 19. In 1938 the *Review* offered a free, personally autographed copy of Balabanoff's pamphlet of poems, "To the Austrian Workers," to all new subscribers. In 1950 she was honored at the party's annual Debs Day dinner, where Norman Thomas himself paid her tribute. See the New York *Times*, October 28, 1950. Ludwig Lore called her "one of the finest human beings I have had the good fortune to meet." See his review of *My Life As a Rebel, Nation* 147 (August 6, 1938): 132.

183. New York *Times*, December 23, 1947; July 8, 12, 1950.

184. On Saragat's party, see Clough and Saladino, pp. 577–580; Hilton-Young, pp. 207–208. In 1951 the Italian Workers Socialist Party merged with a variety of other socialist splinter groups to form a new party, the Italian Social Democratic Party (PSDI).

185. See Balabanoff, *Life*, pp. 42–52; "Mussolini's Past and Present"; "Benito Mussolini: Souvenirs sur l'Homme"; *The Traitor; Wesen und Werdegang des Italienischen Fascismus* (Vienna: Hess, 1931), pp. 117–209; the New York *Times*, December 27, 1925; and the New York *Post*, July 27, 1938.

186. Balabanoff, *The Traitor.*

187. Balabanoff, *To the Victims of Fascism* (New York: n.p., 1936).

188. Balabanoff, *Erinnerungen und Erlebnisse* (Berlin: E. Laub, 1927), *My Life As a Rebel*, and *Ricordi di una socialista* (Rome: De Luigi, 1946).

189. Reviewers of *My Life As a Rebel* all mentioned Balabanoff's candid and frank insights into the nature and origins of Stalinist repression. See *New Republic* 96 (August 24, 1938): 81–82; *Saturday Review of Literature* 18 (July 30, 1938): 7; *Socialist Review* 6 (1938): 20–21; *Spectator* 161 (September 9, 1938): 418; *Time* 32 (August 1, 1938): 43; and *Times Literary Supplement* 37 (July 23, 1938): 486.

190. See William Rose Benet, "The Season's Poetry," *Saturday Review of Literature* 26 (October 16, 1943): 24; for other reviews of *Tears*, see *Nation* 157 (November 27, 1943): 615–618; and the New York *Times*, October 10, 1943.

191. Balabanoff, *Tears*, p. 11.

192. Ibid., pp. 113, 128; also see pp. 67–68.

193. Ibid., pp. 13–14.

194. Ibid., pp. 145–146. Also see, "31 Décembre," pp. 140–144.

195. Goldman, *Disillusionment*, p. 52; *Living*, p. 762.

196. Goldman, *Disillusionment*, p. 39. For Balabanoff's relationship with

Goldman, see *Life*, pp. 253-256; and Richard Drinnon, *Rebel in Paradise: A Biography of Emma Goldman* (New York: Harper and Row, 1976), p. 234.

197. John Reed quoted in Balabanoff, *Life*, p. 246; also see Louise Bryant, *Six Red Months in Russia* (New York: George H. Doran, 1918), p. 169.

198. Swiss socialist and Zimmerwaldian Rosa Bloch, quoted in Senn, *Diplomacy*, p. 163.

NOTES TO CHAPTER 5

1. Ernest Hemingway, *For Whom the Bell Tolls* (New York: Charles Scribner's Sons, 1940), pp. 357-358.

2. Charles F. Gallagher, *La Pasionaria* (Hanover, N.H.: American Universities Field Staff Reports, 1976), p. 1; Merle Wolin, "La Pasionaria," *Viva* 5 (September 1978): 47.

3. There is no biography of Ibarruri in English. Brief sketches of her life appear in both Gallagher and Wolin; also in Rita Mae Kelly and Mary Boutilier, *The Making of Political Women: A Study of Socialization and Role Conflict* (Chicago: Nelson-Hall, 1978), pp. 140-142. The American Communist Party published a propaganda pamphlet during the Spanish Civil War: *Pasionaria, People's Tribune of Spain* (New York: Workers Library, 1938).

4. Hemingway, pp. 309-311. For a discussion of Hemingway's Pasionaria, see Frederick R. Benson, *Writers in Arms: The Literary Impact of the Spanish Civil War* (New York: New York University Press, 1967), p. 219; and John M. Muste, *Say That We Saw Spain Die: Literary Consequences of the Spanish Civil War* (Seattle: University of Washington Press, 1966), pp. 103-104.

5. Hemingway, p. 357.

6. Franz Borkenau, *European Communism* (London: Faber and Faber, 1953), pp. 164, 228.

7. Sheila M. O'Callaghan, *Cinderella of Europe: Spain Explained* (New York: Philosophical Library, n.d.), pp. 163-164. There is little available, in English, on Spanish feminism or the history of Spanish women. The material in this chapter is based on Louis Lespine, *La Femme en Espagne* (Toulouse: Clémence-Isaure, 1919); Kaethe Schirmacher, *The Modern Woman's Rights Movement: A Historical Survey*, trans. Carl Conrad Eckhardt (New York: Macmillan, 1912), pp. 206-211; and Theodore M. Stanton, ed., *The Woman Question in Europe* (New York: G. P. Putnam's Sons, 1884), pp. 330-353.

8. Stanton, pp. 339-340.

9. The best portrait of wealthy Spanish women of the period is seen in Constancia de la Mora, *In Place of Splendor: The Autobiography of a Spanish Woman* (New York: Harcourt, Brace, 1939).

10. Lespine, p. 149.

11. Robert Kern, "Margarita Nelken: Women and the Crisis of Spanish

Politics," in *European Women on the Left*, ed. Jane Slaughter and Robert Kern (Westport, Conn.: Greenwood Press, 1981), p. 148.

12. Stanton, p. 333.

13. For a complete discussion of Iberian misogyny, see C. R. Boxer, *Mary and Misogyny: Women in Iberian Expansion Overseas 1415-1815* (London: Gerald Duckworth, 1975), pp. 97-112.

14. Ibid., p. 101.

15. Ibid., p. 97.

16. Ibid., pp. 99-100.

17. Claude G. Bowers, *My Mission to Spain* (New York: Simon and Schuster, 1954), p. 136; Boxer, pp. 103-104.

18. Zsolt Aradi, *Shrines To Our Lady Around the World* (New York: Farrar, Straus, and Young, 1954), pp. 22-24; William J. Walsh, *The Apparitions and Shrines of Heaven's Bright Queen* (New York: T. J. Carey, 1904), pp. 78-84.

19. *Catholic Encyclopedia*, 1967 ed. See under "Pillar, Our Lady of the"; Frank Jellinek, *The Civil War in Spain* (New York: Howard Fertig, 1969), p. 55; John Langdon-Davies, *Behind the Spanish Barricades* (New York: Robert M. McBride, 1936), p. 35.

20. Langdon-Davies, p. 34.

21. Ibid., p. 35; Jellinek, p. 42.

22. Evelyn P. Stevens, "*Marianismo*: The Other Face of *Machismo* in Latin America," in *Female and Male in Latin America*, ed. Ann Pescatello (Pittsburgh: University of Pittsburgh Press, 1973), pp. 89-101.

23. Ibid., p. 91.

24. Franz Borkenau, *The Spanish Cockpit* (Ann Arbor: University of Michigan Press, 1963), p. 135; Peter Merin, *Spain Between Death and Birth*, trans. Charles Fullman (New York: Dodge, 1938), pp. 208-212.

25. Quoted in Gerald Brenan, *The Spanish Labyrinth* (London: Cambridge University Press, 1943), p. 141.

26. On early socialism in Spain, see Brenan, pp. 216-219; Pierre Broué and Emile Témime, *The Revolution and the Civil War in Spain*, trans. Tony White (Cambridge, Mass.: MIT Press, 1970), pp. 54-73; and G. D. H. Cole, *A History of Socialist Thought* (New York: St. Martin's Press, 1953-1960), 3, bk, 2: 744-773.

27. This portrait of Ibarruri's early life is drawn from her autobiography, *They Shall Not Pass: The Autobiography of La Pasionaria* (New York: International, 1966).

28. Ibid., p. 43.

29. Ibid., p. 17.

30. Ibid., p. 42.

31. Ibid., p. 43.

32. Ibid.

33. Ibid., p. 45.

34. Ibid., pp. 46-47.

35. On the *casas*, see Brenan, p. 219; Broué and Témime, p. 60.

36. Ibarruri, p. 84.

37. Ibid., p. 40.

38. Ibid., p. 41.

39. Ibid., pp. 49-50.

40. Ibid., p. 61.

41. Ibid., p. 66.

42. Ibid., p. 60.

43. Ibid., p. 61.

44. Ibid., p. 62.

45. Gerald H. Meaker, *The Revolutionary Left in Spain, 1914-1923* (Stanford, Calif.: Stanford University Press, 1974), pp. 45-46.

46. Ibid., pp. 34-36; Cole, 4, bk. 2: 535-552.

47. Ibarruri, p. 64.

48. Meaker, p. vii.

49. Ibarruri, p. 66.

50. On the formation of the Spanish Communist Party, see Gallagher, pp. 3-6; Meaker, pp. 249-279; and Paul Preston, "The Origins of the Socialist Schism in Spain, 1917-1931," *Journal of Contemporary History* 12 (1977): 101-132.

51. Ibarruri, pp. 64-65, 68.

52. Meaker, p. 194.

53. Ibid., p. 371.

54. Ibarruri, p. 76.

55. For her stints in prison, see ibid., pp. 67, 93-104, 121, 162-163.

56. The best account of Spanish politics during these years is in Hugh Thomas, *The Spanish Civil War* (New York: Harper and Row, 1961), pp. 3-113.

57. On Asturias, see Jellinek, pp. 173-180; E. Allison Peers, *The Spanish Tragedy, 1930-1936* (London: Methuen, 1936), pp. 168-173; Thomas, pp. 79-85. Ibarruri's account is in her *Autobiography*, pp. 129-133.

58. For a discussion of the Popular Front policy, see David T. Cattell, *Communism and the Spanish Civil War* (Berkeley: University of California Press, 1955), pp. 24-30; Cole, 5: 22-24; Georgi Dimitroff, *The United Front* (New York: International, 1938); and Wilhelm Pieck, *Freedom, Peace, and Bread!* (New York: Workers Library, 1935).

59. For a sampling of accounts repeating this charge, see Luis Bolin, *Spain: The Vital Years* (London: Cassell, 1967), p. 153; James Cleugh, *Spanish Fury: The Story of a Civil War* (London: George G. Harrap, 1962), pp. 45, 102; Brian Crozier, *Franco: A Biographical History* (London: Eyre and Spottiswoode, 1967), p. 165; H. Edward Knoblaugh, *Correspondent in Spain* (London: Sheed and Ward, 1937), p. 23; and O'Callaghan, p. 66. Ibarruri refutes it in her *Autobiography*, p. 180.

60. See Katharine Marjory Atholl, *Searchlight on Spain* (London: Penguin, 1938), pp. 112-113; Henry Buckley, *Life and Death of the Spanish Republic* (London: Hamish Hamilton, 1940), p. 312; and Thomas, p. 121.

61. Allen Guttman, *The Wound in the Heart: America and the Spanish Civil War* (New York: Free Press of Glencoe, 1962), pp. 146, 154.

62. See, for example, Meriel Buchanan, "How Moscow Helps Spanish Reds," *Saturday Review* 162 (October 17, 1936): 492-493, and "What Is Stalin Plotting?" *Saturday Review* 162 (October 31, 1936): 552; Ronald Fraser, *Blood of Spain: An Oral History of the Spanish Civil War* (New York: Pantheon, 1979), p. 154; Langdon-Davies, p. 79; and Arthur F. Loveday, "Spain From Dictatorship to Civil War," *Quarterly Review* 267 (October 1936): 203.

63. The best discussion of communist policy in the war is in Cattell, *Communism and the Spanish Civil War.*

64. Ibid., pp. 20-23; Thomas, p. 8.

65. Cattell, p. 95.

66. Burnett Bolloten, *The Grand Camouflage: The Spanish Civil War and Revolution, 1936-1939* (New York: Praeger, 1961), p. 110.

67. For a complete discussion of the siege of Madrid, see Robert Garland Colodny, *The Struggle for Madrid* (New York: Paine-Whitman, 1958); Geoffrey Cox, *Defence of Madrid* (London: Victor Gollancz, 1937), and "Eye-Witness in Madrid," *Harper's Monthly Magazine* 175 (June-July 1937): 27-37, 151-162; George Hills, *The Battle for Madrid* (New York: St. Martin's Press, 1977); and Dan Kurzman, *Miracle of November: Madrid's Epic Stand* (New York: G. P. Putnam's Sons, 1980).

68. Ibarruri, "Danger! To Arms!" in *Speeches and Articles, 1936-1938* (London: Lawrence and Wishart, 1938), pp. 7-8.

69. Janet Riesenfeld, *Dancer in Madrid* (New York: Funk and Wagnalls, 1938), p. 272.

70. Ibarruri, "The War Must Be Felt!" in *Speeches and Articles*, p. 32.

71. Mikhail Koltzov, quoted in Robert Payne, *The Civil War in Spain, 1936-1939* (New York: Capricorn, 1970), pp. 129-130.

72. Ibarruri, "Our Fighters Must Lack For Nothing!," "The War Must Be Felt!," and "The Defense of Madrid is the Defense of Spain," in *Speeches and Articles*, pp. 9-10, 33, 36-37.

73. Robert Goldston, *The Civil War in Spain* (New York: Bobbs-Merrill, 1966), p. 54; Richard Kisch, *They Shall Not Pass: The Spanish People at War, 1936-1939* (London: Wayland, 1974), p. 103; "Where Are They Now? " *Newsweek* 60 (July 2, 1962): 10.

74. On the activities of Spanish women during the war, see Broué and Témime, pp. 1-5; Cox, *Defence*, pp. 196-197; Kisch, pp. 104-109; Merin, pp. 207-208; and Liz Willis, *Women in the Spanish Revolution* (London: Solidarity, 1975).

75. George Felix, quoted in *From Spanish Trenches: Recent Letters From Spain*, ed. Marcel Acier (New York: Modern Age Books, 1937), p. 83.

76. Quoted in Frank Pitcairn, *Reporter in Spain* (London: Lawrence and Wishart, 1936), p. 46.

77. Borkenau, *Cockpit*, pp. 126-127; Fraser, pp. 286-287; Gabriel Jackson, *A Concise History of the Spanish Civil War* (New York: John Day, 1974), p. 67; Kisch, pp. 20, 104-109; Mary Low and Juan Brea, *Red Spanish Notebook* (London: Martin Secker and Warburg, 1937), pp. 174-198.

78. Fraser, p. 286.

79. New York *Times*, June 13, 1938.

80. Ibarruri, "Rather Be Widows of Heroes than Wives of Cowards," in *Speeches and Articles*, pp. 38-39.

81. Ibarruri, "Our Battle-Cry Has Been Heard by the Whole World!," and "We Shall Win!" in *Speeches and Articles*, p. 24, 34.

82. See Fraser, p. 121.

83. Ibarruri, "Rather Be Widows," pp. 38-39.

84. Ibarruri, *For the Independence of Spain, For Liberty, For the Republic, For the Union of All Spaniards* (Madrid: Communist Party of Spain, 1938), p. 58.

85. Ibarruri, "Defend and Strengthen the People's Front to the Utmost!" in *Speeches and Articles*, pp. 189-190.

86. Ibid., p. 179; Ibarruri, "Employ All Means to Defend and Consolidate the People's Front," *Communist International* 15 (March 1938): 282.

87. Ibarruri, *Autobiography*, p. 59; "Employ All Means," p. 289.

88. Ibarruri, "Employ All Means," p. 289; "Defend and Strengthen," p. 191.

89. Ibid.

90. Ibid.

91. Ibid.

92. Ibid.

93. Ibarruri, "Despite All Defeatist Moods and Difficulties, the Spanish People Will Win!" in *Speeches and Articles*, p. 210.

94. Quoted in Fraser, p. 309.

95. Ibarruri, "Youth in Free Spain Are Ensured a Happy and Industrious Life," in *Speeches and Articles*, pp. 124-125.

96. Ibarruri, *For the Independence of Spain*, p. 29.

97. Ibarruri, "Employ All Means," p. 288; "Defend and Strengthen," p. 189.

98. Ibarruri, "A Reply to Enemies, Slanderers, and Vacillating Elements," in *Speeches and Articles*, p. 140.

99. Bolloten, p. 221; Cattell, p. 87.

100. See, for example, Alvah Bessie, *Men In Battle* (New York: Charles Scribner's Sons, 1939), pp. 28-29; Cox, *Defence*, pp. 16-17, and "Eye-Witness," p. 29; Cecil Eby, *Between the Bullet and the Lie: American Volunteers in the Spanish Civil War* (New York: Holt, Rinehart, and Winston, 1969), p. 80; and New York *Times*, July 7, 1937.

101. Quoted in Wolin, p. 85.

102. Quoted in Fraser, p. 292.

103. Alvah Bessie, *The Un-Americans* (New York: Cameron Associates, 1957), p. 11.

104. See, for example, Edwin Rolfe, "City of Anguish," in *The Heart of Spain*, ed. Alvah Bessie (New York: Veterans of the Abraham Lincoln Brigade, 1952), pp. 212-213.

105. Hemingway, p. 321.

106. Ibarruri, "Spain Will Never Be Fascist," in *Speeches and Articles*, p. 262.

107. Ibid., pp. 253, 256.

108. Ibarruri, "Women of South America, Your Sisters in Spain Think of You, Look to You, and Believe in You!" in *Speeches and Articles*, p. 84.

109. For a full discussion of nonintervention, see Cole, 5: 132-134; Goldston, pp. 69-74; Jackson, pp. 49-62; and Thomas, pp. 209-311.

110. Her meeting with Blum is described in Ibarruri, *Autobiography*, p. 229.

111. Ibarruri, "Reply,"; "Never Be Fascist," and "Forward to Victory," in *Speeches and Articles*, pp. 132-136, 260-261, 50; *For the Independence of Spain*, p. 24.

112. Ibarruri, "Never Be Fascist," p. 258.

113. *Gringoire* (Paris), September 18, 1936, September 25, 1936.

114. *L'Humanité* (Paris), September 13-14, 1936.

115. Cattell, p. 71; Herbert L. Matthews, *Half of Spain Died: A Reappraisal of the Spanish Civil War* (New York: Charles Scribner's Sons, 1973), pp. 159-160.

116. George Orwell, *Homage to Catalonia* (New York: Harcourt, Brace, 1952), p. 63.

117. Ibarruri, *For the Independence of Spain*, pp. 20-21; *Autobiography*, p. 262.

118. For a full discussion of Soviet motives, see Borkenau, *European Communism*, pp. 166-169; David T. Cattell, *Communism and the Spanish Civil War*, and *Soviet Diplomacy and the Spanish Civil War* (Berkeley: University of California Press, 1957); Cole, 5: 22-24; and Isaac Deutscher, *Stalin: A Political Biography* (New York: Oxford University Press, 1967), pp. 423-425.

119. Ibarruri, "What Is Happening in Spain?" *Communist International* 13 (October 1936): 1308-1310. "The Time Has Come to Create a Single Party of the Proletariat in Spain," *Communist International* 14 (September 1937): 642-655.

120. Ibid., p. 643; "Win the War!" in *Speeches and Articles*, pp. 58-59.

121. Orwell, p. 67.

122. For a complete discussion of the events in Barcelona and the liquidation of the POUM, see Thomas, pp. 424-436, 452-455.

123. See Ibarruri, "Why the Communist Party is Opposed to the Policy of Largo Caballero," in *Speeches and Articles*, pp. 94-98.

124. Ibarruri, *Autobiography*, pp. 310-311.

125. See Colonel Segismundo Casado, *The Last Days of Madrid*, trans. Rupert Croft-Cooke (London: Peter Davies, 1939).

126. José Díaz, quoted in *People's Tribune*, p. 30; and André Marty, *Heroic Spain* (New York: Workers Library, 1937), p. 30.

127. Borkenau, *Spanish Cockpit*, p. 121.

128. Vincent Sheean, *Not Peace But a Sword* (New York: Doubleday, Doran, 1939), p. 185.

129. New York *Times*, June 19, 1938.

130. Buckley, pp. 313–314.

131. de la Mora, p. 297.

132. Edith Thomas's poem about Pasionaria is reprinted in David Caute, *Communism and the French Intellectuals 1914-1960* (New York: Macmillan, 1964), p. 120.

133. Charlotte Haldane, "Pasionaria," *Left Review* 3 (April 1938): 926.

134. *Gringoire* (Paris), September 18, 1936.

135. See, for example, Julio Alvarez del Vayo, *Freedom's Battle*, trans. Eileen E. Brooke (New York: Hill and Wang, 1940), p. 153; Kisch, p. 77; Matthews, pp. 87, 116; *News of Spain*, July 23, 1936, April 6, 1938.

136. Bowers, pp. 334–335.

137. Guttman, pp. 10–12.

138. Ibarruri, *Autobiography*, p. 298.

139. Peter Kemp, *Mine Were of Trouble* (London: Cassell, 1957), pp. 80–81.

140. See Ibarruri, *For the Independence of Spain*, p. 68; "Reply," p. 141; and "Trotskyism and Duplicity Are Synonymous," in *Speeches and Articles*, pp. 60–62.

141. de la Mora, p. 297.

142. Atholl, p. 112; Anna Louise Strong, *Spain in Arms* (New York: Henry Holt, 1937), p. 24.

143. Ibarruri, *Autobiography*, pp. 237–240; Matthews, *Half of Spain Died*, p. 68, *The Yoke and the Arrows: A Report on Spain* (New York: George Braziller, 1961), p. 165, and review of *They Shall Not Pass: The Autobiography of La Pasionaria*, by Dolores Ibarruri, in New York *Times Book Review*, November 27, 1966, p. 67.

144. Ibarruri, "Time Has Come," p. 651; and *Implacable War Against Fascism* (Moscow: Foreign Languages Publishing House, 1941), p. 16.

145. Cattell, *Communism and the Spanish Civil War*, p. 63.

146. Elie Faure, "A Portrait of La Pasionaria," *Living Age* 351 (October 1936): 136.

147. New York *Times*, October 3, 1937.

148. *L'Humanité* (Paris), September 13-14, 1936.

149. Riesenfeld, p. 273.

150. Vincent Sheean, "Pasionaria," in Jo Davidson, *Spanish Portraits* (New York: Arden Gallery, 1939), pp. 10–11.

151. Borkenau, *Spanish Cockpit*, p. 121.

152. Thomas, p. 183.

153. Hugh Purcell, *The Spanish Civil War* (New York: G. P. Putnam's Sons, 1973), p. 43.

154. Ibid., p. 23; Jellinek, p. 42.

155. Sheean, "Pasionaria," pp. 10-11.

156. Ibid.

157. Ibarruri, "From Militia to Regular Army," in *Speeches and Articles*, p. 216.

158. Sheean, "Pasionaria," pp. 10-11.

159. *People's Tribune*, pp. 30-31.

160. Ibid., p. 11.

161. Borkenau, *Spanish Cockpit*, p. 193; *World Communism: A History of the Communist International* (Ann Arbor: University of Michigan Press, 1962), pp. 394-395.

162. Ibarruri, *Autobiography*, p. 62.

163. Ibarruri, "Time Has Come," p. 654; "For a United Party of the Spanish Proletariat!" and "A Letter to My Children," in *Speeches and Articles*, pp. 119-120, 144-146; New York *Times*, September 7, 1937.

164. Ibarruri, "We Are Inspired by the Great Example of the U.S.S.R.," in *Speeches and Articles*, p. 42.

165. Ibarruri, "Time Has Come," pp. 651-652.

166. For example, in 1933 before the Comintern's evolution of the Popular Front policy, she continued to hope for a proletarian revolution in Spain. During the civil war, however, she repeatedly championed a "bourgeois democratic" revolution, not a socialist one. See Bolloten, p. 88.

167. Sheean, *Not Peace*, p. 184.

168. Ibarruri, "We Are at War and We Cannot Afford to be Sentimental," in *Speeches and Articles*, p. 158.

169. Fernando Claudin, *The Communist Movement*, trans. Brian Pearce and Francis MacDonagh (New York: Monthly Review Press, 1975), 1: 221.

170. Ibarruri, "Time Has Come," pp. 650, 653; "For a United Party," pp. 99, 113, 119.

171. Strong, pp. 23-24.

172. Borkenau, *European Communism*, p. 164.

173. On this point, see Richard Crossman, ed., *The God That Failed: Six Studies in Communism* (London: Hamish Hamilton, 1950).

174. Ibarruri, "We Shall Fulfill Our Sacred Duty to the U.S.S.R.," *Communist International* 13 (December 1936): 1603-1604.

175. Santiago Carrillo, *Eurocommunism and the State* (Westport, Conn.: Lawrence Hill, 1978), p. 112.

176. Sheean, *Not Peace*, p. 184; Borkenau, *World Communism*, p. 405.

177. Matthews, *Half of Spain Died*, p. 125.

178. Borkenau, *Spanish Cockpit*, pp. 120-121.

179. Quoted in Stanley Weintraub, *The Last Great Cause: The Intellectuals and the Spanish Civil War* (New York: Weybright and Talley, 1968), p. 143.

180. Ibarruri, *The Women Want a People's Peace* (New York: Workers Library, 1941).

181. Strong, p. 24.

182. Ibarruri, "Fascism Shall Not Pass," in *Speeches and Articles*, p. 16.

183. Ilya Ehrenburg, quoted in Murray A. Sperber, *And I Remember Spain: A Spanish Civil War Anthology* (New York: Macmillan, 1974), p. 132.

184. Faure, p. 136.

185. Matthews, review of *They Shall Not Pass*, p. 67.

186. Kurzman, pp. 43-44.

187. In April 1941 a specially created court of political responsibilities tried Ibarruri, in absentia, along with other high officials of the republican regime. She was forbidden to live in Spain for 15 years and was assessed a fine "comprising all her property." See New York *Times*, April 22, 27, 1941.

188. Ibarruri, *Implacable War*, pp. 7-9; *People's Peace*, pp. 35-36.

189. Dolores Ibarruri and Isabel Brown, *Women Against Hitler* (London: Communist Party of Great Britain, n.d.), p. 7.

190. Wolin, pp. 86-87.

191. Ibid., p. 87.

192. Ibid., p. 86.

193. Ibid., p. 85; Ibarruri, *Autobiography*, p. 65.

194. Jesús Hernández, *La Grande Trahison*, trans. Pierre Berthelin (Paris: Fasquelle, 1953), pp. 83-84, 162.

195. Guy Hermet, *The Communists in Spain*, trans. S. Seago and H. Fox (Lexington, Mass.: Lexington Books, 1974), p. 51.

196. Valentin González and Julian Gorkin, *El Campesino: Life and Death in Soviet Russia*, trans. Ilsa Barea (New York: G. P. Putnam's Sons, 1952), p. 19.

197. Ibid., pp. 72-76, 104, 113, 198; Enrique Castro Delgado, *J'ai Perdu la foi à Moscou*, trans. Jean Talbot (Paris: Gallimard, 1950), p. 85.

198. Kurzman, pp. 158, 182.

199. Hermet, pp. 63-65; Benjamin Welles, *Spain: The Gentle Anarchy* (New York: Praeger, 1965), p. 210.

200. Ibarruri, *Liberate Spain From Franco* (London: Communist Party, 1945), p. 7.

201. Ibarruri, "José Díaz," *Labour Monthly* 24 (May 1942): 158; New York *Times*, December 29, 1945; April 16, 1960.

202. Hermet, pp. 59-61.

203. Ibid., p. 65.

204. Carrillo, pp. 11, 132.

205. Hermet, p. 79; R. Neal Tannahill, *The Communist Parties of Western Europe* (Westport, Conn.: Greenwood Press, 1978), p. 77.

206. *Le Monde* (Paris), October 23, 1970.

207. Hermet, p. 79; New York *Times*, June 30, 1976; July 28, 1976.

208. *Le Monde* (Paris), October 23, 1970; New York *Times*, May 14, 1977;

Eusebio M. Mujal-Leon, "Spanish Communism in the 1970s," *Problems of Communism* 24 (March 1975): 43-55.

209. *Yearbook on International Communist Affairs, 1973* (Stanford, Calif.: Hoover Institution Press, 1974), p. 213.

210. New York *Times*, November 21, 1975.

211. Ibid., April 8, 1976; *Yearbook on International Communist Affairs, 1976* (Stanford, Calif.: Hoover Institution Press, 1977), p. 227.

212. New York *Times*, May 14, 1977; "La Pasionaria: An Exile Ends," *Time* 109 (May 23, 1977): 50.

213. New York *Times*, July 14, 1977.

214. Charles F. Gallagher, *Left, Right, and Center in Spain: Is More Than Two a Crowd?* (Hanover, N.H.: American Universities Field Staff Reports, 1978), p. 6.

215. Ibid., pp. 5-6; Carrillo, p. 8; New York *Times*, August 7, 1976.

216. Wolin, pp. 81-83; 88; New York *Times*, May 23, 1977.

217. Wolin, p. 47.

218. Ibid., p. 88.

219. Ibid.; New York *Times*, June 27, 1977.

220. New York *Times*, May 23, 1977.

221. Ibid., June 27, 1977.

222. Ibid., June 26, 27, 1977.

223. Wolin, p. 81.

224. Ibid., pp. 83, 88.

225. Ibid., p. 88.

NOTES TO CONCLUSION

1. E. Victor Wolfenstein, *The Revolutionary Personality* (Princeton, N.J.: Princeton University Press, 1967), pp. 101, 166-167. See also Patrick P. Dunn, "Fathers and Sons Revisited: The Childhood of Vissarion Belinskii," *History of Childhood Quarterly* 1 (1974): 389-407; Max Eastman, *Leon Trotsky: Portrait of a Youth* (New York: Greenberg, 1925), p. 38; and Stefan T. Possony, *Lenin: The Compulsive Revolutionary* (Chicago: Henry Regnery, 1964), p. 381.

2. Erik H. Erikson, *Young Man Luther* (New York: W. W. Norton, 1958), p. 14; Wolfenstein, p. 89. Significantly, the Eriksonian pattern of personality development on which Wolfenstein relies may also be problematic here. Researchers are only beginning to demonstrate how and why his picture of the human life cycle—which actually presents male psychological development as the norm for human psychological development during adulthood—may be inapplicable to the experience of women. See Maggie Scarf, *Unfinished Business: Pressure Points in the Lives of Women* (Garden City, N.Y.: Doubleday, 1980), p. 277ff.

3. Wolfenstein, p. 281.

4. See, for example, Jean Baker Miller, ed., *Psychoanalysis and Women* (Baltimore: Penguin, 1973); and Roy Schaffer, "Problems in Freud's Psychology of Women," *Journal of the American Psychoanalytic Association* 22 (1974): 459-485.

5. The standard Freudian view of female personality development was outlined in the following essays, all to be found in *The Standard Edition of the Complete Psychological Works of Sigmund Freud*, trans. and ed. James Strachey (London: Hogarth Press and the Institute of Psycho-Analysis, 1955). See "Three Essays on the Theory of Sexuality," 7: 123-243; "The Dissolution of the Oedipus Complex," 19: 171-179; "Some Psychical Consequences of the Anatomical Distinction Between the Sexes," 19: 241-258; and "Female Sexuality," 21: 221-243.

6. Sigmund Freud, *A General Introduction to Psychoanalysis* (New York: Garden City Publishing, 1938), p. 42, quoted in Wolfenstein, p. 302.

7. Harold D. Lasswell, *Psychopathology and Politics* (Chicago: University of Chicago Press, 1930), pp. 121-124.

8. See, for example, Alphonse de Lamartine's discussion of the eighteenth-century Girondist Madame Roland. She embraced the French Revolution "like a lover," he explained. Had she felt "loved and happy," she would have been satisfied with being a wife. "Discontent and isolated, she became the leader of a party." *Histoire des Girondins* (Paris: Hachette, 1881), 1: 366-367.

9. Merle Wolin, "La Pasionaria," *Viva* 5 (September 1978): 84; also see Janet Riesenfeld, *Dancer in Madrid* (New York: Funk and Wagnalls, 1938), pp. 271-272.

10. Jeane J. Kirkpatrick, *Political Woman* (New York: Basic, 1974), p. 52.

11. See Victor Goertzel and Mildred George Geortzel, *Cradles of Eminence* (Boston: Little, Brown, 1962), pp. 122-126.

12. Recent studies have noted that mothers who are not dominated by their husbands tend to raise children with a high need for achievement. See David C. McClelland, *The Achieving Society* (New York, Free Press, 1961), p. 404. Other studies have indicated that women with an activist sex role ideology tend to come from families in which neither parent was dominant or where the mother dominated. See Rita Mae Kelly and Mary Boutilier, *The Making of Political Women: A Study of Socialization and Role Conflict* (Chicago: Nelson Hall, 1978), p. 23; Jean Lipman-Blumen, "How Ideology Shapes Women's Lives," *Scientific American* 226 (January 1972): 38; M. Kent Jennings and Kenneth P. Langton, "Mothers vs. Fathers: The Formation of Political Orientations Among Young Americans," *Journal of Politics* 31 (1969): 329-357.

13. Eleanor Marx, *Commonweal*, December 1885.

14. Alexandra Kollontai, "Working Woman and Mother," in *Selected Writings of Alexandra Kollontai*, ed. and trans. Alix Holt (Westport, Conn.: Lawrence Hill, 1977), p. 134.

15. Rosa Luxemburg, "What Does the Spartacus League Want?" in *Selected Political Writings of Rosa Luxemburg*, ed. Dick Howard (New York: Monthly Review Press, 1971), pp. 366-376.

16. See Eleanor Marx's comments in Aaron Rosebury, "Eleanor, Daughter of Karl Marx: Personal Reminiscences," *Monthly Review* 24 (1973): 45.

17. William T. Daly, *The Revolutionary: A Review and Synthesis* (Beverly Hills, Calif.: Sage Publications, 1972), pp. 9-11; Possony, pp. 388-389, 397; and Wolfenstein, p. 234.

18. Wolfenstein, pp. 233-234.

19. Daly, p. 11; E. Victor Wolfenstein, *Personality and Politics* (Belmont, Calif.: Dickenson, 1969), pp. 34-36.

20. On the role of terror and violence in the consolidating stages of the revolutionary process, see Crane Brinton, *The Anatomy of Revolution* (New York: Vintage, 1965), pp. 176-204; Albert Camus, *The Rebel*, trans. Anthony Bower (New York: Alfred A. Knopf, 1956), pp. 125-132; Eric Hoffer, *The True Believer* (New York: Harper and Bros., 1951), p. xii; Vladimir C. Nahirny, "Some Observations on Ideological Groups," *American Journal of Sociology* 67 (1962): 397-405; and Philip Pomper, "Necaev, Lenin, and Stalin: The Psychology of Leadership," *Jahrbücher für Geschichte Osteuropas* 26 (1978): 11-30.

21. Wolfenstein, *Revolutionary Personality*, pp. 169-171.

22. Quoted in J. M. Thompson, *Robespierre* (New York: D. Appleton-Century, 1936), 2: 141.

23. Vissarion G. Belinsky, *Selected Philosophical Works* (Moscow: Foreign Languages Publishing House, 1948), p. 158.

24. Quoted in Peter Merin, *Spain Between Death and Birth*, trans. Charles Fullman (New York: Dodge, 1938), p. 214.

25. See Balabanoff's comments in Nancy Gorman Eshelman, "Angelica Balabanoff and the Italian Socialist Movement: From the Second International to Zimmerwald" (Ph.D. diss., University of Rochester, 1977), p. 330.

26. Yvonne Kapp, *Eleanor Marx* (New York: Pantheon, 1972-1976), 2: 477.

27. Alexandra Kollontai to Bessie Beatty, quoted in Beatty, *The Red Heart of Russia* (New York: Century, 1918), p. 379.

28. Balabanoff, quoted in Eshelman, p. 330.

29. Mary-Alice Waters, ed., *Rosa Luxemburg Speaks* (New York: Pathfinder Press, 1970), p. 17.

30. Dolores Ibarruri, *They Shall Not Pass: The Autobiography of La Pasionaria* (New York: International, 1966), pp. 208, 349-350.

31. Eleanor Marx, quoted in Ronald Florence, *Marx's Daughters* (New York: Dial Press, 1975), p. 45.

32. Angelica Balabanoff, *My Life As a Rebel* (Bloomington: Indiana University Press, 1973), p. 228.

33. Ibarruri, p. 74.

34. Sherry B. Ortner, "Is Female to Male as Nature Is to Culture?" in

Woman, Culture, and Society, ed. Michelle Zimbalist Rosaldo and Louise Lamphere (Stanford, Calif.: Stanford University Press, 1974), p. 81.

35. David B. Lynn, *Parental and Sex-Role Identification: A Theoretical Formulation* (Berkeley, Calif.: McCutchen, 1969), p. 98; Kelly and Boutilier, p. 209.

36. See, for example, Lawrence Kohlberg, "A Cognitive-Developmental Analysis of Children's Sex Role Concepts and Attitudes," in *The Development of Sex Differences*, ed. Eleanor E. Maccoby (Stanford, Calif.: Stanford University Press, 1966), pp. 82–173.

37. For a comprehensive treatment of these basic arguments, see Nancy Chodorow, "Family Structure and Feminine Personality," in Rosaldo and Lamphere, pp. 43–66.

38. Dorothy Dinnerstein, *The Mermaid and the Minotaur: Sexual Arrangements and the Human Malaise* (New York: Harper and Row, 1977), pp. 153, 275.

39. Scarf, pp. 528–529; Chodorow, pp. 43–66.

40. Ibarruri, p. 62; *The Women Want a People's Peace* (New York: Workers Library, 1941), p. 5.

41. New York *Times*, June 27, 1963; June 30, 1963.

42. Rosa Luxemburg, "Against Capital Punishment," in Waters, p. 399.

43. Lenin quoted in Isabel de Palencia, *Alexandra Kollontay: Ambassadress from Russia* (New York: Longmans, Green, 1947), p. 93.

44. Philip Pomper, *Sergei Nechayev* (New Brunswick, N.J.: Rutgers University Press, 1979), pp. 128–129.

45. Sergei Nechayev, "The Catechism of the Revolutionist," in *Revolutionaries on Revolution*, ed. Philip B. Springer and Marcello Truzzi (Pacific Palisades, Calif.: Goodyear, 1973), pp. 184–188.

46. Quoted in Robert Payne, *The Life and Death of Lenin* (New York: Simon and Schuster, 1964), p. 249.

47. Possony, pp. 382–385. The quotation is taken from a widely circulated Chinese Communist Party pamphlet. See Bruce Mazlish, *The Revolutionary Ascetic: Evolution of a Political Type* (New York: Basic Books, 1976), p. 188.

48. Paul B. Axelrod, quoted in Bertram D. Wolfe, *Three Who Made a Revolution* (New York: Dell, 1964), p. 249.

49. Sigmund Freud, "Group Psychology and the Analysis of the Ego," in Strachey, 18: 65–143.

50. Mazlish, p. 6.

51. Rosa Luxemburg to Leo Jogiches, March 25, 1894, March 21, 1895 in *Comrade and Lover: Rosa Luxemburg's Letters to Leo Jogiches*, ed. and trans. Elzbieta Ettinger (Cambridge, Mass.: MIT Press, 1979), pp. 8, 17–18.

52. Eleanor Marx to Olive Schreiner, June 16, 1885 in Havelock Ellis, "Eleanor Marx," *The Modern Monthly* 9 (1935): 287.

53. Alexandra Kollontai, *Love and the New Morality*, trans. Alix Holt (Bristol: Falling Wall Press, 1972), p. 24.

54. Rosa Luxemburg to Marta Rosenbaum, January 4, 1919, in *Briefe an Freunde*, ed. Benedikt Kautsky (Hamburg: Europäische Verlagsanstalt, 1950), pp. 168–169.

55. For an illustration of this theme in the lives of certain women activists, see Blanche Wiesen Cook, "Female Support Networks and Political Activism," in *A Heritage of Her Own: Toward a New Social History of American Women*, ed. Nancy F. Cott and Elizabeth H. Pleck (New York: Simon and Schuster, 1979), pp. 412–444.

56. Eleanor Marx to Olive Schreiner, June 16, 1885 in Havelock Ellis, "Eleanor Marx," *Adelphi* 10 (1935): 350.

57. Scarf, p. 86.

58. Judith M. Bardwick, *Psychology of Women* (New York: Harper and Row, 1971), pp. 157–158.

59. Rosa Luxemburg to Sonia Leibknecht, May 2, 1917 in Rosa Luxemburg, *Letters From Prison*, trans. Eden and Cedar Paul (London: Socialist Book Centre, 1946), p. 16.

60. V. I. Lenin, "An Interview on the Woman Question," in Lenin, *The Emancipation of Women* (New York: International, 1975), p. 107.

61. For one example of this, see Laura Fermi, *Mussolini* (Chicago: University of Chicago Press, 1961), p. 59.

62. Judith Nies, *Seven Women: Portraits from the American Radical Tradition* (New York: Viking Press, 1977), p. xii.

63. Compare Gerda Lerner's comments in "Politics and Culture in Women's History: A Symposium," *Feminist Studies* 6 (1980): 49.

64. Eduard Bernstein, *Die deutsche Revolution: ihr Ursprung, ihr Verlauf, und ihr Werk* (Berlin-Fichtenau: Verlag für Gesellschaft und Erziehung, 1921), p. 171.

65. Balabanoff, p. 239.

66. Eduard Bernstein, *My Years of Exile: Reminiscences of a Socialist*, trans. Bernard Miall (New York: Harcourt, Brace, and Howe, 1921), p. 162.

67. Nadezhda K. Krupskaya, *Reminiscences of Lenin* (Moscow: Foreign Languages Publishing House, 1959), p. 498; Lenin, "The Dual Power," in *The Lenin Anthology*, ed. Robert C. Tucker (New York: Norton, 1975), p. 301.

68. See Milovan Djilas, *The New Class: An Analysis of the Communist System* (New York: Praeger, 1957).

69. Trotsky quoted in James Joll, *The Anarchists* (London: Eyre and Spottiswoode, 1964), p. 11.

NOTES TO EPILOGUE

1. New York *Times*, November 18, 1977.

2. Barbara W. Jancar, "Women Under Communism," in *Women in Politics*, ed. Jane Jaquette (New York: John Wiley, 1974), pp. 217–242.

3. In the early days of the revolution, when Kollontai's support for Lenin was total and unflinching, he had a much different view of her. One observer commented, "I remember how long and heartily Lenin laughed at reading . . . the remark somewhere, 'There are only two communists in Russia, Lenin and Kollontai.' He laughed and then sighed, 'What a clever woman she is.'" See Maxim Gorky, *Days with Lenin* (New York: International, 1932), p. 54.

4. Quoted in Lelio Basso, *Rosa Luxemburg, A Reappraisal*, trans. Douglas Parmée (New York: Praeger, 1975), p. 54.

5. Rosa Luxemburg, "Versäumte Pflichten," *Die Rote Fahne*, January 8, 1919.

6. On the nonhierarchical structure of the PSI, see Robert Michels, *Le Prolétariat et la Bourgeoisie dans le Mouvement socialiste italien*, trans. Georges Bourgin (Paris: Giard, 1921), pp. 243-252; and James Edward Miller, "The Italian Socialist Party, 1900-1914: An Organizational Study" (Ph.D. diss., University of Illinois at Urbana-Champaign, 1974), pp. 91-92.

7. Gerald H. Meaker, *The Revolutionary Left in Spain, 1914-1923* (Stanford, Calif.: Stanford University Press, 1974), pp. 10-11, 464.

8. Elzbieta Ettinger, ed. and trans., *Comrade and Lover: Rosa Luxemburg's Letters to Leo Jogiches* (Cambridge, Mass.: MIT Press, 1979), p. xix.

9. Luxemburg to Jogiches, May 25, 1900 in ibid., pp. 101-102.

10. See Kurt Lewin, "Self-Hatred Among Jews," *Contemporary Jewish Record* 4 (1941): 219-232; and Robert S. Wistrich, *Revolutionary Jews From Marx to Trotsky* (New York: Barnes and Noble, 1976), esp. pp. 20-21.

11. Often women who have succeeded in predominantly male fields like law, politics, or business are reluctant to see other women succeed, because their success would detract from their own status and importance. See Caroline Bird, *Born Female* (New York: Simon and Schuster, 1968), pp. 84-109.

12. Dolores Ibarruri, *They Shall Not Pass: The Autobiography of La Pasionaria* (New York: International, 1966), p. 108.

13. Robin Morgan, *Sisterhood Is Powerful* (New York: Vintage, 1970), p. xvii.

14. Balabanoff quoted in Louise Bryant, *Six Red Months in Russia* (New York: George H. Doran, 1918), p. 169.

15. Rosa Luxemburg to Emanuel and Mathilde Wurm, July 18, 1906, in Rosa Luxemburg, *Briefe an Freunde*, ed. Benedikt Kautsky (Hamburg: Europäische Verlagsanstalt, 1950), pp. 42-44.

16. Lionel Tiger, *Men In Groups* (New York: Vintage, 1970).

17. Albert Camus, *The Rebel*, trans. Anthony Bower (New York: Alfred A. Knopf, 1956), pp. 87, 247, 281.

18. Lenin quoted in *Rosa Luxemburg Speaks*, ed. Mary-Alice Waters (New York: Pathfinder Press, 1970), p. 22.

19. Eleanor Marx, *Commonweal*, December 1885.

Bibliography

GENERAL STUDIES ON REVOLUTION, REVOLUTIONARY WOMEN, THE REVOLUTIONARY PERSONALITY, AND POLITICAL SOCIALIZATION

Abray, Jane. "Feminism in the French Revolution." *American Historical Review* 80 (1975): 43–62.

Arendt, Hannah. *On Revolution.* New York: Viking Press, 1965.

Bachtold, Louise M. "Personality Characteristics of Women of Distinction." *Psychology of Women Quarterly* 1 (1976–1977): 70–78.

Bardwick, Judith M. *Psychology of Women.* New York: Harper and Row, 1971.

Barzun, Jacques. "History: The Muse and Her Doctors." *American Historical Review* 77 (1972): 36–64.

Belinsky, Vissarion G. *Selected Philosophical Works.* Moscow: Foreign Languages Publishing House, 1948.

Berman, Ronald, "I'll Play My Father." *Kenyon Review* 29 (1967): 550–555.

Bianchi, Eugene C. *The Religious Experience of Revolutionaries.* Garden City, N.Y.: Doubleday, 1972.

Bird, Caroline. *Born Female.* New York: Simon and Schuster, 1968.

Brinton, Crane. *The Anatomy of Revolution.* New York: Vintage, 1965.

———. *A Decade of Revolution, 1789–1799.* New York: Harper and Row, 1963.

Camus, Albert. *The Rebel.* Translated by Anthony Bower. New York: Alfred A. Knopf, 1956.

Cantril, Hadley. *The Psychology of Social Movements.* New York: John Wiley, 1941.

Cherniss, Cary. "Personality and Ideology: A Personological Study of Women's Liberation." *Psychiatry* 35 (May 1972): 109–125.

Chernyshevsky, N. G. *A Vital Question; or What Is To Be Done?* Translated by Nathan Haskell Dole and S. S. Skidelsky. New York: Thomas Y. Crowell, 1886.

Chodorow, Nancy. "Family Structure and Feminine Personality." In *Woman, Culture, and Society*, pp. 43–66. Edited by Michelle Zimbalist Rosaldo and Louise Lamphere. Stanford, Calif.: Stanford University Press, 1974.

Christ, Carol P., and Judith Plaskow, eds. *Womanspirit Rising: A Feminist Reader in Religion.* San Francisco: Harper and Row, 1979.

Christophe, Robert. *Danton: A Biography.* Translated by Peter Green. Garden City, N.Y.: Doubleday, 1967.

Cobb, Richard. "Quelques Aspects de la Mentalité Révolutionnaire." *La Revue d'Historie Moderne et Contemporaine* 6 (1959): 83–120.

———. "The Revolutionary Mentality in France, 1793–1974." *History* 42 (1957): 181–196.

Cohen, D. L. "The Concept of Charisma and the Analysis of Leadership." *Political Studies* 20 (1972): 299–305.

Coles, Robert. *Erik H. Erikson: The Growth of His Work.* Boston: Little, Brown, 1970.

Cook, Blanche Wiesen. "Female Support Networks and Political Activism." In *A Heritage of Her Own: Toward a New Social History of American Women,* pp. 412–444. Edited by Nancy F. Cott and Elizabeth H. Pleck. New York: Simon and Schuster, 1979.

Daly, William T. *The Revolutionary: A Review and Synthesis.* Beverly Hills, Calif.: Sage Publications, 1972.

Deutsch, Helene. *Psychology of Women.* 2 vols. New York: Grune and Stratton, 1944–1945.

Diamond, Solomon. *A Study of the Influence of Political Radicalism on Personality Development.* New York: Columbia University Press, 1936.

Dinnerstein, Dorothy. *The Mermaid and the Minotaur: Sexual Arrangements and the Human Malaise.* New York: Harper and Row, 1977.

Dooley, Lucille. "Psychoanalytic Studies of Genius." *American Journal of Psychology* 27 (1916): 363–416.

Dunn, Patrick P. "Fathers and Sons Revisited: The Childhood of Vissarion Belinskii." *History of Childhood Quarterly* 1 (1974): 389–407.

Edinger, Lewis J. "Political Science and Political Biography." *Journal of Politics* 26 (1964): 423–439, 648–676.

Ellwood, Charles A. "A Psychological Theory of Revolutions." *American Journal of Sociology* 11 (1905): 49–59.

Erikson, Erik H. *Childhood and Society.* New York: W. W. Norton, 1950.

——. *Gandhi's Truth.* New York: W. W. Norton, 1969.

——. *Identity, Youth, and Crisis.* New York: W. W. Norton, 1968.

——. *Young Man Luther.* New York: W. W. Norton, 1958.

Fischer, Louis. *The Life of Lenin.* New York: Harper and Row, 1964.

Fowler, Marguerite Gilbert, and Hani K. Van de Riet. "Women Today and Yesterday: An Examination of the Feminist Personality." *Journal of Psychology* 82 (1972): 269–276.

Freud, Sigmund. *The Standard Edition of the Complete Psychological Works of Sigmund Freud.* Translated and edited by James Strachey. 24 vols. London: Hogarth Press, and the Institute of Psycho-Analysis, 1955.

Fromm, Erich. "Sex and Character." In *The Family: Its Function and Destiny,* pp. 399–419. Edited by Ruth Nanda Anshen. New York: Harper and Row, 1959.

George, Alexander. "Power as a Compensatory Value for Political Leaders." *Journal of Social Issues* 24 (July 1968): 29–49.

Getzler, Israel. "Marxist Revolutionaries and the Dilemma of Power." In *Revolution and Politics in Russia,* pp. 88–112. Edited by Alexander and Janet Rabinowitch. Bloomington: Indiana University Press, 1972.

Giffin, Frederick C. *Woman as Revolutionary: Writings by and about Women Who Have Left Their Vivid Mark on History.* New York: New American Library, 1973.

Goertzel, Victor, and Mildred George Goertzel. *Cradles of Eminence.* Boston: Little, Brown, 1962.

Goldsmith, Margaret. *Seven Women Against the World.* London: Methuen, 1935.

Goldstein, Kurt. *The Organism*. New York: American Press, 1939.

Gornick, Vivian, and Barbara K. Moran. *Woman in Sexist Society*. New York: Basic Books, 1971.

Greenstein, Fred I. "Personality and Politics: Problems of Evidence, Inference, and Conceptualization." *American Behavioral Scientist* 11 (1967): 38-53.

———, ed. "Personality and Politics: Theoretical and Methodological Issues." *Journal of Social Issues* 24 (July 1968).

———, and Michael Lerner. *A Source Book for the Study of Personality and Politics*. Chicago: Markham, 1971.

Groth, Alexander J. *Comparative Politics: A Distributive Approach*. New York: Macmillan, 1971.

Heilbrun, Carolyn G. *Toward a Recognition of Androgyny*. New York: Alfred A. Knopf, 1973.

Hobsbawm, E. J. "Revolution is Puritan." *New Society* 13 (May 22, 1969): 807.

———. *Revolutionaries: Contemporary Essays*. London: Weidenfeld and Nicolson, 1973.

Hoffer, Eric. *The True Believer*. New York: Harper and Bros., 1951.

Hufton, Olwen. "Women in Revolution, 1789-1796." *Past and Present*, no. 53 (1971): 90-108.

Huszar, George B. de. *The Intellectuals*. Glencoe, Ill.: Free Press, 1960.

Hyman, Herbert H. *Political Socialization*. Glencoe, Ill.: Free Press, 1959.

Jaggar, Alison M., and Paula Rothenberg Struhl. *Feminist Frameworks: Alternative Theoretical Accounts of the Relations between Women and Men*. New York: McGraw-Hill, 1978.

Jaquette, Jane, ed. *Women in Politics*. New York: John Wiley, 1974.

Jaros, Dean. *Socialization to Politics*. New York: Praeger, 1972.

Jennings, M. Kent, and Kenneth P. Langton. "Mothers vs. Fathers: The Formation of Political Orientations Among Young Americans." *Journal of Politics* 31 (1969): 329-357.

Kelly, Aileen. "Revolutionary Women." *New York Review of Books* 22 (July 17, 1975): 20-22.

Kelly, Rita Mae, and Mary Boutilier. *The Making of Political Women: A Study of Socialization and Role Conflict*. Chicago: Nelson-Hall, 1978.

Kempf, E. J. *Psychopathology*. St. Louis: C. V. Mosby, 1920.

Kirkpatrick, Jeane J. *Political Woman*. New York: Basic Books, 1974.

Lampert, E. *Studies in Rebellion*. London: Routledge and Kegan Paul, 1957.

Lane, Robert E. "Fathers and Sons: Foundations of Political Belief." *American Sociological Review* 24 (August 1959): 502-511.

Langton, Kenneth P. *Political Socialization*. New York: Oxford University Press, 1969.

Lasswell, Harold D. *Power and Personality*. New York: W. W. Norton, 1948.

———. *Psychopathology and Politics*. Chicago: University of Chicago Press, 1930.

———. "The Scientific Study of Human Biography." *Scientific Monthly* 30 (1930): 79-80.

———. "Types of Political Personalities." In *Personality and the Social Group*, pp. 151-161. Edited by Ernest W. Burgess. Chicago: University of Chicago Press, 1929.

——, and Daniel Lerner. *World Revolutionary Elites.* Cambridge, Mass.: MIT Press, 1965.

LeBon, Gustave. *The Psychology of Revolution.* Translated by Bernard Miall. New York: G. P. Putnam's Sons, 1913.

Leites, Nathan. *A Study of Bolshevism.* Glencoe, Ill.: Free Press, 1953.

Lenin, V. I. *The Paris Commune.* New York: International, 1931.

Lipman-Blumen, Jean. "How Ideology Shapes Women's Lives." *Scientific American* 226 (January 1972): 34–42.

Lynn, David B. *The Father: His Role in Child Development.* Monterey, Calif.: Brooks/Cole, 1974.

——. *Parental and Sex-Role Identification: A Theoretical Formulation.* Berkeley, Calif.: McCutchen, 1969.

McClelland, David C. *The Achieving Society.* New York: Free Press, 1961.

Maccoby, Eleanor E., ed. *The Development of Sex Differences.* Stanford, Calif.: Stanford University Press, 1966.

Maniha, John K., and Barbara B. Maniha. "A Comparison of Psychohistorical Differences Among Some Female Religious and Secular Leaders." *Journal of Psychohistory* 5 (1977–1978): 552–549.

Marvick, Dwaine, ed. *Harold D. Lasswell on Political Sociology.* Chicago: University of Chicago Press, 1977.

——, ed. *Political Decision-Makers.* Glencoe, Ill.: Free Press, 1961.

Marx, Karl. *Notebooks on the Paris Commune.* Edited by Hal Draper. Berkeley, Calif.: Independent Socialist Press, 1971.

——, and Frederick Engels. *Writings on the Paris Commune.* Edited by Hal Draper. New York: Monthly Review Press, 1971.

Maslow, Abraham. *Motivation and Personality.* New York: Harper and Row, 1954.

——. "A Theory of Human Motivation." *Psychological Review* 50 (1943): 370–396.

Matrat, Jean. *Robespierre.* Translated by Alan Kendall. New York: Charles Scribner's Sons, 1971.

Mazlish, Bruce. "Clio on the Couch." *Encounter* 30 (September 1968): 46–54.

——. *The Revolutionary Ascetic: Evolution of a Political Type.* New York: Basic Books, 1976.

——, ed. *Psychoanalysis and History.* Englewood Cliffs, N.J.: Prentice-Hall, 1963.

Miller, Jean Baker, ed. *Psychoanalysis and Women.* Baltimore: Penguin, 1973.

Nahirny, Vladimir C. "The Russian Intelligentsia: From Men of Ideas to Men of Convictions." *Comparative Studies in Society and History* 4 (1962): 403–435.

——. "Some Observations on Ideological Groups." *American Journal of Sociology* 67 (1962): 397–405.

Nies, Judith. *Seven Women: Portraits from the American Radical Tradition.* New York: Viking, 1977.

Nomad, Max. *Apostles of Revolution.* New York: Collier, 1961.

——. *Aspects of Revolt.* New York: Bookman, 1959.

——. *Dreamers, Dynamiters, and Demagogues.* New York: Waldon Press, 1964.

——. *Political Heretics.* Ann Arbor: University of Michigan Press, 1963.

Ortner, Sherry B. "Is Female to Male as Nature Is to Culture?" In *Woman, Culture, and Society*, pp. 67–87. Edited by Michelle Zimbalist Rosaldo and Louise Lamphere. Stanford, Calif.: Stanford University Press, 1974.

Payne, Robert. *The Life and Death of Lenin*. New York: Simon and Schuster, 1964.

Pomper, Philip. "Bakunin, Nechaev, and the 'Catechism of a Revolutionary': The Case for Joint Authorship." *Canadian-American Slavic Studies* 10 (1976): 535–550.

——. "Nechaev, Lenin, and Stalin: The Psychology of Leadership." *Jahrbücher für Geschichte Osteuropas* 26 (1978): 11–30.

——. *Sergei Nechaev*. New Brunswick, N.J.: Rutgers University Press, 1979.

Possony, Stefan T. *Lenin: The Compulsive Revolutionary*. Chicago: Henry Regnery, 1964.

Pye, Lucian W. "Administrators, Agitators, and Brokers." *Public Opinion Quarterly* 22 (1958): 342–348.

Rejai, Mostafa. *The Comparative Study of Revolutionary Strategy*. New York: David McKay, 1977.

——, with Kay Phillips. *Leaders of Revolution*. Beverly Hills, Calif.: Sage Publications, 1979.

Renshon, Stanley. *Psychological Needs and Political Behavior: A Theory of Personality and Political Efficacy*. New York: Free Press, 1974.

Riezler, Kurt. "On the Psychology of the Modern Revolution." *Social Research* 10 (1943): 320–336.

Rogers, Carl. *On Becoming a Person*. Boston: Houghton Mifflin, 1961.

Rowbotham, Sheila. *Women, Resistance, and Revolution: A History of Women and Revolution in the Modern World*. New York: Vintage, 1974.

Rubel, Maximilien. "Deux Interviews de Karl Marx sur la Commune." *Le Mouvement Social*, no. 38 (1962): 3–27.

Rudé, George. *The Crowd in History, 1730–1840*. New York: John Wiley, 1964.

——. *Robespierre: Portrait of a Revolutionary Democrat*. New York: Viking Press, 1976.

Salaff, Janet W., and Judith Merkle. "Women in Revolution: The Lessons of the Soviet Union and China." In *Taking State Power*, pp. 500–517. Edited by John C. Leggett. New York: Harper and Row, 1973.

Salert, Barbara. *Revolutions and Revolutionaries: Four Theories*. New York: Elsevier, 1976.

Sampson, Ronald V. *The Psychology of Power*. New York: Pantheon, 1966.

Schaffer, Roy. "Problems in Freud's Psychology of Women." *Journal of the American Psychoanalytic Association* 22 (1974): 459–485.

Scott, Otto J. *Robespierre: The Voice of Virtue*. New York: Mason and Lipscomb, 1974.

Shub, David. "Kropotkin and Lenin." *Russian Review* 12 (1953): 227–234.

Shulim, Joseph I. "Robespierre and the French Revolution: A Review Article." *American Historical Review* 82 (1977): 20–38.

Skocpol, Theda. *States and Social Revolutions*. Cambridge: Cambridge University Press, 1979.

Sorokin, Pitirim A. *The Sociology of Revolution*. New York: Howard Fertig, 1967.

Springer, Philip B., and Marcello Truzzi, eds. *Revolutionaries on Revolution.* Pacific Palisades, Calif.: Goodyear, 1973.

Strauss, Harlan J. "Revolutionary Types: Russia in 1905." *Journal of Conflict Resolution* 17 (1973): 297–316.

Strouse, Jean, ed. *Women and Analysis.* New York: Grossman, 1974.

Taintor, Zebulon C. "Assessing the Revolutionary Personality." In *Revolution and Political Change,* pp. 239–249. Edited by Claude E. Welch, Jr. and Mavis Bunker Taintor. Belmont, Calif.: Duxbury, 1972.

Thomas, Edith. *The Women Incendiaries.* Translated by James and Starr Atkinson. New York: George Braziller, 1966.

Thompson, E. P. "The Moral Economy of the English Crowd." *Past and Present,* no. 50 (1971): 76–136.

Thompson, J. M. *Robespierre.* 2 vols. New York: D. Appleton-Century, 1936.

Tiger, Lionel. *Men in Groups.* New York: Vintage, 1970.

Trotsky, Leon. *Lenin.* New York: Minton, Balch, 1925.

Tucker, Robert C. "The Theory of Charismatic Leadership." *Daedalus* 97 (1968): 731–756.

Valentinov, Nikolay. *Encounters with Lenin.* Translated by Paul Rasta and Brian Pearce. London: Oxford University Press, 1968.

Ward, Reginald Somerset. *Maximilien Robespierre.* London: Macmillan, 1934.

Weinstein, Fred, and Gerald M. Platt. *The Wish to be Free.* Berkeley: University of California Press, 1969.

Willner, Ann Ruth, and Dorothy Willner. "The Rise and Role of Charismatic Leaders." *Annals of the American Academy of Political and Social Science* 358 (1965): 77–88.

Wistrich, Robert S. *Revolutionary Jews From Marx to Trotsky.* New York: Barnes and Noble, 1976.

Wolfe, Bertram D. *Three Who Made a Revolution.* New York: Dell, 1964.

Wolfenstein, E. Victor. *Personality and Politics.* Belmont, Calif.: Dickenson, 1969.

———. *The Revolutionary Personality.* Princeton, N.J.: Princeton University Press, 1967.

Wolman, Benjamin B., ed. *The Psychoanalytic Interpretation of History.* New York: Basic Books, 1971.

Wolpert, J. F. "The Myth of Revolution." *Ethics* 58 (1947-1948): 245–255.

BACKGROUND STUDIES ON SOCIALISM, COMMUNISM, SOCIALIST FEMINISM, AND SOCIALIST THOUGHT

Aveling, Eleanor Marx, and Edward Aveling. "The Woman Question: From a Socialist Point of View." *The Westminster Review* 69, N.S. (1886): 207–222.

Bebel, August. *Woman Under Socialism.* New York: Labor News Press, 1904.

Beer, Max. *Fifty Years of International Socialism.* New York: Macmillan, 1935.

Bernstein, Eduard. *My Years of Exile: Reminiscences of a Socialist.* Translated by Bernard Miall. New York: Harcourt, Brace, and Howe, 1921.

Borkenau, Franz. *European Communism.* London: Faber and Faber, 1953.

——. *World Communism: A History of the Communist International.* Ann Arbor: University of Michigan Press, 1962.

Braunthal, Julius. *History of the International.* 2 vols. Translated by John Clark. New York: Praeger, 1967.

Bunyan, James, and H. H. Fisher. *The Bolshevik Revolution, 1917–1918: Documents and Materials.* Stanford, Calif.: Stanford University Press, 1934.

Cabet, Etienne. *La Femme.* Paris: Le Populaire, 1848.

Carr, Edward Hallett. *The Bolshevik Revolution, 1917–1923.* 3 vols. New York: Macmillan, 1950–1953.

——. *Michael Bakunin.* London: Macmillan, 1937.

——. *1917: Before and After.* London: Macmillan, 1969.

——. *Socialism in One Country, 1924–1926.* 3 vols. New York: Macmillan, 1958–1964.

Chamberlin, William Henry. *The Russian Revolution, 1917–1921.* 2 vols. New York: Macmillan, 1935.

Cole, G. D. H. *A History of Socialist Thought.* 5 vols. New York: St. Martin's Press, 1953–1960.

Conquest, Robert. *The Great Terror: Stalin's Purges of the Thirties.* London: Macmillan, 1968.

Daniels, Robert V. *The Conscience of the Revolution: Communist Opposition in Soviet Russia.* Cambridge, Mass.: Harvard University Press, 1960.

Deutscher, Isaac. *The Prophet Armed: Trotsky, 1879–1921.* New York: Oxford University Press, 1954.

——. *Stalin: A Political Biography.* New York: Oxford University Press, 1967.

Djilas, Milovan. *The New Class: An Analysis of the Communist System.* New York: Praeger, 1957.

Dutt, R. Palme. *The Internationale.* London: Lawrence and Wishart, 1964.

Einaudi, Mario. "Western European Communism: A Profile." *American Political Science Review* 45 (1951): 185–208.

——, Jean-Marie Domenach, and Aldo Garosci. *Communism in Western Europe.* Ithaca, N.Y.: Cornell University Press, 1951.

Engels, Frederick. *The Condition of the Working Class in England.* Translated by Florence Kelley Wischnewetzky. New York: Lovell, 1887.

——. *The Condition of the Working Class in England in 1844.* Edited and translated by W. O. Henderson and W. H. Chaloner. Stanford, Calif.: Stanford University Press, 1968.

——. *The Origin of the Family, Private Property, and the State.* Edited by Eleanor Burke Leacock. New York: International, 1975.

Fainsod, Merle. *International Socialism and the World War.* Cambridge, Mass.: Harvard University Press, 1935.

Fourier, Charles. *Oeuvres Complètes.* 6 vols. Paris: Librairie Sociétaire, 1841–1846.

——. *Théorie des Quatre Mouvements.* Paris: Librairie Sociétaire, 1846.

Galenson, Walter, ed. *Comparative Labor Movements.* New York: Prentice-Hall, 1952.

Gankin, Olga Hess, and H. H. Fisher. *The Bolsheviks and the World War.* Stanford, Calif.: Stanford University Press, 1940.

Gorky, Maxim. *Days with Lenin.* New York: International, 1932.

Gruber, Helmut, ed. *International Communism in the Era of Lenin: A Documentary History.* Ithaca, N.Y.: Cornell University Press, 1967.

Gunther, John. *Behind the Curtain.* New York: Harper and Bros., 1948.

Haimson, Leopold H. *The Russian Marxists and the Origins of Bolshevism.* Cambridge, Mass.: Harvard University Press, 1967.

Haupt, Georges. *Socialism and the Great War: The Collapse of the Second International.* Oxford: Clarendon Press, 1972.

——, and Jean-Jacques Marie, eds. *Makers of the Russian Revolution.* Translated by C. I. P. Ferdinand. Ithaca, N.Y.: Cornell University Press, 1974.

Jancar, Barbara Wolfe. *Women Under Communism.* Baltimore: Johns Hopkins University Press, 1978.

Joll, James. *The Anarchists.* London: Eyre and Spottiswoode, 1964.

——. *The Second International, 1889–1914.* New York: Praeger, 1956.

Kohak, Erazim V. "Turning On for Freedom: The Curious Love Affair of Sex and Socialism." *Dissent* (September-October 1969): 437–443.

Krupskaya, Nadezhda K. *Memoirs of Lenin.* 2 vols. Translated by E. Verney. New York: International, 1930.

——. *Reminiscences of Lenin.* Moscow: Foreign Languages Publishing House, 1959.

Lapidus, Gail Warshofsky. *Women in Soviet Society.* Berkeley: University of California Press, 1978.

Lazitch, Branko, and Milorad M. Drachkovitch. *Biographical Dictionary of the Comintern.* Stanford, Calif.: Hoover Institution Press, 1973.

——. *Lenin and the Comintern.* Stanford, Calif.: Hoover Institution Press, 1972.

Lenin, V. I. *Collected Works.* 45 vols. Moscow: Progress, 1963–1970.

——. *The Emancipation of Women.* New York: International, 1934.

——. *"Left" Communism: An Infantile Disorder.* London: The Toiler, 1920.

——. *The Letters of Lenin.* Edited and translated by Elizabeth Hill and Doris Mudie. New York: Harcourt, Brace, 1937.

——. *Selected Works.* 3 vols. Moscow: Foreign Languages Publishing House, 1960–1961.

Lichtheim, George. *The Concept of Ideology and Other Essays.* New York: Vintage, 1967.

——. *Marxism: An Historical and Critical Study.* New York: Praeger, 1961.

McLellan, David. *Karl Marx: His Life and Thought.* New York: Harper and Row, 1973.

Marx, Karl. *Capital.* 2 vols. London: Swan Sonnenschein, Lowrey, 1887.

——. *Critique of the Gotha Program.* Edited by C. P. Dutt. New York: International, 1973.

——. *The Economic and Philosophic Manuscripts of 1844.* Edited by Dirk J. Struik. New York: International, 1964.

——, and Frederick Engels. *The German Ideology.* New York: International, 1970.

——. *The Holy Family.* Translated by R. Dixon. Moscow: Foreign Languages Publishing House, 1956.

——. *Marx and Engels: Basic Writings on Politics and Philosophy.* Edited by Lewis S. Feuer. Garden City, N.Y.: Anchor, 1959.

——. *Marx-Engels Werke.* 39 vols. Berlin: Dietz, 1961–1968.

Mayer, Gustav. *Friedrich Engels: A Biography.* Translated by Gilbert and Helen Highet. New York: Alfred A. Knopf, 1936.

Mehring, Franz. *Karl Marx: The Story of His Life.* Translated by Edward Fitzgerald. London: George Allen and Unwin, 1936.

Meijer, J. M. *Knowledge and Revolution: The Russian Colony in Zuerich (1870–1873).* Assen, the Netherlands: Van Gorcum, 1955.

Michels, Robert. *Political Parties.* Translated by Eden and Cedar Paul. New York: Dover, 1959.

Plamenatz, John. *German Marxism and Russian Communism.* London: Longmans, Green, 1954.

Raddatz, Fritz J. *Karl Marx: A Political Biography.* Translated by Richard Barry. Boston: Little, Brown, 1979.

Rosenberg, Arthur. *A History of Bolshevism.* Translated by Ian F. D. Morrow. Oxford: Oxford University Press, 1934.

Rover, Constance. *Love, Morals, and the Feminists.* London: Routledge and Kegan Paul, 1970.

Schapiro, Leonard. *The Communist Party of the Soviet Union.* New York: Vintage, 1971.

——. *The Origin of the Communist Autocracy.* London: London School of Economics and Political Science, 1955.

Schirmacher, Kaethe. *The Modern Woman's Rights Movement: A Historical Survey.* Translated by Carl Conrad Eckhardt. New York: Macmillan, 1912.

Scott, Hilda. *Does Socialism Liberate Women?* Boston: Beacon Press, 1974.

Shub, David. *Lenin: A Biography.* New York: Penguin, 1977.

Slaughter, Jane, and Robert Kern, eds. *European Women on the Left.* Westport, Conn.: Greenwood Press, 1981.

Stalin, Joseph. *Leninism: Selected Writings.* New York: International, 1942.

Stanton, Theodore, ed., *The Woman Question in Europe.* New York: G. P. Putnam's Sons, 1884.

Sturmthal, Adolf. *The Tragedy of European Labor, 1918–1939.* New York: Columbia University Press, 1943.

Tannahill, R. Neal. *The Communist Parties of Western Europe.* Westport, Conn.: Greenwood Press, 1978.

Trotsky, Leon. *The History of the Russian Revolution.* Translated by Max Eastman. London: Victor Gollancz, 1934.

——. *My Life.* New York: Charles Scribner's Sons, 1930.

——. *Writings of Leon Trotsky.* 12 vols. Edited by Naomi Allen and George Breitman. New York: Pathfinder Press, 1970.

Ulam, Adam B. *The Bolsheviks.* Toronto: Collier, 1968.

Vandervelde, Emile. *Souvenirs d'un Militant Socialiste.* Paris: Editions Denoël, 1939.

Woodcock, George. *Anarchism.* Cleveland: World, 1962.

ELEANOR MARX

Published Writings

Original Writings

Marx, Eleanor. "The Irish Dynamiters." *Progress* 3 (May 1884): 268-272.
———. "Karl Marx: A Biography." *Progress* 1 (May 1883): 288-294.
———. "Karl Marx: A Biography." *The Social Democrat* 1 (1897): 163-168.
———. "The Liverpool Congress." *Time* 2, N.S. (October 1890): 1088-1097.
———. "March 18: The Paris Commune: A Letter of Eleanor Marx." Edited by
   Allen Hutt. *The Labour Monthly* 22 (March 1940): 158-161.
———. "Marx's Theory of Value." *Progress* 1 (June 1883): 362-366.
———. "A Reply to Ernest Radford." *Progress* 2 (December 1883): 371-374.
———. "The Rev. W. Lansdell, D. D." *Progress* 1 (May 1883): 302-304.
———. "Review of Stepniak's *Underground Russia*." *Progress* 2 (1883): 106-
   110, 172-176.
———. *The Working Class Movement in England: A Brief Historical Sketch.*
   London: Twentieth Century Press, 1896.
———, and Edward Aveling. "The Chicago Anarchists." *To-Day* 7, N.S. (Novem-
   ber 1887): 142-149.
———. *The Factory Hell.* London: Socialist League, 1885.
———. "The Labour Movement in America." *Time* 5, N.S. (1887): 298-304,
   431-446, 554-563, 705-713.
———. "Shelley and Socialism." *To-Day* 9, N.S. (April 1888): 103-116.
———. *Shelley's Socialism: Two Lectures.* London: printed for private distribu-
   tion, 1888.
———. "The Woman Question: From a Socialist Point of View." *The Westminster
   Review* 69, N.S. (1886): 207-222.
———. *The Woman Question.* London: Swan Sonnenschein and Lowrey, 1886.
———. *The Working Class Movement in America.* London: Swan Sonnenschein,
   1891.
Zangwill, Israel, and Eleanor Marx Aveling. "'A Doll's House' Repaired." *Time*
   3, N.S. (March 1891): 239-253.

Works Edited and Translated

Bernstein, Eduard. *Ferdinand Lassalle as a Social Reformer.* Translated by
   Eleanor Marx Aveling. London: Swan Sonnenschein, 1893.
Flaubert, Gustave. *Madame Bovary.* Translated by Eleanor Marx Aveling. Lon-
   don: W. W. Gibbings, 1901.
Ibsen, Henrik. *An Enemy of Society.* Translated by Eleanor Marx Aveling.
   London: Camelot Classics, 1888.
———. *The Lady from the Sea.* Translated by Eleanor Marx Aveling. London:
   T. Fisher Unwin, 1890.
———. *The Wild Duck.* Translated by Eleanor Marx Aveling. Boston: Walter H.
   Baker, 1890.

Kielland, Alexander. "A Ball Mood." Translated by Eleanor Marx Aveling. *Time* 1, N.S. (May 1890): 520–524.

——. "A Good Conscience." Translated by Eleanor Marx Aveling. *Time* 1, N.S. (February 1890): 167–176.

——. "Siesta." Translated by Eleanor Marx Aveling. *The Social-Democrat* 2 (1898): 28–32.

Lissagaray, Hippolyte-Prosper-Olivier. *History of the Commune of 1871.* Translated by Eleanor Marx Aveling. London: Reeves and Turner, 1886.

Marx, Karl. *The Eastern Question.* Edited by Eleanor Marx Aveling and Edward Aveling. London: Swan Sonnenschein, 1897.

——. *Revolution and Counter-Revolution.* Edited by Eleanor Marx Aveling. London: George Allen and Unwin, 1891.

——. *The Secret Diplomatic History of the Eighteenth Century.* Edited by Eleanor Marx Aveling. London: Swan Sonnenschein, 1899.

——. *The Story of the Life of Lord Palmerston.* Edited by Eleanor Marx Aveling. London: Swan Sonnenschein, 1899.

——. *Value, Price, and Profit.* Edited by Eleanor Marx Aveling. London: Swan Sonnenschein, 1898.

Plechanoff, Georgi. *Anarchism and Socialism.* Translated by Eleanor Marx Aveling. London: Twentieth Century Press, 1895.

Newspapers and Journals

Brooklyn *Daily Eagle*
Chicago *Tribune*
The Clarion
Commonweal: The Official Journal of the Socialist League
Contemporary Review
Fraser's Magazine
Labour Echo
Labour Elector
Labour Leader
London *Times*
Die Neue Zeit
New Century Review
New York *Daily Tribune*
New York *Herald*
Newark *Evening News*
The Nineteenth Century
The Pall Mall Gazette
Progress
Quarterly Review
The Social-Democrat
Le Socialiste
Der Sozialdemokrat
Time

To-Day
Woodhull and Claflin's Weekly

Descriptions of Marx by Friends and Contemporaries

Bax, Ernest Belford. *Reminiscences and Reflexions of a Mid and Late Victorian.* London: George Allen and Unwin, 1918.

Bernstein, Eduard. "Eleanor Marx: Erinnerungen von Eduard Bernstein." *Die Neue Zeit* 16, Bd. II, no. 30 (1897–1898): 118–123.

——. "Was Eleanor Marx in den Tod trieb." *Die Neue Zeit* 16, Bd. II, no. 42 (1897–1898): 481–491.

"Burden: Recollections of Jean Longuet." *The New Yorker* 30 (September 25, 1954): 23–25.

Cahan, Abraham. *The Education of Abraham Cahan.* Translated by Leon Stein, Abraham P. Conan, and Lynn Davison. Philadelphia: Jewish Publication Society of America, 1969.

Clayton, Joseph. *The Rise and Decline of Socialism in Great Britain, 1884–1924.* London: Faber and Gwyer, 1926.

Collison, William. *The Apostle of Free Labour.* London: Hurst and Blackett, 1913.

Comyn, Marian. "My Recollections of Karl Marx." *The Nineteenth Century* 91 (1922): 161–169.

Corbin, Caroline Fairfield. *One Woman's Experience of Emancipation.* Chicago: Illinois Assn. Opposed to the Extension of Suffrage to Women, c. 1886.

Ellis, Havelock. "Eleanor Marx." *Adelphi* 10 and 11 (1935): 342–352, 33–41.

——. "Eleanor Marx." *The Modern Monthly* 9 (1935): 283–295.

——. *My Life.* Boston: Houghton Mifflin, 1939.

Glasier, J. Bruce. *William Morris and the Early Days of the Socialist Movement.* London: Longmans, Green, 1921.

Hyndman, Henry Mayers. *Further Reminiscences.* London: Macmillan, 1912.

——. *The Record of an Adventurous Life.* New York: Macmillan, 1911.

Hyndman, Rosalind Travers. *The Last Years of H. M. Hyndman.* New York: Brentano's, 1924.

Lee, H. W., and E. Archbold. *Social-Democracy in Britain.* London: Social Democratic Federation, 1935.

Lessner, Frederick. *Sixty Years in the Social-Democratic Movement.* London: Twentieth Century Press, 1907.

Liebknecht, William. "Eleanor Marx." *The Social-Democrat* 2 (1898): 258–265.

Mann, Tom. *Tom Mann's Memoirs.* London: Labour Publishing, 1923.

Morris, May. *William Morris: Artist, Writer, Socialist.* 2 vols. New York: Russell and Russell, 1966.

Okey, Thomas. *A Basketful of Memories: An Autobiographical Sketch.* London: J. M. Dent and Sons, 1930.

Pankhurst, Sylvia. *The Suffragette Movement.* London: Longmans, Green, 1931.

Paton, John. *Proletarian Pilgrimage: An Autobiography.* London: George Routledge and Sons, 1935.

Robins, Elizabeth. *Both Sides of the Curtain.* London: William Heinemann, 1940.

Rogers, Frederick. *Labour, Life, and Literature: Some Memories of Sixty Years.* London: Smith, Elder, 1913.

Rosebury, Aaron. "Eleanor, Daughter of Karl Marx: Personal Reminiscences." *Monthly Review* 24 (1973): 29–49.

Salt, Henry S. *Company I Have Kept.* London: George Allen and Unwin, 1930.

——. *Seventy Years Among Savages.* London: George Allen and Unwin, 1921.

Sanders, William Stephen. *Early Socialist Days.* London: Hogarth Press, 1927.

Thorne, Will. *My Life's Battles.* London: George Newnes, 1925.

Tillett, Ben. *Memories and Reflections.* London: John Long, 1931.

Webb, Beatrice. *My Apprenticeship.* London: Longmans, Green, 1926.

Winchevsky, Morris. [Leopold Benedict] *Stories of the Struggle.* Chicago: Charles H. Kerr, 1908.

Related Primary Materials

Adler, Friedrich, ed. *Victor Adler Briefwechsel mit August Bebel und Karl Kautsky.* Vienna: Wiener Volksbuchhandlung, 1954.

Allen, Grant. *The Woman Who Did.* Boston: Roberts Bros., 1895.

Arnold, Arthur. "The Political Enfranchisement of Women." *Fortnightly Review* 11, N.S. (1872): 204–214.

Aveling, Edward. *An American Journey.* New York: John W. Lovell, 1887.

——. "The Ape-Men." *Progress* 2 (1883): 209–218, 276–282, 350–353.

——. "Charles Darwin and Karl Marx: A Comparison." *New Century Review* 1 (1897): 232–243, 321–327.

——. *Darwin Made Easy.* London: Progressive Publishing, 1889.

——. "The Eight Hours Working Day." *Time* 1, N.S. (June 1890): 632–638.

——. "Evolution and Definition." *Progress* 1–2 (1883): 257–263, 321–327, 1–8.

——. "The Generalisations of Charles Darwin." *Progress* 1 (1883): 79–85, 138–144.

——. *An Introduction to the Study of Botany.* London: Swan Sonnenschein, 1891.

——. "Progress in Science." *Progress* 1 (1883): 52–56.

——. *The Student's Darwin.* London: Freethought Publishing, 1881.

——. *The Student's Marx.* London: Swan Sonnenschein, 1892.

Baylen, Joseph O. "George Bernard Shaw and the Socialist League: Some Unpublished Letters." *International Review of Social History* 7 (1962): 426–440.

Bebel, August. *Bebel's Reminiscences.* Translated by Ernest Untermann. New York: Socialist Literature, 1911.

Blumberg, Dorothy Rose. "'Dear Mr. Engels': Unpublished Letters, 1884–1894, of Florence Kelley to Friedrich Engels." *Labour History* 5 (1964): 103–133.

Blumenberg, Werner, ed. *August Bebels Briefwechsel mit Friedrich Engels.* The Hague: Mouton, 1965.

——. "Ein Unbekanntes Kapitel aus Marx' Leben." *International Review of Social History* 1 (1956): 54–111.

Bottigelli, Emile, ed. "Engels et Lafargue: Lettres Inédites." *Cahiers Internationaux*, no. 78 (1956): 39–52.

——. *Friedrich Engels-Paul et Laura Lafargue: Correspondance.* 3 vols. Paris: Editions Sociales, 1956–1959.

Burns, John. "The Great Strike." *New Review* 1 (1889): 410–422.

Cronwright-Schreiner, S. C., ed. *The Letters of Olive Schreiner, 1876–1920.* London: T. Fisher Unwin, 1924.

Eckert, Georg, ed. *Wilhelm Leibknecht Briefwechsel mit Karl Marx und Friedrich Engels.* The Hague: Mouton, 1963.

"Engels on Irish Nationalism." *The Monthly Review* 23 (1972): 53–56.

Fontana and Prati. *Saint-Simonism in London.* London: E. Wilson, 1834.

Henderson, Philip, ed. *The Letters of William Morris to his Family and Friends.* London: Longmans, Green, 1950.

Hyndman, Henry Mayers. *Economics of Socialism.* Boston: Small, Maynard, 1921.

——. *England for All.* London: Gilbert and Rivington, 1881.

Institut Marksizma-Leninizma. *Reminiscences of Marx and Engels.* Moscow: Foreign Languages Publishing House, 1961.

Jackson, T. A. "Marx and Engels on Ireland." *The Labour Monthly* 14–15 (1932–1933): 643–648, 710–175, 769–775, 53–60.

Kropotkin, Prince. "Russian Prisons." *The Nineteenth Century* 13 (1883): 27–44.

Lansdell, Henry. "A Russian Prison." *Contemporary Review* 43 (1883): 275–288.

Laurence, Dan H. *Bernard Shaw: Collected Letters, 1874–1897.* New York: Dodd, Mead, 1965.

——. *Bernard Shaw: Collected Letters, 1898–1910.* London: Max Reinhardt, 1972.

Lenin, V. I. *Letters on Britain.* New York: International, 1934.

Liebknecht, Wilhelm. *Karl Marx: Biographical Memoirs.* Translated by Ernest Untermann. Chicago: Charles H. Kerr, 1908.

Lovett, William. *Life and Struggles of William Lovett in Pursuit of Bread, Knowledge and Freedom.* 2 vols. New York: Alfred A. Knopf, 1920.

Mann, Tom. "The Development of the Labour Movement." *The Nineteenth Century* 27 (1890): 709–720.

Marx, Karl. "The Chartist Movement." *The Labour Monthly* 11 (1929): 721–703.

——. "On the Jewish Question." In *Writings of the Young Marx on Philosophy and Society*, pp. 216–248. Edited and translated by Loyd D. Easton and Kurt H. Guddat. Garden City, N.Y.: Anchor, 1967.

——, and Friedrich Engels. *Selected Correspondence, 1846–1895.* Edited and translated by Dona Torr. New York: International, 1936.

——. *Ireland and the Irish Question.* New York: International, 1972.

——. *Letters to Americans, 1848–1895.* Translated by Leonard E. Mins. New York: International, 1953.

——. *On Britain.* Moscow: Foreign Languages Publishing House, 1953.

Marx-Engels Briefwechsel. 4 vols. Berlin: Dietz, 1949–1950.

Owen, Robert. *The Marriage System of the New Moral World.* Leeds: J. Hobson, 1839.

Potter, Beatrice. "The Dock Life of East London." *The Nineteenth Century* 22 (1887): 483–499.

——. "East London Labour." *The Nineteenth Century* 24 (1888): 161–184.

Radford, Dollie. *One Way of Love*. London: T. Fisher Unwin, 1898.

Rocher, Jules, ed. *Lettres de Communards et de militants de la Première Internationale à Marx, Engels et autres dans les journées de la Commune de Paris en 1871*. Paris: Bureau d'Editions, 1934.

St. John, Christopher, ed. *Ellen Terry and Bernard Shaw: A Correspondence*. New York: G. P. Putnam's Sons, 1931.

Selitrenny, L. "The Jewish Working Woman in the East End." *The Social-Democrat* 2 (1898): 271–275.

Shaw, George Bernard. *The Doctor's Dilemma*. New York: Brentano's, 1931.

——. *Pen Portraits and Reviews*. London: Constable, 1931.

——. Sixteen Self Sketches. New York: Dodd, Mead, 1949.

Smith, H. Llewellyn, and Vaughan Nash. *The Story of the Dockers' Strike, Told by Two East Londoners*. London: T. Fisher Unwin, 1889.

"Socialism in England." *Quarterly Review* 156 (1883): 353–393.

Spargo, John. *Karl Marx: His Life and Work*. New York: B. W. Huebsch, 1910.

——. *Sidelights on Contemporary Socialism*. New York: B. W. Huebsch, 1911.

Stepniak. [Sergei Kravchinsky] *Underground Russia*. New York: Charles Scribner's Sons, 1883.

Tillett, Ben. *A Brief History of the Dockers' Union*. London: Twentieth Century Press, 1910.

——. "The Dockers' Story." *English Illustrated Magazine* 7 (1889–1890): 97–101.

Biographies and Works about Marx

Barker, Felix. "Department of Amplification." *The New Yorker* 30 (November 27, 1954): 190–199.

Cherniak, Judith. *The Daughter: A Novel Based on the Life of Eleanor Marx*. New York: Harper and Row, 1979.

Feuer, Lewis S. "Marxian Tragedians." *Encounter* 19 (1962): 23–32.

Florence, Ronald. *Marx's Daughters*. New York: Dial Press, 1975.

Hastings, Michael. *Tussy Is Me: A Novel of Fact*. New York: Delacorte Press, 1971.

Hutt, Allen. "Eleanor Marx." *World News* 1 (May 29, 1954): 425–426.

Kapp, Yvonne. *Eleanor Marx*. 2 vols. New York: Pantheon, 1972–1976.

Read, Piers Paul. *Game in Heaven with Tussy Marx*. New York: McGraw-Hill, 1966.

Tsuzuki, Chushichi. "Japanese Archives Relating to British Labour History (2): Eleanor Marx." *Bulletin of the Society for the Study of Labour History*, no. 8 (Spring 1964): 18–22.

——. *The Life of Eleanor Marx (1855–1898): A Socialist Tragedy*. Oxford: Clarendon Press, 1967.

Background and Related Secondary Materials

Allemagne, Henry-René d'. *Les Saint Simoniens, 1827-1837.* Paris: Grund, 1930.

Arnot, R. Page. *William Morris: The Man and the Myth.* New York: Monthly Review Press, 1964.

Avineri, Shlomo. "Marx and Jewish Emancipation." *Journal of the History of Ideas* 25 (1964): 445-450.

Beer, M. *A History of British Socialism.* 2 vols. London: George Allen and Unwin, 1953.

Briggs, Asa, and John Saville, eds. *Essays in Labour History, 1886-1923.* London: Archon, 1971.

Brittain, Vera. *Lady into Woman: A History of Women from Victoria to Elizabeth II.* New York: Macmillan, 1953.

Brockway, Fenner. *Socialism Over Sixty Years.* London: George Allen and Unwin, 1946.

Buchanan-Gould, Vera. *Not Without Honour: The Life and Writings of Olive Schreiner.* London: Hutchinson, 1948.

Clegg, H. A., Alan Fox, and A. F. Thompson. *A History of British Trade Unions Since 1889.* London: Oxford University Press, 1964.

Cole, G. D. H. *Chartist Portraits.* London: Macmillan, 1965.

——. *The Life of Robert Owen.* London: Frank Cass, 1925.

Cole, Margaret. *Makers of the Labour Movement.* London: Longmans, Green, 1948.

——. *Robert Owen of New Lanark.* New York: Oxford University Press, 1953.

Collins, Henry, and Chimen Abramsky. *Karl Marx and the British Labour Movement.* London: Macmillan, 1965.

Eros, John. "The Rise of Organized Freethought in Mid-Victorian England." *Sociological Review* 2, N.S. (1954): 98-120.

Fishman, William J. *East End Jewish Radicals, 1875-1914.* London: Gerald Duckworth, 1975.

Fiss, Joan. "The Theory and Non-Practice of British Socialism." Ph.D. dissertation, New York University, 1968.

Foner, Philip S. *History of the Labor Movement in the United States.* vol. 2: *From the Founding of the American Federation of Labor to the Emergence of American Imperialism.* New York: International, 1955.

——. ed. *When Karl Marx Died: Comments in 1883.* New York: International, 1973.

Frank, Joseph. *The Levellers.* Cambridge, Mass.: Harvard University Press, 1955.

Fulford, Roger. *Votes for Women.* London: Faber and Faber, 1957.

Gartner, Lloyd P. *The Jewish Immigrant in England, 1870-1914.* Detroit: Wayne State University Press, 1960.

——. "Notes on the Statistics of Jewish Immigration to England, 1870-1914." *Jewish Social Studies* 22 (1960): 97-102.

Gibb, Mildred A. *John Lilburne the Leveller.* London: L. Drummond, 1947.

Gould, Frederick J. *Hyndman: Prophet of Socialism.* London: George Allen and Unwin, 1928.

Halévy, Elie. *A History of the English People in the Nineteenth Century.* 6 vols. Translated by E. I. Watkin. New York: Peter Smith, 1949-1952.

Hammond, J. L., and Barbara Hammond. *The Age of the Chartists, 1832-1854.* Hamden, Conn.: Archon, 1962.

Harrison, J. F. C. *Robert Owen and the Owenites in Britain and America.* London: Routledge and Kegan Paul, 1969.

Hobsbawm, E. J. *Labouring Men: Studies in the History of Labor.* London: Weidenfeld and Nicolson, 1964.

———, ed. *Labour's Turning Point 1880-1900.* Cranbury, N.J.: Associated University Presses, 1974.

Hulse, James W. *Revolutionists in London.* Oxford: Clarendon Press, 1970.

Johnson, Oakley C. *Marxism in United States History Before the Russian Revolution, 1876-1917.* New York: Humanities Press, 1974.

Jones, Gareth Stedman. *Outcast London.* London: Oxford University Press, 1971.

Kendall, Walter. *The Revolutionary Movement in Britain, 1900-1921: The Origins of British Communism.* London: Weidenfeld and Nicolson, 1969.

Lipman, V. D. *Social History of the Jews in England 1850-1950.* London: Watts, 1954.

McArthur, Ellen A. "Women Petitioners and the Long Parliament." *English Historical Review* 24 (1909): 698-709.

McGee, John Edwin. *A History of the British Secular Movement.* Girard, Kans.: Haldeman-Julius, 1948.

O'Neill, William L. *The Woman Movement.* London: George Allen and Unwin, 1969.

Pankhurst, Richard K. P. "Fourierism in Britain." *International Review of Social History* 1 (1956): 398-432.

———. "Saint-Simonism in England." *Twentieth Century* 152-153 (1952-1953): 499-512, 47-58.

Payne, Robert, ed. *The Unknown Karl Marx: Documents Concerning Karl Marx.* New York: New York University Press, 1971.

Pease, Edward R. *The History of the Fabian Society.* London: Frank Cass, 1918.

Pelling, Henry. *A Short History of the Labour Party.* London: Macmillan, 1972.

Pierson, Stanley. *Marxism and the Origins of British Socialism.* Ithaca, N.Y.: Cornell University Press, 1973.

"Portrait of a Bibliophile XIV: Karl Marx and Friedrich Engels." *The Book Collector* 18 (1969): 189-198.

Radice, Giles, and Lisanne Radice. *Will Thorne: Constructive Militant.* London: George Allen and Unwin, 1974.

Rover, Constance. *Women's Suffrage and Party Politics in Britain, 1866-1914.* London: Routledge and Kegan Paul, 1967.

Silberner, Edmund. "British Socialism and the Jews." *Historia Judaica* 14 (1952): 27-52.

Stenton, Doris Mary. *The English Woman in History.* London: George Allen and Unwin, 1957.

Strachey, Ray. *"The Cause": A Short History of the Women's Movement in Great Britain.* Port Washington, N.Y.: Kennikat Press, 1969.

Taylor, Barbara. "'The Men Are As Bad As Their Masters . . .': Socialism, Feminism, and Sexual Antagonism in the London Tailoring Trade in the Early 1830s." *Feminist Studies* 5 (1979): 7-40.

Thomas, Keith. "Women and the Civil War Sects." *Past and Present*, no. 13 (1958): 42-62.

Thompson, Dorothy. *The Early Chartists*. Columbia: University of South Carolina Press, 1971.

Thompson, E. P. *William Morris: Romantic to Revolutionary*. London: Lawrence and Wishart, 1955.

Thompson, Paul. "Liberals, Radicals and Labour in London 1880-1900." *Past and Present*, no. 27 (1964): 73-101.

Torr, Dona. *Tom Mann*. London: Lawrence and Wishart, 1936.

Tsuzuki, Chushichi. *H. M. Hyndman and British Socialism*. London: Oxford University Press, 1961.

Uroyeva, Anna. *For All Time and All Men*. Translated by David Fidlon. Moscow: Progress Publishers, 1969.

Walzer, Michael. *The Revolution of the Saints: A Study in the Origins of Radical Politics*. New York: Atheneum, 1974.

Wilkins, M. S. "The Non-Socialist Origins of England's First Important Socialist Organization." *International Review of Social History* 4 (1959): 199-207.

Winsten, Stephen. *Salt and His Circle*. London: Hutchinson, 1951.

ALEXANDRA KOLLONTAI

Published Writings

Kollontai, Alexandra. *The Activity of the Russian People's Commissariat for Social Welfare*. London: People's Russian Information Bureau, 1919.

——. [Elna Malin] "Die Arbeiterbewegung in Finnland und die russische Regierung." *Die Neue Zeit* 22, Bd. I, no. 24 (1903-1904): 749-757.

——. "The Attitude of the Russian Socialists." *New Review* 4 (March 1916): 60-61.

——. *The Autobiography of a Sexually Emancipated Communist Woman*. Translated by Salvator Attanasio. New York: Schocken, 1975.

——. *Communism and the Family*. San Francisco: Richmond Record, 1918.

——. "Do Internationalists Want a Split?" *International Socialist Review* 16 (January 1916): 394-396.

——. "Exclusion des Zimmerwaldiens—Le Nouveau Parti Socialiste." *Demain, Pages et Documents* 2 (May 1917): 46-48.

——. *A Great Love*. Translated by Lily Lore. New York: Vanguard Press, 1929.

——. *International Women's Day*. Translated by Alix Holt. Highland Park, Mich.: Sun Press, 1975.

——. "Les Internationalistes d'Amérique." *Demain, Pages et Documents* 2 (May 1917): 34-39.

——. *La juventud comunista y la moral sexual*. Madrid: J. Pueyo, 1933.

——. *Love and the New Morality.* Translated by Alix Holt. Bristol: Falling Wall Press, 1972.

——. *Love of Worker Bees.* Translated by Cathy Porter. London: Virago, 1977.

——. *Alexandra Kollontai: Marxisme et Révolution Sexuelle.* Edited by Judith Stora-Sandor. Paris: François Maspero, 1973.

——. *The Peasant and Working Woman in Soviet Russia.* Moscow: International Secretariat on Work Amongst Women of the Executive Committee of the Communist International, 1921.

——. *Red Love.* New York: Seven Arts, 1927.

——. *Selected Writings of Alexandra Kollontai.* Edited and translated by Alix Holt. Westport, Conn.: Lawrence Hill, 1977.

——. *Sexual Relations and the Class Struggle.* Translated by Alix Holt. Bristol: Falling Wall Press, 1972.

——. *Women Workers Struggle for Their Rights.* Translated by Celia Britton. Bristol: Falling Wall Press, 1971.

——. *The Workers Opposition in Russia.* Chicago: International Workers of the World, 1921.

——. "Ziel und Wert meines Lebens." In *Führende Frauen Europas*, pp. 258–286. Edited by Elga Kern. Munich: Ernst Reinhardt, 1928.

Public Documents

Browder, Robert Paul, and Alexander F. Kerensky, eds. *The Russian Provisional Government, 1917: Documents.* 3 vols. Stanford, Calif.: Stanford University Press, 1961.

U.S. Congress. Senate. Subcommittee on the Judiciary. *Brewing and Liquor Interests and German and Bolshevik Propaganda.* 3 vols. 66th Cong., 1st sess., 1919.

Newspapers and Journals

American Socialist
Chicago *Tribune*
International Review
Literary Digest
London *Times*
Die Neue Zeit
New York *Call*
New York *Post*
New York *Times*
New Yorker Volkszeitung
Newsweek
Time
Times Literary Supplement

Descriptions of Kollontai by Friends and Contemporaries

Anthony, Katharine. "Alexandra Kollontay: The World's One Woman Ambassador." *North American Review* 230 (1930): 277–282.

Balabanoff, Angelica. *Impressions of Lenin.* Translated by Isotta Cesari. Ann Arbor: University of Michigan Press, 1964.

——. *My Life As a Rebel.* New York: Harper and Bros., 1938; reprint, Bloomington: Indiana University Press, 1973.

Barmine, Alexander. *One Who Survived.* New York: G. P. Putnam's Sons, 1945.

Beatty, Bessie. *The Red Heart of Russia.* New York: Century, 1918.

Body, Marcel. "Alexandra Kollontai." *Preuves*, no. 14 (1952): 12–24.

Bryant, Louise. *Mirrors of Moscow.* New York: Thomas Seltzer, 1923.

——. *Six Red Months in Russia.* New York: George H. Doran, 1918.

Bursch, F. C. "Who Is Madame Kollontai?" *Woman Voter's Bulletin* 6 (May 1926): 5–7.

Duranty, Walter. *I Write as I Please.* New York: Simon and Schuster, 1935.

Fischer, Ruth. *Stalin and German Communism.* Cambridge, Mass.: Harvard University Press, 1948.

Goldman, Emma. *Living My Life.* New York: AMS Press, 1970.

——. *My Disillusionment in Russia.* New York: Thomas Y. Crowell, 1970.

——. *My Further Disillusionment in Russia.* Garden City, N.Y.: Doubleday, Page, 1924.

Harrison, Marguerite E. *Marooned in Moscow.* New York: George H. Doran, 1921.

Landfield, Jerome. "Kollontai and the New Morality." *Weekly Review* 3 (July 28, 1920): 85–86.

Petrov, Vladimir and Evdokia Patrov. *Empire of Fear.* New York: Praeger, 1956.

Reed, John. *Ten Days That Shook the World.* New York: International, 1919.

Sadoul, Jacques. *Notes Sur la Révolution Bolchévique.* Paris: Editions de la Sirène, 1920.

——. *Notes Sur la Révolution Bolchévique: Quarante Lettres de Jacques Sadoul.* Paris: Editions de la Librairie de l'Humanité, 1922.

Serge, Victor. *Memoirs of a Revolutionary, 1901–1941.* Edited and translated by Peter Sedgwick. London: Oxford University Press, 1963.

Sorokin, Pitirim A. *Leaves from a Russian Diary.* Boston: Beacon Press, 1950.

Related Primary Materials

Balabanoff, Angelica. *Die Zimmerwalder Bewegung 1914–1919.* Leipzig: C. L. Hirschfeld, 1928.

Berkman, Alexander. *The Bolshevik Myth.* New York: Boni and Liveright, 1925.

Blackwell, Alice Stone, ed. *The Little Grandmother of the Russian Revolution: Reminiscences and Letters of Catherine Breshkovsky.* Boston: Little, Brown, 1917.

Breshko-Breshkovskaia, Katerina. *Hidden Springs of the Russian Revolution.* Stanford, Calif.: Stanford University Press, 1931.

Figner, Vera. *Memoirs of a Revolutionist*. New York: International, 1927.

Kropotkin, Peter. *Memoirs of a Revolutionist*. Boston: Houghton Mifflin, 1899.

Lawton, Lancelot. *The Russian Revolution*. London: Macmillan, 1927.

Price, M. Philips. *My Reminiscences of the Russian Revolution*. London: George Allen and Unwin, 1921.

Ransome, Arthur. *Russia in 1919*. New York: B. W. Huebsch, 1919.

Reichenbach, Bernhard. "Moscow 1921: Meetings in the Kremlin." *Survey*, no. 53 (1964): 16–22.

Rosmer, Alfred. *Lenin's Moscow*. Translated by Ian H. Birchall. London: Pluto Press, 1971.

Ross, Edward A. *Russia in Upheaval*. New York: Century, 1919.

——. *The Russian Soviet Republic*. New York: Century, 1923.

Sack, A. J. *The Birth of the Russian Democracy*. New York: Russian Information Bureau, 1918.

Smith, Jessica. *Woman in Soviet Russia*. New York: Vanguard Press, 1928.

Stepniak. [Sergei Kravchinsky] *Underground Russia*. New York: Charles Scribner's Sons, 1883.

Sukhanov, N. N. *The Russian Revolution: A Personal Record*. Translated by Joel Carmichael. London: Oxford University Press, 1955.

Tikhomirov, L. *Russia, Political and Social*. 2 vols. Translated by Edward Aveling. London: Swan Sonnenschein, Lowrey, 1888.

Trotsky, Leon. *Problems of Life*. Translated by Z. Vengerova. London: Methuen, 1924.

——. *The Revolution Betrayed*. Translated by Max Eastman. Garden City, N.Y.: Doubleday, Doran, 1937.

——. *Stalin: An Appraisal of the Man and His Influence*. Translated by Charles Malamuth. New York: Harper and Bros., 1941.

Tyrkova-Williams, Ariadna. *From Liberty to Brest-Litovsk: The First Year of the Russian Revolution*. London: Macmillan, 1919.

Williams, Albert Rhys. *Journey Into Revolution: Petrograd, 1917–1918*. Edited by Lucita Williams. Chicago: Quadrangle, 1969.

——. *Lenin: The Man and His Work*. New York: Scott and Seltzer, 1919.

——. *Through the Russian Revolution*. New York: Boni and Liveright, 1921.

Biographies and Works about Kollontai

Anderson, Thornton. *Masters of Russian Marxism*. New York: Appleton-Century-Crofts, 1963.

Bailes, Kendall E. "Alexandra Kollontai et la Nouvelle Morale." *Cahiers du Monde Russe et Soviétique* 6 (1965): 471–496.

Clements, Barbara Evans. *Bolshevik Feminist: The Life of Aleksandra Kollontai*. Bloomington: Indiana University Press, 1979.

——. "Emancipation Through Communism: The Ideology of A. M. Kollontai." *Slavic Review* 32 (1973): 323–338.

——. "Kollontai's Contribution to the Workers' Opposition." *Russian History* 2 (1975): 191–206.

——. "The Revolution and the Revolutionary: Alexandra Kollontai, 1917–1923." Ph.D. dissertation, Duke University, 1971.

Farnsworth, Beatrice Brodsky. *Aleksandra Kollontai: Socialism, Feminism, and the Bolshevik Revolution.* Stanford, Calif.: Stanford University Press, 1980.

——. "Bolshevism, the Woman Question, and Aleksandra Kollontai." *American Historical Review* 81 (1976): 292–316.

Hauge, Kaare. "Alexandra Mikhailovna Kollontai: The Scandinavian Period, 1922–1945." Ph.D. dissertation, University of Minnesota, 1971.

Lenczyc, Henryk. "Alexandra Kollontai: Essai bibliographique." *Cahiers du Monde Russe et Soviétique* 14 (1973): 205–241.

Palencia, Isabel de. *Alexandra Kollontay: Ambassadress from Russia.* New York: Longmans, Green, 1947.

Pertzoff, Margaret Henderson. "'Lady in Red': A Study of the Early Career of Alexandra Mikhailovna Kollontai." Ph.D. dissertation, University of Virginia, 1968.

Porter, Cathy. *Alexandra Kollontai: The Lonely Struggle of the Woman Who Defied Lenin.* New York: Dial Press, 1980.

Stites, Richard. "Kollontai, Inessa, and Krupskaia." *Canadian-American Slavic Studies* 9 (1975): 84–92.

Background and Related Secondary Materials

Alliluyeva, Svetlana. *Only One Year.* Translated by Paul Chavchavadze. New York: Harper and Row, 1969.

Atkinson, Dorothy, Alexander Dallin, and Gail Warshofsky Lapidus, eds. *Women in Russia.* Stanford, Calif.: Stanford University Press, 1977.

Avakumovic, Ivan. "A Statistical Approach to the Revolutionary Movement in Russia, 1878–1887." *American Slavic and East European Review* 18 (1959): 182–186.

Avrich, Paul H. "The Bolshevik Revolution and Workers' Control in Russian Industry." *Slavic Review* 22 (1963): 47–63.

——. *The Russian Anarchists.* Princeton, N.J.: Princeton University Press, 1967.

——. "Russian Factory Committees in 1917." *Jahrbücher für Geschichte Osteuropas* 11 (1963): 161–182.

Bandera, V. N. "The NEP as an Economic System." *Journal of Political Economy* 71 (1963): 265–279.

Baron, Samuel H. "The First Decade of Russian Marxism." *American Slavic and East European Review* 14 (1955): 315–330.

——. "Plekhanov and the Origins of Russian Marxism." *Russian Review* 13 (1954): 38–51.

Bell, Daniel. "One Road From Marx: On the Vision of Socialism, and the Fate of Workers' Control, in Socialist Thought." *World Politics* 11 (1959): 491–512.

Bobroff, Anne. "The Bolsheviks and Working Women, 1905–1920." *Soviet Studies* 26 (1974): 540–567.

Broido, Vera. *Apostles into Terrorists: Women and the Revolutionary Movement in the Russia of Alexander II.* New York: Viking Press, 1977.

Cohen, Stephen F. *Bukharin and the Bolshevik Revolution*. New York: Alfred A. Knopf, 1973.

Curtiss, John Shelton. *The Russian Church and the Soviet State, 1917-1950*. Boston: Little, Brown, 1953.

Daniels, Robert V. "The Kronstadt Revolt of 1921: A Study in the Dynamics of Revolution." *American Slavic and East European Review* 10 (1951): 241-254.

——. *Red October: The Bolshevik Revolution of 1917*. New York: Charles Scribner's Sons, 1967.

Draper, Theodore. *The Roots of American Communism*. New York: Viking Press, 1957.

Edmonson, Linda. "Russian Feminists and the First All-Russian Congress of Women." *Russian History* 3, pt. 2 (1976): 123-149.

Engel, Barbara Alpern. "From Feminism to Populism: A Study of Changing Attitudes of the Women of the Russian Intelligentsia, 1855-1881." Ph.D. dissertation, Columbia University, 1974.

——. "Women As Revolutionaries: The Case of the Russian Populists." In *Becoming Visible: Women in European History*, pp. 346-369. Edited by Renate Bridenthal and Claudia Koonz. Boston: Houghton Mifflin, 1977.

——, and Clifford N. Rosenthal, eds. and trans. *Five Sisters: Women Against the Tsar*. New York: Schocken, 1977.

Evans, Richard J. *The Feminists*. London: Croom Helm, 1977.

Fedotoff-White, Dimitri Daniel. *The Growth of the Red Army*. Princeton, N.J.: Princeton University Press, 1944.

Ferro, Marc. *The Russian Revolution of February 1917*. Translated by J. L. Richards. Englewood Cliffs, N.J.: Prentice-Hall, 1972.

Fischer, George. *Russian Liberalism: From Gentry to Intelligentsia*. Cambridge, Mass.: Harvard University Press, 1958.

Frank, Victor. "The Russian Radical Tradition." *Soviet Survey*, no. 29 (1959): 97-102.

Futrell, Michael. *Northern Underground: Episodes of Russian Revolutionary Transport and Communications Through Scandinavia and Finland, 1863-1917*. London: Faber and Faber, 1963.

Gasiorowska, Xenia. *Women in Soviet Fiction, 1917-1964*. Madison: University of Wisconsin Press, 1968.

Geiger, H. Kent. *The Family in Soviet Russia*. Cambridge, Mass.: Harvard University Press, 1968.

Gelb, Barbara. *So Short a Time: A Biography of John Reed and Louise Bryant*. New York: W. W. Norton, 1973.

Halle, Fannina W. *Woman in Soviet Russia*. New York: Viking Press, 1935.

——. *Women in the Soviet East*. New York: E. P. Dutton, 1938.

Harcave, Sidney S. *First Blood: The Russian Revolution of 1905*. New York: Macmillan, 1964.

Hayden, Carol Eubanks. "The Zhenotdel and the Bolshevik Party." *Russian History* 3, pt. 2 (1976): 150-173.

Hindus, Maurice. *Humanity Uprooted*. New York: Jonathan Cape and Harrison Smith, 1929.

Jakobson, Max. *The Diplomacy of the Winter War.* Cambridge, Mass.: Harvard University Press, 1961.

Katkov, George. "The Kronstadt Rising." *Soviet Affairs,* no. 2 (1959): 9-74.

Keep, J. L. H. *The Rise of Social Democracy in Russia.* Oxford: Clarendon Press, 1963.

Knight, Amy. "The Fritschi: A Study of Female Radicals in the Russian Populist Movement." *Canadian-American Slavic Studies* 9 (1975): 1-17.

Krosby, H. Peter. *Finland, Germany, and the Soviet Union, 1940-1941.* Madison: University of Wisconsin Press, 1968.

Lemons, J. Stanley. *The Woman Citizen: Social Feminism in the 1920s.* Urbana: University of Illinois Press, 1973.

Lowenthal, Richard. "Unreason and Revolution." *Encounter* 33 (1969): 22-34.

Lundin, C. Leonard. *Finland in the Second World War.* Bloomington: Indiana University Press, 1957.

McNeal, Robert H. *Bride of the Revolution: Krupskaya and Lenin.* Ann Arbor: University of Michigan Press, 1972.

——. "Lenin and 'Lise de K . . . ': A Fabrication." *Slavic Review* 28 (1969): 471-474.

——. "Women in the Russian Radical Movement." *Journal of Social History* 5 (1971-1972): 143-163.

Madison, Bernice. "Russia's Illegitimate Children Before and After the Revolution." *Slavic Review* 22 (1963): 82-95.

Malia, Martin. *Alexander Herzen and the Birth of Russian Socialism.* New York: Grosset and Dunlap, 1965.

Mandel, William M. *Soviet Women.* Garden City, N.J.: Anchor Press, 1975.

Massell, Gregory J. *The Surrogate Proletariat: Moslem Women and Revolutionary Strategies in Soviet Central Asia, 1919-1929.* Princeton, N.J.: Princeton University Press, 1974.

Mawdsley, Evan. *The Russian Revolution and the Baltic Fleet.* New York: Barnes and Noble, 1978.

Mehlinger, Howard D., and J. M. Thompson. *Count Witte and the Tsarist Government in the 1905 Revolution.* Bloomington: Indiana University Press, 1972.

Mosse, W. E. "Makers of the Soviet Union." *Slavonic and East European Review* 46 (1968): 141-154.

Pope, Barbara Corrado. "Angels in the Devil's Workshop: Leisured and Charitable Women in 19th Century England and France." In *Becoming Visible: Women in European History,* pp. 296-324. Edited by Renate Bridenthal and Claudia Koonz. Boston: Houghton Mifflin, 1977.

Porter, Cathy. *Fathers and Daughters: Russian Women in Revolution.* London: Virago, 1976.

Rappoport, A. S. *Home Life in Russia.* New York: Macmillan, 1913.

Rauch, Georg von. *A History of Soviet Russia.* Translated by Peter and Annette Jacobsohn. New York: Praeger, 1962.

Reich, Wilhelm. *The Sexual Revolution.* Translated by Thérèse Pol. New York: Farrar, Straus, and Giroux, 1974.

Riasanovsky, Nicholas V. "Fourierism in Russia: An Estimate of the Petraševcy." *American Slavic and East European Review* 12 (1953): 289-302.

Rosenthal, Bernice Glatzer. "Love on the Tractor: Women in the Russian Revolution and After." In *Becoming Visible: Women in European History*, pp. 370–399. Edited by Renate Bridenthal and Claudia Koonz. Boston: Houghton Mifflin, 1977.

Sablinsky, Walter. *The Road to Bloody Sunday*. Princeton, N.J.: Princeton University Press, 1976.

Sandomirsky, Vera. "Sex in the Soviet Union." *Russian Review* 10 (1951): 199–209.

Satina, Sophie. *Education of Women in Pre-Revolutionary Russia*. Translated by Alexandra F. Poustchine. New York: n.p., 1966.

Saul, Norman E. *Sailors in Revolt*. Lawrence: Regents Press of Kansas, 1978.

Schlesinger, Rudolf, ed. *The Family in the USSR*. London: Routledge and Kegan Paul, 1949.

Schwarz, Solomon M. *The Russian Revolution of 1905*. Translated by Gertrude Vakar. Chicago: University of Chicago Press, 1967.

Selivanova, Nina N. *Russia's Women*. New York: E. P. Dutton, 1923.

Sourine, Georges. *Le fouriérisme en Russie: contribution à l'historie du socialisme russe*. Paris: Dupont, 1936.

Stavrakis, Bette. "Women and the Communist Party in the Soviet Union, 1918–1935." Ph.D. dissertation, Case Western Reserve University, 1961.

Stites, Richard. "M. L. Mikhailov and the Emergence of the Woman Question in Russia." *Canadian Slavic Studies* 3 (1969): 178–199.

——. "Wives, Sisters, Daughters, and Workers: A Review Article." *Russian History* 3, pt. 2 (1976): 237–244.

——. *The Women's Liberation Movement in Russia: Feminism, Nihilism, and Bolshevism, 1860–1930*. Princeton, N.J.: Princeton University Press, 1978.

——. "Women's Liberation Movements in Russia, 1900–1930." *Canadian-American Slavic Studies* 7 (1973): 460–474.

——. "Zhenotdel: Bolshevism and Russian Women, 1917–1930." *Russian History* 3, pt. 2 (1976): 174–193.

Stock, Phyllis. *Better than Rubies: A History of Women's Education*. New York: G. P. Putnam's Sons, 1978.

Strong, Anna Louise. *I Change Worlds*. New York: Henry Holt, 1935.

Venturi, Franco. *Roots of Revolution*. Translated by Francis Haskell. New York: Alfred A. Knopf, 1960.

Von Laue, Theodore H. *Why Lenin? Why Stalin? A Reappraisal of the Russian Revolution, 1900–1930*. Philadelphia: J. B. Lippincott, 1964.

Wheeler-Bennett, John W. *The Forgotten Peace: Brest-Litovsk, March 1918*. New York: William Morrow, 1939.

Wildman, Allan K. "The Russian Intelligentsia of the 1890s." *American Slavic and East European Review* 19 (1960): 157–179.

Winter, Ella. *Red Virtue: Human Relationships in the New Russia*. New York: Harcourt, Brace, 1933.

Wolfe, Bertram D. "Krupskaya Purges the People's Libraries." *Survey*, no. 72 (1969): 141–155.

——. "Lenin and Inessa Armand." *Slavic Review* 22 (1963): 96–114.

Yarmolinsky, Avrahm. *Road to Revolution: A Century of Russian Radicalism*. New York: Collier, 1962.

ROSA LUXEMBURG

Published Writings

Luxemburg, Rosa. *The Accumulation of Capital.* Translated by Agnes Schwarzschild. New Haven, Conn.: Yale University Press, 1951.

——. "The Accumulation of Capital: An Anti-Critique." In *Imperialism and the Accumulation of Capital*, pp. 45–150. Edited by Kenneth J. Tarbuck. London: Penguin Press, 1972.

——. *Ausgewählte Reden und Schriften.* 2 vols. Berlin: Dietz, 1951.

——. *Briefe an Freunde.* Edited by Benedikt Kautsky. Hamburg: Europäische Verlagsanstalt, 1950.

——. *Comrade and Lover: Rosa Luxemburg's Letters to Leo Jogiches.* Edited and translated by Elzbieta Ettinger. Cambridge, Mass.: MIT Press, 1979.

——. *The Crisis in German Social Democracy.* New York: Howard Fertig, 1969.

——. "Démocratie industrielle et Démocratie politique." *Le Mouvement socialiste*, no. 11 (June 15, 1899): 641–656.

——. "Einige Briefe Rosa Luxemburgs." Edited by Werner Blumenberg. *International Review of Social History* 8 (1963): 94–108.

——. "Einige Briefe Rosa Luxemburgs und Andere Dokumente." Edited by Werner Blumenberg. *Bulletin of the International Institute for Social History* 8 (1952): 9–39.

——. *Gesammelte Werke.* 5 vols. Berlin: Dietz, 1970–1975.

——. *The Industrial Development of Poland.* Translated by Tessa DeCarlo. New York: Campaigner, 1977.

——. *J'Etais, Je Suis, Je Serai! Correspondance, 1914–1919.* Edited by Georges Haupt. Paris: François Maspero, 1977.

——. *Letters From Prison.* Translated by Eden and Cedar Paul. London: Socialist Book Centre, 1946.

——. "Letters From Prison." *Partisan Review* 5 (1938): 3–23.

——. "Letters From Prison." *Partisan Review* 10 (1943): 362–371.

——. *The Letters of Rosa Luxemburg.* Edited by Stephen Eric Bronner. Boulder, Colo.: Westview Press, 1978.

——. *Letters to Karl and Luise Kautsky from 1896 to 1918.* Edited by Luise Kautsky. Translated by Louis P. Lochner. New York: Gordon Press, 1975.

——. *Lettres à Léon Jogichès.* 2 vols. Edited by Felix Tych and Victor Fay. Paris: Denoël Gonthier, 1971.

——. *Listy do Leona Jogichesa-Tyszki.* 3 vols. Edited by Feliks Tych. Warsaw: Ksiazka i Wiedza, 1968–1971.

——. *Marxisme Contre Dictature.* Paris: Spartacus Cahiers Mensuels, 1946.

——. "Nach dem ersten Akt." *Die Neue Zeit* 23, Bd. I, no. 19 (February 1, 1905): 610–614.

——. *The National Question: Selected Writings.* Edited by Horace B. Davis. New York: Monthly Review Press, 1976.

——. "Neue Strömungen in der polnischen Sozialistischen Bewegung in Deutschland und Osterreich." *Die Neue Zeit* 14, Bd. II, nos. 32–33 (April 19, May 6, 1896): 176–181, 206–216.

——. *On the Spartacus Program*. Translated by Eden and Cedar Paul. Colombo, Ceylon: Young Socialist Publications, 1966.

——. "Organisationfragen der russischen Sozialdemokraten." *Die Neue Zeit* 22, Bd. II, nos. 42–43 (July 13, 20, 1904): 484–492, 529–535.

——. "Der Parteitag und der hamburger Gewerksschaftsstreit." *Die Neue Zeit* 19, Bd. II, no. 49 (September 4, 1901): 705–711.

——. "Peace Utopias." *Labour Monthly* 8 (1926): 421–428.

——. "Quatre Lettres à Louise Kautsky." Edited by Leon Bozalgetti. *Europe* 7 (1925): 257–273.

——. *Reform or Revolution*. New York: Three Arrows Press, 1937.

——. "Die Revolution in Russland." *Die Neue Zeit* 23, Bd. I, no. 1 (January 25, 1905): 572–577.

——. *Rosa Luxemburg im Kampf Gegen den deutschen Militarismus*. Berlin: Dietz, 1960.

——. *Rosa Luxemburg: Selections From Her Works*. Edited by Virgil J. Vogel. Chicago: Young People's Socialist League, 1946.

——. *Rosa Luxemburg Speaks*. Edited by Mary-Alice Waters. New York: Pathfinder Press, 1970.

——. "Rosa Luxemburg's Unpublished Prison Letters 1916-1918." Edited by Ralph H. Lutz. *Journal of Central European Affairs* 23 (1963): 303-312.

——. *The Russian Revolution* and *Leninism or Marxism?* Ann Arbor: University of Michigan Press, 1961.

——. "The Second and Third Volumes of *Capital*." In Franz Mehring, *Karl Marx: The Story of His Life*. Translated by Edward Fitzgerald. New York: Covici, Friede, 1935.

——. *Selected Political Writings*. Edited by Robert Looker. Translated by William D. Graf. London: Jonathan Cape, 1972.

——. *Selected Political Writings of Rosa Luxemburg*. Edited by Dick Howard. New York: Monthly Review Press, 1971.

——. *Socialism and the Churches*. Translated by Juan Punto. Colombo, Ceylon: Young Socialist Publications, 1964.

——. *Le Socialisme en France*. Edited by Daniel Guérin. Paris: Editions Pierre Belfond, 1971.

——. "Der Sozial-patriotismus in Polen." *Die Neue Zeit* 14, Bd. II, no. 41 (July 1, 1896): 459–470.

——. "Die Theorie und die Praxis." *Die Neue Zeit* 28, Bd. II, nos. 43-44 (1910): 564-578, 626-642.

——. "Von Stufe zu Stufe: Zur Geschichte der bürgerlichen Klassen Polen." *Die Neue Zeit* 14, Bd. I, no. 6 (October 27, 1897): 165-175.

——. *What Is Economics?* Translated by T. Edwards. New York: Pioneer, 1954.

Public Documents

Illustrierte Geschichte der Deutschen Revolution. Berlin: Internationaler Arbeiter-Verlag, 1929.

Zeman, Z. A. B., ed. *Germany and the Revolution in Russia, 1915–1918. Documents from the Archives of the German Foreign Ministry.* London: Oxford University Press, 1958.

Newspapers and Journals

The Labour Leader
London *Times*
Le Mouvement socialiste
Die Neue Zeit
New York *Daily Tribune*
New York *Times*
New York *World*
Die Rote Fahne

Descriptions of Luxemburg by Friends and Contemporaries

Balabanoff, Angelica. *My Life As a Rebel.* Bloomington: Indiana University Press, 1973.
Berger, Maurice. *Germany After the Armistice.* Translated by William L. McPherson. New York: G. P. Putnam's Sons, 1920.
Bernstein, Eduard. *Die deutsche Revolution, ihr Ursprung, ihr Verlauf, und ihr Werk.* Berlin-Fichtenau: Verlag für Gesellschaft und Erziehung, 1921.
Eberlein, Hugo. "The Foundation of the Comintern and the Spartakusbund." *The Communist International* 6 (1929): 436–442.
Fischer, Ruth. *Stalin and German Communism.* Cambridge, Mass.: Harvard University Press, 1948.
Kautsky, Karl. *Rosa Luxemburg, Karl Liebknecht, Leo Jogiches: Ihre Bedeutung für die Sozialdemokratie.* Berlin: Freiheit, 1921.
Kautsky, Luise. *Rosa Luxemburg: ein Gedenkbuch.* Berlin: E. Laubsche, 1929.
Kollontai, Alexandra. *Selected Writings of Alexandra Kollontai.* Edited by Alix Holt. Westport, Conn.: Lawrence Hill, 1977.
Meiner, Felix, ed. *Die Volkswirtschaftslehre der Gegenwart in Selbstdarstellungen.* 2 vols. Leipzig: F. Meiner, 1924–1929.
Radek, Karl. *Rosa Luxemburg, Karl Liebknecht, Leo Jogiches.* Hamburg: Verlag der Kommunistischen internationale, 1921.
Roland-Holst, Henriette. *Rosa Luxemburg: Ihr Leben und Wirken.* Zurich: Jean Christophe, 1937.

Related Primary Materials

Adler, Victor. *Briefwechsel mit August Bebel und Karl Kautsky.* Edited by Friedrich Adler. Vienna: Wiener Volksbuchhandlung, 1954.

Anthony, Katharine. *Feminism in Germany and Scandinavia.* New York: Henry Holt, 1915.

Bebel, August. *Aus meinem Leben.* 3 vols. Stuttgart: Dietz, 1911.

——. *Unsere Ziele.* Leipzig: F. Thiele, 1870.

Bernstein, Eduard. "Probleme des Sozialismus." *Die Neue Zeit* 15, Bd. I (1896-1897): 164-171, 204-213, 303-311.

——. "Das realistische und ideologische Moment im Sozialismus." *Die Neue Zeit* 16, Bd. II, nos. 34, 39 (May 18, June 22, 1898): 225-232, 388-395.

——. "Die Sozialpolitische Bedeutung von Raum und Zahl." *Die Neue Zeit* 15, Bd. II, no. 30 (April 21, 1897): 100-107.

——. *Zur Geschichte und Theorie des Sozialismus.* Berlin: Edelheim, 1901.

Bevan, Edwyn. *German Social Democracy During the War.* New York: E. P. Dutton, 1919.

Blücher, Princess Evelyn. *An English Wife in Berlin.* New York: E. P. Dutton, 1920.

Blumenberg, Werner, ed. *August Bebels Briefwechsel mit Friedrich Engels.* The Hague: Mouton, 1965.

Braun, Lily. *Memoiren einer Sozialistin.* 2 vols. Munich: Albert Langen, 1922.

Franz, Rudolf, ed. "Aus Briefen Konrad Haenischs." *Archiv für die Geschichte des Sozialismus und der Arbeiterbewegung* 14 (1929): 444-484.

Kautsky, Karl. "Finis Poloniae?" *Die Neue Zeit* 14, Bd. II, nos. 42-43 (July 8, 15, 1896): 484-491, 513-522.

——. "Julie Bebel." *Die Neue Zeit* 29, Bd. I, no. 9 (December 2, 1910): 276-278.

——. "Zwischen Baden und Luxemburg." *Die Neue Zeit* 18, Bd. II, no. 45 (August 5, 1910): 652-667.

Kautsky, Karl, Jr. *August Bebels Briefwechsel mit Karl Kautsky.* Assen: Van Gorcum, 1971.

Maximilian, Prince of Baden. *The Memoirs of Prince Max of Baden.* Translated by W. M. Calder and C. W. H. Sutton. 2 vols. New York: Charles Scribner's Sons, 1928.

Mehring, Franz. "Historisch-materialistische Literatur." *Die Neue Zeit* 25, Bd. II, no. 41 (July 17, 1907): 502-509.

Michels, Robert. "Die deutsche Sozialdemokratie: Parteimitgliedschaft und soziale Zusammensetzung." *Archiv für Sozialwissenschaft und Sozialpolitik* 23 (1906): 471-556.

Mlochowski, Apollo. *Les Polonais et la Commune de Paris.* Paris: Librairie générale, 1871.

Nettl, J. P., ed. "Ein Unveroffentlichter Artikel Lenins vom September 1912." *International Review of Social History* 9 (1964): 470-482.

Noske, Gustav. *Erlebtes aus Aufstieg und Niedergang einer Demokratie.* Offenbach-am-Main: Bollwerk, 1947.

Pilsudski, Joseph. *The Memoirs of a Polish Revolutionary and Soldier.* Translated and edited by D. R. Gillie. London: Faber and Faber, 1931.

Popp, Adelheid. *The Autobiography of a Working Woman.* Translated by E. C. Harvey. London: T. Fisher Unwin, 1912.

Russell, Alys. "Social Democracy and the Woman Question in Germany." In Bertrand Russell, *German Social Democracy*, pp. 173-195. London: Longmans, Green, 1896.

Scheidemann, Philip. *Memoirs of a Social Democrat.* 2 vols. Translated by J. E. Michell. London: Hodder and Stroughton, 1929.

——. *Der Zusammenbruch.* Berlin: Verlag für sozialwissenschaft, 1921.

Trotsky, Leon. "Problems of Civil War." *International Socialist Review* 31 (1970): 3-23.

Zetkin, Clara. *Zur Geschichte der proletarischen Frauenbewegung Deutschlands.* Berlin: Dietz, 1958.

Biographies and Works about Luxemburg

Ascherson, Neal. "Love and Revolution." *New York Review of Books* 27 (March 6, 1980): 14-16.

Badia, Gilbert. *Rosa Luxemburg: Journaliste, Polémiste, Révolutionnaire.* Paris: Editions Sociales, 1975.

Basso, Lelio. "Rosa Luxemburg, the Dialectical Method." *International Socialist Journal* 3 (1966): 504-541.

——. *Rosa Luxemburg: A Reappraisal.* Translated by Douglas Parmée. New York: Praeger, 1975.

Carsten, F. L. "Rosa Luxemburg: Freedom and Revolution." *Soviet Survey*, no. 33 (1960): 93-99.

Cliff, Tony. "Rosa Luxemburg." *International Socialism*, nos. 2-3 (1959).

Desanti, Dominique. *Visages de Femmes.* Paris: Editions Sociales, 1955.

Dunayevskaya, Raya. *State Capitalism and Marx's Humanism.* Detroit: News and Letters, 1967.

Florence, Ronald. *Marx's Daughters.* New York: Dial Press, 1975.

Fouchère, Berthe. *La vie héroïque de Rosa Luxemburg.* Paris: Spartacus Cahiers Mensuels, 1948.

Frolich, Paul. *Rosa Luxemburg, Her Life and Work.* Translated by Edward Fitzgerald. New York: Howard Fertig, 1969.

——. *Rosa Luxemburg: Ideas in Action.* Translated by Joanna Hoornweg. London: Pluto Press, 1972.

Geras, Norman. *The Legacy of Rosa Luxemburg.* London: NLB, 1976.

Goldsmith, Margaret Leland. *Seven Women Against the World.* London: Methuen, 1935.

Guérin, Daniel. *Rosa Luxemburg et la spontanéité révolutionnaire.* Paris: Flammarion, 1971.

Held, Walter. "Once Again—Lenin and Luxemburg." *Fourth International* 1 (1940): 47-52.

Lee, George. "Rosa Luxemburg and the Impact of Imperialism." *Economic Journal* 81 (1971): 847-862.

McLean, Edward Bruce. "Rosa Luxemburg's Revolutionary Socialism: A Study in Marxian Radicalism." Ph.D. dissertation, Indiana University, 1964.

Nettl, J. P. *Rosa Luxemburg.* 2 vols. London: Oxford University Press, 1966.

——. "Rosa Luxemburg: Sketch for a Portrait." *Survey*, no. 53 (1964): 48–58.

Nicholls, A. J. "Rosa Luxemburg and Lenin." *History* 51, N.S. (1966): 331–335.

Oelssner, Fred. *Rosa Luxemburg: Eine kritische biographische Skizze*. East Berlin: Dietz, 1951.

Richards, Michael Dulany. "Reform or Revolution: Rosa Luxemburg and the Marxist Movement, 1893–1919." Ph.D. dissertation, Duke University, 1969.

Rothwell, Charles Easton. "Rosa Luxemburg and the German Social Democratic Party." Ph.D. dissertation, Stanford University, 1938.

Schurer, H. "Some Reflections on Rosa Luxemburg and the Bolshevik Revolution." *Slavonic and East European Review* 40 (1962): 356–372.

Shachtman, Max. "Lenin and Rosa Luxemburg." *New International* 2 (1935): 60–64.

——. *Lenin, Liebknecht, Luxemburg*. Chicago: Young Workers League, 1925.

Sweezy, Paul M. "Rosa Luxemburg's *The Accumulation of Capital*." *Science and Society* 31 (1967): 474–485.

Vollrath, Ernst. "Rosa Luxemburg's Theory of Revolution." *Social Research* 40 (1973): 83–109.

Background and Related Secondary Materials

Angress, Werner T. *Stillborn Revolution: The Communist Bid for Power in Germany, 1921–1923*. Princeton, N.J.: Princeton University Press, 1963.

Arendt, Hannah. *Men in Dark Times*. New York: Harcourt, Brace, and World, 1968.

Armstrong, Sinclair W. "The Internationalism of the Early Social Democrats of Germany." *American Historical Review* 47 (1942): 245–258.

Badia, Gilbert. *Le Spartakisme*. Paris: L'Arche, 1967.

——. *Les Spartakistes: 1918: l'Allemagne en révolution*. Paris: René Julliard, 1966.

Barraclough, G. *The Origins of Modern Germany*. New York: Capricorn, 1963.

Bassler, Gerhard P. "The Communist Movement in the German Revolution, 1918–1919: A Problem of Historical Typology?" *Central European History* 6 (1973): 233–277.

Bell, Daniel. "The Rediscovery of Alienation: Some Notes Along the Quest for the Historical Marx." *Journal of Philosophy* 56 (1959): 933–952.

Berlau, Abraham Joseph. *The German Social Democratic Party, 1914–1921*. New York: Columbia University Press, 1949.

Blit, Lucjan. *The Origins of Polish Socialism: The History and Ideas of the First Polish Socialist Party 1878–1886*. London: Cambridge University Press, 1971.

Bloesch, Hans. *Das Junge Deutschland in seinen Beziehungen zu Frankreich*. Bern: Buchler, 1903.

Butler, E. M. *The Saint-Simonian Religion in Germany*. New York: Howard Fertig, 1968.

Clark, R. T. *The Fall of the German Republic*. New York: Russell and Russell, 1964.

Coper, Rudolf. *Failure of a Revolution: Germany in 1918–1919*. Cambridge: Cambridge University Press, 1955.

Craig, Gordon A. *Germany, 1866-1945.* New York: Oxford University Press, 1978.

Deutscher, Isaac. *The Non-Jewish Jew and Other Essays.* London: Oxford University Press, 1968.

Dziewanowski, M. K. *The Communist Party of Poland.* Cambridge, Mass.: Harvard University Press, 1959.

——. "The Polish Revolutionary Movement and Russia, 1904-1907." *Harvard Slavic Studies* 4 (1957): 375-394.

——. "The Revolution of 1904-1905 and the Marxist Movement of Poland." *Journal of Central European Affairs* 12 (1952): 259-275.

——. "Social Democrats versus 'Social Patriots': The Origins of the Split of the Marxist Movement in Poland." *American Slavic and East European Review* 10 (1951): 14-25.

Epstein, Klaus. "Three American Studies of German Socialism." *World Politics* 11 (1959): 629-651.

Evans, Richard J. *The Feminist Movement in Germany, 1894-1933.* Beverly Hills, Calif.: Sage Publications, 1976.

——. *The Feminists.* London: Croom Helm, 1977.

Fishman, William J. *Jewish Radicals: from Czarist Stetl to London Ghetto.* New York: Pantheon, 1974.

Freund, Gerald. *Unholy Alliance: Russian German Relations from the Treaty of Brest-Litovsk to the Treaty of Berlin.* London: Chatto and Windus, 1957.

Friedlander, Henry Egon. "Conflict of Revolutionary Authority: Provisional Government vs. Berlin Soviet, Nov.-Dec. 1918." *International Review of Social History* 7 (1962): 163-176.

Gay, Peter. *The Dilemma of Democratic Socialism: Eduard Bernstein's Challenge to Marx.* New York: Collier, 1970.

Gooch, G. P. *Germany and the French Revolution.* New York: Russell and Russell, 1966.

Gosset, Hélène. "Les Polonais dans la Commune de Paris." *Europe* 29 (1951): 147-156.

Hackett, Amy. "Feminism and Liberalism in Wilhelmine Germany, 1890-1918." In *Liberating Women's History*, pp. 127-136. Edited by Berenice A. Carroll. Urbana: University of Illinois Press, 1976.

——. "The German Women's Movement and Suffrage, 1890-1914: A Study of National Feminism." In *Modern European Social History*, pp. 354-386. Edited by Robert J. Bezucha. Lexington, Mass.: D. C. Heath, 1972.

Haffner, Sebastian. *Failure of a Revolution: Germany 1918-1919.* Translated by Georg Rapp. New York: Library Press, 1972.

Halperin, S. William. *Germany Tried Democracy.* Hamden, Conn.: Archon, 1963.

Hanna, Gertrud. "Women in the German Trade Union Movement." *International Labor Review* 8 (1923): 21-37.

Hayes, Carlton J. "German Socialism Reconsidered." *American Historical Review* 23 (1917-1918): 62-101.

Held, Walter. "The German Left and Bolshevism." *The New International* 5 (1939): 46-48.

Honeycutt, Karen. "Clara Zetkin: A Left-Wing Socialist and Feminist in Wilhelmian Germany." Ph.D. dissertation, Columbia University, 1975.

Hostetter, Richard. "The SPD and the General Strike as an Anti-War Weapon, 1905-1914." *The Historian* 13 (1950-1951): 27-51.

Kieniewicz, Stefan. *The Emancipation of the Polish Peasantry*. Chicago: University of Chicago Press, 1969.

Labedz, Leopold, ed. *Revisionism: Essays on the History of Marxist Ideas*. New York: Praeger, 1962.

Landes, Ruth, and Mark Zborowski. "Hypotheses Concerning the Eastern European Jewish Family." *Psychiatry* 13 (1950): 447-464.

Lewin, Kurt. "Self-Hatred Among Jews." *Contemporary Jewish Record* 4 (1941): 219-232.

Lion, Hilde. *Zur Sociologie der Frauenbewegung*. Berlin: Herbig, 1926.

Lowenthal, Richard. "The Bolshevization of the Spartacus League." In *International Communism*, pp. 23-71. Edited by David Footman. London: Chatto and Windus, 1960.

Lutz, Ralph Haswell. *The German Revolution, 1918-1919*. Stanford, Calif.: Stanford University Press, 1922.

McClellan, Woodford. *Revolutionary Exiles: The Russians in the First International and the Paris Commune*. London: Frank Cass, 1979.

MacDonald, H. Malcolm. "Karl Marx, Friedrich Engels, and the South Slavic Problem in 1848-1849." *University of Toronto Quarterly* 8 (1939): 452-460.

———. "Marx, Engels, and the Polish National Movement." *Journal of Modern History* 13 (1941): 321-334.

Maehl, William. "Recent Literature on the German Socialists, 1891-1932." *Journal of Modern History* 33 (1961): 292-306.

———. "The Role of Russia in German Socialist Policy, 1914-1918." *International Review of Social History* 4 (1959): 177-198.

———. "The Triumph of Nationalism in the German Socialist Party on the Eve of the First World War." *Journal of Modern History* 24 (1952): 15-41.

Marks, Harry J. "The Sources of Reformism in the Social Democratic Party of Germany 1890-1914." *Journal of Modern History* 11 (1939): 334-356.

Massing, Paul W. *Rehearsal for Destruction: A Study of Political Anti-Semitism in Imperial Germany*. New York: Harper and Bros., 1949.

Meynell, Hildamarie. "The Stockholm Conference of 1917." *International Review of Social History* 5 (1960): 1-25, 202-225.

Morgan, Roger. *The German Social Democrats and the First International, 1864-1872*. London: Cambridge University Press, 1965.

Nedava, Joseph. *Trotsky and the Jews*. Philadelphia: Jewish Publication Society of America, 1971.

Nettl, Peter. "The German Social Democratic Party 1890-1914 as a Political Model." *Past and Present*, no. 30 (1965): 65-95.

Neuman, R. P. "The Sexual Question and Social Democracy in Imperial Germany." *Journal of Social History* 7 (1973-1974): 271-286.

———. "Socialism, the Family, and Sexuality: The Marxist Tradition and German Social Democracy Before 1914." Ph.D. dissertation, Northwestern University, 1972.

O'Boyle, Lenore. "The German Independent Socialists during the First World War." *American Historical Review* 56 (1950-1951): 824-831.

Parsons, Talcott. "Democracy and Social Structure in Pre-Nazi Germany." *Journal of Legal and Political Sociology* 1 (1942): 96-114.

Pinson, Koppel. *Modern Germany.* 2d ed. New York: Macmillan, 1966.

Prudhommeaux, André and Dori Prudhommeaux. *Spartacus et la Commune de Berlin, 1918-1919.* Paris: Spartacus, 1949.

Puckett, Hugh Wiley. *Germany's Women Go Forward.* New York: AMS Press, 1967.

Quataert, Jean Helen. "The German Socialist Women's Movement 1890-1918: Issues, Internal Conflicts, and the Main Personages." Ph.D. dissertation, University of California, Los Angeles, 1974.

——. *Reluctant Feminists in German Social Democracy, 1885-1917.* Princeton, N.J.: Princeton University Press, 1979.

Reichard, Richard W. *Crippled From Birth: German Social Democracy, 1844-1870.* Ames: Iowa State University Press, 1969.

——. "The German Working Class and the Russian Revolution of 1905." *Journal of Central European Affairs* 13 (1953): 136-153.

Rjasanoff, N. "Karl Marx und Friedrich Engels über die Polenfrage." *Archiv für die Geschichte des Sozialismus und der Arbeiterbewegung* 6 (1916): 174-221.

Rosenberg, Arthur. *Imperial Germany.* Translated by Ian F. D. Morrow. Boston: Beacon Press, 1964.

Roth, Guenther. *The Social Democrats in Imperial Germany.* Totowa, N.J.: Bedminster Press, 1963.

Rurup, Reinhard. "Problems of the German Revolution 1918-1919." *Journal of Contemporary History* 3 (1968): 109-135.

Ryder, A. J. *The German Revolution of 1918.* Cambridge: Cambridge University Press, 1967.

Sanford, Jutta Schroers. "The Origins of German Feminism: German Women 1789-1870." Ph.D. dissertation, Ohio State University, 1976.

Schapiro, Leonard. "The Role of the Jews in the Russian Revolutionary Movement." *Slavonic and East European Review* 40 (1961): 148-167.

Schorske, Carl E. *German Social Democracy, 1905-1917.* New York: Russell and Russell, 1970.

Schüddekopf, Otto-Ernst. "Karl Radek in Berlin, Ein Kapitel deutsch-russischer Beziehungen im Jahre 1919." *Archiv für Sozialgeschichte* 2 (1962): 87-166.

Schurer, Heinz. "The Permanent Revolution: Metamorphosis of an Idea." *Soviet Survey*, no. 32 (1960): 68-73.

——. "Radek and the German Revolution." *Survey*, nos. 53-55 (1964-1965): 59-69, 126-140.

——. "The Russian Revolution of 1905 and the Origins of German Communism." *Slavonic and East European Review* 39 (1961): 459-471.

Snell, John L. "The Russian Revolution and the German Social Democratic Party in 1917." *American Slavic and East European Review* 15 (1956): 339-350.

——. "Socialist Unions and Socialist Patriotism in Germany, 1914-1918." *American Historical Review* 59 (1953-1954): 66-76.

Strain, Jacqueline. "Feminism and Political Radicalism in the German Social Democratic Movement, 1890-1914." Ph.D. dissertation, University of California, Berkeley, 1964.

Ströbel, Heinrich. *The German Revolution and After.* Translated by H. J. Stenning. New York: Thomas Seltzer, 1923.

Teller, Judd L. *Scapegoat of Revolution.* New York: Charles Scribner's Sons, 1954.

Thälmann, Ernest. *Der revolutionäre Ausweg und die KPD.* Berlin: Schneller, 1932.

Thönnessen, Werner. *The Emancipation of Women: The Rise and Decline of the Women's Movement in German Social Democracy, 1863-1933.* Translated by Joris de Bres. London: Pluto Press, 1973.

Waldman, Eric. *The Spartacist Uprising of 1919.* Milwaukee: Marquette University Press, 1958.

Wendel, Hermann. "Marxism and the South Slav Question." *Slavonic Review* 2 (1923-1924): 289-307.

Wolff, Theodor. *Through Two Decades.* Translated by E. W. Dickes. London: William Heinemann, 1936.

Zborowski, Mark. "The Place of Book-Learning in Traditional Jewish Culture." *Harvard Educational Review* 19 (1949): 87-109.

ANGELICA BALABANOFF

Manuscript Sources

Balabanoff, Angelica. "My Life As a Rebel." Typescript and random notes. New York Public Library Archives.

Lola Maverick Lloyd Papers. General Correspondence, 1936-1939. Schwimmer-Lloyd Collection. New York Public Library Archives.

Scrapbooks. References to Rosika Schwimmer's Associates. Angelica Balabanoff Folder. Schwimmer-Lloyd Collection. New York Public Library Archives.

Published Writings

Balabanoff, Angelica. "Anti-Semitism in Italy." *Socialist Review* 6 (1938): 7-8, 18.

——. "Benito Mussolini: Souvenirs Sur l'Homme." *Europe* 18 (1928): 544-556.

——. *Erinnerungen und Erlebnisse.* Berlin: E. Laub, 1927.

——. *Erziehung der Massen zum Marxismus.* Berlin: E. Laubsche, 1927.

——. *Impressions of Lenin.* Translated by Isotta Cesari. Ann Arbor: University of Michigan Press, 1964.

——. Introduction to Roy Curtis, *Italy: Victory Through Revolution.* New York: Socialist Party, c. 1945.

——. "Italian Socialists and the Crisis." *The Socialist Review* 12 (1915): 625-632.

——. "Lénine et la Création du Comintern." In *Contributions à l'Histoire du Comintern*, pp. 29–37. Edited by Jacques Freymond. Geneva: Droz, 1965.

——. *Marx und Engels als Freidenker in ihren Schriften.* Jena: Urania-Freidenker-Verlag, 1931.

——. "Mussolini's Past and Present." *Socialist Review* 6 (1939): 19.

——. *My Life As a Rebel.* New York: Harper and Bros., 1938; reprint, Bloomington: Indiana University Press, 1973.

——. *Sozialismus als Weltanschauung.* Berlin: Deutscher Freidenkerverband, 1932.

——. "Sozialismus und Freimaurerei." *Die Neue Zeit* 32, Bd. II, no. 8 (May 22, 1914): 345–350.

——. *Tears.* New York: E. Laub, 1943.

——. *To the Victims of Fascism.* New York: n.p., 1936.

——. *The Traitor: Benito Mussolini and His "Conquest" of Power.* New York: Giuseppe Popolizio, 1942–1943.

——. "La Troisième Conférence de Zimmerwald." *Demain, Pages et Documents* 2 (1917): 93–100.

——. *Wesen und Werdegang des Italienischen Fascismus.* Vienna: Hess, 1931.

——. *Die Zimmerwalder Bewegung, 1914-1919.* Leipzig: C. L. Hirschfeld, 1928.

Public Documents

Lademacher, Horst. *Die Zimmerwalder Bewegung.* 2 vols. The Hague: Mouton, 1967.

Schmitt, Bernadotte E. "The Italian Documents for July 1914." *Journal of Modern History* 37 (1965): 469–472.

Newspapers and Journals

Current History
L'Humanité
Labour Leader
Le Monde
Nation
New Republic
New York *Call*
New York *Post*
New York *Times*
New Yorker
Saturday Review of Literature
Socialist Review
Spectator
Time
Times Literary Supplement

Descriptions of Balabanoff by Friends and Contemporaries

Bryant, Louise. *Six Red Months in Russia*. New York: George H. Doran, 1918.

Goldman, Emma. *Living My Life*. New York: AMS Press, 1970.

——. *My Disillusionment in Russia*. Garden City, N.Y.: Doubleday, Page, 1923.

——. *My Further Disillusionment in Russia*. Garden City, N.Y.: Doubleday, Page, 1924.

Harrison, Marguerite. *Marooned in Moscow*. New York: George H. Doran, 1921.

Lore, Ludwig. Review of *My Life As a Rebel*, by Angelica Balabanoff. *Nation* 147 (August 6, 1938): 131–132.

Nomad, Max. *Dreamers, Dynamiters, and Demagogues*. New York: Waldon Press, 1964.

"Observer." "Seldes and Plagiarism." *Socialist Review* 6 (1939): 17–19.

Sadoul, Jacques. *Notes Sur La Révolution Bolchévique*. Paris: Editions de la Sirène, 1920.

——. *Notes Sur La Révolution Bolchévique: Quarante Lettres de Jacques Sadoul*. Paris: Edition de la Librairie de l'Humanité, 1922.

Serge, Victor. *Memoirs of a Revolutionary, 1901–1941*. Translated by Peter Sedgwick. London: Oxford University Press, 1963.

Sorokin, Pitirim A. *Leaves From a Russian Diary*. Boston: Beacon Press, 1950.

Wolfe, Bertram D. *Strange Communists I Have Known*. New York: Stein and Day, 1965.

Related Primary Materials

Bainville, Jacques. *Italy and the War*. Translated by Bernard Miall. New York: George H. Doran, 1917.

Berkman, Alexander. *The Bolshevik Myth*. New York: Boni and Liveright, 1925.

Bonomi, Ivanoe. *From Socialism to Fascism*. Translated by John Murray. London: Martin Hopkinson, 1925.

Destrée, Jules. *En Italie Avant la Guerre, 1914–1915*. Brussels: G. Van Oest, 1915.

——. *En Italie Pendant la Guerre*. Brussels: G. Van Oest, 1916.

Dutt, R. Palme. *The Two Internationals*. London: George Allen and Unwin, 1920.

Eberlein, Hugo. "The Foundation of the Comintern and the Spartakusbund." *The Communist International* 6 (1929): 436–442.

Foerster, Robert F. *The Italian Emigration of Our Times*. Cambridge, Mass.: Harvard University Press, 1919.

Garlanda, Federico. *The New Italy*. Translated by M. E. Wood. New York: G. P. Putnam's Sons, 1911.

Giolitti, Giovanni. *Memoirs of My Life*. Translated by Edward Storer. London: Chapman and Dodd, 1923.

Goblet d'Alviella, E. F. A. *L'Université de Bruxelles pendant son troisième quart de siècle, 1884–1909*. Brussels: M. Weissenbruch, 1909.

Ignotus. "Italian Nationalism and the War with Turkey." *Fortnightly Review* 90 (1911): 1084–1096.

King, Bolton, and Thomas Okey. *Italy To-Day*. London: James Nisbet, 1901.

Labriola, Antonio. *Essays on the Materialistic Conception of History*. Translated by Charles H. Kerr. Chicago: Charles H. Kerr, 1908.

Lemonon, Ernest. *L'Italie Economique et Sociale*. Paris: Félix Alcan, 1913.

Lowell, Abbott Lawrence. *Governments and Parties in Continental Europe*. 2 vols. Boston: Houghton Mifflin, 1896.

Luchaire, Julien. *Confession d'un Français Moyen*. 2 vols. Florence: Leo S. Olschki, 1965.

Malon, Benoît. *Le Socialisme intégrale*. Paris: Félix Alcan, 1890.

Mariani, Emilia. "Le Mouvement Féministe en Italie." *Revue Politique et Parlémentaire* 13 (1897): 481–495.

Michels, Robert. *First Lectures in Political Sociology*. Translated by Alfred de Grazia. Minneapolis: University of Minnesota Press, 1949.

——. *Le Prolétariat et la Bourgeoisie dans le Mouvement socialiste italien*. Translated by Georges Bourgin. Paris: M. Giard, 1921.

——. *Zur Soziologie des Parteiwesens in der Modernen Demokratie*. Leipzig: W. Klinkhardt, 1911.

Mussolini, Benito. *My Autobiography*. New York: Charles Scribner's Sons, 1928.

Nitti, Francesco. *Bolshevism, Fascism and Democracy*. Translated by Margaret M. Green. New York: Macmillan, 1927.

Peluso, Edmondo. "Notes et impressions d'un délégué." *Demain, Pages et Documents*, no. 5 (1916): 341–346.

Por, Odon. "The New University of Brussels." *International Socialist Review* 7 (1906): 209–220.

Price, M. Philips. *My Reminiscences of the Russian Revolution*. London: George Allen and Unwin, 1921.

Ransome, Arthur. *Russia in 1919*. New York: B. W. Huebsch, 1919.

Seldes, George. *Sawdust Caesar: The Untold Story of Mussolini and Fascism*. New York: Harper and Bros.,1935.

Walling, William English. *The Socialists and the War*. New York: Henry Holt, 1915.

Biographies and Works about Balabanoff

Eshelman, Nancy Gorman. "Angelica Balabanoff and the Italian Socialist Movement: From the Second International to Zimmerwald." Ph.D. dissertation, University of Rochester, 1977.

Florence, Ronald. *Marx's Daughters*. New York: Dial Press, 1975.

Modern Encyclopedia of Russian and Soviet History. See under "Balabanoff, Angelica," by Richard Stites.

Slaughter, Jane. "Humanism versus Feminism in the Socialist Movement: The Life of Angelica Balabanoff." In *European Women on the Left*, pp. 179–194. Edited by Jane Slaughter and Robert Kern. Westport, Conn.: Greenwood Press, 1981.

——. "Women and Socialism: The Case of Angelica Balabanoff." *Social Science Journal* 14 (April 1977): 57–66.

Background and Related Secondary Materials

Albrecht-Carrié, René. "Italian Colonial Policy, 1914-1918." *Journal of Modern History* 18 (1946): 123-147.

——. "Italian Foreign Policy, 1914-1922." *Journal of Modern History* 20 (1948): 326-339.

——. *Italy From Napoleon to Mussolini*. New York: Columbia University Press, 1950.

Andrews, Marian. [Christopher Hare] *The Most Illustrious Ladies of the Italian Renaissance*. London: Harper and Bros., 1911.

Askew, William C. *Europe and Italy's Acquisition of Libya, 1911-1912*. Durham, N.C.: Duke University Press, 1942.

Borgese, G. A. *Goliath: The March of Fascism*. New York: Viking Press, 1938.

Borghi, Armando. *Mussolini Red and Black*. Translated by Dorothy Daudley. New York: Freie Arbeiter Stimme, 1938.

Boulting, William. *Woman in Italy*. New York: Brentano's, 1910.

Burckhardt, Jacob. *The Civilization of the Renaissance in Italy*. Vienna: Phaidon Press, n.d.

Cammett, John M. *Antonio Gramsci and the Origins of Italian Communism*. Stanford, Calif.: Stanford University Press, 1967.

Clark, Martin. *Antonio Gramsci and the Revolution That Failed*. New Haven, Conn.: Yale University Press, 1977.

Clough, Shepard B. *The Economic History of Modern Italy*. New York: Columbia University Press, 1964.

——, and Carlo Livi. "Economic Growth in Italy: An Analysis of the Uneven Development of North and South." *Journal of Economic History* 16 (1956): 334-349.

——, and Salvatore Saladino. *A History of Modern Italy*. New York: Columbia University Press, 1968.

Coker, Francis W. *Recent Political Thought*. D. Appleton-Century, 1934.

Collart, Yves. *Le Parti Socialiste Suisse et l'Internationale*. Geneva: Graduate Institute of International Studies, 1969.

Craver, Earlene Joyce. "The Crisis of Italian Socialism and the Origins of the Italian Communist Party, 1912-1921." Ph.D. dissertation, University of Southern California, 1972.

Croce, Benedetto. *A History of Italy 1871-1915*. Translated by Cecilia M. Ady. Oxford: Clarendon Press, 1929.

Cunsolo, Ronald S. "Libya, Italian Nationalism, and the Revolt Against Giolitti." *Journal of Modern History* 37 (1965): 186-207.

Davidson, Alastair. "The Russian Revolution and the Formation of the Italian Communist Party." *The Australian Journal of Politics and History* 10 (1964): 355-370.

Delzell, Charles F. "Benito Mussolini: A Guide to the Biographical Literature." *Journal of Modern History* 35 (1963): 339-353.

——. "The Italian Anti-Fascist Emigration, 1922-1943." *Journal of Central European Affairs* 12 (1952): 20-55.

——. *Mussolini's Enemies: The Italian Anti-Fascist Resistance*. Princeton, N.J.: Princeton University Press, 1961.

Despy-Meyer, Andrée. *Inventaire des Archives de l'Université Nouvelle de Bruxelles (1894-1919)*. Brussels: l'Empereur, 1973.

DiScala, Spencer Michael. "Filippo Turati and Factional Strife in the Italian Socialist Party, 1892-1912." Ph.D. dissertation, Columbia University, 1969.

Drinnon, Richard. *Rebel in Paradise: A Biography of Emma Goldman*. New York: Harper and Row, 1976.

Dunbar, Gary S. *Elisée Reclus: Historian of Nature*. Hamden, Conn.: Archon, 1978.

Eckaus, Richard. "The North-South Differential in Italian Economic Development." *Journal of Economic History* 15 (1961): 285-317.

Evans, Richard J. *The Feminists*. London: Croom Helm, 1977.

Faggi, John A. B. "The Beginnings of the Italian Socialist Party (1890-1900)." Ph.D. dissertation, Columbia University, 1954.

Fermi, Laura. *Mussolini*. Chicago: University of Chicago Press, 1961.

Finer, Herman. *Mussolini's Italy*. Hamden, Conn.: Archon, 1964.

Gerschenkron, Alexander. "Notes on the Rate of Industrial Growth in Italy, 1881-1913." *Journal of Economic History* 15 (1955): 360-375.

Gualtieri, Humbert L. *The Labor Movement in Italy*. New York: S. F. Vanni, 1946.

Haupt, Georges. *Le Congrès manqué: l'internationale à la veille de la première guerre mondiale*. Paris: François Maspero, 1965.

Hentze, Margot. *Pre-Fascist Italy*. New York: W. W. Norton, 1939.

Hilton-Young, W. *The Italian Left: A Short History of Political Socialism in Italy*. London: Longmans, Green, 1949.

Horowitz, Daniel L. *The Italian Labor Movement*. Cambridge, Mass.: Harvard University Press, 1963.

Hostetter, Richard. *The Italian Socialist Movement: Origins (1860-1882)*. Princeton, N.J.: Van Nostrand, 1958.

Keene, Frances, ed. *Neither Liberty Nor Bread: The Meaning and Tragedy of Fascism*. Port Washington, N.Y.: Kennikat Press, 1969.

Kelly-Gadol, Joan. "Did Women Have a Renaissance?" In *Becoming Visible: Women in European History*, pp. 137-164. Edited by Renate Bridenthal and Claudia Koonz. Boston: Houghton Mifflin, 1977.

Kirkpatrick, Ivone. *Mussolini: Study of a Demagogue*. London: Odhams, 1964.

LaVigna, Claire. "Anna Kuliscioff: From Russian Populism to Italian Reformism, 1873-1913." Ph.D. dissertation, University of Rochester, 1971.

——. "The Marxist Ambivalence Toward Women: Between Socialism and Feminism in the Italian Socialist Party." In *Socialist Women*, pp. 146-181. Edited by Marilyn J. Boxer and Jean H. Quataert. New York: Elsevier, 1978.

Leonetti, Alfonso, ed. *Mouvements Ouviers et Socialistes: L'Italie*. Paris: Les Editions Ouvrières, 1952.

Lowe, C. J., and F. Marzari. *Italian Foreign Policy, 1870-1940*. London: Routledge and Kegan Paul, 1975.

Mack Smith, Denis. *Italy: A Modern History*. Ann Arbor: University of Michigan Press, 1959.

Megaro, Gaudens. *Mussolini in the Making.* New York: Howard Fertig, 1967.

Miller, James Edward. "The Italian Socialist Party, 1900-1914: An Organizational Study." Ph.D. dissertation, University of Illinois at Urbana-Champaign, 1974.

Monelli, Paolo. *Mussolini: The Intimate Life of a Demagogue.* New York: Vanguard Press, 1954.

Nation, Robert Craig. "The Zimmerwald Left: The Roots of International Communism in the First World War." Ph.D. dissertation, Duke University, 1975.

Neufeld, Maurice F. *Italy: School for Awakening Countries.* Ithaca, N.Y.: Cayuga Press, 1961.

Noether, Emiliana P. "Italian Intellectuals Under Fascism." *Journal of Modern History* 43 (1971): 630-648.

Nolte, Ernst. *Three Faces of Fascism.* Translated by Leila Vennewitz. New York: New American Library, 1969.

Patrucco, Armand Italo. "The Critics of the Italian Parliamentary System, 1860-1915." Ph.D. dissertation, Columbia University, 1969.

Procacci, Giovanna. "Italy: From Intervention to Fascism, 1917-1919." *Journal of Contemporary History* 3 (1968): 153-176.

Putnam, Emily James. *The Lady.* Chicago: University of Chicago Press, 1910.

Renzi, William. "Italy's Neutrality and Entrance into the Great War: A Reexamination." *American Historical Review* 73 (1968): 1414-1432.

———. "Mussolini's Sources of Financial Support, 1914-1915." *History* 56 (1971): 189-206.

Rodocanachi, E. *La Femme Italienne.* Paris: Hachette, 1922.

Rosmer, Alfred. *Le mouvement ouvrier pendant la première guerre mondiale.* 2 vols. Vol. I: Paris: Librairie du Travail, 1936. Vol. II: Paris: Mouton, 1959.

Rossi, A. *The Rise of Italian Fascism, 1918-1922.* Translated by Peter and Dorothy Wait. New York: Howard Fertig, 1966.

Salomone, A. William. *Italy in the Giolittian Era.* Philadelphia: University of Pennsylvania Press, 1960.

———, ed. *Italy: From the Risorgimento to Fascism.* Garden City, N.Y.: Doubleday, 1970.

Salvemini, Gaetano. *The Origins of Fascism in Italy.* Edited by Roberto Vivarelli. New York: Harper and Row, 1973.

Sarfatti, Margherita G. *The Life of Benito Mussolini.* Translated by Frederic Whyte. London: Thronton Butterworth, 1925.

Senn, Alfred Erich. *Diplomacy and Revolution: The Soviet Mission to Switzerland, 1918.* Notre Dame, Ind.: University of Notre Dame Press, 1974.

———. *The Russian Revolution in Switzerland, 1914-1917.* Madison: University of Wisconsin Press, 1971.

Seton-Watson, Christopher. *Italy From Liberalism to Fascism, 1870-1925.* London: Methuen, 1967.

Sforza, Carlo. *Contemporary Italy: Its Intellectual and Moral Origins.* Translated by Drake and Denise DeKay. New York: E. P. Dutton, 1944.

Sprigge, Cecil J. S. *The Development of Modern Italy.* New Haven, Conn.: Yale University Press, 1944.

Tannenbaum, Edward R., and Emiliana P. Noether. *Modern Italy: A Topical History Since 1861.* New York: New York University Press, 1974.

Thayer, John A. *Italy and the Great War: Politics and Culture, 1870-1915.* Madison: University of Wisconsin Press, 1964.

Webster, Richard A. "From Insurrection to Intervention: The Italian Crisis of 1914." *Italian Quarterly* 5-6 (1961-1962): 27-50.

Wiskemann, Elizabeth. *Italy.* London: Oxford University Press, 1947.

DOLORES IBARRURI, "LA PASIONARIA"

Published Writings

Ibarruri, Dolores. "Against the Enemies of the People." *Communist International* 13 (September 1936): 1127-1134.

——. "Employ All Means to Defend and Consolidate the People's Front." *Communist International* 15 (March 1938): 282-290.

——. *For the Independence of Spain, For Liberty, For the Republic, For the Union of All Spaniards.* Madrid: Communist Party of Spain, 1938.

——. "I Become 'La Pasionaria.'" *The Nation* 203 (July 25, 1966): 94-98.

——. *Implacable War Against Fascism.* Moscow: Foreign Languages Publishing House, 1941.

——. "José Díaz." *Labour Monthly* 24 (May 1942): 158-159.

——. *Liberate Spain From Franco.* London: Communist Party, 1945.

——. "Reply to Enemies, Slanderers, and Wavering Elements." *Communist International* 14 (November 1937): 808-813.

——. "The Spanish People Will Conquer Despite All Defeatist Sentiments and Difficulties." *Communist International* 15 (April 1938): 380-385.

——. *Speeches and Articles, 1936-1938.* London: Lawrence and Wishart, 1938.

——. "Stalin, Leader of Peoples, Man of the Masses." *Communist International* 17 (January 1940): 36-44.

——. *They Shall Not Pass: The Autobiography of La Pasionaria.* New York: International, 1966.

——. "The Time Has Come to Create a Single Party of the Proletariat in Spain." *Communist International* 14 (September 1937): 642-655.

——. "We Shall Fulfill Our Sacred Duty to the U.S.S.R." *Communist International* 13 (December 1936): 1603-1604.

——. "What Is Happening In Spain?" *Communist International* 13 (October 1936): 1308-1310.

——. *The Whole People Resolved to Win the War.* Barcelona: Communist Party of Spain, 1938.

——. *The Women Want a People's Peace.* New York: Workers Library, 1941.

——, and Isabel Brown. *Women Against Hitler.* London: Communist Party of Great Britain, n.d.

Newspapers and Journals

Current History
Gringoire
L'Humanité
Le Monde
New Republic
News of Spain
Newsweek
New York *Times*
Time

Descriptions of Ibarruri by Friends and Contemporaries

Atholl, Katharine Marjory. *Searchlight on Spain*. London: Penguin, 1938.

Bessie, Alvah. *Men In Battle*. New York: Charles Scribner's Sons, 1939.

——. *The Un-Americans*. New York: Cameron Associates, 1957.

——, ed. *The Heart of Spain*. New York: Veterans of the Abraham Lincoln Brigade, 1952.

Borkenau, Franz. *The Spanish Cockpit*. Ann Arbor: University of Michigan Press, 1963.

Bowers, Claude G. *My Mission to Spain*. New York: Simon and Schuster, 1954.

Buckley, Henry. *Life and Death of the Spanish Republic*. London: Hamish Hamilton, 1940.

Castro Delgado, Enrique. *J'ai Perdu la foi à Moscou*. Translated by Jean Talbot. Paris: Gallimard, 1950.

Claudin, Fernando. *The Communist Movement*. 2 vols. Translated by Brian Pearce and Francis MacDonagh. New York: Monthly Review Press, 1975.

Davidson, Jo. *Spanish Portraits*. New York: Arden Gallery, 1939.

Faure, Elie. "A Portrait of La Pasionaria." *Living Age* 351 (October 1936): 135-137.

Fischer, Louis. *Men and Politics*. New York: Duell, Sloan, and Pearce, 1941.

González, Valentin, and Julian Gorkin. *El Campesino: Life and Death in Soviet Russia*. Translated by Ilsa Barea. New York: G. P. Putnam's Sons, 1952.

Haldane, Charlotte. "Pasionaria." *Left Review* 3 (April 1938): 926.

Hemingway, Ernest. *For Whom the Bell Tolls*. New York: Charles Scribner's Sons, 1940.

Hernández, Jesús. *La Grande Trahison*. Translated by Pierre Berthelin. Paris: Fasquelle, 1953.

Langdon-Davies, John. *Behind the Spanish Barricades*. New York: Robert M. McBride, 1936.

Leonhard, Wolfgang. *Child of the Revolution*. Translated by C. M. Woodhouse. London: William Collins, 1957.

Mora, Constancia de la. *In Place of Splendor: The Autobiography of a Spanish Woman*. New York: Harcourt, Brace, 1939.

Riesenfeld, Janet. *Dancer in Madrid*. New York: Funk and Wagnalls, 1938.

Sheean, Vincent. *Not Peace But a Sword.* New York: Doubleday, Doran, 1939.
Strong, Anna Louise. *Spain in Arms.* New York: Henry Holt, 1937.

Related Primary Materials

Acier, Marcel, ed. *From Spanish Trenches: Recent Letters From Spain.* New York: Modern Age, 1937.
Alvarez del Vayo, Julio. *Freedom's Battle.* Translated by Eileen E. Brooke. New York: Hill and Wang, 1940.
——. *Give Me Combat: The Memoirs of Julio Alvarez del Vayo.* Translated by Donald D. Walsh. Boston: Little, Brown, 1973.
——. *The Last Optimist.* New York: Viking Press, 1950.
——. *The March of Socialism.* Translated by Joseph M. Bernstein. London: Jonathan Cape, 1974.
Bolin, Luis. *Spain: The Vital Years.* London: Cassell, 1967.
Buchanan, Meriel. "How Moscow Helps Spanish Reds." *Saturday Review* 162 (October 17, 1936): 492–493.
——. "What is Stalin Plotting?" *Saturday Review* 162 (October 31, 1936): 552–553.
Carrillo, Santiago. *Eurocommunism and the State.* Westport, Conn.: Lawrence Hill, 1978.
Casado, Colonel Segismundo. *The Last Days of Madrid.* Translated by Rupert Croft-Cooke. London: Peter Davies, 1939.
Cattaneo, B. "Women in the Struggle for Peace and Liberty, Against Fascism." *Communist International* 15 (May 1938): 432–437.
Cox, Geoffrey. *Defence of Madrid.* London: Victor Gollancz, 1937.
——. "Eye-Witness in Madrid." *Harper's Monthly Magazine* 175 (June-July 1937): 27–37, 151–162.
Crossman, Richard, ed. *The God that Failed: Six Studies in Communism.* London: Hamish Hamilton, 1950.
Dimitroff, Georgi. *The United Front.* New York: International, 1938.
Ercoli, M. [Palmiro Togliatti] *The Spanish Revolution.* New York: Workers Library, 1936.
Etchbéhère, Mika. *Ma guerre d'Espagne à moi.* Paris: Editions Denoël, 1976.
Fernsworth, Lawrence A. "Mass Movements in Spain." *Foreign Affairs* 14 (July 1936): 662–674.
Fischer, Louis. *The War in Spain.* New York: The Nation Printing, 1937.
Fonteriz, Luis de. *Red Terror in Madrid.* London: Longmans, Green, 1937.
Gannes, Harry, and Theodore Repard. *Spain in Revolt.* New York: Alfred A. Knopf, 1936.
Godden, G. M. *Conflict in Spain, 1920–1937.* London: Burns, Oates, and Washbourne, 1937.
Greaves, H. R. G. "A Soviet Spain?" *Political Quarterly* 7 (July 1936): 399–407.
Hemingway, Ernest. "The Spanish War." *Fact*, no. 16 (July 1938): 7–72.
Humphries, Rolfe, trans. "The Balladry of the Civil War." *International Literature*, no. 3 (1937): 31–39.

Kemp, Peter. *Mine Were of Trouble.* London: Cassell, 1957.

Knoblaugh, H. Edward. *Correspondent in Spain.* London: Sheed and Ward, 1937.

Koestler, Arthur. *Spanish Testament.* London: Victor Gollancz, 1937.

Krivitsky, W. G. *In Stalin's Secret Service.* New York: Harper and Bros., 1939.

Lespine, Louis. *La Femme en Espagne.* Toulouse: Clémence-Isaure, 1919.

Loveday, Arthur F. "Spain From Dictatorship to Civil War." *Quarterly Review* 267 (October 1936): 189-207.

Low, Mary, and Juan Brea. *Red Spanish Notebook.* London: Martin Secker and Warburg, 1937.

Maisky, Ivan. *Spanish Notebooks.* Translated by Ruth Kisch. London: Hutchinson, 1966.

Manning, Leah. *What I Saw in Spain.* London: Victor Gollancz, 1935.

Marty, André. *Heroic Spain.* New York: Workers Library, 1937.

Merin, Peter. *Spain Between Death and Birth.* Translated by Charles Fullman. New York: Dodge, 1938.

Morrow, Felix. *Revolution and Counter-Revolution in Spain.* New York: Pathfinder Press, 1974.

Orlov, Alexander. "How Stalin Relieved Spain of $600,000,000." *Readers' Digest* 89 (November 1966): 37-47, 50.

——. *The Secret History of Stalin's Crimes.* New York: Random House, 1953.

Orwell, George. *Homage to Catalonia.* New York: Harcourt, Brace, 1952.

Peers, E. Allison. *The Spanish Tragedy, 1930-1936.* London: Methuen, 1936.

Pieck, Wilhelm. *Freedom, Peace, and Bread.* New York: Workers Library, 1935.

Pitcairn, Frank. *Reporter in Spain.* London: Lawrence and Wishart, 1936.

Regler, Gustav. *The Great Crusade.* New York: Longmans, 1940.

Shaw, Rafael. *Spain From Within.* London: T. Fisher Unwin, 1910.

Sinclair, Upton. *No Pasaran! A Story of the Battle of Madrid.* Published by the author, 1937.

Soria, George. *Trotskyism in the Service of Franco.* New York: International, 1938.

Spender, Stephen, and John Lehmann, eds. *Poems For Spain.* London: Hogarth Press, 1939.

Toynbee, Arnold J. *Survey of International Affairs.* London: Oxford University Press, 1936-1937.

Trotsky, Leon. *The Spanish Revolution (1931-1939).* New York: Pathfinder Press, 1973.

Wolfe, Bernard. *The Great Prince Died.* New York: Charles Scribner's Sons, 1959.

Wolfe, Bertram D. *Civil War in Spain.* New York: Workers Age, 1937.

Biographies and Works about Ibarruri

Gallagher, Charles F. *La Pasionaria.* Hanover, N.H.: American Universities Field Staff Reports, 1976.

Matthews, Herbert L. Review of *They Shall Not Pass: The Autobiography of La Pasionaria,* by Dolores Ibarruri. New York *Times Book Review* (November 27, 1966): 66-67.

Wolin, Merle. "La Pasionaria." *Viva* 5 (September 1978): 44–47, 82–88.

Workers Library. *Pasionaria, People's Tribune of Spain.* New York: Workers Library, 1938.

Background and Related Secondary Materials

Aradi, Zsolt. *Shrines to Our Lady Around the World.* New York: Farrar, Straus and Young, 1954.

Benson, Frederick R. *Writers in Arms: The Literary Impact of the Spanish Civil War.* New York: New York University Press, 1967.

Bolloten, Burnett. *The Grand Camouflage: The Spanish Civil War and Revolution, 1936–1939.* New York: Praeger, 1961.

Boxer, C. R. *Mary and Misogyny: Women in Iberian Expansion Overseas 1415–1815.* London: Gerald Duckworth, 1975.

Brenan, Gerald. *The Spanish Labyrinth.* London: Cambridge University Press, 1943.

Broué, Pierre, and Emile Témime. *The Revolution and the Civil War in Spain.* Translated by Tony White. Cambridge, Mass.: MIT Press, 1970.

Carr, Raymond. *Spain, 1808–1939.* London: Oxford University Press, 1966.

Cattell, David T. *Communism and the Spanish Civil War.* Berkeley: University of California Press, 1955.

——. *Soviet Diplomacy and the Spanish Civil War.* Berkeley: University of California Press, 1957.

Caute, David. *Communism and the French Intellectuals 1914–1960.* New York: Macmillan, 1964.

Cleugh, James. *Spanish Fury: The Story of a Civil War.* London: George G. Harrap, 1962.

Colodny, Robert Garland. *The Struggle for Madrid.* New York: Paine-Whitman, 1958.

Crozier, Brian. *Franco: A Biographical History.* London: Eyre and Spottiswoode, 1967.

Eby, Cecil. *Between the Bullet and the Lie: American Volunteers in the Spanish Civil War.* New York: Holt, Rinehart, and Winston, 1969.

Ford, Hugh D. *A Poets' War: British Poets and the Spanish Civil War.* Philadelphia: University of Pennsylvania Press, 1965.

Fraser, Ronald. *Blood of Spain: An Oral History of the Spanish Civil War.* New York: Pantheon, 1979.

Gallagher, Charles F. *Left, Right, and Center in Spain: Is More Than Two a Crowd?* Hanover, N.H.: American Universities Field Staff Reports, 1978.

——. *Reflections on the Spanish Elections.* Hanover, N.H.: American Universities Field Staff Reports, 1977.

Goldsborough, James O. "Eurocommunism After Madrid." *Foreign Affairs* 55 (July 1977): 800–814.

Goldston, Robert. *The Civil War in Spain.* New York: Bobbs-Merrill, 1966.

Guttmann, Allen. *The Wound in the Heart: America and the Spanish Civil War.* New York: Free Press of Glencoe, 1962.

Hermet, Guy. *The Communists in Spain.* Translated by S. Seago and H. Fox. Lexington, Mass.: Lexington Books, 1974.

Hills, George. *The Battle for Madrid.* New York: St. Martin's Press, 1977.

Jackson, Gabriel. *A Concise History of the Spanish Civil War.* New York: John Day, 1974.

——. *The Spanish Republic and the Civil War, 1931-1939.* Princeton, N.J.: Princeton University Press, 1965.

——, ed. *The Spanish Civil War.* Chicago: Quadrangle, 1972.

Jellinek, Frank. *The Civil War in Spain.* New York: Howard Fertig, 1969.

Kaplan, Temma. "Spanish Anarchism and Women's Liberation." *Journal of Contemporary History* 6 (1971): 101-110.

——. "Turmoil in Spain: The Communist Party and the Mass Movement." *Radical America* 11 (March-April 1977): 53-72.

——. "Women and Spanish Anarchism." In *Becoming Visible: Women in European History*, pp. 400-421. Edited by Renate Bridenthal and Claudia Koonz. Boston: Houghton Mifflin, 1977.

Kern, Robert W. "Anarchist Principles and Spanish Reality: Emma Goldman as a Participant in the Spanish Civil War." *Journal of Contemporary History* 11 (1976): 237-259.

——. *Red Years/Black Years: A Political History of Spanish Anarchism, 1911-1937.* Philadelphia: Institute for the Study of Human Issues, 1978.

Kisch, Richard. *They Shall Not Pass: The Spanish People at War, 1936-1939.* London: Wayland, 1974.

Kurzman, Dan. *Miracle of November: Madrid's Epic Stand, 1936.* New York: G. P. Putnam's Sons, 1980.

Matthews, Herbert L. *Half of Spain Died: A Reappraisal of the Spanish Civil War.* New York: Charles Scribner's Sons, 1973.

——. *The Yoke and the Arrows: A Report on Spain.* New York: George Braziller, 1961.

Meaker, Gerald H. *The Revolutionary Left in Spain, 1914-1923.* Stanford, Calif.: Stanford University Press, 1974.

Mujal-Leon, Eusebio M. "Spanish Communism in the 1970s." *Problems of Communism* 24 (March 1975): 43-55.

Muste, John M. *Say That We Saw Spain Die: Literary Consequences of the Spanish Civil War.* Seattle: University of Washington Press, 1966.

O'Callaghan, Sheila M. *Cinderella of Europe: Spain Explained.* New York: Philosophical Library, n.d.

Payne, Robert. *The Civil War in Spain, 1936-1939.* New York: Capricorn, 1970.

Preston, Paul. "The Origins of the Socialist Schism in Spain, 1917-1931." *Journal of Contemporary History* 12 (1977): 101-132.

Purcell, Hugh. *The Spanish Civil War.* New York: G. P. Putnam's Sons, 1973.

Puzzo, Dante A. *The Spanish Civil War.* New York: Van Nostrand Reinhold, 1969.

Rosenthal, Marilyn. *Poetry of the Spanish Civil War.* New York: New York University Press, 1975.

Smith, Rhea Marsh. *Spain: A Modern History.* Ann Arbor: University of Michigan Press, 1965.

Sperber, Murray A. *And I Remember Spain: A Spanish Civil War Anthology.* New York: Macmillan, 1974.

Stevens, Evelyn P. "*Marianismo*: The Other Face of *Machismo* in Latin America." In *Female and Male in Latin America*, pp. 89–101. Edited by Ann Pescatello. Pittsburgh: University of Pittsburgh Press, 1973.

Thomas, Hugh. *The Spanish Civil War.* New York: Harper and Row, 1961.

Toynbee, Philip, ed. *The Distant Drum: Reflections on the Spanish Civil War.* New York: David McKay, 1976.

Walsh, William J. *The Apparitions and Shrines of Heaven's Bright Queen.* New York: T. J. Carey, 1904.

Watt, D. C. "Soviet Military Aid to the Spanish Republic in the Civil War, 1936–1938." *Slavonic and East European Review* 38 (June 1960): 536-538.

Weintraub, Stanley. *The Last Great Cause: The Intellectuals and the Spanish Civil War.* New York: Weybright and Talley, 1968.

Welles, Benjamin. *Spain: The Gentle Anarchy.* New York: Praeger, 1965.

Willis, Liz. *Women in the Spanish Revolution.* London: Solidarity, 1975.

Index

Accumulation of Capital (Luxemburg), 127
Adler, Victor, 116, 126
Alexander II, Tsar, 57, 62
American Socialist Party, 69, 186
anarchism, 33, 80, 162, 202
Anton Sáenz, Francisco, 235–36
Armand, Inessa, 68, 78
Asturias uprising, 207
Autobiography of a Sexually Emancipated Communist Woman (Kollontai), 95
Aveling, Edward: moral character of, 28, 34, 48, 50; and New Unionism, 38; relationship with Eleanor Marx, 27–29, 33, 35, 42, 47–50, 261; translates *Capital*, 39; trip to U.S., 33–35

Baez, Joan, 267
Bakunin, Michael, 153, 162
Balabanoff, Angelica: and Antonio Labriola, 158; attitude toward power, 252; and Bolshevik Revolution, 150, 170–76; compared with Eleanor Marx, 159, 177, 178, 181; compared with Ibarruri, 193, 203, 226, 230; compared with Kollontai, 150, 154, 155, 159, 177, 183–84, 184, 185–86; compared with Luxemburg, 8, 149, 150, 153, 154, 177; condemnation of Bolsheviks, 176–78, 179; criticized by colleagues, 179; death, 187; early work in Switzerland, 158–61; education, 154, 155, 156, 157–58, 179, 249; effect of Jewish heritage on, 154; faith in masses, 165, 177–78, 181; and Gregory Zinoviev, 173; importance of love and friendship to, 166, 259, 261; importance of role models for, 247–48; importance of teaching to, 156, 158, 183, 187, 257; and Italian Socialist Party, 151, 158, 161–67, 170, 174–76, 181, 185; and Lenin, 170, 171–72, 172–73, 174, 179, 184, 258; motivations of, 160, 254; and Mussolini, 150, 161–62, 165–67, 186–88, 261; on need for violence in revolutions, 174, 177; on theory, 170, 179–82; position in historiography, 150, 161, 189; praise for Luxemburg, 177; praised by colleagues, 181, 189; publications, 179–80, 182, 187–89; relationship with father, 154, 248; relationship with mother, 154–56, 247; socialization, 154–56; spirit of rebelliousness in, 154–55, 248; and Stalin, 185, 188; and Trotsky, 181, 185; used as symbol, 262–63; views on feminism, 159, 163, 183–84; vision of socialism, 177, 178, 249; work among women, 159–60, 163, 183–84; and World War I, 150, 167–70; years in exile, 184–89; and Zimmerwald movement, 150, 168–73, 181
Basques, 198–99, 200, 202, 226
Bax, Belfort, 31
Beatty, Bessie, 84
Bebel, August: and Balabanoff, 180, 181; and Luxemburg, 116, 121–22, 125; views on women, 6, 44, 85, 104; *Woman Under Socialism*, 6, 44, 104
Bebel, Julie, 105
Belinsky, Vissarion, 251

About the Author

MARIE MARMO MULLANEY is an Assistant Professor at Caldwell College in Caldwell, New Jersey, and Chairperson of the Department of History and Political Science. She has also taught at Douglass College, New Brunswick, New Jersey, one of the nation's leading centers for research and teaching in women's studies; Rutgers College, New Brunswick; and University College, Rutgers, Newark.

Dr. Mullaney's articles and book reviews in both women's history and modern European history have appeared in *Historian*, *Library Journal*, *Journal of the Rutgers University Libraries*, *Alternative Futures: The Journal of Utopian Studies*, *Red River Valley Historical Journal of World History*, and *International Social Science Review*.

A Danforth Fellow, she holds a B.A. from Seton Hall University in South Orange, New Jersey, and an M.A. and a Ph.D. from Rutgers University.